YESTERDAY, TODAY AND TOMORROW

THE GROWTH OF THE ITALIAN CANADIAN BUSINESS COMMUNITY

YESTERDAY, TODAY AND TOMORROW

THE GROWTH OF THE ITALIAN CANADIAN BUSINESS COMMUNITY

ICCO CANADA/MANSFIELD PRESS

TORONTO/MILAN

Printed in Canada

Library and Archives Canada Cataloguing in Publication

Title: Yesterday, today and tomorrow : the change, growth and development of the Italian Canadian business community in Toronto and the GTA from the 20th century until today.
Other titles: Yesterday, today and tomorrow (2020)
Names: Paina, Corrado, 1954- editor.
Description: Edited by Corrado Paina.
Identifiers: Canadiana 2020037267X | ISBN 9781771262569 (softcover)
Subjects: LCSH: Business enterprises—Ontario—Toronto—History—20th century. | LCSH: Business enterprises—Ontario—Toronto—History—21st century. | LCSH: Toronto (Ont.)—Economic conditions—20th century. | LCSH: Toronto (Ont.)—Economic conditions—21st century. | CSH: Italian Canadians—Ontario—Toronto—History—20th century. | CSH: Italian Canadians—Ontario—Toronto—History—21st century. | CSH: Italian Canadians—Ontario—Toronto—Economic conditions—20th century. | CSH: Italian Canadians—Ontario—Toronto—Economic conditions—21st century.
Classification: LCC HF3230.T67 Y47 2020 | DDC 338.7089/510713541—dc23

Book Concept—Corrado Paina, ICCO Canada
Interviews—Denis De Klerck, Bruno Magliocchetti
Photographer—Giulia Storti
Editor—Denis De Klerck
Proofreading—Gianfranco Guida, Tiziana Tedesco, Mary Chirico
Cover Design—Fabiola Iavarone
Book Design—Mansfield Press
Project Coordinator—Corrado Paina

Mansfield Press Inc.
25 Mansfield Avenue,
Toronto, Ontario, Canada M6J 2A9
www.mansfieldpress.net

THIS BOOK IS DEDICATED TO

MARISA PIATTELLI

SERGIO MARCHIONNE

RON FARANO

ANTONIO VALERI

Dear Reader,

I am delighted to welcome this marvelous book that pays homage to the many hundreds of thousands of courageous Italians that left their families, towns and country; some for adventure, others for economic opportunities, to make Canada their new home. Their story is the story of many other immigrants who came to Canada, but it is also unique, because Italians are unique.

Many came from humble beginnings at a very young age, learned English or French or both, found employment or started thriving businesses that allowed them to raise their families. It was with hard work and integrity that they took ad vantage of the opportunities that their new country offered. While many began in the construction and service industries they quickly expanded to other areas and are now leaders in industry, academia and politics. Italian Canadians have contributed to the building of a modem Canada; not only our infrastructure and houses, but our culture, ethics and our cuisine!

This collection speaks of the industriousness, the perseverance and the creativity of the Italian immigrant and how they've played a key role in designing the Canadian Italian partnership. Today, Italy and Canada are world leaders in aerospace, life sciences, green economy, sustainability and agriculture. The Canada EU Trade Agreement (CETA), is a natural alliance founded on these linkages that will continue to allow both countries to prosper and meet the challenges of the future.

It has been an honour and a joy to represent Canada in Italy for the past four years, and my heart now bears a large green stripe.

Sincerely,

Alexandra Bugailiskis
Ambassador of Canada to Italy

TABLE OF CONTENTS

WOODBRIDGE

PREFACE
HON. MAURIZIO BEVILACQUA, P.C.
MAYOR
CITY OF VAUGHAN

The story of the Italian community in Canada has often been told because it so neatly illustrates the promise this country represents to the rest of the world. We are a nation built on the energy, initiative, and imagination of immigrants. We provide a safe harbour for people around the world seeking a better life and in return we ask newcomers to contribute to building a compassionate, equitable, and adventurous society. Italian Canadians have responded to this grand bargain with such intelligence and determination that they have become a model of how an immigrant community can find success, and in the process, transform the country they settle in.

Yesterday, Today and Tomorrow is filled with such stories and clearly shows that there is not a sector of the economy that hasn't been touched by the Italian Canadian spirit and influence. From humble beginnings they created a self-supportive community, providing social services to each other when none were available. Manual labourers acquired skills they applied to designing and building houses, eventually creating companies that developed entire communities in the GTA. Today if you look at the media, sciences, fashion, law, politics, entertainment, manufacturing or investment, you will find Italian Canadians in leadership positions. Seventy years ago, genuine Parmigiano-Reggiano, espresso, and even garlic were considered exotic items by the average Canadian. Today, the Italian approach to food has not only transformed the hospitality industry by dominating restaurant menus, it has become the default Canadian cuisine for many people when they gather for a meal at home.

It's easy to take the Italian contribution to our culture for granted because it is everywhere around us and part of the daily life of all Canadians. But it's worth remembering where it came from. Yesterday provides us with many moving stories of a community pulling together to overcome hardships. Today we see the fruits of those efforts all around us. Tomorrow will bring new adventures and new challenges but also a new generation of Italian Canadians with a rich and inspiring history to draw from. Who knows what they will contribute next?

ICCO CANADA

FROM THE ITALIAN CHAMBER OF COMMERCE OF ONTARIO TO ICCO CANADA

CORRADO PAINA

Some claim the famous Italian industrialist James Franceschini founded the first Italian Chamber in Canada, in the city of Toronto. If one wants to know more about Franceschini and other Italian business leaders one would have trouble finding documentation. Italian settlement has been the subject of many books and research papers by academics, historians and community leaders. Nevertheless, one can find few meaningful documents on the Italian business community in Canada, with a few exceptions, such as the ICCO Canada's former magazine, *Partners*.

SERGIO MARCHIONNE, 2006

NIVO ANGELONE, CORRADO PAINA, SERGIO MARCHIONNE

The entire geography of the GTA has been transformed by Italian builders. The Prime Minister admitted that Toronto Italians own the city for having built it, but most historians and sociologists have overlooked the footsteps of Italian originators—the entrepreneurs, merchants, and traders. This has metamorphosed the GTA economy—from corner fruit sellers and street musicians to great law people, financiers, and builders, including countless small business owners. And what of the contribution of Italians in Canadian science, innovation and health? Is it not correct to say Italians have integrated to become one hundred per cent Canadian? Does that imply historical precedents are erased with forgetfulness?

The award given by ICCO Canada to Sergio Marchionne in 2006 was certainly one of the highlights in the history of the Chamber. This book is in fact dedicated to Sergio Marchionne, a citizen of two worlds. It is difficult to imagine anyone more indicative of the nature, culture, and spirit of North America and Italy, to be perfectly at ease in two nations. Marchionne set a precedent, as a social and political human entity, sewing one suit from two cloths, two identities. Is it true that Mario Cuomo was asked about his identity: "Italian or American?" His answer: "I bring with me 2500 years of history—2,000 from Italy, 500 from America." Marchionne navigated two languages, and, more importantly, two sophisticated cultural and business realms. We grew up learning that the Risorgimento was one of the pinnacles of Italian history. We studied Mazzini, Cavour and Garibaldi, "the hero of two worlds." That sentence, that title, no Italian can ever forget. If Garibaldi was the hero, Sergio Marchionne was the citizen of two worlds.

Sergio Marchionne has at times been strongly criticized but media publications never stop talking about his legacy. I cannot say the same is happening here in Canada. Scholars and visiting overseas students ask for documents, books, newspapers, magazines about the Italian business community. We have very little at the Chamber—because there is not much in Canada. "Yesterday, Today and Tomorrow" doesn't have all the answers but it does hold significant information that leads to further questions. My hope is this book will inspire scholars, journalists and the general public to dig deeper into the phases of settlement, development and eventual integration of the Italian business community in Toronto, the GTA and hopefully, all of Canada. How can we overlook the Italian contribution to Canadian history from the Italians in Northern Ontario, Ottawa, Montreal, Edmonton, and Vancouver? In 2006 the Italian Chamber of Commerce of Toronto became the Italian Chamber of Commerce of Ontario (ICCO). That same year, the annual Business Excellence Awards acknowledged Marchionne's work, as well as the mandate of an Ontario Minister of International Trade of Italian origin: Joseph Cordiano.

This year the ICCO became the Italian Chamber of Commerce of Ontario Canada (ICCO Canada.) I've worked with some great people these last 14 years, including great presidents: Clemente Benelli, Nivo Angelone, George Visintin and current co-presidents, Tony Altomare and Pat Pelliccione. I've worked with great board members, both past and present. We are at a crossroads and COVID-19 has taught us that we cannot stop change.

You can never step twice in the same river. The hurried passenger might overlook two plaques at the entrance of the Princes' Gates at the Canadian National Exhibition. The little square in front of the gates was rebuilt, thanks to an ICCO Canada sponsored contest, resulting in a joint force of architectural firms from Milan and Toronto. Our name is now among those of important organizations and city leaders, all of whom have contributed to the building of this city. Of this province. Of Canada.

An organization that claims to be a leader must know the history of its community. This year saw the publication of "Land of Triumph and Tragedy," an interesting and long-overdue book by Marino Toppan and Paola Breda on fallen Italian workers. As noted in the magazine *Spacing*, Hoggs Hollow was one of the 25 most important events in Toronto—a historical moment for our community and urban development, in which five Italian workers died at a watermain project under the Don River.

"Yesterday, Today and Tomorrow" talks about Italian politicians, builders, and law people. It talks about the beginning and development of fashion, of the agri-food and hospitality industries. We are at a crossroad—what will be the identity of the Chamber? It will, in my opinion, be one that follows the development of the business community. Science and enterprise are more frequently melding to create a new DNA. Or perhaps revisiting a prior DNA: in the Renaissance there was a poet that was both city leader and banker. Some of the first poets were lawmen.

Culture and business. This is the future. Science, poetry, business. The ICCO Canada is working to be a Chamber of the future. A new mission statement is emerging, positioning the Chamber as a catalyst for developing business and cultural alliances among visionaries, entrepreneurs, and global organizations in Canada and in Italy.

Finally, this book is also dedicated to three other people who each made lasting contributions to the Italian Canadian community and to the civic life of this country. Marisa Piattelli was a city leader, a social entrepreneur and a member of the ICCO Canada board. Ron Farano was a champion of the ICCO Canada from its earliest days in the 1960s, as was Antonio Valeri, the managing director. Both men helped lead it from its infancy to its maturity. Their guidance will always be remembered.

Our community has many business leaders, most of them unknown to the community at large. It is time to know more by learning about Yesterday, Today, and Tomorrow.

TOP RIGHT: MARISA PIATTELLI

BOTTOM RIGHT: RON FARANO

BAR
CARR & CO'S
LUNCH

AN IMMIGRANT FAMILY ARRIVES IN TORONTO (1910) PHOTO: CITY OF TORONTO ARCHIVES

FRANK IACOBUCCI

SOME REFLECTIONS ON ITALIAN CANADIANS

(Remarks originally offered at the Italian Chamber of Commerce of Ontario Canada Business Excellence Awards May 25, 2017)

"Like many immigrant communities before and after them and like many other countries, the Italians were victims of widespread prejudice and discrimination. In the popular consciousness of the time, immigrant—and specifically Italian—quarters were usually associated with dirt, diseases, overcrowding, ignorance, immorality and vice."

When Corrado Paina asked me to offer some remarks this evening, we both thought it was appropriate for me to share some reflections on Italian Canadians especially since we are celebrating the sesquicentennial of Canada. Now I am not 150 years old but I am over one half that age and have witnessed great changes for Italian Canadians—much for the better.

I thought I'd give a brief overview of the settling in Canada of Italians interspersed with personal experiences of my family and myself. My personal experiences are not meant to be unique but simply to illustrate the events that occurred and the transformation that has taken place. Now for a little history.

EARLIEST ITALIAN CONTACT WITH NORTH AMERICA

Italians were among the earliest Europeans to have visited and settled in what is now Canada. Not counting Columbus, the earliest Italian contact with North America was Giovanni Caboto (John Cabot), an Italian navigator from Venice, who in 1497 explored the coasts of Newfoundland on behalf of England and King Henry VII.[1] In 1524, Giovanni de Varrazzano charted the Atlantic coast of North America between the Carolinas and Newfoundland, on behalf of France. Also under the patronage of the Kings of Portugal and Spain, the Florentine Amerigo Vespucci was another early Italian explorer after whom America is named. Why so many Italians? They were great navigators in those times whose skills were practised on the Mediterranean Sea. But Italy, unlike England, France, Spain and Portugal, was not a colonizing nation, mainly, so it seems, because it was not on the Atlantic coasts. Other early Italians in Canada included those serving as mercenaries in the military of New France, or later in the British army during the war of 1812. Some of these latter mercenaries elected to stay, accepting lots granted by Britain in Quebec's Eastern townships and Southern Ontario.[2]

Montreal was home to one of the country's earliest Italian colonies. In the early to mid-19th Century, there were a significant number of Italians living in the city, many working in the hotel trade and others as street musicians.[3] Overall, however, the numbers of Italian Canadians remained very small—it is estimated that by 1881 there were approximately 2000 people of Italian origin living in Canada.[4] Immigration from Italy to Canada gradually accelerated in the late 19th Century, as large numbers of Italian peasants began emigrating to Canada, the United States, South America and Western Europe. By the turn of the century, the number of people of Italian origin living in Canada had grown to almost 11,000.[5]

FIRST BIG WAVE OF ITALIAN IMMIGRATION: 1900-1914

Between 1900 and the outbreak of World War I, almost 120,000 Italians entered Canada. Remarkably, about 80% of them were young males, most of whom went to work in seasonal and heavy labour jobs in mines, lumber-camps, building projects and especially the railways. Included in this group were one of my paternal aunts and her husband who went to Vancouver in about 1912. In Canada, a major part of these workers were absorbed into the two principal railroad companies, the Canadian Pacific and the Grand Trunk.[6] These men came predominantly from Italy's rural South, especially the regions of Calabria, Abruzzo and Sicily, beginning a trend that would continue with successive waves of Italian immigration to Canada. Friuli also joined the southern regions as a major source of Italian emigration from Italy. As most of you know, factors inducing emigration from these regions included overpopulation, the fragmentation of peasant farms, poverty, poor health and education and political dissatisfaction.[7]

The largest center of Italian immigration in Canada remained Montreal, where the 1911 census recorded over 7000 people of Italian origin. Toronto followed, with over 4600. In Toronto, the College Street colony emerged as Toronto's major Little Italy, bounded by Manning Ave in the East, Crawford in the West, College in the North, and Dundas in the South. While some of these urban immigrants worked as tradesmen, artisans or merchants, most were working physically demanding, dirty and dangerous jobs. The most common occupations were construction, excavation, brick and cement work.[8]

In addition to Montreal and Toronto, significant numbers of Italians went to northern Ontario during this period. Hundreds went to the twin cities of Port Arthur and Fort William (now amalgamated as the city of Thunder Bay), filling jobs in freight yards, grain elevators, and coal docks. Between 1906 and 1909, Italian labourers in the twin cities were involved in numerous large-scale strikes in protest of the poor pay, long hours and dangerous working conditions to which they were subjected.[9]

Many of these immigrants were more properly labelled 'sojourners' than immigrants, as they did not anticipate settling in North America permanently. As the Canadian Superintendent of Immigration observed in 1910 "They [Italians] are usually looking for work as railway navies and are to a great extent birds of passage and have no desire to make Canada a permanent home[10] Gradually, increasing numbers made the transition from sojourner to permanent settler.

Like many immigrant communities before and after them, like many other countries, the Italians were victims of widespread prejudice and discrimination. In the popular consciousness of the time, immigrant—and specifically Italian—quarters were usually associated with dirt, diseases, overcrowding, ignorance, immorality and vice. In 1911 Toronto's medical officer of Health, writing in the Globe, suggested Italian neighbourhoods represented a threat to the rest of the city, noting the "congested districts of unsanitary, overcrowded dwellings which are a menace to public health, affording hotbeds for germination of disease, vice and crime."[11] The Port Arthur Daily News had described the Italian working-class as "a horde of ignorant and low-down mongrel swashbucklers and peanut vendors."[12] This sentiment found expression among Anglo-Saxons across the political spectrum: even Canadian socialist icon J.S. Woodsworth warned in his book "Strangers Within Our Gates" that "we must see to it that the civilization and ideals of South-eastern Europe are not transplanted to and perpetuated on our virgin soil."[13]

INTERWAR PERIOD AND WORLD WAR II: ITALIAN IMMIGRATION DRIES UP

Immigration was slowed by the outbreak of World War I, and remained low throughout the inter-war period and the Depression. My father went to Vancouver from Abruzzo in 1922 and my mother from Calabria in 1925, well before

CAMP PETAWAWA

Pier 21 in Halifax. When Mussolini joined the Axis powers in World War II, Canadian hostility towards fascism became directed at Italian Canadians, who were designated 'enemy aliens.' As enemy aliens, my mother and father had to report monthly to the RCMP. When I was 5 or 6 years old, I remember going with my mother on some of the monthly visits. Many men lost jobs (including my father who had been working at the airport), had their businesses vandalized, and found their civil liberties suspended under the War Measures Act.[14] Most infamously, hundreds of Italian Canadians were interned for years at Camp Petawawa in Ontario. Included in this group was my older brother's father-in-law who was in Petawawa for over two years and lost his bakery business in Vancouver. While a minority of these men had connections to fascist groups in Canada, most did not: the large majority of naturalized Canadians were not disloyal to Canada, and most simply had (often tenuous) connections to various lodges and clubs of the Italian Canadian community.[15] For example, my brother's father-in-law joined a fascist club because he was selling Panini from his bakery to club members. Of course they were not given any due process whatsoever in the loss of their liberty. The interned men had to work on roads, or deep in woods clearing brush and cutting timber, for which they were paid 20 cents a day; as I said, many lost their businesses, and letters from home were censored with no family visits.[16] Among those interned was James Franceschini, Canada's first Italian-born millionaire, who had made his fortune after founding Dufferin Construction in 1918. Franceschini ultimately had many of his properties confiscated by the government.[17]

Because of the stigma associated with Italian heritage during this period, many Italian Canadians chose to anglicize their names: Rossini became Ross, Riccioni became Richards, Giacomo became Jackman.[18]

SECOND BIG WAVE: 1950-1970

As Italy joined the ranks of liberal democracies and was integrated into Western security arrangements following WWII, the barrier to further Italian immigration to Canada was removed. The number of Italian immigrants to Canada exploded, with approximately half a million arriving between 1950 and 1970. The large numbers were a result of 'chain migration': Italian families, immediate and extended, were large and links extended to neighbouring villages. Thus, as one writer notes, an entire commune would sometimes come, over the course of a decade or two, from Italy to a new home in Canada.[19] Each year tens of thousands of Italian immigrants moved through the port of Halifax, with as many as two-thirds bound for Toronto, which overtook Montreal as the largest Italian Canadian community, and ultimately one of the largest settlements of Italians living outside Italy.[20] A great many went to work on the Gardiner expressway, or other construction and labour jobs in the Toronto suburbs, since Italians were shunned by British or Irish dominated unions, and not recruited to work in prized downtown Toronto jobs.[21]

Like the immigrants in the Northern Ontario twin cities at the turn of the 20th century, Toronto's Italian labourers played a significant role in labour rights struggles. A major turning point was 1960: a tunnel was being dug under the Don River along the route of the aqueduct intended to serve the then burgeoning urbanization of North York. The tunnel collapsed during a night shift, killing five Italian workers. Only two months later, in a dockyard near Weston Road, an Italian digger was buried alive in a landslide.[22] These incidents came to be seen as emblematic of the mistreatment of Italian workers, leading to major strikes and demonstrations that were covered by the English-speaking press as the "revolt of the immigrants."[23] The labour agitation resulted in government commissions and reviews of lax labour regulations, and ultimately embryonic collective agreements.

In addition to Toronto, the Italian immigrants would go on to establish Italian communities in Montreal, Sault Ste. Marie and Thunder Bay. Large numbers also made their way to British Columbia, where 40,000 had settled by the late 1950s, including 20,000 in Vancouver, with men at work in lumbering, mining, fishing and farming. In contrast to the general pattern of Italian immigrants coming largely from the South, the Italian community in B.C. comes mostly from the North (Trentino, Friuli, Veneto).[24]

Men ostensibly arrived under one year contracts for hard physical labour, but the great majority in fact were coming as permanent settlers, later sponsoring their wives, children and other relatives. Family "chain migration" from Italy was so extensive that by 1958, Italy surpassed Britain as a source for immigrants. In fact, the Italians were marked as the largest ethnic group in the nation after the English, French and Germans.[25] This massive wave of Italian immigration only slowed when new regulations were introduced in 1967 that based admissibility on universal criteria, and confined family sponsorship to a limited range of relatives.

Unfortunately, Italian immigrants continued to be the subjects of discrimination and prejudice. As Bagnell notes, even in the 1960s, "so many decades after the ignominy of the war years, the derision lingered, less coarse or explicit, but fixed and ingrained."[26] One of the more endemic (and harmful) manifestations of this prejudice found expression in the education system, where vocational guidance counsellors steered Italian Canadian children away from university academic study and instead to trades and clerical jobs (euphemistically labelled 'streaming').[27]

Here I inject another personal episode. In 1957 while at UBC I was an undergraduate in Commerce. I was asked by my Economics Statistics professor (Tadek Matuzewski) what I wanted to do in life. As I had done well in his statistics course, I was one of his lab assistants. When I told him I wanted to be a lawyer, he said I shouldn't because "I didn't have the right name." He suggested we go talk to John Deutsch, then Chairman of the Political Economy Department and later President of Queen's University. Fortunately Deutsch said Canada "was changing" and I should go to law school if that is what I wanted. But I still wondered why would anyone's last name be a barrier to what career he or she wished to pursue.

Now let me highlight Italian Canadians in contemporary Canada.

PROFILE OF ITALIAN CANADIANS TODAY

According to the 2011 census (the most recent statistics I found), just under 1.5 million Canadians claim full or partial Italian ancestry.[28] About 60% of Italian Canadians live in Ontario, 21% in Quebec and 10% in B.C. By far the largest concentration of Italian immigrants is in Toronto, where there are nearly half a million people of Italian origin. The second largest community is Montreal, where there are over a quarter million. As a percentage of population, the Canadian community with the highest proportion of Italian residents is Sault Ste. Marie, where fully 20% of residents claim Italian heritage. In descending order, other large concentrations of Italian Canadians are found in the following communities: Vancouver, Hamilton, St.Catherines-Niagara, Ottawa, Windsor, Calgary, Edmonton, London, Winnipeg, Thunder Bay, Sudbury, Oshawa.

Of the Italian immigrants who came following WWII, over 75% of the first generation were employed in low-income occupations. This, however, changed dramatically with the second and subsequent generations. Already by the 1980s, the children of Italian immigrants had achieved a level of higher education equal to the national average. Today, Italian Canadians are well-represented across professions, especially business, academics, education, politics, law, and medicine, and have a higher rate of homeownership than the national average.[29] While certain stereotypes persist (e.g., that Italian Canadians are indelibly associated with the mobsters), the level of prejudice against Italian Canadians has lessened dramatically as they have advanced and become fully integrated into broader Canadian society.

As a small example of the transformation of both the attitudes and engagement of Canadians of Italian origin, I point out that I was appointed successively by then Prime Minister Mulroney to be Deputy Minister of Justice and Deputy Attorney General of Canada, Chief Justice of the Federal Court of Canada and a Justice of the Supreme Court of Canada. I mention this for two reasons. First, without the outstanding record of contributions and achievements of Italian Canadians, I don't believe I would have been appointed to those positions. Second, the appointments reflect the importance of diversity and equality as a reality for Canada. As Italian Canadians we must all do our part to ensure that Canada continues to go forward, not backward in that respect. To conclude, I wish to say that I profoundly cherish my Italian ancestry and I am immensely proud of my fellow Italian Canadians. And on July 1 I will celebrate not only Canada's 150th but also those Italians who came to our country to contribute to its growth and development and paved the way for us and succeeding generations.

BILLIARDS
CIGARS
IGARETTES
Smoke
Ogden's
Cut Plug
Smoke
Ogd

COLLEGE ST. TORONTO, 1930; PHOTO: JA

THE 1930s: SUFFERING, TRIUMPH AND CHALLENGES

FRANK GIORNO

The stock market crash of October 1929 started a panic on the New York, Toronto, and Montreal stock exchanges and billions of dollars were lost. Hundreds of thousands of workers were laid off. Unemployment rose to a record 30% by 1933 in Canada. Even those who were employed struggled as their earnings shrunk by up to 60%. One in five Canadians became dependent upon government relief for survival. The unemployment rate remained above 12% until the start of the Second World War in 1939.

Ontario's economic position during the early depression years was very unstable. Government policy favoured protecting taxpayers and their demands for less government rather than protecting those who were in actual need.

R.B. Bennett's Conservative party won the 1930 election against William Lyon Mackenzie King's Liberals, promising to fight the Great Depression. Failure to keep his promise resulted in his defeat by King in 1935.

The Italian communities during the 1930s survived because of strong family networks and thrift, so they could absorb some of the economic shock of unemployment and deprivation. Churches provided aid: Our Lady of Mount Carmel in the Ward on Simcoe St.; St. Agnes (Dundas St. W. and Grace) serving the College St. area; St. Mary of the Angels on Dufferin, serving the St. Clair and Dufferin community. For those on the Danforth, Holy Name, was the church of choice. The United Church of Canada and other protestant churches established missions to care for these "new" Canadians in the hope their generosity would attract the Italian immigrant to join them.

Young males made up 80% of the Italian Canadians immigrating to Canada to work on railroad construction and maintenance, highway construction and paving, mining and forestry in the Ontario hinterland north of Toronto. Many Italian men who settled in large urban cities like Toronto worked construction as city road repairers, home builders, or in heavy industry. The Canada Foundry plant in the Lansdowne and Dupont area where railway engines were built, and the Canadian General Electric factory, are a couple of examples.

ITALIAN FAMILY IN 'THE WARD' (1913) PHOTO CREDIT, CITY OF TORONTO ARCHIVES

Some, using their savings from their hinterland heavy construction work, started up small businesses. Fruit markets and grocery stores were opened. Others engaged in barbering and hairstyling, shoe repair, tailoring, dressmaking, bar, restaurant, or hotel management.

The work history of Vincenzo (James) Franceschini provides an overview of Italian Canadians who opened businesses.

Franceschini arrived in Toronto 1906 as a 16-year-old from Abruzzo, Italy. He started off working at Canada Foundry, producing fabricated steel and iron products, including locomotives.

Franceschini later worked for contractors who built or repaired the city of Toronto sidewalks and road projects. Around 1910, Franceschini and friends opened up a small excavation company. Franceschini knocked on doors in the Ward district of Toronto to find those who needed foundations dug, or expansions built.

The Ward was an immigrant reception area because of its proximity to Union Station. It was comprised of Jewish, Ukrainian, Polish, Italian, German, and Slavic peoples. The neighbourhood ran from Queen St. north to College St., and from Yonge St. west to Spadina Avenue.

Dufferin Construction was formed in 1912 and secured a contract to build the roads system for the Ontario Hydro Generation station at Eugenia, Ontario. The company nearly went bankrupt as work dried up during WWI. Through persistence and hard work, Franceschini accumulated income working at the newly built Kodak Plant at Weston and Eglington. He also went to Noble, Ontario to build tracks for the newly finished explosive factory near Parry Sound.

With his savings he bought back his road building equipment, including a steam shovel, and in 1915 Colonel Sam McLaughlin hired Dufferin Construction to build the road network at the Canadian General Motors facility in Oshawa.

In the 1917 provincial election, the United Farmers of Ontario [UFO] ran on the need for better roads to break up the railway monopoly, offering a less expensive way of bringing their products to market. The UFO defeated the Liberals and the Conservatives and Premier E.C. Drury formed the first UFO government in Ontario. Dufferin Construction became the preferred highway builder. From 1917 to 1923, Dufferin Construction worked on the King's Highway System, building Highway 2, 3, 5, and others. The Toronto Star lauded Franceschini as a two-time millionaire by age 34 in a 1924 article. By 1939, Dufferin had become the largest highway construction company in Canada, expanding into Quebec and the Maritimes.

JAMES FRANCESCHINI PHOTO CREDIT, MCCREATH FAMILY ARCHIVES

CONSTRUCTION AND CONTRACTING BUSINESS

In addition to Dufferin Construction, a number of other Italian Canadian construction or specialty contracting companies existed in the 1930s. Jack Del Zotto created a small company in 1934 that his three sons, Angelo, Elvio and Leo, evolved into Tridel, one of the largest developers in Canada. There were 12 construction and contractor companies listed in the 1931 Toronto City Directory. By 1934 there were 15. In 1936 the number increased to 27.

FRUIT VENDORS, GROCERY STORES AND FOOD PRODUCTS

By far the largest sector of Italian Canadian business was in the food sector, ranging from fruit stores, grocery stores, market gardens, confectionary stores, restaurants, cafes, and ice cream parlours.

Italian Canadian grocery stores clustered in the four major Italian Canadian neighbourhoods in Toronto. As described by John Zucchi in his book "History of Italians in Toronto 1875-1935," the four principal areas were The Ward, College Street, Danforth and St. Clair Ave W.

Other stores known as market gardens were opened by Italian Canadians beyond what was then, the city limits. For example, Pirri's Fruit and Vegetable Market was located at 2533 Yonge St., between Eglinton and Lawrence. Frank

Palumbo was located even further north at 3229 Yonge St. Another market garden location was along Varsity Avenue in the Township of York by the Humber River.

Pasquale Bros. opened in 1917, on Elm Street in the Ward. By the 1930s, the success of Pasquale Bros. enabled them to purchase a property at 111 King St. W. in the heart of Old Toronto. Soon, their food products, under the Unico brand, such as canned tomatoes, tomato paste and other products catering to the Italian community were being mass produced and supplied to fruit and grocery stores all over Toronto.

The strategy Pasquale Bros. pursued was to be a wholesale food provider for everyone in the city. Christmas ads in the Globe and Mail, the Toronto Star, and Toronto Telegram offered season's greetings and were an effort to ingratiate themselves with Anglo-Saxons and English-speaking Irish and Scots.

Today the Longo, Pusateri, and Badali names from the 1930s still prosper, as do the Pasquale Bros.

SELF-CARE

The other major area of Italian Canadian participation was in the self-care business, such as barbershops, hairdressers, shoe repair, shoeshine, and clothing sectors.

By 1938 there were 27 Italian Canadian barbershops and five beauty salons in Toronto. Though they were mostly pegged to the Italian Districts in Toronto, some Italian barbershops were also operating in non-Italian neighbourhoods such as mid-Toronto, north of College to St. Clair, or downtown in the Toronto business heartland, serving the non-Italian business community

Shoe repair and shoeshine stores were another area of heavily Italian Canadian involvement. In 1936 there were 26 shoe repair stores in Toronto. Unlike previous patterns of being situated near Italian Canadian districts, most of the shoe-shiners were located near Union Station, the Royal York Hotel, the King Edward Hotel, and the downtown business district.

Clothing needs were easily met. For special occasions, such as marriages, funerals, first communions, and on those occasions where dressing well was a factor, there were tailors, dressmakers and children's wear stores to provide that distinguished look.

HOTELS AND BOARDING HOUSES

By the 1930s, the Hotel Glionna, an important landmark for the nascent Italian community, was long gone. But the legacy of the Glionna family, the operators of the hotel until 1917, touched many aspects of Toronto life. According to John Zucchi, Francesco Glionna's grandchildren became Toronto's first Italian Canadian doctor and lawyer. His son Donato Glionna was an organizer for the Liberal Party and also started up two social organizations. They also became artists and designers, university professors, musicians, and athletes.

Though their hotel closed, Italian-run hotels and boarding houses continued to operate, such as Angelo's Hotel on the corner of Elm and University. It would exist as a hotel and later a restaurant and small theatre known as Old Angelo's. In 1934, Leonard Franceschini, got a license to open a bar at the Royal Cecil Hotel on Jarvis Ave. south of Dundas St. E. In addition to hotels there were several boarding houses operated by Italian Canadians that provided a respite for the seasonal workers of Ontario's hinterland. Up north building roads, working in forestry, pulp and paper, or mining, some returned south for the winter and then flocked back up north in the spring.

WOMEN EARNING A LIVELIHOOD

Italian Canadian women worked in factories in the Spadina needle trade as seamstresses; they also worked as domestics. Some Italian Canadian women were listed in the City Directory during the 1930s as the owners, or at least the managers of grocery stores. Somewhat unusually, Mrs. Mary Fasano was listed as the owner of an auto repair shop at 1670 St. Clair Ave. West, where she also provided a bicycle repair service.

ARTISTS

There were also Italian Canadian artists of note like Vincent De Vita, who had immigrated to Canada by way of the United States. In the 1930s, De Vita was friends with the Group of 7 and focused on the Canadian outdoors, but in a much more subdued manner.

In the 1930s, Ettore Fattori had a workshop on 112 Bond Street near St. Michael's Cathedral and was renowned for his religious themed paintings and design. Fattori produced the "Rosary Color Book," drawings by Ettore Fattori, originally published in 1949 by the Catechetical Guild. In 2008, a website (familyfeastandferia.com) revived interest in Fattori's religious colouring book and his other religious artworks.

ITALIAN CANADIAN SPORTS HEROES OF THE DEPRESSION

Boxing became a passion for Italian Canadians, as Frankie "Kid" Genovese and Steve Rocco became the great Italian hopes in Toronto. Genovese fought memorable bouts against Sammy Luftspring and Baby Yack. Genovese was named to the 1932 Canadian Olympic Boxing Team for the Los Angeles Olympics. It was a proud moment for Italians. The COC, strapped for funds, only sponsored a handful athletes to L.A. The Kid was not one of them. The Italian community held fundraisers to pay for his train ticket and lodgings so he could participate for Canada.

A year after the Olympics on August 9, 1933, the Jewish and Italian communities spearheaded by boxers from local boxing clubs beat back an effort by the Beaches Swastika Club to disrupt a minor baseball game at Christie Pits. The game was between the St. Peter's CYO team and the mainly Jewish Elizabeth Recreation team, better known as the Lizzies. The event today is known as "The Riot at Christie Pits."

For ordinary folk, community recreation could be found in Italian billiard rooms, also known as pool halls, but many also provided tables in the back to play Italian card games, which were periodically raided by Toronto Police as part of Toronto's Blue Laws.

The 1930s also saw the rise of Italian Canadians playing hockey. Peter Palangio born in 1908 in North Bay, Ontario, played for the Montreal Canadiens in 1926-1929 and Palangio also played for the Chicago Black Hawks' 1938 Stanley Cup-winning team—the first Italian Canadian to be a Cup winner. Several years later, in 1944, another Italian Canadian made history in the NHL. Armand "Bep" Guidolin, a 16-year-old from Timmins, Ontario, became the youngest player to skate in an NHL game. Guidolin later went on to coach Bobby Orr in the Ontario Hockey League and the NHL.

MUSIC

For Italian Canadians, and all Toronto music lovers, several popular Italian Canadian musicians offered world class entertainment during the depression-ravaged decade.

In 1926, Edoardo Ferrari-Fontana moved to Toronto and opened a voice studio where he taught operatic singing until shortly before his death in 1936. Ferrari-Fontana founded the Music and Arts League of Toronto, which flourished 1927-36, and presented operatic concerts annually at Eaton Auditorium or Hart House.

A number of exciting Italian Canadian jazz bands helped Torontonians dance the depression away. Guy Lombardo and his Royal Canadians established themselves as one of the top jazz bands in Canada, frequently playing Toronto. The Palais Royale and the Palace Pier were the places to go for live music and dancing. Big bands such as Duke Ellington, Count Basie, and the Dorsey Brothers played there. From 1933 to 1950, "Canada's King of Swing," Bert Niosi, and his orchestra, were the house band at the Palais Royale.

Several music schools were opened by Italians in Toronto, such as Michele Angelo at 269 College St. and Joseph Carboni at 4 Alexandria St. Frank Fusco taught at the Toronto Conservatory of Music at University of Toronto. Antonio Glionna taught violin at 1 Grant Street in the area of Broadview and Gerrard St. East known as Riverdale.

POLITICAL INVOLVEMENT

Political parties began wooing the Italian community for their votes. The Liberal Party held many grass roots meetings. On June 17, 1934, James Franceschini held a massive rally for the Conservative Party of Ontario at his horse farm near Dufferin and Wilson. It was one of the largest political rallies in Ontario on behalf of Conservative Premier George Henry. The Toronto Star and Globe and Mail estimated 10,000 people attended on a Sunday. Shuttle buses were hired to carry people from St. Clair and Dufferin to the farm.

Franceschini exhorted Italian Canadians to vote Conservative because Premier George

Henry gave Dufferin Construction road building contracts that allowed him to hire Italian Canadian labourers. Despite Franceschini's plea, Mitchell Hepburn became Premier in June 1934 and the Liberals formed the government.

At the municipal level, and further afield from Toronto, Hubert Badanai, in 1938, was elected Mayor of Fort William, the first Italian to be mayor of a Canadian City.

International politics also played a major role in the community. Before Mussolini's Ethiopian invasion in 1935, he had strong support in Toronto and elsewhere. Sir Winston Churchill hailed Mussolini. "I could not help being charmed, like so many other people have been, by his gentle and simple bearing and by his calm, detached poise in spite of so many burdens." Churchill went on to say if he had been Italian, he would have supported Mussolini.

In Toronto, the Empire Club featured fascist luncheon speakers like Professor William Sherwood Fox, who praised Mussolini for upholding Christian moral values threatened by communists and capitalists.

"The fascists are the best men of the younger generation of Italians, ... best educated, the most self-sacrificing in their patriotism and the most industrious," said Fox. "... the one human being who is responsible for the stemming of the tide of bolshevism in its westward flow is Mussolini," Fox added.

Canon Henry John Cody, University of Toronto President, brought Italian professors and Italian Studies courses to the University. In appreciation, Canon Cody was awarded the Victor Emmanuel Medal, as was James Franceschini of Dufferin Construction.

Things that were innocent activities previously, like receptions and addresses of Italian fascists at the Empire Club luncheon series, or the February 1934 reception for Parini, Mussolini's Minister for Overseas Italians, by Franceschini at Myrtle Villa, took on ominous overtones in retrospect.

On September 1, 1939, the day after war broke out, C.D. Howe, the Minister of Munitions and Supply asked Franceschini to build four destroyers for the war effort at the old Toronto Shipyards he purchased in the 1920s. Then on June 10, 1940, the world for Italian Canadians dramatically changed. Belonging to the Fascist party was OK on June 9, 1940, illegal on June 10, 1940. All fascist organizations defined by the War Measures Act in Canada were deemed illegal, including the Casa D'Italia consulate and the Dopolavoro (after work) social club. Casa D'Italia was seized by the Custodian of Enemy Property.

The Mackenzie King government and RCMP were concerned about a "5th Column" inside Canada. The RCMP relied on evidence provided by two Italian Canadians—Camilo Vetere, who was the secretary of the Montreal Fascio, and Agosto Bersani, a discredited priest and minister of the Italian United Church of Canada. James Franceschini, along with hundreds of other Italian Canadians were arrested and sent to Camp Petawawa, the infamous internment camp.

Still, many prominent Canadians and media outlets were supportive of the Italian Canadian community and stood up for them—people like Ontario Premier Mitchell Hepburn, Colonel Sam McLaughlin of GM Canada, The Globe and Mail, John Diefenbaker, then a young MP and prairie lawyer, Sir James Dunn, owner of Algoma Steel and Dalton McCarthy, lawyer, and founder of McCarthy Tetrault, as the firm is known today.

The highly principled Justice James Hyndman was named to head a Royal Commission into the guilt or innocence of the internees. He ruled that internees condemned by Camilo Vetere and Agosto Bersani, with no other evidence, were to be freed.

A large number of Italian Canadian internees were released by Justice Hyndman in 1940, 1941 and 1942. All Italian Canadian internees were released in 1943 after Mussolini was ousted from power by King Victor Emmanuel. In May 2021, Prime Minister Justin Trudeau apologized to the Italian community for their treatment during the second world war.

The generation of the 1930s helped pave the way for the success of postwar Italian immigrants and provided them with a community, churches, stores, and a sense of belonging. The 1930s were a time of suffering, triumph, and disaster for Italian Canadians in Toronto. The hard work, loyalty, and devotion to succeeding in Canada helped pave the way for the future success of Italians who immigrated to Toronto in the postwar period in construction, the food industry, and many other sectors of the Canadian economy.

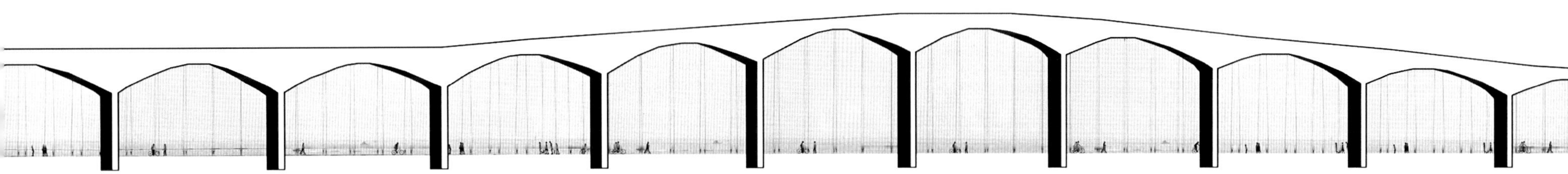

THE INEVITABLE GROUP IMPACT: THE ITALIAN IMMIGRANTS' CONTRIBUTIONS TO THE CONSTRUCTION SECTOR

MONICA CONTRERAS

Canada became an economic and progressive world power after the Second World War in large part due to the contribution and arduous work of immigrants. "According to the 2016 Census almost 22% of the Canadian population are foreign-born immigrants, with 8.3% identified as Italian descent.[1]" For more than 150 years, young unskilled and semi-skilled workers left the newly unified country of Italy during three identified waves of immigration.

PHOTO CREDIT, SHUTTERSTOCK

The contributions of Italian immigrants to Canada in city-building are tangible in Canada's larger urban centres of Montreal and Toronto, and to a lesser extent Vancouver and smaller urban industrial towns such as Hamilton, and even remote communities such as Sault Sainte Marie. Contributions extended beyond the construction sector from the building of railways to the extraction and processing of mines in Sudbury, Kirkland Lake and Cape Breton Island in Nova Scotia, to the pulp and paper mills in British Columbia, to agricultural lands, to the manufacturing and production of consumer goods from textiles, fashion to heavy machinery.

"The construction sector is one that has always been an important driver of the overall Canadian economy and also serves as an accurate barometer for how strong or weak the national economy is at any given time. Canada is widely recognized as one of the world's largest markets for commercial, residential and infrastructure development.[2]" In the construction sector the contribution by Italian immigrants extends into every crevasse, from manufacturing to the expansion of infrastructure, housing, and skyscrapers, as well as all the specialized trades in wood, stone and interior finishes and the artisanal carvers, painter and specialty finishes across Ontario and Quebec. The construction sector contributes 7.2% to Canada's GDP, and in Ontario was a labour force of 568,800.[3]

Beyond immigrants' common stories of hardship, pain, the loss of community, family roots, and unfulfilled dreams, the Italians that came to Canada faced systemic barriers with each wave of immigration.

The first wave between 1870 and 1914 left due to the country's instability and underemployment. The second "smaller" wave took place between 1920 to 1930 (approx. 40,000)[4] to fill the need of cheap labour for railroad-building and mining, which came to a total halt during the great depression. Prime Minister Mackenzie King signed a treaty with Italy in 1947, opening the borders to Italian immigration which brought forward the third and largest wave between 1948 and 1969. During the parliamentary debates over immigration, David Croll, a liberal member of Parliament for Toronto's Spadina, saw immigration from Italy as an opportunity to increase the Canadian labour force, in particular manpower for the growth of the greater Toronto area. The attitude of third wave Italians is a subject of much interest as this group came from fascist occupation, poverty, and devastation after WWII. They were desperate and ambitiously looking for a better life beyond post-war Europe.

The first and second wave of Italian immigrants had to overcome the extreme overcrowding of Toronto's St. John's Ward (1901-1928), the "padrone" tyranny (during the railroad expansion of the late 1800s and early 1900s), and the shame, social humiliations and economic collapses caused by the internment camps during WWII.

The third wave of Italian immigrants entering the construction sector had to face the exploitation from the first/second-wave Italian-owned construction builders and trades, unsafe working conditions, fraudulent cheques, kick-backs and the turmoil of setting up the construction unions in the 1960s. It is worthy to note that many Italians self-organized and led the union movements, such as Marino Toppan, Gus Simone and Bruno Zanini[5]. "The residential sector was saturated with hundreds of small and financially vulnerable contractors and subcontractors, whose often short existence was facilitated by developers trying to keep costs down by creating the conditions for unrealistic bidding wars. The relative ease by which tradesmen became independent sub-contractors and vice-versa contributed to the constant evolution of small firms, which perpetuated the sector's systemic underbidding, and the subsequent unethical and exploitative practices of businesses trying to keep afloat."[6]

Pierre Elliott Trudeau's multiculturalism (1976) promised a fair and just society, yet all immigrants, including Italians, continue today to face the hidden, polite prejudice of Canadian society. There is still an on-going distrust amongst the various ethnic business sectors, partially promoted by the media's focus on criminality that associates the "mafia" with being Italian. This is "Italo phobia" as identified by Professor Robert Harney[7], where the slightest behavioural characteristic of an individual is perceived as pervasive malevolence of a race.

"By the 1960s, more than 15,000 Italian men worked in Toronto's construction industry, representing one third of all construction workers in the city."[8] Currently, it is estimated that 35% of those involved in the construction industry are of Italian ancestry.

By 2020 the construction sector had an abundant representation of Italian Canadians at all the levels of the real estate development sector and its power centres. In any large construction site, one encounters Italian Canadian site workers, semi-skilled to highly skilled trades, manufacturers, suppliers, engineers, architects and designers. With project teams they are represented at all levels of project management as owners of construction companies, manufacturing businesses, real estate development and professional companies.

An inventory of the supporting systemic factors that supported the Italian immigration waves penetration of the construction sector can be used as a model to guide our government to re-think current immigration policies towards the ones that supported the Italian Canadians' success.

Canada offered Italian immigrants stable political governmental structures, open job opportunities because of economic investments and growth without restrictions due to classification of gentry or distinction of class. In Canada, each immigrant can rise to any level of prosperity by their leadership, vision and entrepreneurial abilities regardless of humble origin, and their progeny can continue further intellectual growth by access to public education.

The most significant policy for the construction sector was the sponsorship system which allowed families and their paesani to emigrate into supportive "familiari"[9] (kinship) networks. This phenomenon of chain migration[10] and the corresponding chain settlement grouping patterns allowed for the construction sector to expand by the pools of paesani working together in construction teams, and the use of this large group of immigrants to staff new companies or seek and find the talented semi-skilled immigrants to join innovative construction sector businesses.

The majority of Italians arriving in Toronto faced lack of literacy and language skills, and this inability to communicate, made it difficult to look for and negotiate for a job. As the Italian community grew, newcomers were reliant on their paesani. Surrounded by Italian speakers in construction groups, the next barrier to overcome, and the determining factor for the ability to engage in entrepreneurship, was to learn to speak and write in English. In 1962, COSTI (Centro Organizzativo Scuole Tecniche Italiane) was established to help Italian immigrants to learn English to practice their trades, obtain their professional qualifications and pass licensing exams.[11]

Leadership and entrepreneurial roles demanded mastery of the English language, and most importantly in the construction sector, the ability to read construction drawings and specifications, manage the working crews, and acquire acculturative knowledge[12] to successfully obtain contracts, financial coordination of loans and work with other Canadian-trained construction professionals. The Italians who "made it" in the construction sector achieved the required mastery and

SEWER DIGGING 1890S, PHOTO: CITY OF TORONTO ARCHIVES

were equipped with courageous vision, talent, entrepreneurial strengths, and a resolve to distinguish themselves in this new land, at all costs.

The first story is the one about Dufferin Construction, Quebec Paving, Dufferin Aggregates, Dufferin Concrete and various other road-building equipment companies founded by Vincenzo ("anglicised" to James) Franceschini (1890-1960). In 1905, at 15 years old, he arrived at Ellis Island and went to Toronto the next day. He came equipped with business and enterprise experience obtained from apprenticing in his father's china business in Italy.

Stories of Franceschini abound in many eyewitness publications. As a sojourn labourer during his adolescence, he acquired the command of the English language, the skills to lead a team of men to build, and a belief that technology would give you the speed needed for construction efficiency. He started Dufferin Construction in 1912, becoming a Canadian citizen by 1913 and marrying Annie Pinkham of Irish-Scottish descent, which softened participation in Canadian "society." In 1917 he bought a steam shovel, and with his partner Charles Johnston, a university-educated engineer, named the company in 1918. His brother Renaldo ("anglicised" to Leonard) joined the company in 1923. Reviewing the trajectory of his business one can see that James was a brilliant entrepreneur, successful in pursuing opportunities during the Depression in road-building and obtaining successful bids from all levels of government. Beyond investing in the latest technology to save construction time and winning contracts, he also cut off reliance on external suppliers and acquired an entire vertical supply chain of companies.[13]

Franceschini's success story and his integration into Canadian culture was interrupted by his internment in 1940 at Camp Petawawa, when he was 50 years old. The office of the Custodian of Enemy Property seized and sold off parts of his business during his internment, partially to appease the competition in Quebec. He was released after a year on compassionate grounds due to an advancing cancer but was not cleared of wrongdoing until 1945.

Franceschini was able to rebuild Dufferin Construction with his trusted management team. Many other Italian-born entrepreneurs were not able to rebuild. There is no statistical data on the financial damages of internment. Italian families tell stories of business "lost" during the war and that generation went on to live more "quiet" lives of reduced economic circumstance and political visibility after the war.

When Franceschini died in 1960, his brother and two nephews took over the company. In 1961 Dufferin was acquired by St. Lawrence Cement. It eventually became owned by Holcim Inc. in 2009. Currently, it is operating under CRH Canada Group Inc. (since 2015). Dufferin Construction ranks 28th in Canada according to Construct Connect[14] and it remains a successful construction division that continues to build large infrastructure projects throughout Canada.

Condrain was founded in 1954 by Alfredo De Gasperis and his brother Angelo who had arrived in Canada in 1952, and was later joined by younger brother Antonio. By 1971, Condrain built the Erin Mills Community with Cadillac Developments and grew exponentially. Similarly, to Dufferin, Condrain acquired a series of vertical supply chain companies. Condrain eventually set up Aspen Ridge Homes in 1992 as a design/build development company for high-end communities and in 1996 Metrus Construction was set up to design/build commercial, retail, and industrial buildings. Currently the Condrain Group sits in the top 20 list of Canada's Leaders in Construction.[15]

Condrain participated in a triumvirate along with Remington (Rudy Bratty) and Marel Contracting and the Pemberton Group (Muzzo family) to expand the boundaries of the City of Toronto for housing. It is the lore that many of the trio's projects were done relying on the Italian honour of handshake deals.

ALFREDO DE GASPERIS

In 1957, the City of Toronto's zoning by-law allowed high-rise apartment buildings to meet the demands of the population growth. During this boom, fast-paced construction and extreme competition for bids cried for any magic on site that could effectively reduce the costs of time and therefore reduce labour costs—it was the name of the game. These conditions were ripe for both design and business innovations to penetrate the construction sector. This is not unlike our current focus on digital technology that can reduce costs for construction.

A boom in construction inspired the Italian leaders in the sector to bring their experience from low-rise construction, look to iconic projects in Europe and the USA, and introduce new materials, methods and other construction efficiencies. This seeded the growth of many of today's Italian Canadian construction and development companies such as Condrain (De Gasperis family), Tridel (DelZotto family), Pemberton Group (Muzzo family) Remington (Bratty family), and Orlando Corporation (Fidani family).

Drywall was invented by the US Gypsum Company in 1916, as an innovation to the "sackett board" (made of wool) felt invented in 1894. It was sold initially in small tiles and the sheetrock as fire-proof board, but it failed to penetrate the sector. It was during the post-WWII boom, with labour and lath & plaster shortages, that drywall took over as a residential wall finish. In Toronto, Elio and Marco Muzzo Sr., (founders of Marel Contracting) used drywall to reduce labour and hasten the speed of low residential construction. When one visits these houses and sees their interior design, the rooms' sizes and their proportion were worked to full board sizes in a perfect mathematical efficiency of space and materials.

Mastering the use of concrete for the construction of high-rises is attributed to Fazlur Khan, structural engineer with Skidmore, Owings & Merrill (SOM). During the 1960s, Khan developed detailed concrete design charts for tall buildings, called the 'shear-wall-frame interaction.' This was a milestone in engineering standards influencing Toronto's engineering firms such as the Yolles Group to design structural shells without reliance on steel and with symmetrical and repetitive floors plans. This "industrialization of building construction accelerated in this period, with bold experiments in structural form taking place on an unprecedented level, most notably in reinforced concrete design."[16] This fast-tracked construction, reducing the overall labour and material costs.

In conjunction with the possibilities of concrete, flying forms were used in European, US, and in Latin American high tower construction. The use of flying forms (or table forms) in Toronto's high-rise towers was an additional transformative innovation. A "flying form" is a pre-cast concrete formwork, usually made of typical span lengths, that require complex engineering calculations to be self-supporting, repetitive, and can be re-used and hoisted floor by floor to efficiently form concrete slabs and walls—an innovation that reduces the need for sequential forming labour and fast-tracks the construction. Today passers-by may notice that most of the high-rise buildings use flying forms and form systems that sojourn from project to project, with their corresponding trades, following standardised sizes and proportions. It is a factor in why so many buildings look similar as they rise.

"The extremely efficient construction made possible through the local perfection of the flying form has made high-rise housing a defining feature of Toronto and its suburbs for nearly half a century." "Toronto's flying-form innovators are regarded to have been the developer/builders the Greens (Greenwin Development)

RUDY BRATTY

and the DelZottos (Tridel), as well as Nick Di Lorenzo" (Concrete Formwork Contractor). They were supported by engineers who worked on early flying-form buildings, which included Jablonsky and Yolles.[17] The adoption of the "flying form technique revolutionized the high-rise construction industry and enabled Greenwin to build over 10,000 residential units across Toronto throughout the '60s and '70s."[18]

In an interview, in George Brown College's memorial video for Angelo DelZotto (Tridel), he states that "we were the first to start the flying forms and revolutionized the way buildings went up in the city."[19] At the construction site, additional systemic solutions were required to facilitate the use of the flying forms, including training for the trades, and the support by the concrete forming contractors. "Nick Di Lorenzo was the dominant contractor," importing the flying-form technique from Europe and the tall cranes that made it possible."[20]

The use of the flying forms spearheaded by the Italian Canadian construction sector with the support of the professional disciplines, including architects, engineers, and the trades, demonstrated a transformative fast-track building process. This innovation was quickly adopted by the sector and continues to support city-building today.

Another innovation was a new site management technique of multi-trade teamwork for concrete forming. Teamwork for forming concrete allowed the substitution of steel and brick by project designers and supported efficiency and speed of sequential work which consequentially lowered labour costs. Formwork teams confused the unions that were based on single trade organizations, as forming teams consist of crane operators, steel rod-setters, carpenters, and concrete labourers. The unions had to keep up and create representation for these new multi-disciplinary and specialized trades.

In his obituary, the Globe & Mail stated that "Harold Green also pioneered, in co-operation with labour unions, a new way to organize workers on the construction site called "formwork."[21] "A pragmatic example was Nick Di Lorenzo," at the "end of the 1960s his company was considered the largest in the residential field" in concrete forming and he stated, "I came out with the idea of flying form, the gang form and started to import those big cranes and I also had the idea of making teamwork of men. With this idea forming cost was reduced to 50 per cent."[22]

To conceive and own an idea that can be translated to a patent gives an entrepreneur the power to realize their vision and benefit from the economic launch of the invention, but it also reflects their priorities. While there is not an exhaustive list of Italian construction sector patents, it is important to mention a few who held them, what benefits they yielded and speculate about their priorities.

Mariano ("anglicised" to Murray) Elia held a Canadian patent CA 1015993 with a 'field of invention' of "construction safety fences and posts used for mounting the construction safety fence at the site."[23] While the invention itself is ingenious, as safety fencing must be effective in place on all upper levels of a level change in a construction site, it is the nature of the effort and the focus on the invention which is interesting in Elia's story. Construction safety is a very sore subject and not one to bring up in polite company. One can venture that Elia cared about the safety of his workers.

Elia (1917-2006) arrived in Canada as a 12-year-old in 1929 and evolved from a construction worker with his father, to founding Dell Holdings (later the Elia Corporation) through hard work and steadfast determination, including working with bank funding to exponentially buy land and build housing subdivisions and high-rise buildings.[24]

Elia's story aligns with all the other Italians that succeeded in the construction sector by transforming it with innovative practices. However, his support of an academic legacy sets him apart from the rest. The Mariano A. Elia Chair in Italian Canadian Studies at York University was established (1984) and the Dr. Mariano A. Elia Chair in Head and Neck Cancer Research at Toronto's Princess Margaret Hospital (1998).

Joseph (Joe) Zentil (1929-2018) has a similar trajectory to other construction sector leaders mentioned such as Franceschini, Elia, De Gasperis, Muzzo and Bratty. Within a few months of arriving in Canada in 1948, Joe became a plumbing apprentice, before eventually receiving his Master Plumber license in 1954, while taking night classes in accounting, physics and drafting at Harbord Collegiate. "His plumbing company was a one-man show to start but, would grow to 35 employees in 1956 and 250 by 1966. In the 1970s and 1980s, Zentil Plumbing & Heating was considered one of the largest mechanical contracting companies in Canada, with over 400 employees."[25] Zentil held a patent, US4004767A, credited to inventor Dennis J. Chilton, between 1977 and 1994 for "a pipe-supporting assembly comprising a hanger and a saddle."[26] We can surmise that the hold and use of this patent allowed the company to differentiate itself from his competitors and contributed to its prosperity.

In the early 1960s, Zentil became an active member at York Racquets Tennis Club. This passion led him to establish in 1975 the Mayfair Tennis Clubs (now Mayfair Clubs) with partners Harold Soupcoff, and Garry Zentil (his now-deceased son). The clubs transitioned in the 1990s from tennis and squash to become full-service fitness and health & wellness centres.

In 1995, the company incorporated as University Plumbing & Heating Ltd., and Joe Zentil retired in 2010. Paul Zentil (surviving son) carries on Zentil Property Management which remains "a privately owned real estate development and property management company."[27]

Riccardo ("anglicised" to Richard) Lovat (1928-) came from an extensive line of miners, therefore he was interested in all aspects of tunneling including the safety for the work, the equipment used and the speed of tunneling. Richard attended the Istituto Tecnico Industriale di Belluno and trained as a mechanic. Between 1944 and 1949 he gained valuable experience in Switzerland working in tunnel construction until 1951 when he immigrated to Canada. Unlike other leaders, Lovat came equipped both with an education, extensive experience, and three generations of knowledge transfer.

From 1951 to 1963, Lovat worked in various capacities for an underground construction contractor in Toronto, and in 1963, he founded Richard's Machinery and Repair Ltd., which provided repairs to heavy equipment. He explored innovations for new boring equipment, patented his own technology, and built his first Tunnel Boring Machine [TBM] for a sewer project in Welland, Ontario. In 1972, the Lovat Tunnel Equipment Inc. [LTE] officially was founded to meet the need for safer and more efficient tunnelling capacity. Richard holds seven US patents. The first patent was groundbreaking as "the tunnel making machine of the present invention is adapted not only to tunnel through the earth, but also to concurrently form a concrete wall in the tunnel."[28] Lovat also holds 10 Canadian patents with extensive innovative impact on the tunneling sector.[29]

LTE supplied tunnelling equipment worldwide in competitions with major global tunnelling manufacturers. "The capabilities of this equipment have earned Lovat and the company much acclaim, including acknowledgement in the Guinness Book of Records for being the fastest tunnel drilling equipment in the world, and two world records for wedge block tunnel lining."[30] LTE was first acquired by Caterpillar Tunneling Canada Corp in 2008, and subsequently by Lovsuns Tunneling Canada Ltd. in 2013.

Another contemporary management innovation in the construction sector is the Design Build [DB] project delivery process. DB is done through a single contract between the developer or landowner and the design-build team consisting of contractor, architect, and engineers. This simple but fundamental difference saves money and time by transforming the relationship between designers and builders into an alliance which fosters collaboration and teamwork. DB should be more authentically represented as a re-discovery from history, traditionally referenced as being a "master-builder," going back all the way to Ancient Greece to the process that built those beautiful temples and agoras. DB continued through medieval history and the renaissance until professional designations created specialized construction team members and separated the design and construction delivery into factions.

MARIANO ELIA AS A YOUNG MAN

Orey Fidani (1929-2000) was the son of Carlo Fidani who founded Fidani & Sons in 1948, a construction firm that eventually became Orlando Corporation. It has become Canada's largest landlord of commercial and industrial properties with over 40,000 million square feet. Fidani was a visionary land developer who "pioneered the design-build concept in Canada and that became the Orlando Corporation's business in the 1960s and 1970s."[31]

Orlando's design-build development method included a vertically integrated approach from land ownership, servicing, municipal approvals, bespoke design and construction, leasing, and property management. The first launch was

600 acres of land on Airport Road directly across from the airport in 1964 to develop over 25 years, that eventually served 330 clients and continues today.[32]

Chain migration works both ways. The Canadian construction sector is intricately linked to the Italian companies working in Italy and in the European sector. Italian finishing materials (tiles and flooring), equipment (cranes) and products (furniture, fittings, and equipment) have influenced Canadian design and therefore continue to impact the Canadian construction sector. These bridges between Canada and Italy continue today.

Vic De Zen (1941-) arrived in Canada in 1962 equipped with tool & die experience. With two colleagues, Domenic D'Amico and Lorenzo De Meneghi, he pooled their financial resources and founded Royal Plastics in 1970. In just a decade, Royal Plastics was manufacturing windows, vertical blinds, vinyl siding and innovating in the sector. "Prior to Royal's arrival, the extrusion business was cornered by European companies. De Zen imported $2 million in Italian-made extruders and vacuum-sizers (cooling devices for extruded plastics) and went nose to nose with the offshore plastics people."[33]

In 2001, he founded the ZZEN Group which manages and operates De Zen's real estate holdings of land (acquired over 40 years ago). ZZEN initiated a building portfolio which is primarily focused on commercial and industrial buildings in Vaughan. De Zen left Royal Plastics in 2004 amidst a conflict-of-interest scandal and was cleared of wrongdoing in 2008. The company was sold in 2006 to Georgia Gulf Corporation. In 2008, De Zen launched the Vision Extrusion Group of Companies (9 plants and 1,000 employees) which manufacture doors, fencing and decking. Currently De Zen continues the path of innovation and has noted that "Vision Extrusion is upgrading its machinery and investing in new technologies to automate production and reduce waste."[34]

Thor & Partners' Nicola Capomasi is the new type of immigrant into the construction sector in Toronto. A master stone conservation technician from Padua, Italy, he moved to Canada in 2015 with family, staff, equipment and a long list of experience, expertise, completed projects, and accomplishments.

Thor & Partners started as a general cleaning company in 1978, eventually evolving into a restoration company that uses innovative technology to restore interior and exterior architectural materials using environmentally sustainable methods that do not damage surfaces and therefore are key to property preservation. The company includes a range of new methods, from laser technology for removal of surface pollution, to retail cleaning products and water-based sealers for natural material surfaces.

Nicola states that "I import every month something from Italy. We opened a bridge in my field and there is a lot of traffic going both ways."[35] Nicola Capomasi won the ICCO Italy-Canada Business Excellence Award.

Another significant systemic factor that supported the construction sector is that Italian Canadians have preserved their traditional family relationships and generational knowledge transfer. During the 1960s, streaming of children of Italians to trades and lower-level administrative jobs was not acceptable by Italian Canadian families. The cultural framework was to give their progeny the most education possible, "sistemazione," and set them up in the family businesses or to start businesses by mentoring, apprenticeship, and other forms of early socialization knowledge transfer.

Knowledge transfer relies on strong values of the family structure. Several contributing factors affect knowledge transfer, while one significant feature diverges into two different yet aligned results. The contributing factors include an early socialization into the construction sector—working in the family business on weekends, after school and during the summers. A family cohesiveness with strong emotional attachment—taking part in events, shadowing the elder at work, and watching the work ethic. The variant is when there is an implicit understanding that succession training is part of one's destiny, which includes creating dreams and plans that align with what is expected or necessary for the future of the business—like studying business, engineering or law to get ready to take the reins of the family company. And when there is no implicit understanding that succession is needed, the freedom of choice to start your own business to continue the family success is a valid force.

Most of the company success stories in the construction sector are family businesses, with many of them starting with father and sons, brothers working together and subsequent generations of trained professionals. Builders and developers such as Condrain, Dufferin, Greenpark, Orlando, Pemberton, Remington, and Tridel all currently have third generation family members in leadership and/or in participating roles continuing the family businesses.

Tridel is an example of generational knowledge transfer and a courageous quest for continuing to explore new ways of doing things and innovation models for survival. Jack DelZotto, a brick layer, came to Canada in 1927 and began DelZotto Construction, building single family homes in 1934. His sons Angelo, Elvio, and Leo along with Harvey Fruitman rebranded and formed Tridel and built their first high-rise luxury apartments in Etobicoke in 1961, six years before the Condominium Act was adopted (1967). "So, while Tridel may have not created the first condominium in Canada, Ontario or Toronto, we were the first in creating a new category, lifestyle."[36]

In 1968 Tridel, in joint venture with Alcan Aluminum, founded Aluma Systems Corp. launching "an extruded aluminum form for the pouring of concrete for construction, a system that saved time and money because the forms did not have to be taken apart and reassembled to be moved between floors. The venture proved successful, and in the early 1970s Tridel bought out Alcan's share of Aluma."[37] Through a series of public share exchanges by 1986, the DelZotto brothers regained 85% controlling interest in Tridel and struggled to achieve financial stability between 1993 and 2000.

The transformation that emerges after 2000 is worthy of mention. With an aggressive push at innovation, Tridel took on a leadership position in condominium developments in the GTA, now including leadership roles by its third generation. Tridel, "through its Construction Technology Division, also develops, sells, and leases shoring, forming, scaffolding, and concrete construction accessories, systems, and equipment throughout North America,"[38] along with the design "of large building complexes, sustainable construction and LEED rated communities (since 2006), bespoke development partnerships, and most recently Tridel Connect, a smart home technology initiated at Ten York condominiums."[39]

From large conglomerates such as Dufferin Construction, Condrain, Elia Corporation, Zentil, Tridel, Orlando Corporation and ZZen, there are many more Small/Medium Enterprises (SMEs) that are also construction sector success stories, like Nicola Capomasi's Thor & Partners. They are currently working on the restoration of the exterior stone walls of the Canadian Parliament buildings in Ottawa, part of one of the biggest renovation projects in Canadian history.

The aptly named Second Generation Furnishings—an SME founded in 1985 by Dino DiStefano (1957-) and Robert Antonel (1958-) who are second generation Italian Canadians—is a cabinet-making enterprise which has expanded from a 4-man crew to a robust custom cabinetry enterprise that employs 30 staff and has completed projects

ELVIO, ANGELO AND LEO DELZOTTO

for 800 schools, many community centres, libraries, universities, restaurants, long-term care facilities and offices. Their fathers Tarcisio DiStefano came to Canada in 1951 after a long sojourn in France, and Gino Antonel came in 1953 as a trained cabinet maker. Both fathers met as carpenters in North Bay while working on construction projects and moved to Toronto to find better weather and work, launching New Way Carpentry. New Way Carpentry completed housing projects from foundation to cabinetry, and both Dino and Robert got their site training, "understanding what was expected of us—hard work, discipline, responsibility and dedication,"[40] during the summers. Unfortunately, Antonel passed away young, and DiStefano, along with a partner, held on to the reins of the company tighter without any expectations for the sons to join.

Both sons studied architectural technology, (DiStefano at Humber College and Antonel at Seneca College), and with the knowledge transfer's foundational preparation and work experience, they started Second Generation from "zero," initially relying on work flowing from friends and family. Through steadfastness and careful progress, while perfecting their now renowned "Second Generation Quality,"[41] whereby there are no site rejects "nothing comes back crumpled and broken,"[42] they scaled up from small classroom projects to their first new school, Our Lady of Peace in Maple, completed in 1987.

They invested heavily in new equipment, staying at the cutting edge of sector technology since 1993, with equipment from Germany and Italy, including computerized panel saws, CNC machinery, edge banders and compressors. Currently their production system flow is duplicated to have redundancy and keep maintenance without interrupting their work breakdown schedules of production. Technology allows Second Generation to stay competitive within the bidding world of public sector institutional projects without having to affect their quality.

Second Generation's management structure is as serious, organized, and adaptable as its founders. DiStefano oversees production and deals with staff while Antonel administers the business, prepares the bids, and manages the contracts. They "meet three times a day"[43] to collaborate and discuss all aspects of projects and both formally and informally invite input from staff on "how to improve and discuss ideas which we can then mock-up and learn from."[44]

By the sheer numbers it was inevitable that Italian immigrants would change Canada. When you walk around Toronto, just look up towards the horizon and as far as you can see you will find the evidence of Italian immigration's impact on our built environment—not just the furniture, fittings, buildings and the vast infrastructure below, but all the waves of innovation and all the striving of current large conglomerate and small/medium businesses that make this city-building possible.

There are several memorial monuments in Toronto that speak to the immigration experience, that represent the construction workers, or stand in remembrance of their tragic deaths. Currently there are four that are specific to the Italian experience, and they speak to all facets of collective memories.

One statue lies in front of the Woodbridge Pool and Memorial Arena in Vaughan. The Italian Workers Memorial is found in small piazza/garden designed by Nino Rico Inc. Architect, created in 1993 by Giovanni Fanton, a local sculptor of Italian descent. It is a dramatic and painful representation of the strained muscles of the Italian construction worker trying to save the life of a co-worker on a job site. This monument commemorates almost 1,000 Italian workers who have died in construction related accidents.[45]

The second statue is found at the Villa Colombo gardens at the Lawrence Avenue and Dufferin Street campus. It is isolated in a calm area of the garden with a surrounding wrought iron fence. 960 names are etched on 11 pillars, of Italian lives lost in work-related accidents. Erected in 2016, the space is designed by Giannone Petricone Architects and built by Dominus Construction Group.

The third is both a Toronto Historical Plaque and quilt designed by Laurie Swim depicting the five Italian construction workers that perished in the Hogg's Hollow cave-in in 1960. The quilt is permanently displayed in the main mezzanine at the York Mills subway station.

The fourth monument is in front of the Joseph Piccininni Centre on St. Clair West. Sculpted by Frank Varga, erected in 1998, it depicts an immigrant family, looking hopeful towards a distant future.

While these memorials in the evolutionary journey of the construction sector may be lost in the city streets, the heirs of family businesses continue to strive and engage in knowledge transfer for the benefit of the next generation. It is important to remember, and also inspire the immigrant's children to understand the power of their collective impact. I imagine a small group of children, like my own, at school, surrounded by houses and high rises, in a school room with beautiful cabinetry, Italian flooring and high-tech windows, being told stories about courageous visionaries—how they found their talent, developed their entrepreneurial strengths, and engaged in daring innovations to build their city.

It has often been said that the Italian community played an outsized role in building the GTA. From roadwork, to home-building, to architecture and design and the creation of entire neighbourhoods, Italian Canadians have left, and continue to leave, an indelible mark as city-builders. It would be impossible to list all the smaller builders and designers who have made important contributions to our built environment, but it is worth mentioning a few of the larger developers who have made a lasting impact.

MARIO ROMANO

Castlepoint Numa might be best known for the L Tower designed by Daniel Libeskind situated beside the iconic O'Keefe Centre in downtown Toronto (now known as Meridian Hall), yet their influence is scattered throughout the GTA. Founded by cousins Mario and Alfredo Romano, Castlepoint has built over 8000 homes and is the largest private sector landowner in Toronto's waterfront. They are particularly known for heritage preservation and revitalizing areas in decline as well as their active involvement in the arts and culture of the city. Mario Romano also happens to be a gifted jazz pianist.

The Greenpark Group, founded by Carlo Baldassarra, and run as a family business, is Canada's largest homebuilder and they have been instrumental in the development of over 55 communities and 75,000 home units. Their work includes both commercial and residential construction with projects in Canada, the United States and Europe.

The Cortel Group is another family-run collective of businesses that develop high-rise and low-rise residential and commercial projects in Toronto and across the province. Based in Vaughan, the company is still run by Mario Cortellucci, its founder and president.

For the last 25 years ARGO has been a developer, designer and builder of communities in Ontario. The president, Fabio J. Mazzocco has overseen the construction of over 6000 households.

Rosehaven Homes was created in 1992 when Giovanni Guglietti purchased 20 lots in Waterdown Ontario and turned them over to his sons Marco and Silvio to develop. Since then, the company has grown their portfolio to include 8000 homes in Southern Ontario and the GTA.

Elvio De Meneghi has focused on family-oriented community development through Lormel Homes. Lormel communities include Woodbridge Retreat in Woodbridge, Millwood in Burlington, Fletcher's Park and The Crossing, both in Brampton. Other projects can be found in Etobicoke, Innisfil and Bradford.

Over 30 years Benny Marotta has built the portfolio of the Solmar Development Group to include residential and commercial properties. They do everything from single detached homes, to semis, townhomes and luxury high-rise condos. Their projects include the Erin Glen Community in Erin Ontario, the Park Avenue Place towers in Vaughan, and the Oro at Edge Towers in Mississauga. Marotta's daughters Angela and Melissa are actively involved in the family business which now includes the Two

CARLO BALDASSARA

Sisters Vineyards, an award-winning winery in Niagara on the Lake.

While it's impossible to list all the builders and developers who contributed to creating the landscape of the GTA, it is clear that the Italian Canadian community has made, and continues to make, an enormous contribution to the cities we live in and the places we call 'home.'

FLAIRE CONDOMINIUMS, GIANNONE PETRICONE ASSOCIATES

ITALIAN CANADIAN CONTRIBUTIONS TO ARCHITECTURE AND DESIGN IN TORONTO

LUIGI FERRARA

The contributions of Italian Canadians to architecture and design in the city of Toronto have been numerous despite the many obstacles which Italian immigrants and their descendants experienced in this country. Italian immigration to Canada had various causes, from the aftermath of war, to the escape from rural poverty, to the avoidance of social and political turmoil. The inability to eke out a living in Italy resulted in mass migration from the peninsula to both North America and South America with differing results for the immigrants. Whereas in South America, Italians joined the elite of their societies, in North America Anglo-Nordic prejudice posed a greater challenge to social mobility and achievement. The contrast in opportunities afforded to the same immigrant pool in these different contexts is indicative of the type of systemic racism prevalent in North America.

The Italian immigrants who had been pushed out of Italy as it underwent its transformation from a feudal to a modern industrialized society was composed of a high quotient of skilled tradesmen and artistic craftsmen. Carpenters, masons, bricklayers and concrete formers came to Canada along with skilled craftsmen and artisans in stone cutting, sculpting, stained glass and metalwork. These new immigrants integrated themselves into the labour force that was building a modern Canada in the construction and building product manufacturing industry. Three successive waves of immigration, the first two at the turn of the century and after the Second World War, placed a high value on the education of their children which resulted in a second generation of professionals: legal, financial, medical and in architecture, engineering and design as well.

The status of the Italian Canadian immigrants was marred during the Second World War by the internship of the first wave of successful Italian Canadian immigrant entrepreneurs. The internship set the community back socially and financially during the '40s and '50s and it was only in the 1960s that the extreme prejudice that had plagued the community in the first half of the 20th century began to dissolve. Canada itself transformed into the multicultural society that its Prime Minister Wilfrid Laurier had predicted it would become at the century's dawn and which, he had claimed, would make it one of the greatest countries of the 20th century.

The city of Toronto, considered by many to be a dull "Presbyterian" backwater, began a gradual evolution towards its current globalized identity. This was in great part due to the influence of its many thriving ethnic communities. Jewish, Finnish, Polish, Baltic nationals, Germans and Eastern Europeans arrived in the city and were bringing a new European design consciousness to the Canadian mainstream. Whether it was the Bata family who attempted to recreate the high modernism of their Czech business empire or Nordic Europeans, such as Janis Kravis, transplanting their modernist ethos to the Toronto design scene with shops like Karelia, Toronto was becoming the focus of what Canadian collector and architectural historian John Martins-Manteiga described as "Dominion Modernism." This phenomenon would see the various streams of European culture influence the development of a new Canadian modernist architecture and design tradition.

At this time Toronto was being transformed by a new wave of ethnically diverse architects and immigrants. Figures such as Peter Dickenson brought Festival of Britain modernism to the city. Eberhard Zeidler brought a German hi-tech design sensibility, and the second-generation children of immigrants from Japan and China such as Raymond Moriyama and Doug Lee integrated their cultural sensibilities with the local strain of modernism. In a quick decade the nature and character of Canadian architecture rapidly shifted from colonial provincialism to a progressive and modernist stance.

The Italian influence on this change filtered into Canadian architecture initially through a class of sub-trades, who with the newly minted community of Jewish Canadian architects and engineers, worked with Italian construction firms and sub-contractors to pioneer new technologies such as flying forms and reinforced concrete in the city. This enabled a shift to high-rise concrete building technology, away from the limiting steel and masonry construction techniques that were prevalent. This phenomenon turned the city into one of the world's highest concentrations of high-rise and modernist concrete buildings. In this period, one of the most talented young Italian Canadian architects emerged—a partnership between brothers Venchiarutti and Venchiarutti. The two broke onto the scene by winning the public competition for the park pavilions on the Toronto Islands. These pavilions were designed with reinforced concrete "pilotis" with folded plate concrete rooves and brick clad structures beneath them. A far cry from Toronto's pre-war Arts and Craft styled park pavilions, they combined a robust Corbusier modernism with the flair of the best of the post-war Italian organic architecture promoted by famous Italian architecture critic Bruno Zevi. This muscular style stood in contrast to the Miesian minimalism characteristic of Canadian corporate architecture created by firms such as the Parkin Partnership. The Venchiarutti's went on to design key icons of Canadian modernism that combined a material palette of Muskoka stone walls with wood and concrete in a harmonious way. Opportunity for architects of this first generation was extremely

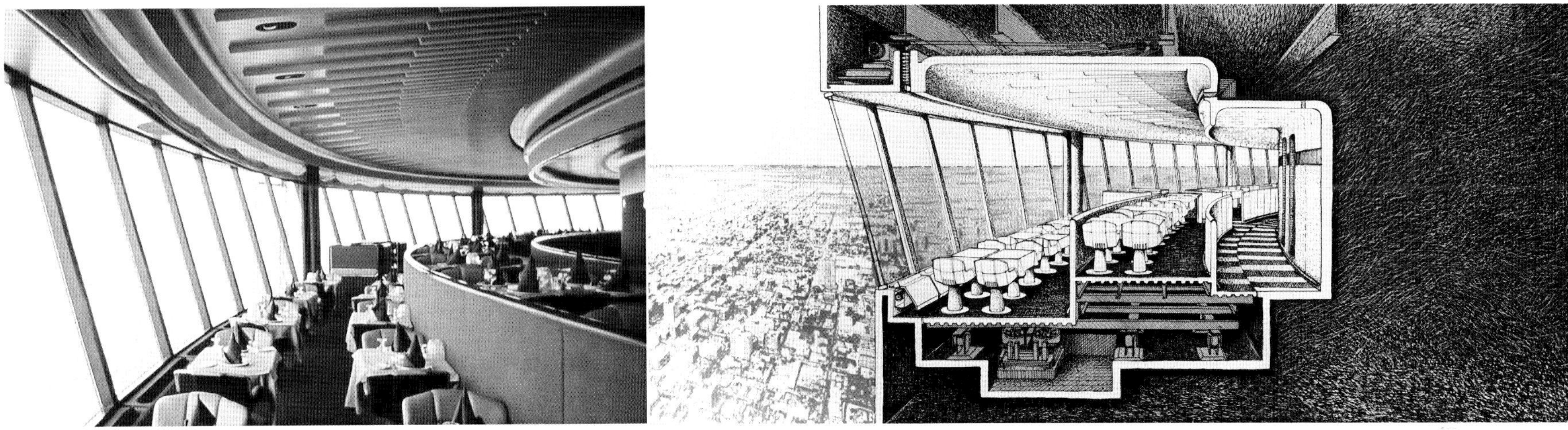

CN TOWER, ALDO & FRANCESCO PICCALUGA

limited. Without access to a class of patrons, Italian Canadian architects were dependant on competitions to secure commissions. The Italian Canadian community was reticent to patronize members of their own community and had limited clout economically as they had not yet transformed themselves from constructors into developers. They generally relied on their connections in the Jewish professional community for architectural services. Because of this, talented young architects like the Venchiaruttis needed to rely on patrons external to the community for opportunity, a sad pattern which would plague the next generations as well.

The challenge for these early Italian Canadian architects was to be able to repeat their initial successes. The lack of social capital of the Italian community and its relative immaturity meant that many talented Italian Canadians were given the choice to struggle for success with their own firms or to work for other architects if they wanted to participate on large scale projects, with the latter being the most prevalent route. It was ultimately a third wave of professional immigration that began during the '70s that would radically transform Toronto's architecture and design scene, bringing with it pivotal Italian Canadian figures who would bring both "rationalist" and "post-modern" architectural styles to the forefront of the Toronto design scene.

Most significantly in 1968, brothers Aldo & Francesco Piccaluga brought their world caliber design and craftmanship to the city. Inspired by the profile of our then Prime Minister Pierre Elliot Trudeau, as the children of Italian diplomats raised in Damascus, they arrived in Toronto after initially intending to go to Montreal, post-Expo 67. Friends suggested Toronto over Montreal as it was more economically vibrant. The brothers began working for Bregmann and Hamman and other local architects due to their extraordinary space planning skills. Aldo had studied in Rome under brilliant architect/engineer Pier Luigi Nervi while Francesco was self-taught. Aldo was soon registered and the talented brothers were recognized by Australian-Canadian architect Ned Baldwin who gave them the signature project of designing a totally prefabricated building interior for the revolving restaurant in the CN Tower. The design the Piccalugas came up with was a sumptuous late modernist environment of natural materials contrasting with high tech metals and super sophisticated lighting. Upon its completion, the design for the restaurant received as much acclaim as the tower itself, being hailed as an example of high-tech luxuriousness. Their Italian calibre quality design ethos with its novel approach to prefabrication, material experimentation, new colour palettes, and elegant innovative detailing lit the Canadian interior design and

DE BERARDINI'S HAIR SALON, ALDO & FRANCESCO PICCALUGA

architecture scene on fire. The two brothers were amongst the first to internationalize the supply chain for the design and construction process, working with manufacturers in Italy to save their clients time and money and to bring unusual and beautiful new products, surfaces and craftsmanship into the country.

Like most Italian Canadian architects and designers, the Piccalugas relied heavily on Anglo-Canadian patrons for their commissions, or alternatively, on a new breed of independent and small-scaled Italian Canadian entrepreneurs to provide them with the opportunity to create their brilliant projects. The De Berardini's Hair Salon, which opened with the new Eaton Centre, was an exquisite bombshell of Joe Colombo-inspired integrations of architecture and product design. Certainly, no hair salon had been conceived with such aesthetical emphasis and total design unity in the country's history. More influentially, a series of remarkable eyewear shops began to appear in Canadian malls beginning in Yorkdale. The Karim Optical stores combined Venetian stucco, used for the first time in Canada, with intricate marble inlay and dramatic lighting effects.

These projects stunned the public and the professional community with their incredible design quality and originality. It was as if a new standard of interior design had descended from a UFO onto the local retail landscape. Soon, the overall professional community was rapidly struggling to catch up with this new sophisticated Italian Canadian design. No retail interior in the city would ever be the same and everyone opening a store or launching a chain would have the challenge of matching this new design quality level.

During the 1980s the brothers began to teach part time at the University of Toronto's School of Architecture inspiring the next generation of Italian Canadian designers coming through the ranks at that time. They were working on the first truly rationalist and post-modern buildings in the city, a set of small social housing projects that were extraordinarily unique and whose thoughtful space planning and contextual design integrated the housing into its local context, while remaining distinctly contemporary. Having been influenced by Carlo Scarpa, the brother's signature mixed-use project on John Street took historic Richardsonian houses and renovated them as if they were a museum installation in a castle in Verona, connecting them with metal glazed structures and injecting modern detailing into the historic buildings in a manner that was both uniquely Canadian and equally European in style. The Piccalugas became experts in taking a project's limitations and turning them into grist for unique architecture, product design and urbanism, and while they taught briefly at UofT they significantly influenced the next generation of Italian Canadians architects as well as being trailblazers for the city's design community.

Contemporaneously, Francesco Scolozzi, originally from Bologna, headed to Harvard for his master's in urban design in 1971-72, after having graduated from the School of Architecture in Florence in 1967. At Harvard he married his wife Doris, who was Berlin-born and whose family had experienced the communist takeover in Germany after the Second World War. While Scolozzi was teaching in Florence and Bologna he found commissions difficult to obtain under the communist leadership of the city. He tapped, at Doris's suggestion, Canadian friends and secured a job working for Canada's most famous architect, Arthur Erickson, working on the competition for the Ottawa National Gallery. After the competition there was a lack of work and Boris Zerafa took Scolozzi under his wing at Webb Zerafa Menkes

Housden Architects. While Zerafa is typically regarded as an Egyptian Canadian architect his mother was a Florentine concert pianist and he spoke Italian. During his legendary career, which grew out of the office of Peter Dickenson, he would mentor many Italian Canadian architects, supporting them as they interned for their licence. Scolozzi obtained his licence in 1981 and quickly received numerous projects that were the result of a wave of investment from Italy into Canada. During that period the third wave of immigrants and Italian capital headed to Canada to avoid social upheavals. His seminal project for the office of the Italian Trade Commission led to the first branch office design for the Banca Commerciale Italiana, winning an OAA award in 1983 for its sleek post-modern rationalism. This office building which he designed for V&A properties in the downtown core remains one of Toronto's signature post-modern buildings and, unlike many of its confreres, has not dated at all after many years.

Scolozzi's talents were recognized by many in the architectural field, but maintaining an office in Toronto proved difficult, as he found securing commissions challenging. Like most Italian Canadian architects, he could not rely on the Italian Canadian development community for work. After the recession of 1991 he turned his attention to securing work in China where his capabilities were more appreciated than was the case in the Canadian context. From 1996-2015 he developed the 30,000,000 square foot campus for the Foreign Language University in Dalian and the Conference Centre for the Communist Party in Shanghai and major office headquarters in Beijing. All of these projects reflected a blend of European urbanism with the corporate architectural quality found in North America. According to Scolozzi, the key ingredient that architects of Italian heritage brought to Canada and to the world in general, was a tradition of humanism that infused their architectural projects—a tradition that could be seen in the design of his own house in Rosedale, influenced by the Swiss Italian architect Mario Botta with its clarity of planning, symmetry and light-filled spaces.

The same kind of architectural excellence was to be found in the work of Rocco Maragna, who while born in central Italy, came to Toronto as a child and graduated from Central Tech high school in drafting. Maragna was amongst the first of the second wave of Canadian-educated architects, and was lucky enough to have been mentored by his high school teacher, as were many Italian Canadian immigrants of this period. Teachers saw incredibly talented pupils, from very humble backgrounds and cared for their future success and tried to provide them opportunities that their family couldn't. Maragna, through the intervention of his teacher Mr. Quinn, secured a summer job in the office of the brilliant Canadian architect Ron Thom. He had always been enamoured by the quality of the Italian Canadian craftsmen that worked on his Massey College project. This inspired Maragna to begin his study of Italian architecture. From grades 11 to 13, and throughout university, he worked at the Thom Partnership and at Webb Zerafa Menkes Housden where he, like Scolozzi, was mentored by Boris Zerafa. In this period, he also traveled to Taliesen West and stayed with infamous Italian environmental architect Paolo Soleri at Arcosanti, which left an indelible influence on him. By 1971 he graduated from the University of Toronto's architectural school and then went to Venice to study at the Universita Internazionale dell'Arte, led by Giuseppe Mazzariol. While at the UIA he was granted a teaching assistantship and dedicated himself to 'solving' Venice's persistent phenomenon of 'acqua alta,' by proposing a system of floating devices. In Venice, Maragna met Louis Kahn who was working on his project for the Palazzo dei Congressi. He also met Manfredo Tafuri and Carlo Scarpa, working as their teaching assistant. He returned to Canada in 1972 and worked for Thom and then Zerafa in 1973-74, working on Canadian architectural landmarks such as the Royal Bank, Trent University and the Prince Hotel.

After the death of his father in 1975, he left for Harvard for his Masters in Urban Design, which he finished in 1977 with a thesis on the Boston waterfront and a landmark paper on urban mobility as a utility, conceptualizing car sharing years ahead of its ultimate implementation. In that year he began his own practice starting with elegant home additions and renovations and the landmark renovation of St. Fidelis Church. This renovation of an industrial building into a religious building, rich in iconic imagery,

ST. FIDELIS CHURCH, MARAGNA ARCHITECT

reflected the heritage of Italian Canadian workers' capabilities in its design. If there is a building that could be labelled as representative of Italian Canadian culture, St. Fidelis would be that building; humble and honest in its expression, elevating the work of the skilled trades into a language of high architecture.

In an effort to support his mother after the death of his father, Maragna began moonlighting. He started working with developer George Mann, who recognized his skills, on the project for Delisle Court. This mixed-use retail and office project, which was constructed with the same bricks as those at Massey College, was one of Toronto's most urbane and innovative complexes. Inspired by the Italian piazza, but adapted to the Canadian climate and lifestyle, Maragna created a three-dimensional square covered by a generous sky-light that created multi-level retail and offices integrating them into a public realm that was active and full of life. The project was a tremendous success and led to a series of signature commissions, such as the elegant modernist Palladian villa in Etobicoke, the earthquake relief project in Friuli in 1976, and a number of high schools, amongst which those named after Archbishop Romero and Marshall McLuhan stand out.

Further religious projects, such as St. Peter's in Vaughan and the Erin Mills Twin Arenas, reflect the prodigious talent that Maragna demonstrated in creating public buildings. While his work was recognized and applauded abroad, such as his plans for a new city in Chengdu, China and his award-winning entry for the Museum of Modern Art in Damascus, at home, in Toronto, commissions became rarer. Like other Italian Canadian architects, he could never rely on the patronage of the Italian Canadian community itself for bread and butter projects such as office or condominium buildings. Maragna's lack of social capital, as the child of humble immigrant parents from Abruzzo, underscored the tremendous difficulty most Italian Canadian designers of that generation faced. No matter how talented they were they were not socially connected enough for institutional commissions and lacked a patronage structure within their own community.

The next wave of architects and designers emerged from the generation that was born of the post-World War II immigration. They were born and educated in Canada and studied at Canadian universities during the '80s and '90s. They were influenced and inspired by the study of Italian traditions of design that had finally made its way into the curriculum of architecture and interior design schools. Through the development of study abroad programs in Italy, through advocacy of students and enlightened professors such as Rick Haldenby, Italian design culture was finally being taught in school. I personally remember our older professors telling us that we should not study abroad in Italy as it would corrupt us, suggesting that we study abroad in Nottingham, of all places. This gives a sense of the systemic racism of architecture schools of the period. This generation was the first to be able to manage some sustained success and penetrate both the professional and academic hierarchies enabling them to contribute in a more robust way to the Toronto architectural and design scene.

Figures such as Alex Temporale, whose father had sculpted most of the famous sculptures lining University Avenue and whose own work reflected a Zevi-like Wrightian organicism, or Anthony Mancini, whose partnership with

Dublin-born architect Jonathan Kerns created one of the city's best boutique design practices, working on sacred and small scale institutional projects, or UofT grad David Pontarini, whose elegant and fastidious condominium designs like the Florian and One Bloor Street expressed a new generation of suaveness associated with the Italian design ethos. Figures like Silvio Baldassare and Rosario (Roy) Veracalli, worked their way into the leadership of Canadian firms, rising to positions of authority based on merit and capabilities, having succeeded in creating leading-edge commercial and residential projects of exceptional award-winning quality. UofT graduates like Enzo Corazza and Berardo Graziani were able to build a solid practice designing condominium projects, including Canada's tallest residential tower, the Aura. And while this group of men were seeing a measure of success and some limited support from members of the increasingly sophisticated Italian Canadian development community, most of these architects developed their firms by initially gaining the confidence of clients outside the immigrant community who appreciated their high quality design skills or by winning competitions that recognized and celebrated their capabilities. All of them had been shaped by their formative study abroad and the mentorship and inspiration of their Italian Canadian and Italian counterparts. In Silvio Baldassare's case, he reached out to his design hero, Renzo Piano, to collaborate and win the commission for Toronto's courthouse. The result will be a collaboration between the firms NORR and Piano to create a landmark building for our city.

THE AURA, GRAZIANI & CORAZZA ARCHITECTS; PHOTO: TENSZ

But perhaps the most remarkable success story of all has been that of Anna Simone and Elaine Cecconi who, being doubly challenged as women designers of Italian background, courageously founded their own interior design firm and transformed it into an internationally significant enterprise offering design services, merchandising and products, which most significantly, has resulted in them becoming a recognizable brand name. Anna Simone knew from three years old that she wanted to become an interior designer and would reply so when asked by her relatives what she wanted to do when she grew up. Inspired by her dad who was in construction, and by her uncle who made furniture, and even more importantly, by a mom who inspired her creativity, she learned early on how to creatively use space in a house that was 900 square feet with eleven people living in it. She was educated at Humber College but pursued further study at the University of Manitoba and Ryerson. Her familiarity with construction sites gave her an advantage with understanding the vocabulary of trades. She was also inspired by Italian culture, especially by music and opera, which were a big part of her life.

Her professional career began by working with noted architects Robinson and Heinrichs, who, after designing the world renowned Colonnade building, rethought Le Corbusier's Unité d'Habitation into a more urbane format. Their firm had begun to specialize in housing for the elderly. She was especially fond of this topic and conducted research on it as she also had a deeply connected relationship with her grandfather. From there, she moved to work with Marshall Cummings, Canada's premiere commercial interiors design firm, whose pioneering female leadership also provided mentorship and inspiration about what could be possible. There, she met Elaine Cecconi, the daughter of Italian Canadian immigrants from Timmins. With a similar origin story and philosophy of design, they worked together at

ANNA SIMONE AND ELAINE CECCONI

the firm and after 10 years broke away to start a practice of their own. Their partnership was immediately successful, and they pioneered an approach of deeply understanding client and user needs, and then addressing them through a humanized modern design palette. Breakthrough projects included the Albert Sung stores, Rodney's Oyster House, Enoteca, and the Merchandise Building Loft condo rehabilitation project. The Merchandise Lofts was the first time that an interior design firm led a project, rather than architects, and the evolving Cecconi Simone brand helped it win 'community of the year' from the Home Builder's Association. Their signature model dwelling at the Interior Design Show integrated an herb garden into the kitchen. It was Italian Canadian touches like this that turned the firm into a media sensation with the public waiting in 2-3-hour line-ups to see the home. This experience led them to create one of the first licenced furnishing lines with Eaton's and then to set up their own store, ONI ONE, where people could purchase their designs for home accessories and furniture directly. This path of innovation took courage and grew out of their relentless focus on becoming better designers. Celebrity came after the fact. After 38 years, both Simone and Cecconi are still trailblazing, looking at the design of hospices and working on landmark projects.

The success of Cecconi Simone coincided with the emergence of a cool "Italianità" in the city. This reflected a changing demographic and changing perceptions from other ethnic groups. Suddenly things Italian were coming into fashion and the Italian strength in design, food and fashion was being appreciated by other cultures. Italy was no longer looked at by locals as an inferior southern European culture but as a purveyor of luxury and quality. The work of Giannone Petricone Associates fit right into this new reality. Their sophisticated projects for restaurants such as Bar Italia, Fresh, Buca and their commercial spaces for Chiat Day, Publicis exuded that high-quality architectural design style that could be found in works of Carlo Scarpa, Luigi Moretti and Gio Ponti from the '60s. This modernist revival also penetrated their larger scale condominium projects for the Gianonne family-owned development company The Fram Group. Suddenly cool "Italianita" could be found in Port Credit and Don Mills, in new and vibrant mixed-use projects that were re-inventing the suburbs and bringing urbanity to them. This influence of the community was seen in the leadership of architecture and design schools as well, with Pina Petricone becoming the program director for UofT's architecture school, Marco Polo becoming Chair of Architecture at Ryerson and myself, serving as Dean of George Brown's Centre for Arts, Design and Information Technology, and leading the programs for Design Exchange, Canada's Centre for Design and Innovation.

A new breed of young Italian architects and designers were making their mark in a variety of interesting ways and extending their influence internationally. My own career involved being elected President of the World Design Organization. Design success spread into the associated professions such as graphic design, where figures such as Rene De Santis, who designed the Toronto flag as a student at George Brown College, went on to found Montana Steele, one of the most successful real estate marketing agencies in the city. By the 2000s it was now common to have projects branded with Italian connotations—The Treviso, the Burano, to name of a few of the dozens of projects that traded on Italian design quality and prestige. A new younger generation of Italian Canadian graphic design talent, such as Melissa Agostino and Nick Monteleone, were beginning to have an impact on the design industry. Alumni of the venerable Concrete Design Communications firm led by Diti Kataona and John Pylypzcak, they brought an experimental and playful approach to graphic design, with Melissa leading the design of *Azure* magazine, Canada's leading design publication.

Azure, another fundamental contribution

to the Canadian design scene, was a result of Italian immigration. From its founding in the '80s, it evolved into the foremost consumer design and architecture magazine, and by the second decade of the 21st century was a North American leader in design journalism. This is significant as Canada never really had a design publication culture. Early in my career I learned from the famous editor and architect Vittorio Gregotti, who I interviewed as an architecture student while studying abroad, that without a design press there could never exist a design culture. He asked me if there were great Canadian architects and I replied that there were many. He asked where he could find books about them and I said that there were none, to which he replied "no books, no architecture." It is for this reason that capturing stories such as those in this article are critical to record leadership and achievement.

Leadership on the part of Italian Canadians can be found in many areas moving into this new century. Recent projects, like Roberto Chiotti's exquisite St. Gabriel's church, combine theology with sustainability principles to create one of the most remarkable sacred spaces in the world. Anyone watching the play of light on the walls of this church is transported into a spiritual understanding and relationship with nature that is uniquely inspiring. This turn of the millennium flourish of Italian Canadian design is hopeful for the Italian Canadian community and it is certainly advancing the cause of design in general. The success, however, masks a continuing and difficult reality that most of these younger architects and designers still face.

REGENT PARK, BLOCK 22
GIANNONE PETRICONE ASSOCIATES

As a pattern, Italian Canadian architects and designers seem to be able to generate an initial flurry of recognition and attention for their work, but over time they find themselves unable to grow the scale of their projects and evolve their ideas, as there is still no fertile ground for elevating their careers in the local context. The talent quotient in the community has been extremely high but the opportunity array is inversely proportional to their skills and capabilities. As a group they would have accomplished much more, especially if the vibrant Italian Canadian developer community had embraced them and supported their careers. Over time, the truth is, with few exceptions such as Diamante Developments and the Fram Group, the community as a whole has never really patronized Italian Canadian talent. Rather they have used the services of architects higher up in the echelons of Canada's "vertical mosaic" to help them gain approvals from city authorities. Even when Italian Canadians began to enter the boards of major public institutions, they did not lever that power to commission outstanding work from the community as other communities have. The sad truth is that Italian Canadian community organizations have never once commissioned a significant Italian Canadian architect or designer to design the community's civic institutions. This sorry state of affairs is why Italian Canadian architects and designers have never been able to create the masterpieces, the likes of which Raymond Moriyama did, whose first commissions came directly from the Japanese Canadian community. They helped him establish his reputation, allowing his firm to grow within the larger Canadian context. Italian Canadians, on the other hand, have had to rely on the kindness of people outside the community to recognize their talent, people who were willing to give them a chance. And while the talented designers in the community have found a way to make their way forward, who knows what would have happened if there had been recognition, support and patronage of the best talents within the community?

ST LAWRENCE MARKET
JOB
FREE
NOW

PHOTO CREDIT: JEFF SMITH

AGRI-FOOD

MARK CIRILLO

EARLY SETTLERS

When people tell the story of the Italian community in Ontario, it often starts in the early 1950s, the postwar era when tens of thousands of Italians made the long boat-and-rail journey here every year. And certainly, the 1950s-1960s were the heyday of Italian immigration in Canada. But the earliest Italians in Canada came here more than a century ago: between 1900-1914, 50,000 arrived, primarily to work on the Canadian railroad and in mines. Many of these sojourners returned home seasonally or for good after completing their work contracts, but others remained in Canada, settling primarily in Toronto or Montreal where they established Canada's earliest "Little Italies."

Although the Italian population in Toronto was relatively small during this period, less than 2% overall, its impact on the fruit and vegetable trade was enormous. Statistics show that between 1905-1935 more than half the total number of fruit vendors in the city was Italian, a large percentage of whom came from the Termini Imerese area of Palermo.

The ingenuity and business acumen of these early-settler grocers, and their expertise in produce, allowed them to expand trade with US suppliers and introduce new fruits and vegetables to the Toronto market. Staples like bananas and peaches, for example first appeared in Ontario during this time.

Amongst the many Italian grocers opening for business around this time was Pasquale Brothers, founded by brothers Edward and Panfilo Pasquale. The brothers came here from Abruzzo in 1911 and opened their first shop here six years later.

Like the many immigrants at the time, the brothers lived and worked in St John's Ward—commonly known as the Ward District—an area flanked by Queen, College, and Yonge Sts, and and University Avenue. The Ward was a lively, densely populated neighbourhood, teaming with little shops whose owners typically lived on the premises. The shops were tiny, as were the dwellings in the neighbourhood, and there was no refrigeration at the time, so shopping for food was a daily ritual.

This was before Toronto Harbour had been filled in: the city's shoreline was just south of Front St, where the city wharf and rail station were both located—gateways for many types of goods sold in Toronto shops. The Queensway Food Terminal had not yet been built: a smaller predecessor of the terminal was located on Lombard Street, just a few blocks north of the St Lawrence Market.

So, when Edward and his wife Donna had the opportunity to move the family business to 111 King St East (at Church), a short walk to these strategic points on the 1920s Toronto map, they took the plunge. By this time imported goods had become Pasquale Brothers' specialty, particularly olive oil and olives, dried legumes, sott'olio products, rice, aged cheese and cured meats. These products were shipped here in large containers and sold in bulk or repackaged for sale at Pasquale Brothers.

"My grandfather was as strong as an ox," says Edward's granddaughter Anna Marie Kalcevich, who ran the company with her husband John Kalcevich from 1973-2016, before passing it on to her daughter Christina. "I remember hearing stories that he could lift 100 lb bags with his teeth!"

With bigger retail and living spaces, more storage than they had in the Ward, and better access to the supply chain, Edward and Donna's business grew steadily. Many of their customers were Italian, of course, but from its early days the company serviced a multicultural audience, particularly European immigrants: Greek restaurateurs looking for kalamata olives, Portuguese customers shopping for salted cod, Northern and Eastern Europeans seeking Danish Feta, and so on.

Packaging and distributing products were an important part of the business from early on. "When you imported, you wanted a name on your products. My grandfather probably started the Unico brand a few years after the store opened in 1917, and later he created the Marca Gallo brand for his line of olives and tomatoes from Spain," says Anna Marie.

Home deliveries were a normal part of the business, by foot or streetcar until Edward purchased his first car and, as demand for their products grew, Pasquale Brothers also started wholesaling to other grocers. Packing and wholesale was done at King St. right up to the 1950s, when the distribution business grew too big to contain at the store.

The wholesale arm of the business finally moved to an industrial unit on Wingold Avenue, just north of the Beltline Railway, in 1956, where it operated until relocating to its current address on Keele Street in Concord, on the east side of CN MacMillan Yard, in 1967.

WAR YEARS

1935-1950 was a difficult period for Italian Canadians, who found themselves on the "enemy aliens" list of the War Measures Act, and suffered prejudice, financial hardship, and even internment, regardless of whether they were sympathetic to Mussolini or not. They lost their jobs, their businesses, and in many cases Anglicized their names to conceal their Italian heritage.

The story goes that Edward Pasquale's last shipment of Italian olive oil made it to Toronto Harbour just before trade between the countries ceased in 1940, and he was fortunate enough to secure authorized seller status to keep the business going during the war years. But thousands of food rations and price controls came into effect during the period, as the Canadian government encouraged citizens to "eat patriotically." Needless to say, the effects on the food business were profound.

As a result, Pasquale Brothers was forced to source more and more products like cooking oils, preserved goods and legumes domestically. This would ultimately prove beneficial in the postwar era, as the Unico brand evolved into a blended portfolio of locally sourced and imported Italian products. It was a template that many other brands like Primo, Lancia Bravo, Aurora Foods, Jan K. Overweel and others, would adopt in their own ways in later years.

POST WWII - CIBO DI CASA

With the unprecedented economic boom of the post-war era came the need for an influx of labour in Canada. By the end of the 1940s, restrictions on immigration had been removed, and ads seeking "Young Men Ages 18-35," began appearing in little towns all over Italy. Amongst the many thousands who responded to them were Joe Porco from Cosenza, who would later open Joe's Grocery and Meat Market on Gerrard St. East; and Amerigo Borgo from Vicenza, founder of Quality Cheese.

Both men worked alongside many of their paesani on the railway in Western Canada, surviving harsh winter conditions unlike anything they'd seen before in Italy, before eventually settling in Toronto, where a burgeoning Italian community was forming.

Amerigo learned the cheesemaking trade from his father while he was growing up in Vicenza, a city famous for producing Asiago cheese. But by the time he was old enough to help in the family business the area had fallen on hard times, and there was wasn't enough work to be had for young men. After fulfilling his contract on the Canadian Railroad, he worked construction jobs in Toronto, before eventually finding employment with several local cheese producers like Silani Cheese. Around this time, he met Marco Contardi, a master cheese maker from Puglia, and with financial backing by silent partner Louie De Angelis, Amerigo's future father-in-law, the two soon launched their own cheese business.

This was before Ontario's supply management system was established in the 1960s, when cheesemakers bought milk directly from local farmers. So, they needed a location that was accessible both to farms and to the city, where most of their customers would be. They found a piece of land just outside Orangeville, in Grand Valley, and named the dairy after the area where it was established: Grande Cheese.

Most of the Italian cheesemakers who came to Toronto at that time were from the South and were skilled at making pasta filata. And that's what Grande Cheese made, turning it into cheeses like scamorza, caciocavallo and provolone, and also making ricotta.

The men who worked for Grande were skilled at the craft of making cheese by hand, but few knew the technical aspects of coagulating milk properly—this was Amerigo's responsibility, a skill he learned in Vicenza. It wasn't till the late 1960s, when Grande Cheese moved to a larger facility on Milvan Drive in Etobicoke, that they also started making a style of cheese like the one Amerigo's father had taught him. It came to be known as "Friulano" here in Ontario because it was a Northern-Italian style of cheese.

The majority of customers for Grande's products were independent Italian grocers like Joe Porco, small family businesses that were opening all over Southern Ontario in the 1950s-1960s as the community rapidly grew. Joe's son John, who grew up and worked in the family store, has fond memories of those days.

"We used to have people coming into our store who had just arrived in Toronto. They'd go up and down the street and they were told by their paesani, 'go and find a store with a Unico sign, they'll have good Italian food.' And they'd come into the store and tell my father, 'Abbiamo sentito che qua si trovano prodotti italiani,'" says John.

By now the Ontario Food Terminal had moved to the Queensway, and when he was old enough, John would join his father very early in the morning, loading up their small truck with the day's produce. When they arrived back at the store paesani would often be waiting for them, having preordered cases of peaches, tomatoes, peppers—whatever was in season. John also

ONTARIO FOOD TERMINAL

recalls the sense of pride these first-generation Italian Canadians had in sharing traditional foods they would make with the produce, often bringing samples back to Joe's Grocery for the Porco family to try themselves.

In January and February, the family would make soppressata and sausages at the store, just as they had done back in Cosenza. It became so popular people would come from all over Ontario just to purchase it.

The iconic sign on the front of Joe's Grocery was part of an ingenious marketing strategy that helped solidify Unico as the leading brand for Italian products in Ontario during this time.

The idea was deceptively simple—Unico would pay for a shop's sign in exchange for displaying their logo on it. Because these independent grocers and bakeries were the only places Italians could find foods from back home (deli meats, cheeses, sott'olio products, olives, etc.), the Unico sign quickly became a symbol of Italian food in Ontario—a kind of stamp of authenticity.

John Porco, who went on to work for Unico when he finished college, working his way from sales representative all the way up to his current role as Chief Operating Officer, says the program encouraged loyalty on the part of independent merchants like his father towards the Unico brand.

"We also got our name out there and became something of a preferred brand in these stores. And things evolved from there," he says.

Anna Marie Kalcevich, who was involved in the Unico sign program, says it was an ongoing initiative: sales reps came in regularly with requests for new signs and they were rarely turned down. As they proliferated all over the city, Unico became synonymous with Italian food culture, perceived by many Ontarians as an "Italian" rather than a local brand.

Many of Ontario's iconic food businesses were founded during this time: grocers like Longo's, Highland Farms, Fortino's and Pusateri's; growers like Mucci Farms and Sunset Produce; producers and distributors like Aurora, Primo and Sofina Foods; and in the canning sector, industry leader Sun-Brite Canning Ltd.

Invariably they were family businesses trying to re-connect with cibo di casa (food from home) in some way: importing Italian products, producing or preserving them locally, and transplanting Italian fruits and vegetables to Ontario.

The story of Aurora Importing is similar to that of Unico half a century earlier. Nunzio Tumino and his wife opened a traditional Italian grocery store on Queensway in the early 1960s and slowly began importing their own products. Over the next few decades the importing and distribution side of the business eventually grew to a point where it needed be separated from retail.

The story goes that Nunzio got into the importing business accidentally. On the request of a local wholesaler, he brought 400 bags of chestnuts back to Toronto upon returning from a visit to his home in Sicily. But the wholesaler reneged on their agreement and Nunzio was stuck selling and distributing the chestnuts himself. Luckily, he had knack for it and turned the problem into an opportunity—and just like that the importing business was born.

An interesting exception to the rule, a company that did things differently from the start and would evolve into one of the most successful food retailers in the Greater Toronto Area, is Longo's.

Like many of the early Italian settlers who

JOE'S GROCERY

came to Ontario 50 years earlier, brothers Tommy, Joe and Gus came from Termini Imerese. They were farmers in Italy and had deep expertise in produce. Older brothers Tommy and Joe found work with Canadian grocers Loblaws and Miracle Mart shortly after arriving in Toronto, and when the opportunity arose in 1956 the three brothers established their own independent fruit market near Yonge and Castlefield Sts.

Then as now, the neighborhood was primarily Anglophone, meaning that the brothers' customer base was predominantly non-Italian. Though their English wasn't perfect, the brothers got by on the quality of their fruits and vegetables, and quickly learned what Anglophone products (butter, yogurt) they needed to stock in addition to top quality fresh produce.

The entrepreneurship the brothers demonstrated in these early days has been a hallmark of the company, which has never shied from opening up new markets and opportunities: opening a supermarket surrounded by farmland in 1980s Oakville; launching Toronto's first online grocery service, Grocery Gateway, in 2004; and recently starting Pronto Eats, a cashless, convenience-based downtown food kiosk that utilizes the Ritual app for mobile ordering.

PAN-ITALIAN CUISINE

In the book *Italians in Toronto*, John E. Zucchi argues that for the most part, the city's Italian immigrants developed a strong sense of national identity after they came to Canada.

Back home their paesani were people from the same town primarily, and to some extent the province or region. Italy's geographic and cultural diversity, the unique and remote character of so many of its little towns, resulted in great differences of dialect, customs, outlook, history, and of course, cuisine.

But emigration changed things. Suddenly Italians from all over the peninsula came together in one place, and over time a new Italian Canadian culture started to emerge. At home for example, customs around gardening, wine and cold-cut making, and preserves, and the ubiquitous cantina in the basement, were influenced partly by one's home region, but also by one's Canadian "paesani," who came from diverse regions of Italy and brought their own food traditions here.

A kind of Canadian pan-Italian (rather than strictly regional) cuisine was also seen at the bakeries, trattorias, pizzerias and banquet halls that started to appear in the 1960s. And at Italian hot tables that were popularized in the 1970s-1980s,

ABOVE: GUS LONGO OUTSIDE OF WOODBINE STORE

BELOW: TOM LONGO, 1960

where one would find "classic Italian" dishes like melanzane alla parmigiana, and Canadian variations like vitello alla parmigiana or breaded veal sandwiches with tomato sauce.

This pan-Italian culture was even reflected in business names. The use of "Venezia" to make a place seem a little fancy, for example: Ristorante Venezia, or even Marcelleria Venezia.

Importers played an important part in the story. In the early days their focus was on food from home—traditional essentials like olive oil, passata, legumes, and regional specialties like fichi secchi or alici sotto sale. But as the Italian Canadian community became more affluent, it presented the opportunity to market new (or previously unavailable) Italian products.

An early purveyor of such products was Adriano Bertozzi, who came to Canada from Parma, and wanted to bring products like Parmigiano-Reggiano, Aceto Balsamico and polenta to Canada. Adriano grew up with these products in Emilia Romagna, but most Italian Canadian immigrants came from regions like Calabria, Sicily, Lazio, Abruzzo, Veneto and Friuli, where these products were little known. To market these foods to Italian Canadians, Adriano had to educate consumers about their value, demonstrate how to use them properly, and of course, justify their price.

So, if the first wave of importing was about giving immigrants access to their traditional foods (cibo di casa), the second was more about sourcing new (or previously unavailable) Italian products that would be of interest to Italian Canadians.

TUMINO'S; PHOTO: AURORA IMPORTING

Rina Tumino, daughter of Nunzio who worked alongside her father for many years in the Aurora business, recalls the countless consumer food shows and in-store demos in the 1980s-1990s, marketing new products like Sundried Tomatoes, La Bomba Hot Peppers and Pesto Genovese.

"My father had a knack for bringing things in and doing well with them," she says. "He just had an innate understanding of the market." But adoption often required a year or more marketing efforts to gain traction.

NUNZIO AND RINA TUMINO

"Even when we did some advertising, it was always a struggle to get the message in 30 seconds. It couldn't just be, 'buy this product.' We had to explain what the product was and how easy it was to use," says Rina. And of course, importing was only half the story. Like Unico before them, companies like Aurora and Primo, and later Jan K. Overweel, developed blended product portfolios of imported and locally produced goods.

The motivations for sourcing and producing local were varied: keeping costs down; protecting against supply and cost fluctuations abroad; simplifying and accelerating the supply chain and making it more flexible in terms of quantities; and avoiding duties and other trade restrictions.

Often the strategy was about supplementing rather than replacing imported goods. For example, a distributor could offer both locally grown and imported plum tomatoes. This gave consumers more choice; it also gave distributors and retailers access to diverse markets and exposed them to less risk in terms of costs and supplies.

ITALIAN FOOD GOES MAINSTREAM

Broadly speaking, two contradictory trends have occurred in the Italian food business since the 1980s. On the one hand, the population of first- and second-generation ethnic Italians is slowly dwindling, diminishing the demand for traditional Italian Canadian foods. Yet, from a revenue perspective, Italian food sales in Ontario have never been better. The cause of this apparent paradox is the growth of Italian food sales outside of the Italian Canadian community.

"We have a population of 35 million people in Canada," says Jan K. Overweel president Pat Pelliccione. "If you're going to limit your focus to ethnic Italians, even with the second generation, you're looking at two million people tops. That's less than 10 percent of the Canadian population." In other words, if sales are dropping amongst 10% of the population but growing amongst the remaining 90%, revenue is quite likely to go up.

It was during the 1970s that grocery chains like Loblaws, Dominion, Food City and Steinberg first started to carry Italian "ethnic" products. These were the Trudeau years, when the idea of Canadian multiculturalism was popularized, and the domestic palette slowly began to mature. Immigration played a big part, exposing French- and Anglo-Canadians to international flavours, and creating new consumer segments for the large grocery chains to market to.

Italian food—simple, healthy, inexpensive and delicious—was a perfect fit for grocery chains looking for new flavours and trends to offer. And Unico, the most recognizable Italian food brand in Ontario at the time, with the widest variety of products, was in the right place at the right time to capitalize on the opportunity.

The company partnered with Loblaws on an Italian foods media campaign in the late 1970s and it was a great success. Pretty soon other large-scale retailers followed suit, catapulting Unico to a period of unprecedented growth.

Unico was the leading distributor of Italian food products at the time (domestically produced and/or imported) but many others began to appear or grew exponentially during the 1980s-1990s: Primo Foods, Lancia Bravo, Aurora Importing, Numage Trading, Jan K. Overweel and more.

SUN-BRITE FOODS, LEAMINGTON ONTARIO

Multiculturalism was just one of the contributing factors that led mainstream grocery chains to start carrying Italian products. Another was the large-scale migration of Italian Canadians to the suburbs from the 1980s onwards. Independent Italian grocers began to disappear during the era, as more and more first- and second-generation suburban Italians began shopping at supermarket chains. To compete for this growing segment, supermarkets had to stock a sufficient selection of Italian products.

It was also during 1980s that mainstream English media in the US, Britain and Canada first discovered the health benefits of the Mediterranean diet. Numerous studies proved that a low-meat diet, comprised primarily of legumes, fruits and vegetables, whole grains, and olive oil rather than unhealthy fats like butter, reduced the risks of chronic and fatal diseases. Many mainstream articles carried stories on the subject, plus recipes and tips for using products like olive oil, pasta, beans, tomatoes, and so on.

Of course, there are many countries on the Mediterranean, but it was Italian cuisine in particular that enjoyed the most coverage, and the ensuing benefits, from this new interest in the Mediterranean diet. While many food trends have come and gone since, the Mediterranean diet is still considered one of the healthiest, a belief that continues to bolster Italian food sales in Ontario to this day.

Two additional causes of Italian food "going mainstream" in the 1980s-1990s are worth mentioning: increased travel to Italy, and the rise of food media outlets like the Food Network. As exposure grew, more and more non-Italians discovered the incredible diversity of Italian cuisine and the simplicity of its traditional recipes (which, importantly, makes them easy to learn).

A new interest in "authentic" food culture was beginning to take hold: consumers started seeking out DOC types of products they heard about on TV or saw in a magazine recipe, and booking culinary tours to Italy to experience the real thing. Italian Canadians themselves discovered foods and traditions that had been lost over the decades since immigration, and new ones (e.g. burrata) that had appeared since their parents and grandparents came here.

Back in Italy, marketing boards and consortiums were forming to meet this new demand. A dynamic cycle developed between Italian producers and marketers on the one hand, and North American media and consumers on the other—a trend that would only accelerate in the 2000s with the rise of digital media.

Behind the scenes at the local supermarket, an interesting debate was forming between grocery chains and the distributors who supplied them with Italian products. Even as importers continued to source more and more "authentic Italian" products for the Ontario market, they also argued that categories like olive oil, pasta and legumes had simply become part of the local diet, and therefore should not be hidden in an ethnic "Italian" section of the supermarket. It raised a question still debated in the industry today: is Italian food ethnic anymore?

A GLOBALIZED, DIGITIZED FOOD CULTURE

When senior grocery consultant Mary Dalimonte recalls the early Italian food ads she used to see growing up in Toronto's Italian Canadian community, it was typically a local brand like Primo, Lancia or Unico advertising staples like olive oil, beans and pasta.

"Now you look at an Italian themed ad," she says, "and you've got everything from cooking to finishing olive oils. An incredible selection of olives, pastas, tomatoes, antipasti. You've got cheeses wrapped in grape leaves, aged 24, 30 or 36 months, different grades of Parmigiano-Reggiano, Vacca Nera.

"You look at deli too: it used to be domestic prosciutto, Genoa salami and mortadella. Now most places have 3 or 4 imported prosciuttos, culatello, imported mortadella, prosciutto cotto, and more. The expansion of Italian food at Ontario supermarkets is very prevalent today."

It extends to prepared foods as well, which has become a major category in today's grocery business. "When I was growing up you couldn't walk into your local Loblaws and buy a real Italian lasagna," Mary says.

The breadth and diversity of the Italian food offering in Ontario today is a complex story, with many contributing factors.

On the importing side, it starts in Italy itself of course, where food production, particularly food products geared for export, has never been higher. In 2019 Italian food imports to Canada alone were over one billion CAD, a 500% increase compared to 20 years ago.

Food exporting has become a high-stakes, well-oiled machine in Italy, with massive trade fairs like Cibus and TuttoFood bringing together

PREPARED FOOD AT PUSITERI'S; PHOTO: RICK O'BRIEN

thousands of producers at a time to meet with international distributors. Their work is bolstered by the Italian Trade Agency, who host international delegates at these shows and trade missions across Italy, in addition to its 'Made in Italy' program, which sponsors advertising and original content, and brings Italian producers to key food fairs across the globe.

Not surprisingly, as the industry has expanded, so too has the number of importers in Ontario: in addition to established brands like Unico-Primo, Jan K. Overweel, Aurora, Bertozzi, Numage and La Molisana, there are many smaller niche players in today's market like MSM, Sarafino, Lugano and Taste For Luxury.

Further complicating the scene are the many regulations today's importers have to navigate —like tariffs protecting local producers and guidelines that have been implemented by the Canadian Food Inspection Agency (CFIA) over the past few decades.

Pat Pelliccione says that Jan K. Overweel, one of Canada's largest food importers, employs 12-14 QA people full-time, and their primary focus is CFIA compliance. He's a big supporter of the agency's agenda, both as a barrier against unfair competition and as a champion of public health but acknowledges that compliance makes things more complicated than they were back in the 1990s when his family took over the business.

"Distribution at the time was still the Wild West," he says. "Importers were bringing in whatever they wanted, labels didn't have to conform, a lot of games were being played. We decided to focus on categories that required some capital for entry so we could assure a reasonable margin.

"So, we had to set up inventory control procedures and software to control lot tracking of inventory in case of recalls, and lot tracking of best-before-dates so we could create a first in, first out method of shipping. We invested a lot of up-front money into infrastructure like racking, which was unheard of at the time in our industry."

The company also had to develop its own software to standardize the tracking and billing process in order to secure access to the large grocery chains. A grocer might purchase two wheels of cheese of different weights, for example, but want the invoice to show two "cases" of cheese, both of equal weight.

"So I would need to quickly pick that up in a scan, while still being able to control if there's a recall (what lot it came from, who was the supplier, etc.)—software like this didn't exist, so we had to develop it."

That's a lot different than when he was working part-time for his dad at Primo. "Stuff came in, maybe you had to change the format or branding, and then you go to market. Our generation didn't get those opportunities."

Aside from the time and expense it took to develop and maintain its own automated digital processes, there are also new risks that didn't exist a generation ago. In late 2019 for example, Jan K. was subject to a Russian cyber attack that halted its software for several months, forcing them to rely on fax, email, phone calls and other manual processes.

Perhaps the biggest change for contemporary producers, importers and retailers compared to a generation ago is the behavior of the modern consumer. Globalization and digital media have radically changed consumer expectations and buying habits, and the effects are seen in the Italian food sector like all others.

In the past, importers would source new products and introduce them to the domestic market; building awareness and educating local retailers and their customers about the benefits of these products was critical to success. But today the relationship is often inverted—thanks to social media, food blogs, culinary websites and other digital media, it's often consumers themselves who discover new products online, and go looking for them at local retailers, who, in turn, look to importers like Jan K. Overweel to source them.

That could be an Italian Montasio, Fontina or Prosciutto di Parma—but increasingly, it could also be a Spanish Manchego, a Dutch Gouda or a Swiss Gruyere. "Our customer base is not just the ethnic Italian segment anymore," says Pat Pelliccione. "It's the whole Canadian multicultural mosaic."

PAT PELLICCIONE

More than ever, today's consumers are educated and well travelled, and like Canadian society itself, they have an eclectic, multicultural palette. To service this market Jan K. Overweel increasingly 'Shops the World,' as its tagline says, not just Italy, building on the network, expertise and systems it originally built for Italian food importing.

Similarly, the company's manufacturing facilities have diversified their product offering beyond traditional Italian products. Today the same local facility produces Milano biscotti and English-style shortbread biscuits; and the meat plant that produces Emma brand mortadella also white-labels a long list of non-Italian products like cooked ham, smoked turkey and pepperettes, for companies like Loblaws and Maple Leaf.

BERTOZZI IMPORTING, PHOTO: RICK O'BRIEN

Distributors like Primo-Unico and Aurora have had analogous growth with products like preserved legumes and tomatoes, which first appeared on Ontario shelves as "Italian" foods. Today they are staple foods for a variety of consumer segments in Ontario—some traditional (e.g. Middle Eastern or West Indian), others more lifestyle based (e.g. vegetarian or vegan). In the case of Unico, the company has broadened its positioning from "Italian" to "Mediterranean" foods, a reflection of the diversity of its customer base and a more accurate depiction of the broader geographical area from which it sources its products from today.

In the cheese business, Amerigo Borgo decided to leave Grande in the late 1990s to found Quality Cheese, with his sons Albert, Joseph and William. Amerigo's background and expertise in producing traditional Italian cheeses was the starting point for the company, and today it's still regarded as the best local pasta filata and ricotta producer by many experts. Quality Cheese's innovative spirit and dedication to R&D have taken it well beyond traditional Italian cheese (its award-winning brie is a good example of this).

This is not to say that all Italian Canadian brands have or will diversify beyond Italian products. It's a sign of the maturity of today's market that there are many different types of business. Bertozzi Importing, for example, prides itself in continuing the mandate of founder Adriano Bertozzi, whose passion was to bring high quality, artisanal Italian products to the Canadian market.

Bertozzi's approach has always made it a more natural partner for independent retailers and artisanal restaurants than grocery chains. And with the rise of digital media, the company has a whole new way to sell, directly to consumers, via its proprietary website, Nonna's Pantry.

Bertozzi's products continue to find a market in the modern digital marketplace because they are unique. They have what marketers like to call "stories": small batch products, traditional production methods, often made by iconic family businesses like Giusti, Beppino Occelli, and Melegatti.

Rosanne Longo, Spokesperson and Brand Ambassador for Longo's and Grocery Gateway, says this search for unique, authentic food experiences is one of the most important trends in the contemporary food market. Unlike early generations of Italian Canadians who sought foods from their homeland, today's consumers have more complex criteria for their purchasing decisions. These "foodie" consumers are looking for new culinary experiences, novel foods or foods from diverse cultures, interesting products they read about online or tasted on a trip abroad. So it is that while sales of certain Italian Canadian staples like Genoa salami and Friulano cheese slowly decline in sales, interest in others, like imported Mortadella, DOP cheeses, and locally produced burrata and fior di latte, steadily rise.

Another important driver Rosanne sees in today's grocery market is the need for convenience. In the Italian food sector like others, this means a shift towards semi- or fully prepared foods rather than raw ingredients. Today Unico sells more diced tomatoes than whole ones, and more canned beans than dried; and sales of its ready-made pasta sauces have never been stronger. And while grocers like Longo's continue to sell bushels of fresh, in-season produce, today's consumer is more likely to buy preserves than make them from scratch at home.

Additionally, like most major retailers, Longo's has increased its prepared foods offering to meet rising demand. It's also developed innovative new offerings like Pronto Eats and Recipe Kiosks that solve the need for convenience based on different consumer needs and lifestyles (e.g. professional singles, busy parents, empty nesters).

A third trend Rosanne thinks will impact the grocery business into the future is consumer demand for more choice. There are many causes for this, including the amount of information now available to food shoppers. "Guests are more focused and knowledgeable about where their food comes, and what's in it, than ever before," says Rosanne.

Factors contributing to purchase decisions today include health and nutrition; ethics (treatment of animals, environmental impact); alternative diets (Keto, Atkins); religious beliefs; ethnicity; and a myriad of mainstream and niche food fads. Today's multicultural, globalized, digitized food economy is complex and ever-evolving; to succeed into the future, food businesses must be attuned and responsive.

DIGESTIVO

"Canada is self-reliant in terms of our food supply chain," says Rosanne Longo. "And the COVID-19 pandemic only solidified that. Despite the panic buying you saw in the early days, there was really nothing to worry about."

If the early days of the COVID crisis proved the reliability of the local food supply chain, the history of the Italian food sector proves the fundamental role Italians have played in the development of our food supply chain.

"You want to see the influence of Italians on the produce sector?" asks Mary Dalimonte. "Just walk the floor of the Food Terminal one morning and look at all of those multi-generational Italian family businesses."

One of those businesses is F.G. Lister, established in 1931, owned and operated today by Tony Fallico. Tony came to Toronto from Cosenza as a young child in 1963, and began working at the Terminal in 1971, before he had even started high school. He remembers leaving his Little Italy home at 3:30 am to arrive on time for his shift at the Terminal's Farmer's Market at 4 am.

"The farmers would come in from Newmarket and Holland Marsh. I'd help them load and unload and sell their produce. That's where I met people like the Longo and Coppa families, all the people who are still my customers today."

Long-standing family businesses like F.G. Lister, some quite literally the descendants of early Italian settlers who dominated the local produce business over a century ago, supply other multi-generation family retailers like Longo's, Coppa's and Highland Farms. These retailers in turn are supplied by multi-generational businesses like Jan K. Overweel, Unico (Sun-Brite), Numage, Aurora and others. Not to mention figures like Mary Dalimonte, who have worked their entire careers for companies like Sobey's, Metro and Loblaws—bringing native Italian food sensibilities to the executive level in these institutions and helping to introduce Italian products to the grocery chains.

It would be impossible to recount the history of the Ontario food business without acknowledging the critical contribution Italians have made to agriculture, food production, importing, distribution and retail. And at this uncertain moment, as the food sector (like all other sectors) struggles to navigate the unchartered waters of COVID-19 era, one thing is for certain: Italian food businesses will, as always, lead the way.

LONGO'S NEWMARKET

BENVENUTI A "LA MENSA"
HOMEMADE GELATO BARS & DELICIOUS PASTA
*ALL PASTAS CONTAIN EGG + FLOUR
BIBITE GRAB&GO

SUD FORNO, YONGE & TEMPERANCE ST. PHOTO: GIANNONE PETRICONE ASSOCIATES

SETTING THE TABLE: DINNER AND A GLASS OF WINE, ITALIAN STYLE

DENIS DE KLERCK

In 1826, the French epicure and gastronome, Jean Anthelme Brillat-Savarin, published his influential book "The Physiology of Taste." His most famous aphorism, quoted approvingly by Chairman Kaga on the TV series Iron Chef, is "Tell me what you eat, and I will tell you what you are." One wonders what he would have made of Canadians based on their cuisine. Traditional Indigenous culture gave us pânsâwân, a type of dried smoked meat from bison, elk or moose but also, the more commonly consumed maple syrup. The Inuit contributed fermented meats as well as 'muktuk,' a popular snack of whale skin and blubber. As for the rest, most Canadians would list poutine, Nanaimo bars, butter tarts and Montreal-style bagels as national signifiers, though these items hardly add up to a national cuisine. In fact, when we tell Brillat-Savarin what we commonly eat, in order for him to learn what we are, he would likely conclude that most of us are at least partly Italian, based on the items found in a typical Canadian pantry and on restaurant menus across the country.

Thanks to that influence you can now enjoy a salad with balsamic vinaigrette at McDonald's and find a surprisingly decent espresso at Tim Hortons. But it wasn't always like this. The austerity during and after the Second World War didn't do the culinary world any favours. Neither did the North American prosperity of the '50s, which introduced new refrigerators, ovens, electric can openers and carving knives, powders and potions—instant everything—designed to relieve the beleaguered housewife of her daily chores. As novel as TV dinners and Jello molds were back in the day, these innovations contributed very little of lasting value to local food culture.

By contrast, France and Italy, two adjoining countries with an outsized influence on the hospitality industry, built their gastronomic reputations on the foundations of their local cuisines. Perfected over generations, that kind of home cooking is, understandably, a great source of pride for local people, not to mention a great source of argument on how to cook things properly according to tradition and according to the seasons. These are cultures that take the pleasures of the table seriously, as central to a well-lived life.

The post-war period brought a huge influx of immigrants to Canada from Italy, primarily from the south. Because so many of them were escaping poverty to build a new life, practical matters, like how to feed a family, were among the first things to be addressed. Planting a garden was an effective supplement to domestic finances, as was fishing in the Humber River, making homemade wine, foraging for dandelion greens or hunting for morel mushrooms on Toronto Island. Poverty doesn't give everyone a keen appreciation of nature's bounty, but Italians have always excelled at the cultivation and preparation of the family meal because the family meal is important to the culture. If Italians have been successful in the hospitality industry, it is because they know that beyond the food itself, breaking bread with someone is an important social and communal ritual, something that translates well as an attitude to have when running a restaurant.

The clichéd portrait of an Italian Canadian restaurant of the 1950s would likely include a red checkered tablecloth with a candle slowly weeping down an empty straw-covered Chianti bottle. There is pizza and spaghetti bolognese and maybe a veal sandwich on the menu. While these remain great gifts to Canadian cuisine, it is the Italian Canadian approach to food in general, drawn from their home life, which will likely have the most lasting effect on the Canadian dinner table.

Toronto didn't have a restaurant culture to speak of until after the Second World War. For one thing, people didn't eat out (or order in) as often in those days. For another, British immigrants were predominant in the city until the early '60s, and though they brought many skills to their new country, culinary sophistication was not one of them. The great wave of immigration that began in the late '50s, with Italians dominating the influx, began a process that would utterly transform Toronto's relation to food, which surely is one of the best arguments for keeping our borders open and allowing newcomers to influence our daily lives. Toronto is now one of the most multicultural cities in the world and Italians, and the food culture they brought with them, remain one of the most prominent examples of successful integration.

The Italian contribution to shifting our relation to food began with an earlier generation of immigrants who opened small, corner groceries selling fruits and vegetables. The Pasquale Brothers were particularly important. They opened their doors in 1917, selling groceries, and quickly found a market packaging and distributing the "ethnic" foods that recent immigrants couldn't find elsewhere in the city. The Unico brand they created, and the speciality items they imported, soon dominated corner groceries across the city.

By the 1950s, the first wave of post-war immigration began and Italian hospitality began to leave an indelible mark on the culinary landscape of the GTA with many businesses that still thrive today. These early businesses tended to focus on simple menus with affordable items geared toward working people. Fine dining was typically associated with French cuisine and those that could afford it, while Italian food was for everyone else. This accessibility, usually thanks to small family-run businesses, laid the groundwork for what eventually became the acceptance and even dominance of the Italian approach to food.

On Clinton Street, in the heart of Little

Italy, San Francesco began selling pizza, veal sandwiches, and assorted delicatessen items out of a small converted row house in 1954. Bitondo Pizzeria opened directly across the street in 1964 and to this day, since seating is limited in both places, clients can take their veal sandwiches or panzerotti across the street to the Monarch Tavern and wash their meals down with a cold glass of beer.

Around the corner, on Claremont Avenue, the Papa-Bertucci family opened La Rinascente Grocery in 1967. When they added homemade breaded veal cutlet sandwiches to the grocery staples they were selling, they found themselves with an immediate hit on their hands. It wasn't long before the grocery business gave way to this new demand and the family re-christened their operations as California Sandwiches. Today there are thirteen locations across the GTA.

Another classic old-school Italian Canadian food destination is Commisso Italian Bakery. Opened in 1957, the bakery runs 24 hours a day, 365 days a year. It is part convenience store and part bakery but what keeps people coming back, at all hours of the day, is the 'tavola calda,' which features porchetta, arancini, lasagna or veal cutlets among other things. Over the years it has become popular with truck drivers servicing the surrounding industrial area and also with hungry late-night revellers who know they can always find a hot meal after the bars close down and restaurant options become limited.

Other pioneers include the Galipo family who, in 1959, created Sicilian Ice Cream, Toronto's oldest gelateria, developing a street-side business that would eventually grow into being a commercial producer of gelato, even while maintaining their cafe on College St. in Little Italy. La Paloma, another classic gelateria, first opened their doors in 1967 in the other Little Italy on St. Clair West.

In the west end of the city, Vesuvio Pizzeria and Spaghetti house opened their doors for business in Toronto's Junction neighbourhood in 1957. Owned by the Pugliese family, Vesuvio set a template for Italian restaurants in the city and introduced countless people to the joy of having a piping hot pizza delivered directly to their home. Camarra's Pizza, near Dufferin and Lawrence opened in 1958 and quickly became a mainstay of classic old-school pizzerias.

In 1954 Giacomo Zuccarini opened the Sidewalk Caffè at College and Yonge St. and although it didn't last long as a restaurant Zuccarini's great contribution was to import Toronto's first espresso machine. Sensing an opportunity, the Zuccarini Importing Company was created and Giacomo,

ABOVE: THE ORIGINAL DIPLOMATICO PATIO; PHOTO: ROCCO MASTRANGELO

BELOW: VESUVIO, CIRCA 1963; PHOTO PIERA PUGLIESE

MICHAEL CARLEVALE

representing the Gaggia line of espresso machines, set about educating the city and its restaurateurs on how to make a proper cup of coffee. A few years later Mike Di Donato began importing San Marco espresso machines, eventually switching and becoming the sole distributor of Faema machines in Canada. Today of course, coffee culture is a huge part of the hospitality industry, largely thanks to the early evangelizing of Zuccarini and Di Donato.

By the 1960s, small cafes and pizza parlours were becoming more common and some, like Cafe Diplomatico on College St., with its expansive patio, became neighbourhood institutions giving the Italian community a common place to gather. As time went on the approach to food in these restaurants became more sophisticated and more conscious of meeting a demand beyond the Italian community. The Primucci family for example, opened their first pizzeria in 1963 in Scarborough. Pizza Nova gained quick success by focusing on quality ingredients and standardizing their product for consistency. Instead of remaining a small 'mom and pop' operation like so many others, they began franchising their concept in 1969. Today, with over 140 stores, Pizza Nova vividly demonstrates the growth and acceptance of Italian food as part of daily life.

The 1960s also signalled the beginnings of a more adventuresome restaurant culture in Toronto. In 1962, father and son, John and Charles Grieco, opened La Scala, the first Italian restaurant in the city to focus on fine dining. The authentic Northern Italian menu departed decisively from the 'Chef Boyardee' conception of Italian food and their introduction of fine Italian wines, not previously available in Ontario, helped transform how Italian cuisine was viewed in the city. It quickly became a favourite of Queen's Park politicians and the moneyed class and set a standard that other restauranteurs could aspire to.

By the 1970s, a nucleus of talent began to form in Toronto restaurants that would transform how the hospitality industry was viewed. Fine dining based on French cuisine executed with military precision by Swiss-trained chefs began to give way to more adventurous menus served in less formal dining rooms. While food was still important, restaurants became places for people to see, and be seen in—the social nature of communal dining was an attraction in itself, aside from the items on the menu.

This shift in attitudes was most clearly seen with the opening of Noodles in 1973, a restaurant envisioned by George Minden, the owner of the Windsor Arms Hotel. Minden tasked his Swiss-trained chef Herbert Sonzogni with creating an authentic Italian menu. The dining room avoided Italian restaurant design clichés and was brash, with chrome and hot pink neon lighting. Toronto hadn't seen anything like this before. Sonzogni's adventurous menu and the unusual decor was such a departure from the norm that it prompted Joanne Kates to propose a restaurant review column to the Globe and Mail newspaper. That the Globe didn't have a regular restaurant column prior to this is a testament to the paucity of restaurants worth writing about. Noodles became the first review that Kates wrote for the paper and by the time she stepped down from her role as restaurant critic 38 years later, the culinary landscape of the GTA was completely transformed.

The '70s also demystified Italian cuisine to the home cook by introducing the local television audience to the opera-loving chef Pasquale Carpino. Immigrating to Toronto from Cosenza, Calabria in 1958, Carpino worked in local restaurants while studying opera at the Royal Conservatory of Music. Carpino branched out into television when Johnny Lombardi gave him his own cooking show, "La Cucina Italiana con Pasquale" on CHIN television. During the '80s and early '90s Carpino was a

FRANCO PREVEDELLO; PHOTO: RICK O'BRIEN

television fixture, hosting the popular shows "Pasquale's Kitchen" and "Pasquale's Kitchen Express." Carpino was not only one of the first television celebrity chefs, he was instrumental in normalizing Italian cuisine and making it part of the standard repertoire of non-Italian home cooks.

By the 1980s, Toronto was well on its way to become the food-obsessed city that it is today. The population had grown and it had become the financial centre of the country. The Toronto International Film Festival, established in 1976, brought international glamour to the city. It was also the beginning of the celebrity chef. While Pasquale Carpino gained his celebrity through television, the new celebrity chefs gained renown by developing adventurous menus in destination restaurants. Scaramouche opened its doors in 1980 with co-chefs Jamie Kennedy and Michael Stadtländer who would both go on to train and influence a whole generation of young cooks. The hospitality industry had suddenly become a popular sub-culture with the comings and goings of chefs and restaurants documented breathlessly in the reviews of Joanne Kates at the Globe and Mail and James Chatto and others at Toronto Life magazine.

The 1980s was really the decade that the hospitality industry came of age in Toronto and no one exemplified this maturity more than Franco Prevedello. He has been the owner, partner, landlord, and/or consultant of countless restaurants, and the mentor to literally hundreds of people in the hospitality industry. Like all great restaurateurs, Prevedello combines a deep understanding of food and wine with a flair for the theatrical nature of hospitality. Before going out on his own, Prevedello spent time working at the Westbury Hotel, La Scala and Winston's, which in its day, catered to the most influential people in the country. No doubt mastering the art of serving a demanding clientele was a good training ground for the string of home runs Prevedello accomplished with his restaurants beginning in the eighties.

In short order Prevedello opened Biffi Bistro, Pronto, and Bindi Ristorante, before taking a break to run the Trillium Restaurant in the Ontario Pavilion at Expo 86 in Vancouver. Upon his return he opened Centro, which was really the jewel in the crown, and it quickly became the spiritual home of the glitterati. For years it was the high water mark for fine dining in Toronto and people like Marc Thuet, Chris McDonald, David Lee, Michael Bonacini and many others spent time working there before establishing their own stellar careers. Prevedello continued his restaurant successes beyond the '80s with Splendido Bar and Grill, Acrobat, Terra, Acqua and Nota Bene, but his work in the '80s really showed how far Toronto had come and how much those travelling in his orbit had to up their game to compete.

Michael Carlevale was another restaurateur that brought the Italian dining experience to new heights in those years. An American, transplanted from Boston, Carlevale was a self-taught cook and in 1978 he opened Carlevale's on Avenue Road. Two years later, with his friend Joey Bersani, he opened Bersani and Carlevale a little further south on Avenue Rd. The popular restaurant served lunch and dinner and take out Italian food and was highly regarded. Though he had other restaurant projects like Carlevale's at the Y, the Greek-Mediterranian Byzantium on Church Street and the ill-fated Boston Club, which ultimately drove him to bankruptcy, he will be remembered for Prego della Piazza, his restaurant, with its beautiful patio, tucked in behind a church at the corner of Avenue Road and Bloor. From its opening in 1987 to its closing in 2008, Prego gave Carlevale a theatre to perform in, appropriate to his talents. He was flamboyant, generous and deeply intelligent and the restaurant quickly gained a clientele drawn to the stylish energy of the place. Like Centro, it attracted a moneyed crowd and

ROBERTO MARTELLA; PHOTO: RICK O'BRIEN

quickly became the spot for celebrity sightings due to its proximity to the Toronto International Film Festival.

Also, like Franco Prevedello at Centro, Carlevale had a knack for spotting and cultivating talent. He chose Massimo Capra to run the Prego kitchen and when Prego expanded, Capra oversaw both Enoteca, the adjoining wine bar, and Black and Blue, the high-end steak house. After ten years Capra left Prego to open his own highly regarded restaurant Mistura and is now one of Canada's best known celebrity chefs, juggling a career as a TV personality, cookbook author, restaurateur and consultant.

In the 1980s Franco Prevedello, Michael Carlevale, Mark McEwen, Jamie Kennedy, Michael Stadtländer, and a few others, did more than anyone else to attract new talent to the hospitality industry. Apprenticing under any of them was just as valuable as a college degree and there is no question that their example and influence improved the restaurant culture of the city. They made the business seem glamorous, artistic, cosmopolitan, and even moral in its celebration of authentic farm-raised ingredients treated with artisanal techniques.

By the '90s this attitude had filtered down from fine dining, 'destination' establishments to less formal trattorias and cafes, and knowing where your food came from, how it was raised, and what wine to pair with it became a popular concern. This was the decade that saw the creation of The Food Network on television, which enhanced the average person's knowledge of regional cuisine, while raising their expectations for quality and authenticity in the restaurants they frequented.

It was out of this environment that places like Grano, Bar Italia and Terroni, despite their humble beginnings, developed loyal followings and cultural influence. When Roberto Martella opened Grano in 1986 he didn't aspire to create a high-end restaurant, even though Franco Prevedello was his landlord and something of a mentor. Grano began as a simple bakery and deli, and as it grew in popularity it expanded into a larger operation. While Grano celebrated the fundamental simplicity and honesty of good Italian cooking, Martella, through his interest in community engagement and the force of his personality, turned his culinary enterprise into a cultural initiative by offering Italian language lessons and hosting a well-regarded speaker series. Eugene Barone did a similar thing at Bar Italia, taking a run-down pool hall and adding an inventive menu by Andrew Milne-Allen that celebrated the simplicity of Italian culinary traditions. With his success Barone expanded Bar Italia by commissioning the architects Giannone Petricone Associates to design a multi-level restaurant that combined an Italian spirit of food and hospitality with countless community events, hosting everything from live music, political meetings, book launches, and World Cup soccer parties, to early iterations of the Hot Docs film festival. Milne-Allen, has long been an influential chef, beginning in the

’70s as co-owner of The Parrot on Queen St. Despite being a native New Zealander, he is best-known for his grasp of Italian cuisine. Besides his work at Bar Italia, he was also instrumental in establishing Trattoria Giancarlo and later gaining national acclaim for the Italian menu of his renowned restaurant, Zucca, on Yonge St.

Like Grano and Bar Italia, Terroni had humble beginnings, starting as a small store on Queen St. selling dried goods and southern Italian staples. Their food service went from four stools to 25 stools, and finally, to successful restaurant locations in Toronto and Los Angeles. Their popularity comes from their fidelity to simple Italian cuisine and their willingness to import wine and specialty items from Italy to create an authentic dining experience.

From one generation to the next, the history of the hospitality industry in the GTA demonstrates a remarkably quick maturity, led more often than not, by Italian Canadian entrepreneurs who transformed our notions of what constitutes honest food and genuine hospitality. A full history of this contribution would require a book as it is impossible to list the many personalities and restaurants that played an important role in our conception of what constitutes good food. One could mention people like Dante Rota, Freddy Lo Cicero, or Claudio Aprile as influences, yet barely scratch the surface. How can one speak of the hospitality industry and not mention Trattoria Giancarlo, Porretta’s Pizza, Biagio’s, La Fenice, Joso’s, Noce, and countless others?

EUGENE BARONE (LEFT) IN THE ORIGINAL BAR ITALIA WITH ANDREW MILNE-ALLEN (RIGHT)

Restaurants provide sustenance and the pleasures of the table but they have also played a vital social role, giving neighbourhoods throughout the city individual focal points where communities can gather and get to know one and other. This is especially important for immigrant communities. That was the case in 1963 when brothers Rocco and Mike Di Donato opened up San Marco, a small cafe on St. Clair Avenue, and then Lorenzo’s at Bay and Dundas. Eventually, Mike went on to proselytize for Faema and Italian coffee and become one of the city’s premier restaurant suppliers. Rocco moved Lorenzo’s to the Galleria Mall and had a long successful career as a restaurateur. From humble beginnings both men brought something to the city that wasn’t here before and provided the seeds for the next generation. In fact Rocco’s son Nick Di Donato has become one of the most successful entrepreneurs the Toronto hospitality industry has ever seen. As President and CEO of the Liberty Entertainment Group, Di Donato has overseen the creation of countless restaurants and nightclubs. He is renowned for breathing new life into historic properties such as the Liberty Grand Entertainment Complex on the Canadian National Exhibition grounds and Toronto's historic Casa Loma—two of the city's most unique special event venues. He did the same with the 40,000 square foot Coral Gables Country Club in Miami. His Cibo wine bars can be found in Toronto and Miami and his restaurant Don Alfonso 1890 has been internationally acclaimed.

Di Donato's example of a second generation Italian Canadian successfully building on the experience of the first generation is also clearly seen with Janet Zuccarini whose father Giacomo was a pioneering importer to the restaurant trade. Her success with Trattoria Nervosa in Yorkville has led to the creation of the Gusto 54 restaurant group which has an ever-growing portfolio of properties in Toronto and Los Angeles, with plans to expand to other markets.

Modern Canadian restaurants now go out of their way to advertise seasonal menus based on what is available in their region at any given time. Sourcing local and seasonally appropriate ingredients is now considered an essential mark of authenticity for the restauranteur who hopes to be taken seriously. Gastronomy has become a national hobby, yet despite the popularity of television shows and the rise of the celebrity chef, so much of what we value in the modern approach to food was already present in the way Italian Canadians cultivated, prepared and shared their daily bread. Robert Gentile, to take one example, is justly famous for his approach to Italian food at his Buca restaurants. While his presentation might show the hallmarks of professionalized food service, his salumi room of in-house cured meats and game owes less to haute cuisine than it does to the humble cantina filled with jarred tomatoes and homemade salumi hanging from the rafters. The immigrant cantina might have been seen as impossibly rustic in the 1950s when North America was otherwise discovering the modern miracle of frozen TV dinners and other convenience foods, but it has come to represent a respect for the integrity of ingredients that the best restaurants now take for granted.

The ability to think about where food comes from, and utilize that knowledge, is something Italians have always done well. Torontonians, without a distinctive regional cuisine to fall back on, have leaned heavily on the food culture Italians brought to Canada. While Franco Prevedello and his acolytes were busy shaping the high ground of Toronto hospitality, the city was growing at an exponential rate. A few short decades after Giacomo Zuccarini and Mike Di Donato began selling espresso machines and the idea of Italian cafe culture to skeptical Torontonians, the city found itself wired to the corporate Italianicity of Starbucks and Second Cup and dependant on restaurant chains like Boston Pizza, Il Fornello, Pizza Pizza, and East Side Mario's, not to mention countless individual restaurants that draw all or part of their menu from Italian cuisine.

BUCA; PHOTO: RICK O'BRIEN

Toronto was once predominately white Anglo Saxon Protestant but in searching for our own local tradition, no one looks to the British food we used to eat. And while we may love Chinese food, we order in, or we go to China Town to get it. When we want Indian food, we go to Little India. When we just want everyday food, we find it all around us. It's in our pantries, at the corner store, or available at the local cafe on the corner. These days, more often than not, it's Italian.

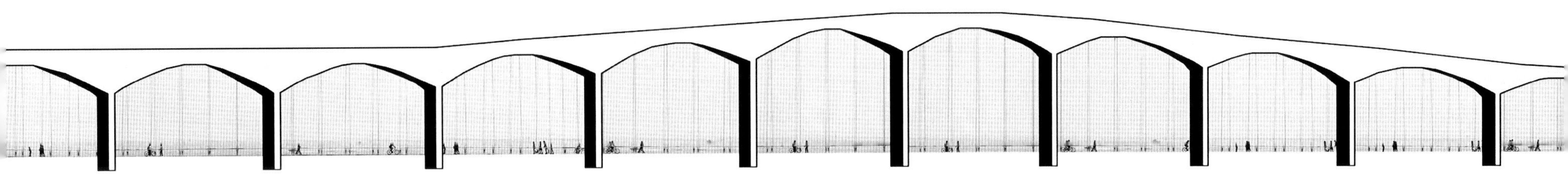

PHOTO: JILL WELLINGTON

ITALIAN CANADIANS IN THE ONTARIO WINE INDUSTRY

ROBERTO FRACCHIONI

It should come as no surprise that many Canadians of Italian descent have been involved in the founding and development of the Ontario wine industry. We all know how fundamental wine is to the Italian culture, to social gatherings, and even to our health. “Il vino fa buon sangue,” we like to say, trusting that good wine makes good blood.

History tells us that Italian immigration to Canada occurred in two main waves—the first was from 1900 to 1914 and the second was between 1950 and 1970. The majority of Italians who arrived in Canada during the first wave were young men, who set to work as labourers, tradesmen or artisans. Those who made their way to the Niagara Peninsula in Ontario and Okanagan Valley in British Columbia were also happy to find work on orchards, vineyards and farms, often starting their own.

The Italians who arrived in Niagara soon realized that although their beloved libation was being produced in the area, it was certainly not up to their standards. The native species of vitis labrusca they found growing in Canada—including Concord, Coronation, and Niagara grapes—were far inferior to the noble varietals of Europe and the Italian grapes they knew so well, such as Sangiovese, Barolo, Barbera, Brunello, Montepulciano and Nebbiolo, just to name a few.

More concerning, were the harvesting and fermentation methods used in Ontario at the time. While they did indeed result in the rapid production of an alcoholic beverage derived from grapes, in the minds of the Italians, it could hardly be considered "vino."

In Italy, a land where seemingly every type of fruit and flower grows in effortless abundance, making wine is not complicated: collect some vines from your neighbour, stick them in a field, pick the fruit when ripe, smash 'em up, and "fatto!"—you have some good wine. In mid 20th century Canada, however, wine making proved to be more of a challenge.

Faced with a future of sipping only the sweet, cloying Ontario wine, so characteristic of the region in those days, one can imagine the passionately frustrated Italians contemplating a return to "Il Bel Paese," where, despite the hardships they fled in the first place, there would at least be "vino buono."

However, people who choose to leave home with little to no money, cross an ocean and stake a new life in a country where they barely speak the language—are not generally the type to give up easily. These early Italian Canadians were ambitious, optimistic, hard-working, innovative, and entrepreneurial. Above all, they needed something to drink.

VINES IN A SUITCASE

Wine can be a great motivator, especially when it is such a beloved necessity of life, as wine is to any Italian. Those who settled on the farms of the Niagara Peninsula tirelessly studied the climate, the soil and the sunlight. They sampled, they toiled, they tinkered with formulae. The great game-changer on the road to producing great Ontario wines, however, proved to be the introduction of the legendary grapes of the vitis vinifera.

While many of the varietals of the vitis vinifera were not hardy enough to withstand Canada's harsh weather, the ones that did improved the quality of Ontario wines immensely. Some of the most successful grapes proved to be Chardonnay, Gamay, Reisling and Cabernet Franc.

By experimenting and grafting these old-world vines onto the existing root stocks in the area, the Italian Canadian pioneers managed to overcome the short growing season, the unpredictable rain, and the long cold winters. With determination, trial and error, and a whole lot of prayers to St. Vincent (the patron saint of wine), they ultimately revolutionized wine production in Ontario.

There are many Italian Canadians who were especially influential in the emergence of Ontario's wine industry—equally responsible for successfully transplanting the process of fine wine cultivation to Ontario and producing the culture of appreciation that followed. These include some of the first humble farmers who carved out small plots of grapes to make a few "damigiane" for their families each year, to businessmen who made their money in the city, in real estate, construction or finance, and were able to follow their dreams of building sophisticated wineries as homage to their passion for wine.

Despite the many occasions of an Italian boarding a plane to Canada with a few small vines wrapped in a damp rag and discreetly tucked into their bag, later to be planted in a backyard garden, grafted to a Concord grape root, or delicately nurtured within a makeshift greenhouse, the first large-scale planting of Italian vines in Ontario is often attributed to Donald Ziraldo, the co-founder of Inniskillin Wines and one of the founding fathers of the modern age of Ontario wine.

In 1974, Ziraldo planted a 30-acre vineyard in the Niagara Peninsula exclusively with old

DON ZIRALDO PHOTO: V. PIOTROWSKA

world vinifera vines—Reisling, Chardonnay and Gamay, which were harvested in 1977. He was determined to produce a high quality wine that was grown and produced 100% in Ontario. Together with his business partner and winemaker Karl Kaiser, Ziraldo obtained the first licence to open a winery in Ontario since the prohibition.

Ziraldo's harvests were a success and he went on to expand his range of varietals. He is also considered the godfather of Ontario icewine. By the 1980s, Ziraldo was pioneering a uniquely Canadian product using Vidal grapes and capitalizing on the crisp, icy shoulder seasons, while using innovative methods of production, processing and promotion.

Ziraldo not only succeeded in creating one of the most iconic wineries in Niagara, but he also open the doors—and the eyes—of other ambitious Italians to the possibilities of re-creating the wine and the cultural celebration of their native country. Many were happy to create good Ontario wine with the soul of an Italian Barolo, while others focused on the unique character of the Ontario terroir or developing the professionalism of the industry itself that is now known the world over.

One such person is Leonard Pennachetti, founder of Cave Spring Cellars. Len's grandfather, Giuseppe Pennachetti, was among the early wave of Italians who left his hometown of Fermo, Italy and moved to Niagara where he worked as a mason. After a successful career in the construction trade, Giuseppe retired to pursue his passion—winegrowing. "On lands of modest quality and with the native labrusca grape (a variety that was the order of the day), Giuseppe would prune and tie his hobby vineyard with his son John Sr. and grandson Leonard. The wines that came from these vines were made with heart, but wanting in quality, and the family knew that better was possible."

According to Cave Spring's website, "In 1973, the Pennachetti family acquired its first farmland at Cave Spring on Niagara's Beamsville Bench. To realize the region's full viticultural promise, they focused on planting time-honored European grape varietals, and cultivating these vines with a mixture of traditional and modern techniques. In 1978, the Pennachettis were among the first to plant Riesling and Chardonnay vines on the Niagara Peninsula, helping to pioneer this emerging North American wine region."

Today, Len refers to Cave Spring Cellars as "The house that Riesling built," hearkening back to that first 1978 harvest.

LEONARD PENNACHETTI

With successful harvests and excellent vintages under their belts, both Leonard Pennachetti and Donald Ziraldo worked hard to broaden the playing field and establish a reputable wine industry in Ontario. In 1974, they established the Wine Council of Ontario and by 1988, they helped develop the Vintners Quality Alliance (VQA), "to set out geographic appellations and introduce strict production standards that became law in 1999," further building credibility and professionalism among the fledgling industry. Both Ziraldo and Pennachetti held leadership roles among the two boards, further demonstrating their commitment and zeal for the Ontario wine industry.

Another character for whom Niagara winemakers share their eternal gratitude, is Angelo Locilento. Upon immigrating to

Canada and building a successful career in banking, Locilento witnessed the struggles of his countrymen in their attempts to produce drinkable wines in their garages, as their parents and grandparents had done. Whether it was out of empathy for his neighbours or due to his shrewd business acumen—or both—Locilento saw a niche in the market that he could fill. In 1978, he created a company called Vin Bon, that imported Italian grapes and grape juice to Toronto. The products were sold to desperate hobby winemakers across the Greater Toronto Area for use in their household cantinas.

Vin Bon quickly expanded to include the sale of wine making equipment, and became a one-stop shop for home producers of wine. This business proved to be very successful and the company has since been franchised and now boasts over 40 locations. Eventually, in 1990, Angelo and his son Philip opened their own winery, Cilento Wines, in Woodbridge. The winery produces VQA wines—using 100% Niagara grapes—proving how far the industry has come.

THE ERA OF WINERY RESTAURANTS

As we like to say, "Il pane apre tutte le bocche." Bread opens all mouths. Not only is the Italian tradition of sharing a meal important for familial and friendly bonding whereupon a few glasses of wine can get the real stories out of people, food pairing is an ideal way to introduce and market wine, particularly to consumers with palettes predisposed to imported wines and who are wary about their own homegrown vintages.

It was the aforementioned Len Pennachetti, along with his wife Helen, who in the early 1990s, chose to create Ontario's first winery restaurant at Cave Spring Cellars. Called On The Twenty, it was dedicated to celebrating the culinary bounty of the region and pairing it with the flavours of their award-winning wines. Coming from an Italian heritage, the model of providing fine food and wine available at the same location not only made sense, but it seemed wrong not to do it.

Like most visionaries, the Pennachettis were immediately met with naysayers, who couldn't believe they could make a winery restaurant profitable, let alone, legal. Ironically, at that time, it was not possible for wineries to obtain a liquor license. Len and Helen were undaunted, and they overcame legal and logistical hurdles in order to successfully obtain the right to sell alcohol at their new winery restaurant. They began restoration of the south end of the building that housed the winery, a run-down, falling apart century-old stone and brick building and by 1993, they had turned it into what is still one of the most prized restaurants in the Niagara region.

ROSSANA MAGNOTTA

Winery restaurants and destination wineries have since proliferated. Where chefs and winemakers work together, amazing things can happen. Trius Winery Restaurant and Kitchen 76 at Two Sisters Vineyards are shining examples where the quality of the food and the wine are each strong enough to stand alone, but, why would they? "Anche in paradiso non è bello essere soli." One would not be alone, even in Paradise.

THE JOURNEY CONTINUES

The descendants of those first paesani who immigrated to Canada have made some legendary achievements and innovations. Proving that opportunity arises from adversity, Gabe and Rossana Magnotta struggled with the LCBO and were forced to start selling their wine directly to the public. Consumers went wild for it and the industry was once again revolutionized.

Domenic Di Pietrantonio forged a path to the new wine country of Prince Edward County. He founded Casa Dea winery more than 20 years ago and still visits it almost daily. The Colaneri family specializes in the appassimento style of wines to produce rich, full-bodied Ontario wines at their Colaneri Estate Winery. At Del-

GARY PILLITTERI

Gatto Estates, Pasquale (Pat) Del-Gatto came over from Santa Croce in southern Italy, to bring his expertise as a fourth generation winemaker. And last but never least, Angela and Melissa Marotta of Two Sisters Vineyards, have thrived among a traditionally male dominated industry. Together, they have created a beautifully authentic Italian experience in the heart of Niagara, while producing Italian inspired wines that evoke the passion of Sophia Loren and the grace of Miuccia Prada.

The list goes on with the De Simone Family, Tony and Jared Mastronardi, Santino Paglione, the Pillitteri Family—these are just a few of the many Italian Canadian winery owners who continue to influence and improve the Ontario wine industry, year after year. While many have gone unrecognized, it is always heartwarming to see some of them garner the accolades they deserve, such as Len Crispino.

Crispino served for a decade as Ontario's Chamber of Commerce President and CEO. He also held the role of assistant deputy minister in the Ministry of Economic Development and Trade; and spent three years as Ontario's chief trade representative to Italy. Throughout his career, Crispino worked tirelessly to promote Ontario's products—and burgeoning wine industry—to Italian businesses. His efforts were so appreciated that he was awarded the Order of Merit by the Italian Government for strengthening ties between Canada and Italy.

It was during this time, and his many trips to Italy, that Crispino fell in love with a wine called Amarone. After promoting the work of winemakers for so many years, this was the wine that inspired Crispino to become a winemaker himself. In 2000, he and his wife Marissa and brother-in-law Louis Cimicata, purchased 40 acres of prime land in Niagara, planted vines suitable for the production of Amarone, and started Foreign Affair Winery.

By 2004, the first harvest was collected and the experimentation began. Much like the farmers who came before him, Crispino had many trials and errors in order to achieve success. He and his Foreign Affair team did succeed in producing an Amarone style wine however, by introducing Ontario winemakers to the ancient Italian art of appassimento—a style of drying grapes that produces a rich, complex and deep wine, reminiscent of the cantine of Veneto.

Behind these winery owners, are countless Italian Canadians who are master winemakers, winery managers and directors. Many more are employed in promoting, marketing and strengthening the industry itself. Some were first generation Canadians trying to make a living in the new world doing what they loved, others were born here but were always drawn to the world of food and wine, often crediting their parents and grandparents for instilling this passion within them, transplanted from their roots in Italy.

MARISSA AND LEN CRISPINO

Of course, not all wineries in Niagara are Italian-inspired, or Italian-run. The region pulses with the multicultural influences of French grapes, California technology, and kitschy Canadiana. Yet it was the Italian Canadians who truly seized the opportunity to take what Ontario was doing and make it better—who set into motion what would one day become not only an internationally recognized region producing award-winning wines, but one with wines good enough that even your choosy, opinionated, wine-loving Zio would want to drink.

VERONICA & INES DI SANTO PHOTO CREDIT: MIKE COLON

FROM GARMENT WORKERS TO FASHION DESIGNERS IN A GENERATION

ROSA FRACASSA

Italian labels such as Armani, Valentino, Prada, Dolce and Gabbana and Gucci are icons of fashion. The runways of Milan and Rome have made Italian fashion synonymous with quality, luxury and style. Italian Canadians have been influenced by these examples through their love of style and their heritage, but most importantly through the seeds of culture passed on from their families, and many times particularly from their mothers. Former Toronto Mayor, David Miller, said, "accomplishments of Italians have helped to shape every aspect of life in every part of the city."[1] Italian immigrants and their children have integrated into the social fabric of this country; many children of immigrants have felt compelled to achieve higher goals in order to make their parents' sacrifices worthwhile.[2]

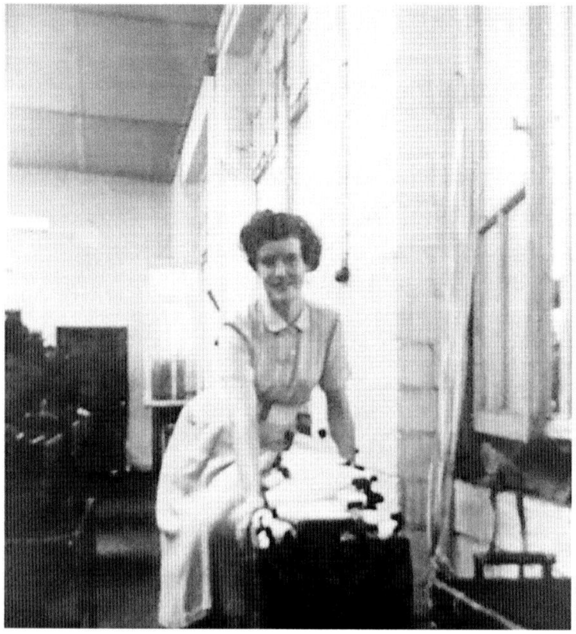

MIRELLA MEROTTO; PHOTO COURTESY DENNIS MEROTTO

Early contributions of Italian immigrants to the apparel industry were primarily as garment workers, while children of Italian immigrants have shaped the Canadian fashion industry and its creative economy as fashion designers through their design labels.

GARMENT WORKERS

Threads of Italian immigration of the 1950s to the 1970s are woven into the subconscious of Italian Canadian designers. The sartorial heritage of first and second generation Italian Canadians was spun from the standards of Italian design and style, to the influence of women who worked in the garment industry as weavers, knitters, embroiders, sewing machine operators, laundresses, and sample makers, to men who worked in the industry as tailors and pressers. After World War II, Italy suffered from a devastated and broken economy; Italians in north-eastern Italy from the regions of Veneto and Friuli-Venezia-Giulia, and the central region of Lazio, continuing south through Abruzzo, Molise and Campania and moving toward southern Italy, including Puglia, Calabria and Sicily, saw mass emigration patterns to Canada, and particularly to Toronto. In the 1950s many Italian workers had come to Canada through worker programs for short term contracts. The Canadian government's sponsorship system allowed relatives to sponsor family members to Canada en masse; in fact, between 1946 and 1967 nearly 90% of all Italian immigrants were sponsored by family members already settled in Canada.[3] More than 81,000 Italian adult women entered Canada during the 1950s, which represented over 30% of Italian immigration in this period.[4] Italian women came from small towns to cities like Toronto. Women in small town Italy were typically responsible for domestic work that included cooking, cleaning, childcare, as well as weaving, and sewing clothes. Women and young girls also farmed as time and distance from family farm plots permitted. In the winter months, they worked on embroidery and crochet as well as the crafting of linens which could be sold or made into a contribution to the daughter's dowry. Many families all over Italy sent their young daughters to the local seamstress to learn patternmaking and sewing or to train as a hairdresser. The apprenticeship training system was often paid for indirectly with sewing work completed for the employer's clients, for which the teacher would be paid. This enabled Italian immigrant women to come to Canada as trained domestics, hairdressers, seamstresses and experienced artisan specialists.

Italian immigrant women were industrious and well organized; they played a key role in bridging familial and motherly responsibilities, keeping cultural traditions alive while contributing to the family's economy. They looked after the household, including the cleaning and cooking, raised the children and often looked after immigrant borders the family may have been hosting. Women preserved fruits and canned vegetables and looked after the vegetable garden. As child-rearing permitted, women entered the workforce as sewing machine operators, seamstresses, laundresses, alterationists, and worked in various factories in the garment district, as well as performing assembly work and light manufacturing. Many women who had a sewing machine at home took on sewing contracts that were either completed throughout their daily routine or in the evenings after household responsibilities were completed and children were put to bed. Women used their skills to sew for private clients who requested custom clothing, completed alterations, embroidery, specialized appliqué and other needle crafts as part of the home sewing network. This allowed wives and mothers to contribute to household expenses, to cover the cost of groceries, clothing and household items. During child-rearing years, working from home was particularly convenient, as it allowed women to care for their children and family whilst contributing to the household budget. Often women's income helped to sustain the family financially during men's periods of unemployment due to seasonal work, especially the construction industry, which typically shut down during cold months of the year.

Many Italian immigrant women worked in factories in the garment industry, often with other Italian women who were related or who had emigrated from the same town or region in Italy. The managers and supervisors in the garment manufacturing factories, knitting mills, leather shops and other needle trade facilities were often of Italian origin too, allowing for easy communication of work-related conversations with employees not fluent in English. Italian immigrants were the third-largest ethnic group in Canada in the '60s and '70s, their presence had an impact on the social fabric of their new country;[5] they were key contributors to the needle trades, including leather and clothing manufacturing and knitting mills where they represented between 34-40% of the work force.[6] Their sartorial skills helped make the apparel industry a key part of the Toronto economy.

LOU MYLES (LUIGI COCOMILE)

Synonymous with sharp style, quality fabric and excellent craftsmanship, a Lou Myles suit is recognized globally. Lou Myles was one of the most well-known men's clothiers in Canada, and arguably, North America. Lou Myles Disegnatore offered men the option of building a quality wardrobe with stylish suiting that was referred to as "Eastern Cool" by his California clients: Eastern Cool—that came from Canada![7]

Luigi Cocomile was born in Toronto in 1928, a few months after his parents, Giuseppe and Lucetta Cocomile, originally from the cities of Cosenza and Catanzaro, emigrated from Calabria, Italy. Giuseppe was a cobbler, making $9 a week, trying to support his wife and family of three children. Growing up, Luigi Cocomile appreciated clothing and loved style. According to daughter, Toronto realtor Kimmé Myles (Cocomile), by age 13, he was buying a suit a month with the money he was making as a precocious swashbuckling street kid, bookmaking and shooting craps to help support his family. Although he grew up poor in the Italian "ghetto" of Toronto, it was still important to look good and have a sense of style, even while gambling in the neighbourhood. He liked clothes and the style of the 1940s/50s; he would watch old movies and study the style of some of his favourite icons—Cary Grant, for example. By age 15, Cocomile quit school, working the streets full time, until 1956, when he and a friend lost everything gambling. That night he decided he needed to change his life and "get a real job." He started making $45 a week working at Coward Clothes, at Danforth and Woodbine. At first, he thought it would be

LOU MYLES NEWSPAPER AD

the perfect job—he could build up his wardrobe and make a modest living while standing around looking good. His clients trusted him and he soon doubled his weekly sales. His role grew to managing the store and contributing to product-buying decisions.

In 1960, Cocomile opened his own shop —*Lou Myles Disegnatore* on Yonge Street. Luigi used the name Myles, derived from his last name, Cocomile. In post-WWII Toronto, Italians were foreigners and not necessarily well liked. It was just "easier" to be Lou Myles.[8] The Yonge street area was gritty in those years, perhaps a little unsavoury and unpleasant, with a developing music scene—but Myles saw it as colourful, full of atmosphere and part of life itself. The Lou Myles style sold widely. In

1962, Myles and his wife Yvonne mortgaged their home and purchased 363 Yonge Street. The shop had a wood panelled men's club feel that periodically closed to the public so celebrity clients could shop freely. Myles began to develop his clientele, which included sports athletes and corporate leaders—a clientele of men "who wanted to look fantastic," as he put it.[9]

Through his suits Myles brought back a lost elegance by incorporating standards he referred to as the big four: fabrication, quality, silhouette, and attitude.[10] By the mid-60s Myles started to attend fabric shows in Europe and work directly with mills in Italy and Spain to develop his own quality fabrics, custom colours, and textures. The cut, feel, and sophistication of a Lou Myles suit stood out from others—technical details such as more fitted jackets and pants, a higher tighter armhole, functional surgeon cuffs and classy vests added up to "sharp" style.[11] By 1970, Myles opened his own factory, to refine his product even further; this allowed him to better control production and quality. Behind the scenes he could easily work directly with his tailors; Vittorio Romeo, for example, worked with Myles to translate his ideas into fabric and to refine his designs through sampling.[12] In the Downsview neighbourhood factory, Myles employed more than 80 seamstresses and tailors, mostly immigrants of Italian heritage with traditional tailoring training. The company produced upwards of 400 suits a week. Myles also produced men's shirts in a Spadina area factory. Before long the Lou Myles suit was being sold in major cities across Canada and the US under the Myles label and wholesaled through private label.

By the mid-70s Myles' company grossed sales well into the millions. His suits were worn by the likes of Bobby Orr, Magic Johnson, Mohammad Ali, Tony Bennett, Frank Sinatra, George Bush, Marcel Marceau, Koby Bryant, David Bowie, Bob Dylan, the Beatles, Pierre Trudeau, Ed Mirvish, as well as many doctors, lawyers, politicians and teachers. Vic Damone often flew to Toronto for his fittings, while Myles was frequently flown to cities all over the US to measure and fit customers who couldn't come to him: in Detroit he fit the automotive executives; in NYC he held appointments and fittings with mobster John Gotti, and in Los Angeles he fit the film celebrities that didn't have time to come to Toronto. His reputation grew through word of mouth, not promotional campaigns.

Myles later moved his production to Millway Avenue, in Vaughan. In addition to made-in-Canada suits, Lou Myles shops also sold haberdashery such as silk ties, leather belts and shoes from Fratelli Rossetti, along with ready-to-wear rainwear and sweaters from Italian labels, such as Sicons, then designed by Giorgio Armani. The Lou Myles suit could be recognized by the square shoulders, a nipped-in waist and lower jacket flare. Although his suits changed with the times, in the six decades of his company, they never wavered in delivering iconic styling and elegant silhouettes, not tainted by what Myles referred to as "gimmicky" trends of fashion. He felt that a suit should last as long as you wanted it to; if it was a quality suit, if the silhouette was right, "you would look right no matter when you bought it."[12] The Lou Myles suit was traditional craftsmanship at its best—he didn't use glues or quick methods to achieve tailoring. It was through technical details and traditional methods, such as handsewn horsehair canvas, a sculptured chest and suppressed waist with just the right flare for the jacket skirt—this made the Lou Myles suit a fashion icon of style for decades. Though his focus was menswear, he also produced suiting for women and his work won awards by the American Custom Tailors and Designers Association. He was recognized by both the province of Ontario and the City of Toronto for being a leader in his field and contributing to the success and development of business in the province.

In the early 2000s, Myles amalgamated the retail shop with the manufacturing facility and wholesale showroom; he could cater both to retail customers and wholesale clientele in one location. Myles was a self-taught menswear designer with no formal training. His eye for style and detailing, an appreciation for traditional craftsmanship and fabrication, and an acute sense of elegance inspired by British tailoring made Lou Myles, born Luigi Cocomile, a sartorial legend. He continued to go to work every day well into his eighties and passed away in July 2015.

EMILY ZARB

Emily Zarb was known for her wrapped and draped separates, body-conscious dresses and large knitwear sweaters for both men and women. She started her own label after graduating from Ryerson Polytechnical Institute, in the '80s. Emily's mother, Gina (Mafrici) Zarb and aunt Maria (Mafrici) Ardito, immigrated to Toronto in 1961 from a small Calabrian town called Delianuova. The Mafrici sisters had both apprenticed as seamstresses; growing up they were also taught to weave and knit by their family. When the sisters arrived in Toronto an elder cousin secured garment factory work for them. Eventually their advanced hand skills allowed them to move to high-end alterations at companies such as Creeds, Mr. Smith and Holt Renfrew. Their handwork, embroidery and alteration expertise kept them working until they were almost 80 as they weren't easily replaceable. Growing up, Emily Zarb was taught how to sew and knit; in fact, the Zarb! Knitwear collection, with its emphasis on pattern, detail and texture, became Zarb's trademark.

Within a couple of years of starting her label, Zarb was selling to major retailers, such as Saks and Barneys in the US. In 1987, she represented Canada at the International Linen Festival in Monte Carlo. In 1988, she went from wholesaling her designs to opening her own boutique on Queen St. West in Toronto. She also spent time teaching Design Theory and Draping at the International Academy of Merchandising and Design in Toronto, using standards of quality craftsmanship taught to her by her mother and her aunt. Zarb says that "her crafts skills and maker instincts have given her inner confidence and comfort, the security and the instincts that are foundational to the basics of life." In 1995, after much success and media attention, Emily Zarb decided to leave the fashion industry and move on to a second career.

FRANCO MIRABELLI

Franco Mirabelli's designs are driven by clean, simple lines and the use of beautiful fabric—he has described his womenswear designs as "sleek, modern and sophisticated."[13] Mirabelli is the youngest of three brothers, the only one born in Canada, after his family immigrated to Toronto in the mid 1950s from Lamezia Terme, in Calabria, Italy. After settling in Toronto his father worked in the construction sector, while his mother, Maria, worked in the garment industry. Through adolescence, Maria's family sent her to apprentice with the town seamstress who offered to teach young girls sewing, tailoring and pattern drafting. Her advanced sewing and pattern-making skills served Maria well in Toronto where she started doing piecework, quickly advancing to sample-maker at various companies in the Spadina garment district. As a young child Mirabelli absorbed his mother's appreciation for thoughtful design and quality work. He recalls that, while his mother worked all day, in the evenings she would often have her own clients come to their home for alterations and custom clothing. She would buy leftover fabric ends at work, often making clothes for Mirabelli. He can recall arguing with her about what he did and did not want to wear because his clothes weren't what the other kids at school were wearing.

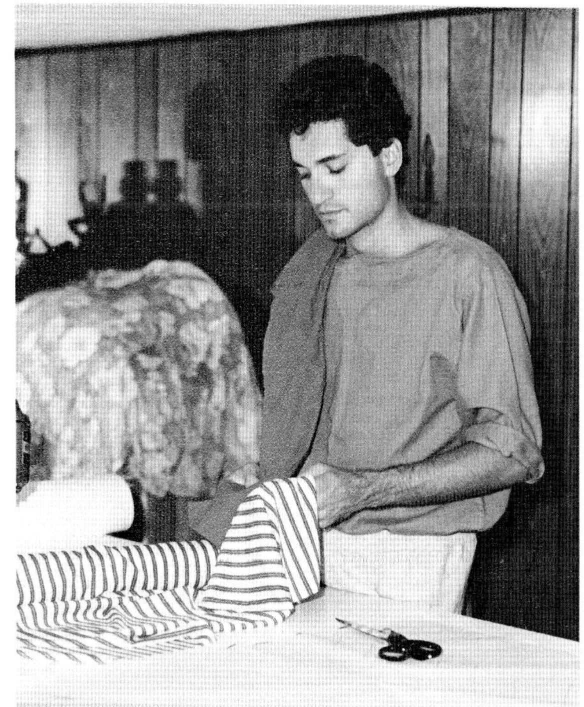

PHOTO COURTESY OF FRANCO MIRABELLI

While in high school, Mirabelli worked at a menswear shop on St. Clair and Dufferin. During high school summers, he also worked at Spadina garment factories which gave him experience and behind-the-scenes access to the industry. From the beginning he demonstrated an innate sense of fine detailing and quality design. He was influenced by his mother's work and inspired by one of his favorite Italian designers, Gianfranco Ferré. After high school Mirabelli attended college but never felt it was the right fit. Instead, having visited New York City, inspired by both the social scene and shops on 5th Avenue, he made his way to the NYC Fashion Institute of Technology to study fashion. On graduation day, he was hired as an assistant designer by Donna Karan, one of the head designers at Anne Klein. After a few years in NYC, Mirabelli was homesick and returned to Toronto; he was full of his own ideas and decided to launch his own label. With his parents' support, he set up his first studio in their basement. With his mother's help, he started his own label, Franco Mirabelli—cutting garments in his basement studio, producing samples with his mother's expertise, and working with a network of home sewers to create his made-in-Toronto line. Mirabelli quickly outgrew his basement studio and opened his first boutique in Mirvish Village on Markham Street in downtown Toronto.

Mirabelli's designs gained attention from Women's Wear Daily. He focused on using beautiful, quality fabrics—many from Italy. Clean lines, precise production values, quality buttons and zippers, all gave his clothing a refinement and sophistication that appealed to high-end retailers. The Franco Mirabelli clothing line was selling in boutiques across Canada and the United States. The label could be found in cities such as Dallas, Los Angeles, and New York. Internationally, the ready-to-wear label was sold in Mexico, Dubai, Bermuda and Puerto Rico. In Canada, Mirabelli and his team were busy running the retail operation with several boutiques in Toronto. He was also one of the first to bring an apparel studio and production workshop to the Wingold area, the now saturated apparel wholesale and design district in Toronto. The ready-to-wear collection is produced in Toronto, with a few pieces from Italy; each collection is executed with luxurious fabrics and high-end details that create elegant and modern pieces.

Mirabelli's work was recognized by notable fashion publications such as *Vogue, Elle Canada, Chatelaine* and many others. Mirabelli was a regular contributor to City-TV's Cityline and CTV's Marilyn Denis Show. He has made regular appearances on Fashion Television with Jeanne Beker. His design work also extends to various corporate clients, such as the Four Seasons Centre for the Performing Arts. In 2006 he designed original uniforms for staff at Canada's first and only opera house, located in Toronto. Mirabelli has been recognized by the industry with several awards including an Industry Achievement Award for Excellence in Fashion Design and a Designer of the Year Award.

Sadly, Maria Mirabelli recently passed away due to the COVID-19 outbreak. Franco Mirabelli recalls his mother bringing him to fabric stores as a child, and playing hide-and-seek with other bored children there with their mothers. Maria opened the door to the industry for Mirabelli with summer jobs she secured for him. She inspired and supported him by working by his side during the many years he produced his collection. Mirabelli's appreciation for textiles, quality, and a passion for style are all attributes that came from his background and time spent with his mother.

DENNIS MEROTTO

Dennis Merotto, has been called "the invisible man" by the National Post—he's been quietly designing womenswear, with a focus on dresses, for various labels over the past 30 years.[14] Merotto grew up in Sudbury, Ontario. His parents emigrated from a town called Lidor, from the Treviso area in Italy. His mother Mirella first immigrated to Switzerland; she learned how to sew and worked in the garment industry. His father Aldo was in the grocery business. Mirella and Aldo met and married in Sudbury where they made their home. Mirella worked as a seamstress in Merotto's grandfather's tailoring and alteration shop, Andreatta's Tailors, alongside his uncle. As a child Merotto spent a lot of time in the shop illustrating images from his mother's collection of Italian magazines, purchased from the local newsstand. He was a natural illustrator, an artistry that would serve him well in his future career. After briefly attending a business program, Merotto detoured and pursued a fashion-focused education.

After graduating from Sheridan College, Merotto began his career working with Deborah Kuchme, designing women's dresses; this gave him the opportunity to travel to New York and learn more about the industry. His focus on dresses continued when he went to work for Tom D'Auria. Merotto's designs focused on private label product development for retailers such Eaton's, Lipton's, Brettons and Braemar. His illustration skills have been a key part of his

ability to communicate his ideas and create designs which reflect modern tailoring and simplicity, those that flatter a woman's body and wrap her in comfortable, beautiful fabrics. After Braemar was bought by an American company, Merotto, who had a previous stint at the company, returned to work at Lida Baday as senior designer for nine years. The Lida Baday collection was sold all over the US and Canada. Merotto's work as head designer focused on building a complete collection for the label while working with retailers to ensure the brand was a success.

In 2010 Merotto decided to start his own label. He opened a showroom in New York City, hired sales agents and created lookbooks. His collection was well received, though retail presented its challenges. It was difficult for small companies to compete with large retailers. A couple of years ago Merotto decided to downsize and he now works with two to three retailers on small collaborative collections and offers made-to-measure services. His redeveloped business model allows him to offer a more personalized experience to his clients. Merotto's dress designs recall the images in Italian magazines of confident women, carefree and at ease. They have a structure and edginess that is stylish and bold, yet harken back to a simple modern elegance featuring beautiful Italian textiles. His designs balance the tension between feminine lines and elusive masculinity.

PHOTO COURTESY OF DENNIS MEROTTO

DOMINIC BELLISSIMO

Dominic Bellissimo has the reputation of creating innovative outerwear that over the years has had the attention of the fashion industry and international clientele. Bellissimo designs both men's and women's outerwear with ease, in a variety of luxurious fabrications.

Bellissimo's parents, both from Vallelongo, Vibo Valentia, Calabria, married by proxy in 1950; while his mother was still in Vallelongo, his father had immigrated to Argentina, looking for work. While there, his father worked at a knitting mill. In 1957, his parents immigrated to Toronto and settled in the Etobicoke area. Bellissimo's mother was well-trained in handwork, such as knitting, crocheting and embroidery. In his high school years Bellissimo started to learn about clothing and began to appreciate fashion. After high school, he attended the fashion program at Sheridan College where he had the reputation of being gifted beyond his years—his design aesthetic was well-developed and his craftsmanship was highly refined and detailed.

After he graduated, he began working at Lindzon as a technical pattern grader. Soon after he became Head Designer for women's outerwear, overseeing design and concepts for key Canadian clients such as Eaton's, Simpsons, Lipton's, Bretons, Holt Renfrew and Creeds, as

PHOTO COURTESY OF DOMENIC BELLISSIMO

well as several US clients. He quickly found his niche in outerwear. Bellissimo explains that, "The coat is a standalone piece not restricted by the aesthetic of an entire collection or other pieces adorned by the wearer; nothing needs to go with it! The coat is a way to make an entrance and an exit—it is the first piece seen when one enters and the last piece you see when one exits." Paul Lindzon, president of Lindzon, says, "Dominic knows how to use shearling in ways no other designer can—to him, it's not just outerwear, but a versatile fabric that belongs in a modern wardrobe."[15]

In the early 1990s Bellissimo began working with Beker Fashions as head designer of outerwear. He also introduced the new outerwear brand "Dominic Bellissimo" in wools, leather and shearling. He oversaw the entire process from concept and design through material selection, production, quality assurance and quality control, to managing supplier and client relationships. Early in his career, Bellissimo was already being recognized for his designs through several awards; in 1987, he won the Craven Award, "Up and Coming Designer of the Year"; in 1998 he was awarded The Woolmark Award; and for three years in a row he was the recipient of the Matinee Ltd Fashion Foundation Grant.

Bellissimo's coats are showpieces; his wide use of fabrications, including leather, suede, wools and various types of fine detailing, coupled with interesting design, bring the pieces to life. His outerwear, embellished by the texture of fabric selection and colour choices, give each piece exceptional detailing and artistry. His pieces include structural details such as enveloping hoods, cape collars, and cut-away coat fronts that are often softened with trims, ruffles, elegant button choices, clasps and various fastenings. He is passionate about the use of leather, and especially the use of shearling; he was often referred to as the "King of Shearling."[16]

In 1992 Bellissimo worked for ITA, managing the Dominic Bellissimo brand. He oversaw all aspects of production and manufacturing of the label that was sold all over Canada as well as in key US retailers, such as Nieman Marcus, Bloomingdale's, Berger Christiansen's Fur Salon and others. Bellissimo's upbringing and Italian heritage have influenced his work; quality, fine hand-detailing echo the skillful artisanship of his parents' work. His collections harmoniously combine style, colour sense and craftsmanship and they have been featured in *Vogue, Elle, Harper's Bazaar*, the *Robb Report* and other leading industry commercial and trade publications. Over the years, his clientele included CEOs, philanthropists, and many celebrities such as Neve Campbell, Catherine Zeta-Jones, Queen Latifah, Jeremy Irons, Richard Gere and many others.

Today, Bellissimo works with Gimpex, as the head designer for leather, cloth and shearling, where he continues to create innovative outerwear with an eye toward environmentally responsible manufacturing processes. He has been recognized by Jeanne Beker as a Canadian designer who has "made their mark" in the industry[17] and continues to be a leader in Canada, designing leading-edge outwear.

INES DI SANTO AND VERONICA DI SANTO

Ines Di Santo is a world-renowned bridal and evening wear designer headquartered in Toronto. Di Santo launched her company in 1984 and since then has been praised by the media and recognized by every major bridal magazine. Ines Di Santo gowns have been on red carpets all over the world, worn by celebrities and tastemakers who appreciate romantic sophistication and luxurious styling.

Di Santo was born in Italy—her mother is

from Naples and her father, from Tuscany. After her parents married, they immigrated to Buenos Aires looking for employment opportunities. In Argentina, her mother had her own men's shirt factory, while her father worked in print and artwork, with a focus on fashion magazine covers. Growing up, Di Santo had an arts-focused education, while dreaming about fashion. Through high school she studied art and upon graduating, returned to Italy and studied in Milan for a year before studying fashion in Paris. After returning to Buenos Aires for a short time, she immigrated to Canada and settled in Toronto.

Di Santo started her career at one of Toronto's premier bridal boutiques, Ritché, on Avenue Road, where she first worked as a fit model, then transitioned to the cutting room, doing pattern making, embroidery and design. In 1984, she launched her own label, CHEZ MOI, and hosted her first show at Casa Loma, a historical venue in Toronto; Ines was shocked after the first show to find she had enough dress orders to keep her busy for the next year. She later launched the namesake brand—Ines Di Santo. In 1998, she launched her collection in New York City and received orders from five US retailers. Her gowns reflect her passion for love and romance, making women feel beautiful on one of the most special days of their lives. Every season she participates in all aspects of the collection design and production process along with her team.

The company launches four collections a year, two fashion shows, and Jewel Box, a collection of five opulent couture gowns that are designed without limit of imagination. Di Santo's partner is her daughter Veronica who recalls that since the age of eight she has always been involved in her mother's work. She has childhood memories of walking to the atelier after school and spending long days and nights absorbing her mother's work ethic and appreciation for high fashion and art. After graduating from university, Veronica decided to join the company: "I saw the opportunity for me to grow into the business and I very much enjoyed the sense of adventure and accomplishment. Having grown up around fashion, I had an intimate knowledge of the business and loved the creative opportunities of the industry."

From the very beginning Di Santo's inspiration has been to ensure that each bride embraces their individuality and a personal style that remains "true to who they are," especially on their wedding day.[18] Di Santo is obsessed with the female form and her talent is working with a bride's shape to make her look and feel her best on her wedding day, says Veronica. While incorporating traditional capes, statement sleeves, pearls, ribbons, floral motifs, lace details, antique jewellery, ruffles and bows, her collection always feels fresh and modern.

The Di Santos work with a team of approximately fifty employees at the atelier in Toronto, where they oversee the production and detailing of each gown. The fabric and lace is imported from Europe, but the gowns are proudly made in Toronto with a diverse team of employees from all over the world. Ines Di

VERONICA & INES DI SANTO, PHOTO CREDIT: KATHY THOMAS

Santo is a collaborator at heart; she worked with Ward Simmons, Vice President of Marketing for Baccarat, a French heritage brand. Together they launched Jewel Box, a mini collection of opulent gowns where each gown was paired with Baccarat's Torsade Cristal Couture shoes designed by Diego Dolcini. She has also launched a jewellery collection in collaboration with American jeweller, Ciner, and has collaborated with Bruno Malli to offer a capsule shoe collection for her clients.

JOSEPH TASSONI

Joseph Tassoni, born in Montreal, is a second generation Italian Canadian who grew up in Oakville, Ontario. His maternal side of the family originally came from the Veneto area of

Italy while his paternal side originally emigrated from the Agrigento and Trapani areas of Sicily. Tassoni was interested in clothing from the age of five, when he created outfits for his three sisters. After high school he studied fashion at Ryerson University. Following his studies, Tassoni honed his apparel skills at various companies. He first began working in the industry at Pink Tartan, then moved to Holt Renfrew private label and Tevrow and Chase where he worked as a junior pattern drafter. He then went to Joseph Mimran & Associates Inc. in various capacities from design, to production, to marketing and sales, including junior menswear designer for Joe Fresh Style. Through the years he launched a consulting agency working for many brands, such as, as Head Designer for the heritage women's outerwear line, La Parka.

In 2017, the Joseph Tassoni brand was launched. Tassoni's mantra is producing classic garments sourced and manufactured in Canada, with quality fit and comfort and innovative design detailing. In March 2017, he unveiled his line at Toronto Fashion Week, themed "Queen of the North"; each outerwear piece is classic and elegant yet detailed with interesting shapes and cuts, fabrications and colours and topped with colourful accents. Tassoni also designed a capsule collection of men's suiting and outerwear pieces for Canada's 'Fashion Santa,' Paul Mason. The outerwear collection is produced across the Greater Toronto Area and sold across Canada. The pieces are not bound by trends or fast fashion; they are investment garments meant to be timeless and to last for years. Comfort, fit and wearability are of the upmost importance.

JOSEPH TASSONI, PHOTO CREDIT: ANDY VANDERKAAY

Tassoni is inspired by his family, and by his favorite designer, his mother, who made clothes for him and his sisters when they were growing up. He feels that women have not always had the benefit of proper fitting garments made locally. He is trying to change this by promoting Canadian-made quality and craftsmanship and advancing the state of the fashion industry in Canada.

DEAN CATEN AND DAN CATEN

Dean and Dan Caten, otherwise known as Dsquared2, took an international approach to their fashion career; their motto, "Born in Canada, living in London, made in Milan"[20] reflects their brand's development—its headquarters are in Milan while the identical twin brothers live in London.

Dean and Dan, originally born Catenacci, were born in the north Toronto neighbourhood of Willowdale, into a large family of nine children with an English mother and an Italian immigrant father from Casalvieri, Frosinone, Italy, a small hilltop town north of Naples, south of Rome. Their father immigrated to Toronto and worked as a pipe fitter and welder. Although they didn't really speak Italian at home, they were influenced by their Italian culture and heritage. Growing up, the standard of dress was important; although the family was a low-medium income household, their father didn't want them to wear jeans to school because he felt jeans were for poor people, so they wore dress pants instead—a look that didn't allow them to fit in with their peers. They've often joked in interviews that "I think that's why we love denim, because we weren't allowed to wear it."[21] Their brand is known for its stylish denim, graphic accents, chunky belts, bold jewellery, metallic embellishments and graphic accents and prints that exude playfulness and sensuality.

Dan and Dean grew up in an immigrant neighbourhood and have openly described being bullied. Their Italian last name was shortened to "Caten"; "dad did not want his kids to be harassed so we shortened our names...," recalls Dean.[22] The twins have five sisters and two brothers; with such a large family they were often lending their fashion advice to their older siblings, even though they were younger. "We could do it on a budget, which allowed us to be more creative, and they trusted us because they knew we knew better than them," said Dan in an interview with CTV in 2009.[23]

The brothers took Home Economics in high school and would go home to sew after school—they clearly appreciated fashion and clothing from their youth. After graduating, the brothers completed a six-week summer program at Parson's in New York City. They returned to Toronto, and with secured financial backing, started DEanDAN their first women's wear label. In 1988, they were hired by Ports International (Ports 1961) in Toronto, as creative directors to update the company while they also designed the company's lower-end leisure brand, Tabi International.[24] It was at Ports that they learned how to cut a pattern, tailor a jacket and critique their own work. During this time, they also had the opportunity to travel to Europe to experience the industry at the Paris and Milan fabric shows. Despite their success at home, the brothers had their hearts set on Europe—a natural move given their interest in the European fashion scene and their Italian heritage. In 1991, they decided to move to Milan to launch their company.

For the first few years they worked in PR, promotion, hosting events and styling; they were getting to know the players in the industry. They began working as designers for the house of Gianni Versace and later for the denim brand, Diesel. With financial backing from Renzo Rosso, of OTB—Only the Brave, holding company, which included Diesel— the brothers were able to launch their first collection and namesake brand, Dsquared2. The brand launched their menswear collection called "Homesick Canada" in 1994, in Paris, and later their womenswear collection, in 2003. Their Homesick Canada line recalls their Canadian roots; it included lumberjack coats and maple leaf symbolism, which have been included in many of their collections over the years. Homesick Canada was a success. The following year, the Catens created a collection called "Napoli," inspired by their father's Italian roots.

Celebrity interest in the brand soon spiralled. After seeing a friend wearing Dsquared2 denim, Madonna asked Dean and Dan to design her wardrobe for the "Don't Tell Me" video and to create 150 pieces for her 2001 "Drowned World Tour."[25] Two years later, they worked with Christina Aguilera on the "Justified and Stripped" Tour. In the meantime, their denim is a favourite among many celebrities, including Justin Timberlake, Lenny Kravitz, Ricky Martin and Nelly Furtado. Over the years, the brothers have also worked with the Black Eyed Peas, Jennifer Lopez, Britney Spears, Beyoncé and many others.

Their shows are runway extravaganzas, including Rhianna appearing on stage in an American muscle car and Bill Kaulitz descending from the ceiling in a caged elevator

DAN AND DEAN CATEN, PHOTO: DFISUN

reminiscent of the Rocky Horror Picture Show. Music is a key source of inspiration for their collections, the brothers say; they often put together the playlist for their runway shows as they are sketching styles.[26] Their runway soundtracks led them to host Sirius XM Radio's "Dean and Dan on Air: Style in Stereo" on BPM station, a talk show that includes music selected from their runway shows, fashion and style interviews and conversations. They have also hosted "Launch my Line" on Bravo Television, a reality design competition show.

The brothers have also worked with other companies to create a complete lifestyle brand which has included various collaborations: a collection of branded MAC cosmetics; an eyewear collection with Marcolin; men's footwear produced by Italian factory and brand Galizio Torresi; a women's footwear collection which is produced internally and a men's and women's fragrance line that includes bath and body products. Their fragrances "Wood for Him" and "Wood for Her" are meant to recall, "Canadian forests, the healthy air and the sense of freedom you can experience only in those limitless woods."

The brothers have designed apparel for athletes: official football uniforms for Juventus, travelling clothes for Manchester City players and senior members of the squad and official off-field uniforms for the Barcelona soccer team. In 2010, they were invited to costume the Winter Olympics opening and closing ceremonies in Vancouver. They also dressed the Canadian team for the Rio Olympics, where they won best-dressed country.[27]

Dsquared2 has over 80 boutiques worldwide, including, Miami, Doha, Los Angeles, New York, Rome, Kiev, Istanbul and many other major cities. Their sales grossed over 240 million Euros in 2018—and their success keeps growing.[28]

Dean and Dan are one of the few immigrant success stories in Italian fashion. In 2017, Dean and Dan and their siblings were invited to Casalvieri, Frosinone, for celebrations in recognition of their success in the Italian fashion industry. They were granted honourary citizenship and the keys to the city; the events were marked with a visit to their paternal grandmother's home where their father grew up and stories from citizens who knew their grandmother and their father.[29] Interestingly, the Caten's success story has come full circle, their father came to Canada to become someone, and instead Dean and Dan took their career journey back to Italy to do the very same thing—to become someone in the global fashion industry.

Canada's apparel history is a complex and diverse quilt that stretches across the country and incorporates many diverse backgrounds and traditions. The story of Italian immigrant garment workers and of first and second generation Italian Canadian fashion designers has contributed to the history of fashion in Canada, and the greater Toronto area, in a meaningful and colourful way. From menswear, to womenswear, to outerwear to bridal wear, Italian Canadians have been shaping the story one stitch at a time, one design at a time. There are many more stories still to be told—of patternmakers, tailors, manufacturers, merchandisers and stylists, to name just a few.

In "Canadese: A Portrait of Italian Canadians," Kenneth Bagnell reminds us that, "In spite of many famous Italian Canadians, [...] the history of Italian Canadians is not the story of the famous, but of solid citizens on ordinary streets."[30] It is the story of garment workers who contributed to the economy and were devoted to their families and it is the story of artisans and designers who made inroads in the industry, setting standards of style, creativity and workmanship.

DSQUARED2, MILAN, PHOTO: ©ANTON OPARIN/123RF.COM

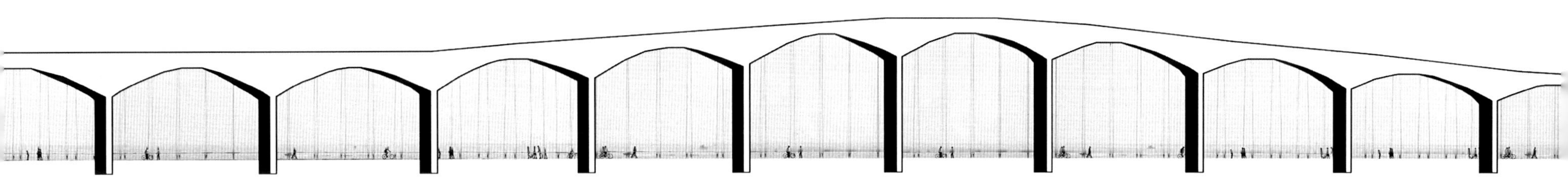

PHOTO CREDIT: DAVID ARTHUR

LAW

EVA H.D.

The entanglement of Italian and Canadian culture goes back centuries; in 1496, Giovanni Caboto's imperial adventurings assisted Britain, then under the rule of Henry VII, in making its spurious colonial claims to what is now known as Canada. Of course, just as the geographic region of contemporary Canada comprised at that time multiple nations and ethnic and linguistic groups, none of whom identified as Canadian, neither was there extant one distinct political unit known as Italy—which would eventually undergo a series of unifying spasms between 1859 and 1870, ending with the conquest of Rome.

ENRICO DE PASQUALE

For this reason, recasting any from that period as "Italian" in the sense of being from a cohesive state called "Italy" is problematic and inaccurate. However, Italians, such as they were, were certainly among the non-Indigenous mercenaries and colonists who arrived on these shores in the 17th century.

Even so, Italians did not start arriving in Canada in significant numbers until the late 1800s; by the turn of the 19th century, nearly 11,000 citizens of the newly-minted Italian megastate had settled in Canada, primarily sticking to the aspiring metropolises of Toronto and Montreal. More than three quarters of Italian Canadians hail from the south of Italy, where high rates of poverty and overpopulation encouraged the first major wave of Italian immigration to Canada, which was followed by a second significant influx post WWII. During that conflict, Italian Canadians were subjected by the Canadian government to the discriminatory designation of "enemy aliens" and several hundred citizens of Italian background were forcibly confined, under the War Measures Act, a mass suspension of civil liberties, at an internment camp in Petawawa, Ontario. Although support for Mussolini was relatively widespread among the Italian Canadian population, active fascists in this group of internees were in the minority.

Despite this negative experience, Italian Canadians were able, in the postwar decades, to eventually escape the stereotyping and degradations of white supremacy, unlike, for example, many Indigenous Canadian communities, who remain effectively interned to this day. This ability to assimilate within the traditional power structures of colonial Canadian society has in turn allowed hardworking Italian newcomers and their descendants to put down roots and create prosperous, successful communities; at this time, approximately 1.6 million people in this country identify as having Italian origins, making Italian Canadians almost 5% of the Canadian population as a whole. Presently, almost 30% of these live in the Greater Toronto Area. But what does it mean to be an Italian Canadian in the 21st century; what ties, if any, remain with Italy; is heritage a question of language, culture, or some other intangible? For Italian Canadians currently practising law in the GTA, the answers to these questions are as diverse as the still-thriving community itself.

Having legal representation available from within one's own ethnic or linguistic group is important; having a network of professional support in this context, perhaps equally so.

In 1984, CIAO, the Canadian Italian Advocates Organization was born, an organisation predicated on the notion that Italian Canadian lawyers, and the Italian Canadian community at large, would benefit from such support. Its first president, John A. Capo, led the organization for almost a decade from its inception in 1984; co-founder Enrico De Pasquale, a long time board member of the Italian Chamber of Commerce of Ontario Canada, served as CIAO's second president, from 1993-1997. CIAO includes among its membership numerous individuals who have been appointed to the Ontario Court of Justice, such as Justices Sal Merenda, Joseph DeFilippis, Antonio DiZio, Roger Yachetti, Elvio DelZotto, and Justice Dino DiGiuseppe, as well as Justice Lucia Favret, who also served as CIAO's president from 1997 to 1999.

Other prominent members include Frank N. Marrocco, Q.C., Treasurer of the Law Society of Upper Canada; he was the first lawyer of Italian heritage to hold this position. In 1997, CIAO honoured its ex officio director, the late Ronald W. Ianni, Q.C., with a gala event which also doubled as a fundraiser for the organization, as well as for a scholarship bearing Ianni's name at the Faculty of Law, University of Windsor, where he had served as Dean and President, capping off a long and distinguished legal and academic career. CIAO initiatives continue to include a focus on education, through seminars and workshops; mentorship; student scholarships, for which they fundraise at various wine and cheese events throughout the year. There is a 'Law Day' mock trial program, which honours the 1982 signing of the Canadian Charter of Rights and Freedoms; various formal and informal networking nights, at which lawyers and judges have an opportunity to mingle and share a bite to eat or a glass of wine; and a series of awards nights to honour past and present members of distinction, who have risen to some of the highest positions in the field of law.

CIAO's Award of Distinction has been won in the past by such prominent figures as the late Justice James Greco, who, upon his retirement from the Ontario Court of Justice in 2003, held the distinction of being its longest-serving member. The award was won the following year, 2001, by Madame Justice Giovanna Roccamo of the Superior Court of Justice; other notable awardees include Pasquale Santini, Armando De Luca, Q.C., Alfredo Petrone, Q.C., and John Capo. Justice Frank Iacobucci, who went on to serve on the Supreme Court of Canada, was formerly a CIAO board member; in his name, CIAO founded the Frank Iacobucci Scholarship.

As Iacobucci, former president of the National Congress of Italian Canadians who continues to practice at the prestigious Toronto firm of Torys LLP, focusing on Indigenous issues, noted earlier in this book, he himself was actively discouraged by his university advisor from pursuing a legal career. Since then, he has risen to the highest level of professional success in his chosen field, also serving as interim President at U of T, as well as Dean of the Faculty of Law—thus influencing countless career trajectories of Italian Canadian young people, including his son, Edward, currently Dean of the University of Toronto Law School.

Known, despite his distinguished academic and judiciary career, as 'down to earth,' and an honorary citizen of Abruzzo and Mongone, where his parents were born, how is his journey similar to those of younger first and second generation Italian Canadian lawyers such as Toronto's Andrew Furgiuele and Jessica Zita, and in what ways does it differ? How will newer Italian immigrants, like lawyers Giovanna Asaro and Sara Riboldi shape and inform the Italian Canadian legal community in years to come?

Iacobucci, who was named a Justice of the Supreme Court of Canada in 1991, has helped to blaze the trail that young lawyers such as Furgiuele and Zita have followed. The story of their experiences, as multifarious and varied as the Italian Canadian community itself, is a microcosm of the transformative trajectory of Italian Canadians throughout the twentieth, and into the twenty-first century. It is a story of displacement, hard work, sacrifice—and ultimately, of positive change.

Giovanna Asaro, a first generation Canadian whose family immigrated to Toronto from a small village in northwest Sicily in 1965, when she was a baby, was also the first in her family

FRANK IACOBUCCI

to pursue a legal career. Neither of her parents had been allowed to pursue education past a grade school level: her father, she recounts, "had been pulled out of school at the age of seven to work in the vineyards as he had several older sisters who would eventually need dowries." Essentially illiterate, his dream in coming to Canada was to escape being a labourer who would never find independence working for wealthy land owners.

The youngest of six children, her mother, on the other hand, "had the privilege of finishing elementary school," before she was forbidden by her parents from continuing her education. Asaro notes that her parents were extremely supportive of her pursuit of higher education; they focussed on instilling in their children a

ANDREW FURGIUELE

strong work ethic, as well as highlighting the importance of family and integrity. As a woman intent on pursuing a career as a professor of literature, and then turning her focus to the law, Asaro points out that she was seen as exceptional within her family and the Sicilian community. But she stresses that, although her pursuits were perceived to be untraditional, the attention she received was never negative—the larger community was generally supportive, proud that Asaro had, as she puts it, "ambition and the smarts."

Andrew Furgiuele, a criminal defence lawyer with DFR Litigation in Toronto who was called to the Bar in 2008, describes his experience as being much more 'Canadian'—he considers the current Italian community in the GTA to be far more assimilated than the one of generations past. "I think as the Italian community has become more entrenched in the professional fabric of the city, the need for a cohesive community has dissipated somewhat. Put another way, the 'Canadian' part of the Italian Canadian community has, for people my age and experience, become more dominant. I don't believe that was the case 40 years ago, when the CIAO began and acted as a necessary resource for immigrants and young Italian Canadians who felt much more outside the mainstream of society," he says.

As a woman from a large Italian Canadian family, Jessica Zita, whose grandparents came over from Puglia after the Second World War, was also the first person in her family to enter the law. Growing up, "it was not seen as an option," she says. "No one knew any lawyers. The idea was to work hard, and maybe if you work your ass off, own your own business someday. I didn't know that law was a career you could pursue, and I definitely did not think it was available to me." The law, as a career, she notes, was not accessible to her in any meaningful way. In terms of career aspirations, she explains that within her family, these expectations are very much tied to gender. "It's very much in my family, get married in your twenties, have babies. That's what the women do. There isn't much pride, there isn't any pride from the Italian side of the family, in terms of what I've accomplished in my career. What's prized is getting married and having babies."

Zita, an up-and-coming downtown Toronto defence lawyer, notes that it is not only her cultural background, but her experience of gender within that culture that have helped her to excel in the contemporary legal world. "There is a difference being an Italian Canadian woman and a man in the Italian Canadian community," she clarifies. "Men and men's experiences are definitely prized more. You know, being a woman with something to say, you need to be particularly tough. Italian Canadian culture is very tough, which is good in some ways. That attitude has helped me in my career."

As with many immigrants who came to Toronto in the latter half of the twentieth century, Italian Canadians in the past faced a significant amount of discrimination from the WASP Canadian establishment. This is a familiar story to Furgiuele, who heard stories of family members facing discrimination growing up. However, he is quick to add, "the trail was blazed for me. Aside from a joking, off-hand comment here and there referencing the Mafia, I haven't felt any discrimination at all. I have never found any glass ceilings in my way." This is due in large part, he believes, to the accomplishments of the immigrant generations who preceded him. "Italian Canadians should be proud of their ancestors who did blaze that trail and became distinguished and successful professionals in this country," he underlines. That being said, in the multicultural makeup of contemporary Toronto, a city still struggling with deeply embedded racist and colonial prejudices, Furgiuele notes, being Italian does not set a person at the same disadvantage that being a member of a marginalized visible minority might. "Assimilation was easier for us—and for me. I spoke English from birth, I identify as Caucasian, and I'm a heterosexual male without any disabilities. There was nothing in terms of race/gender/sexual orientation that stood in my way the way it does for others. The law never appeared out of bounds for me and no one ever made me feel as though it was out of bounds for me. That would have been different if I was born 50 years earlier."

At the same time, the need remains strong for individuals to be able to seek counsel from a member of their own cultural and linguistic community, if they so choose. Says Furgiuele, a first-generation Canadian who speaks Italian, in his own words, "passably well," this bilingualism has been helpful in his career. He explains: "I believe it is vitally important for an individual to feel comfortable and confident in the lawyer they choose. If culture or language is part of that, then that makes sense to me." With this in mind, while professional organizations like the ICCO Canada or CIAO can be helpful to young lawyers in terms of networking or helping them get their career off the ground—particularly if they do not have other supports readily available to them, Furgiuele is quick to point out that he views these options as helpful tools, "but not as a be-all-and-end-all in terms of assisting you on your career path."

Overall, do younger lawyers, those who have taken up the legal profession in the 90s, 2000s, and 2010s, still feel the need for that type of community engagement? Furgiuele himself has chosen to provide support through a different avenue; he is a founding member of the Recent Call Committee of the Criminal Lawyers' Association, a group dedicated to helping young lawyers—regardless of their cultural background—sharpen their skills. Reflecting on what might have changed for Italian Canadian lawyers since the early 1980s, when CIAO was founded, few see Italian Canadian legal professionals as a cohesive community, envisioning more of a loose association of individuals who may or may not share cultural values and experiences. Much of this comes down to no longer sharing the negative experience of establishment prejudice and bigotry, due to changes in the Canadian cultural and political landscape, even as other strains of pernicious systemic racism come to the forefront of public dialogue. However, for relative newcomers like Sara Riboldi, these questions are far removed from lived experience: Riboldi first visited Canada as a tourist when she was a young university student, in the early 1990s, already studying law in her native Italy. Later, in her late twenties, she returned to Toronto to make a life and career for herself in the city. Riboldi, a member of the bar in both Italy and Canada, uses Italian regularly in her work, a mixed practice, where she specializes in conflict of laws between Italian and Canadian jusrisdictions, estate law, and international business law.

Not a member of the CIAO herself, Jessica Zita remarks that for her, it's "very important to

JESSICA ZITA

give back to the Italian Canadian community." However, she notes, "it's a real generational shift—if this was 40 years ago, I would certainly be a part of a cultural organization, whereas now, there's less of a focus on that, certainly among European immigrants. That doesn't seem to be how people coalesce now. I think there's a greater movement towards inclusivity."

Where that puts the future of an organization like CIAO, she remains unsure, but underlines the value of such ties "as the city becomes more geographically disparate, in terms of immigrant communities."

Presently, there are numerous ways for young Italian Canadians to situate themselves within an ever-diversifying broader Italian Canadian community: some speak the language fluently, while others have only a passing familiarity with it; some cling to the traditions brought over by family members of previous generations, while others are happy to shed the constraints of seemingly superannuated religious and community expectations. Whereas Iacobucci was (now infamously) told that he shouldn't pursue a career in law due to his lack of "the right name," Furgiuele, decades later, notes that although there were no lawyers in his immediate family, his family and community were, like Asaro's "very supportive, including of the choice to focus on criminal defence." Although conceding that he lacked a professional role model within the community, Furgiuele does not consider this a drawback. He articled for the prominent Italian Canadian defence lawyer Frank Addario; that connection, however, was not formed through mutual ties to the Italian Canadian community. Rather, says Furgiuele, "Frank's firm—at that time, he was the lead criminal law partner at Sack Goldblatt Mitchell LLP—was at the top of my list for a number of reasons. The Italian Canadian connection was not one of those reasons."

For Sara Riboldi, although she was also familiar with stories of discrimination encountered by Italian immigrants, when she took up the practise of law in Toronto twenty years ago, such experiences seemed relics of the past. "Fortunately," she says, "I encountered no discrimination; I feel like I came from a new generation of professionals." Still, as Riboldi notes, it is always difficult to present oneself with an accent; this can make court environments difficult. "I have certainly encountered some 'attitude' in that context," she laughs.

Meanwhile Giovanna Asaro describes her experience as a law school student as one in which her Italian cultural identity was never seen as something that set her apart, or was a basis for being excluded from the 'establishment'. "I perceived that more as an issue of gender and then only once I was in law school—I was a woman and, despite the near 50/50 ratio of male and female students at Osgoode in the late 1980s, law was still a very male profession. We banded together at Osgoode as women and had our own group."

For Jessica Zita, however, practising law as someone who looks visibly 'other' has been an altogether different experience: "You know, I feel very attached to the Italian Canadian community, to that part of my heritage," she says. "I'm always asked if I'm Middle Eastern. It definitely brings me closer to my identity as an Italian Canadian. I look Italian. I feel very close to that." She mentions having come up against some prejudices and preconceptions, in workplace scenarios, due to her heritage. "Certain comments, a look, whatever... I try to use it to my advantage. Like, okay, if you want, I'll be the loud Italian woman. I'll do that."

In terms of community support for her pursuit of the law, she says, "This was uncharted territory. No one in the community encouraged me. I will say that once I was a lawyer, because of my last name, people from the Italian Canadian community would recognize me, mentor or assist me in significant ways, and have been very, very helpful."

Zita is keen to underline the importance the Italian Canadian community holds for her. "There's a real warmth there, and even though I don't speak the language, you know, there are cultural aspects, I talk a certain way... it's recognizable." The value, both emotional and professional, of being embraced by her community, she emphasizes, is very real. While Giovanna Asaro considers aspirational thinking to be something that, "in the 21st century, falls outside of cultural lines," in the sense of searching out professional role models from one's own ethnic or cultural community, Jessica Zita disagrees. Frank Iacobucci, she says, remains an inspirational figure for young Italian Canadians. "I think that despite assimilation, there is always value in pointing to those who come from your specific cultural background to achieve the sorts of careers that you hope to achieve yourself."

For her part, Riboldi underlines the importance of the ICCO Canada as a mainstay of the community, a key organization for networking, preventing professional isolation, and providing support. Although she characterizes both ICCO Canada and CIAO as generally male-dominated communities, she does not consider the gender divide to be a significant weakness of the Italian Canadian community; rather, she considers it an issue that will naturally adjust as more women enter into and excel at the field of law.

Giovanna Asaro, a longtime member of CIAO, agrees, noting that she would however be very interested in joining an organization specifically for Italian Canadian women in the law. As Jessica Zita puts it, if, when she was growing up, there had been a "Francesca Iacobucci, that would have made a huge difference. I would have found that inspiring. There just aren't that many Italian lawyers. And there are even fewer Italian women lawyers."

Riboldi is curious to discover what the future holds for the CIAO and ICCO Canada organizations: the main question is, she notes, an existential one. "Are they currently useful, and will they continue to be useful, providing a service to the community?" If the CIAO, she says, continues to provide their membership with easy access to information, and a good professional network, it could be extremely effective and helpful. Among issues to watch for, she points first and foremost to CETA (the Comprehensive Economic and Trade Agreement), increasing the numbers exchange and fostering trade between Italy and Canada. She warns, however, that if it's just a question of historical affinity, then the organization's survival seems less assured.

The ICCO Canada, on the other hand, naturally has a broader reach, and continues to depend on new arrivals, especially in Toronto, where there are so many Italians, both newcomers, and third and fourth generation Canadians. Riboldi remarks that the perceived relationship to culture within the Italian Canadian community has changed significantly over the years; instead of strengthening her involvement specifically with the Italian Canadian legal community, she has participated in the founding of several cultural organizations, including the Accademia dei Ragazzi, a non-profit initiative created to assist parents with language learning for children and young people. In this case, Riboldi's legal acumen has been essential in dealing with the legislative technicalities of founding a non-profit. Luxarte Cultural Productions, her other project, is a cultural exchange for visual artists and filmmakers, which brings Italian artists here, at the same time highlighting and promoting Canadian artists in Italy, where they are underrepresented. Riboldi feels that cultural exchange between the two countries is severely limited by the lack of Italian Cultural Affairs outreach in Canada, and vice versa; she cites as an example the Group of Seven, who deserve a much higher profile in the Italian art world. Furthermore, she says, although acknowledging that back in the Toronto of the early 90s, "just finding a bottle of decent olive oil was difficult, I am tired of being identified with food culture." Asaro points out that "any ties that individuals may have to Italy or their Italian heritage will vary significantly from actual ties those individuals deliberately seek out and forge," adding that she continues to keep her Italian cultural heritage alive as an avid consumer of Italian podcasts, films, and books. This is, in her opinion, how Italian Canadian culture will continue to be fostered and passed down in the generations to come.

SARA RIBOLDI

Whether as a participant in official groups and organizations, or privately, the bottom line, says Riboldi, is that "Italian culture is not just for Italians: it's for everybody."

As for her vision for the future, Jessica Zita concludes that what's truly needed in the Italian Canadian legal community is an organization of Italian women in law. How would she participate in such an organization? "I would speak up for them," she laughs. "I'm Italian—I'm good at speaking up."

PHOTO: LUIS VALIENTE

POLITICS

ANGELO PERSICHILLI

The brilliant journalist Ross Howard, in a September 1, 1987, Globe and Mail story, described the expensive and difficult fight waged by the rich and influential Italian Canadian community leader Dott. Laureano Leone to win the provincial Liberal nomination and the campaign that followed in Toronto's Downsview riding. Dott. Leone, a pharmacist, was revered and respected in the Italian Canadian community and beyond, "but," wrote Howard, "he has never received legitimacy for the title of 'deputato' (Member of Parliament) by which he is known when he visits his native Italy."

This statement might sound offensive, belittling the aspirations of a respected Canadian of Italian origin. But it is not—it reflects the importance of a Member of the Parliament and of politicians in general in Italy. Institutionally, the role of MPs and ministers is the same in Canada, but in Italy the reality is completely different, in terms of substance and pageantry.

This is an important element in helping one understand the motivations behind the involvement of the community in Canadian political life.

In Italy, politics rules everything, including business. In Canada, it is the other way around: business and lobbies are the epicentre of power. Politicians with influence are prime ministers, premiers, and some ministers—all the rest is choreography. The role of most MPs and MPPs in Canada is like that of cheerleaders during a game: very pleasant to look at, but when the game starts, they are not on the field.

One Canadian leader who has strongly emphasized the constitutional importance of MPs is former Liberal prime minister John Turner. During many interviews and private conversations I've had with him, he has always stressed the "sovereignty of the Parliament" and the need to give "more freedom to MPs." He once said the role of the House leader should be eliminated, and MPs should be forced to toe the party line only for the budget vote.

The neglect for the role of MPs permeates all political organizations, and all the leaders are aware of it.

During the ninetieth birthday party in Ottawa for former Prime Minister Turner, six other former prime ministers—Jean Chrétien, Paul Martin, Joe Clark, Stephen Harper, Brian Mulroney, and Kim Campbell—praised him for his passion in promoting the centrality of the role of the Parliament and MPs and the need to get them more involved in the decision-making process, as stipulated in the Constitution.

Canadians of Italian origin, like Dott. Leone, were aware of the erosion of the role of MPs and the substantial difference in attitude between Italy and Canada but, still influenced by the role of the politicians in their home country, they pursued political careers in Canada in search of power and, most importantly, success.

Becoming an MPP or an MP was, for young Italian Canadians, a vindication of their immigrant parents and a symbol of success for their community: "Siamo arrivati!" (We've made it!) Still, as Ross Howard wrote, the title was enjoyed as a trophy to display to relatives and friends in Italy more than here in Canada.

When I first arrived in Canada, I was assigned the job of reporting about an important weekend event in the community where the guest was the Minister of Multiculturalism. I was excited. I had only been in Canada a few days and I was already being asked to interview a minister! Immediately I phoned my parents and friends, telling them about my important interview. What I didn't tell them was what really happened during the weekend.

The Italian "cultural" presentation was nothing more than a hundred people gulping down overcooked spaghetti floating in tomato sauce in a paper dish. And, of course, meatballs. I decided to wait for the minister outside the "pavilion" where the temperature was...only 34 degrees Celsius. After a few minutes, a taxi stopped right outside the hall. The passenger paid the cab fare and approached me: "Is this the Italian pavilion?"

"Yes," I answered, not without some embarrassment. But I immediately added with pride, "We are waiting for the Minister of Multiculturalism."

"I am the minister," the gentleman said.

I compared this scene with the image of police cars, sirens screaming and lights flashing, preceding the limousine of an Italian minister; the chauffeur quickly leaving the car and opening the door for the minister; then the messenger boy carrying a bunch of papers; and, when the welcoming lineup was assembled, the minister leaving the limousine: always austere, elegant, concerned.

This Canadian minister, after paying his cab fare (and obtaining the receipt) looked at me, and I offered myself as a guide. Back inside the pavilion, moving slowly through the sweating crowd, with the minister in tow, I tried to get the attention of one of the organizers, but everybody was more interested in the meatballs than in the minister.

After a few failed attempts to make someone aware of the minister's presence, I introduced the guest to a fellow generously sweating from every pore but wearing a tie. He shook hands with the minister and left.

Spotting another man with a tie, I again introduced the minister and, once more, asked to be directed to one of the event organizers. This time I was luckier. The fellow with the tie indicated a man singing on the other side of the room.

The minister was still tagging along behind me. I introduced him to the singing organizer, who seemed more interested in introducing the spaghetti to the minister than the minister to the crowd.

He asked for two more plates of spaghetti and two glasses of red wine. The minister became interested; looking at the spaghetti, he started rolling it with his fork. He stopped when he realized that the entire contents of the dish, excluding the meatballs, were wrapped around the fork, and the end of his jacket sleeve was soon to be involved in the process.

A few minutes later, the chief organizer arrived. I introduced him to the minister and stole away. When I looked back, the minister was no longer following me. Only years later I understood this somewhat rude welcome: the community had begun to recognize the difference between Italy and Canada.

After his election to the Ontario's Legislative Assembly, Dott. Leone learned the sad reality too. He told me many times, later, that he had never felt so "useless and uninfluential" until he became "deputato" in Canada."

Still, for most Italian immigrants, from the beginning of the last century until just a few decades ago, the politician was a symbol of power, and closeness to an MP or MPP was a social achievement for the parents and a beacon for success for the young generations.

This difference is now well known to many young Italian Canadians. They are still involved in Canadian politics, but their aim has changed. They believe, not without reason, that "serving the people" by becoming a parliamentarian is an empty statement. Many have realized that their Ottawa offices are only expensive holding places between two sitting in the House when they are called to raise their hand; their constituency offices are where MPs and MPPs offer social assistance to their voters, mainly around immigration, or to deal with Compensation Board issues.

There are still some talented young Italian Canadians looking for a place in the House, but for many of them, their ambitions are greatly reduced because they are now fully aware of their role there.

This long preamble was necessary to better understand the involvement of the Italian Canadian community and, for that matter, many other ethnocultural communities, in Canadian politics. Let's return now to the historical involvement of Italian Canadians in the political life of Canada.

The relationship between the Italian community and politics in Canada can be divided into four stages. The first goes from the arrival of the first immigrants in the beginning of last century to the late 1950s; the second, from the late 1950s to the mid-1970s; the third stage, from the mid-1970s to the turn of the millennium; while the fourth goes from 2000 to the present.

We'll start from the beginning, keeping in mind that up until the 1970s, the influence of the Italian community in the Canadian political system was non-existent. The first immigrants from Italy had only one major goal: to give financial stability to their family by finding a stable and lucrative job. Politics and politicians were far from their reach and their mind.

One of the signs of success for an Italian Canadian immigrant was, in the early 1900s, proximity to a political figure. Inviting one of them to a community event or, rarely, to a family celebration, and having that invitation accepted, was a huge social accomplishment, a photo opportunity for pictures to show to friends along with the picture of their ancestors. A visual accomplishment akin to "That's where we came from; that's where we are now." The fulcrum of the then limited political activities were the social-cultural clubs.

As the Canadian Encyclopedia notes, "the first successes of Italians in politics occurred in northern Ontario and the West Coast rather than major cities," with some members of the community, through the 1930s, being "elected to local councils and mayoral offices in Fort William, ON, Mayerthorpe and Coleman, AB, and Trail and Revelstoke, BC."

The most successful was the owner of an auto dealership, Umberto Badanai, who became alderman in Fort William (now Thunder Bay) and was later elected mayor. In 1958 he became the first Canadian of Italian origin to be elected to Parliament as a candidate of the Liberal Party. Coincidentally, Joe Comuzzi, another auto dealership owner, also in Thunder Bay, was elected a federal MP when he ran as a Liberal candidate in 1988. Once I told him that when I was in Thunder Bay, I realized he was very much respected by most of the people I spoke to. He reacted with one of his typical ironic comments. "I am surprised" he quipped. "Voters hate three categories of professionals:

JOE VOLPE

SERGIO MARCHI

politicians, lawyers, and car salesmen. I am all three of them and I don't understand why they still trust me. Even when I left the Liberal Party and joined the Conservatives."

Early in the twentieth century, local community organizations and social clubs were increasingly the centre of social activities, but they were acting in isolation. The only common threads were the geographic areas they came from in Italy. This also fragmented the community and, of course, reduced its influence beyond their local areas.

Things started to change in 1974, when the National Congress of Italian Canadians was created in Ottawa. It was a long and difficult growing process, and this is not the proper place to analyze it. However, with the creation of the congress, Italian regional barriers started to fade. It was thanks to the people working in this national organization that immigrants from, say, Sicily and Friuli started to interact more efficiently, making the community stronger from an economic and social perspective.

Most important, this development changed the strength of the community in the political arena. This happened at the same time that young Italian Canadians decided to get more involved in the political life of their new country. The community became more immersed in political activities, joining local political organizations and volunteering help to organize events and, later, electoral campaigns. In this second stage, the community became more familiar with the partisan political process that was useful for the young, ambitious generations. Slowly they became more confident in the process, more aware of the opportunities available to them and, eventually, more aggressive in moving up in the political organizations.

Before the 1970s, some Italian Canadians were involved in political activity, even with a degree of success, but the outcome was based more on personal achievement than community involvement. In fact, they were successful not because of the community, but despite the community. It was popular at the time to anglicize not just one's given name from Giovanni to John, but also one's last name.

The first cabinet member of Italian origin was Philip Gaglardi (likely the English phonetic pronunciation of Gagliardi). Elected in British Columbia in 1952 as a member of the Social Credit Party, he joined the same year the provincial government in Victoria.

For the first federal minister born in Italy (excluding the 1976 appointment of Monique Bégin, who was only born in Rome), we must wait until 1981, when Pierre Trudeau appointed Charles Caccia Minister of Labour. Caccia was elected to Parliament in 1968, but was systematically ignored by Trudeau for a ministerial appointment. Nonetheless, his election can be considered the end of the second chapter of the relationship between Italian Canadians and politics, and the beginning of the third one.

At that time the political involvement of the Italian Canadian community was shaped by two names, Trudeau and Progressive Conservative leader John Diefenbaker. Most Italian Canadian voters hated the second but loved the first. The reality is that the community was taken for granted by both parties: Conservatives made no serious effort to (re)gain the votes of Italian Canadians, while the Liberals did little to keep them.

However, it is while the Italian Canadians were close to the federal Liberals that the community entered the third stage of involvement. At this time, when parents had achieved financial security and their kids finished their education cycle, many decided that licking stamps for the local MP or MPP was no longer exciting; they decided to take political destiny into their own hands and run for office. There were some early, if isolated, successes in the 1960s, like that of Joe Piccinini on the Toronto City Council and the previously cited MP, Charles Caccia, of the Toronto riding of Davenport. These two names were beacons for many young Canadian Italians, an increasing number of whom decided to seek political office.

As mentioned, the political involvement of the community was with the federal Liberal Party; however, this federal support was not automatically downloaded to the provincial Liberals.

In the 1970s, the target of these aspiring politicians was mainly the Provincial Parliament of Queen's Park. Remo Mancini, from Windsor, was elected a Liberal member in 1975, but it was with the provincial New Democratic Party that the community scored its first important political breakthrough. In the same year, three other Italian Canadians—Odoardo Di Santo, Tony Lupusella, and Tony Grande—all NDP candidates, were elected to Queen's Park.

GREG SORBARA

PHILIP GAGLARDI

They were joined by a young Liberal, Michael Spensieri, in 1981. Later, Tony Silipo and Rosario Marchese were appointed to cabinet by then NDP leader Bob Rae, and in 1990, Giorgio Mammoliti and Tony Rizzo.

However, in the 1980s, the young Italian Canadian Liberals took over Queen's Park, reaching their peak in the 1987 election when, under the leadership of Premier David Peterson, there were over twenty MPPs of Italian origin in the Provincial Parliament. The first ministers of Italian origin in the Legislature were Greg Sorbara, from Vaughan, appointed in 1985 by Peterson, along with Vincent Kerrio from Niagara Falls. They were later joined by Remo Mancini. To see a consistent presence of Conservative MPPs of Italian origin at Queen's Park, we must wait until the mid-1990s. Under the leadership of Mike Harris, there were five such members in the PC caucus. Among them, the late Al Palladini, another car dealership owner who, defying all the odds, became one of the most successful Italian Canadian provincial politicians.

Federally, however, the community's involvement was stalling, limited to a few senatorial appointments. Pietro Rizzuto was appointed in Montreal, followed by Peter Bosa in Toronto.

The 1980s, however, was the decade when Italian Canadians changed their target, aiming at the federal politics. As a now retired MP told me at the time, "We are not going to ask for appointments anymore, we are going to take them."

JOHN TURNER; PHOTO: GAGE SKIDMORE

As former Conservative prime minister Joe Clark has said, it was then Liberal leader John Turner who opened the doors of federal politics to members of minorities in general, and Italian Canadians in particular. It was a powerful involvement that lasted almost two decades. In 1984, John Nunziata and Sergio Marchi joined Charles Caccia (Toronto) and Carlo Rossi (Montreal) in Ottawa, but the struggle to gain more seats continued.

In a few years, many other Italian Canadians won the race. Joe Volpe and Tony Ianno gained their nominations, successfully challenging two seated Liberal MPs in Toronto, but the struggle expanded to many other areas. To name just a few, Albina Guarnieri, after another difficult nomination, won in Mississauga; Tony Valeri in Hamilton; Joe Comuzzi in Thunder Bay; Maurizio Bevilacqua in Vaughan; and Joe Fontana in London. The movement was well alive also in Montreal with the election of Nick Discepola and Alfonso Gagliano. In Ottawa, in the early 1980s, five per cent of the members were of Italian origin.

Vincent Della Noce was also elected in Montreal in the Conservative Party, but the involvement of the Italian Canadian community was almost exclusively with the Liberal Party. This increasing engagement, instead of pleasing Liberal leaders, raised some concerns in the top echelon of the party. Obviously, they enjoyed the community's votes, but they were not prepared to elect MPs of Italian origin.

This involvement, and the increasing concerns of the Liberal leadership, didn't go unnoticed in the national media. "Third force challenges Liberal elite," Hugh Winsor wrote in the Globe and Mail in 1984. "Gloves are off in the nomination row," The Toronto Star declared in November 1992, when community leaders opposed the parachuting of former mayor of Toronto Art Eggleton into the riding of York Centre, considered an "Italian Canadian riding." One of the most influential and respected leaders of the Liberal Party at that time, Sen. Keith Davey, was quoted in the April 1993 issue of Toronto Life as saying that "left to its own device, the party in Toronto would have twenty Italian candidates, seven Sikhs, seven Greeks and a WASP in a pear tree."

The Italian Canadian contingent, however, while enjoying the support of the community in their election to Parliament, soon realized it was another story to be appointed to the cabinet. In fact, in Ottawa they were still considered "Italians," subject to the unofficial rule that only one Italian Canadian MP at a time would get a cabinet appointment. For Prime Minister Jean Chrétien, the chosen one was his trusted supporter Sergio Marchi. (Although Chrétien also appointed Alfonso Gagliano in Montreal.)

Despite this limitation, however, the Italian Canadian contingent—some called them the "pasta caucus"—found a way to be relevant in the national politics of the Liberal Party. They took advantage of the deepening feud between Chrétien and then Minister of Finance Paul Martin. Most joined the former against the latter. Their involvement was important to Martin's successful quest for the top, and they were rewarded. When Martin became prime minister, he had eight Italian Canadian MPs in his first government. Joe Volpe, a loyal supporter of the new leader, was rewarded with important government appointments, including the immigration portfolio and the unofficial but powerful position of Minister for Ontario. Volpe was for Martin what Marchi had been for Chrétien in Ontario.

That was the apex of the Italian Canadian involvement in national politics. When Martin lost the government to Conservative leader Stephen Harper, he left the Liberals divided and without solid leadership.

Two Italian Canadian MPs, Volpe and Bevilacqua, even ran, unsuccessfully, for the party leadership (Nunziata had tried first in 1990), but by then the lengthy honeymoon between the community and the Liberal Party had started to fade. First, the long years in opposition did not stimulate the ambitions of the young Italian Canadians; at the same time, the two names that had created the special bond between the Liberals and the community, Diefenbaker and Trudeau, had lost their significance among the younger generations.

There is no doubt that the Italian Canadian community had, and still has, a huge influence in Canadian politics at all levels, even if this influence has morphed according to the ever-changing context. Will the political involvement still evolve? How?

While the contribution of the community to Canadian politics is now less visible and more subtle than in the 1980s and 1990s, it is still very significant. Some believe the community is now more integrated. I agree, but at the same time, I believe the community is less "assimilated" than it was before, or as many believed it was going to be. Let me clarify that.

Assimilation requires a homogenous context into which one assimilates. Unlike in the United States, this is not possible in Canada because, since its creation, our leaders decided to maintain the cultural roots of immigrants.

In Jim Lotz's book "Prime Ministers of Canada," we read of John A. MacDonald, Canada's first prime minister, saying, "A British subject I was born—a British subject I will die." His successor, Alexander Mackenzie, said he had "no sinecure in trying to keep together a crowd of French Liberals, Irish Catholics, Methodists, Free Traders, Protectionists, Eastern Province Men, Western men, Central Canada men, Columbians, Manitobans, all jealous of each other and striving to obtain some advantages or concession."

Things have changed in the era of globalization, but the attachment to the community cultural roots persists. Only a few decades ago, we heard about a "distinct society," while the concept of funding cultures, even if officially limited to linguistic recognition, still lingers in the political context. French-English dualism remains heavily present in the country, and this creates difficulties for the non-English and non-French citizens in finding a stable Canadian identity, especially in Ottawa. It is easier to become American or Canadian, but it's more difficult to become francophone or anglophone.

A few years ago, I wrote a column that a former prime minister didn't like. He invited me to his residence at 24 Sussex to "understand how" I had reached those conclusions. It was a nice, long, and cordial conversation. Just before I left, he asked me if, the following week, I was going to Alberta for the G8 Summit. To my affirmative answer, he said: "Good, we are going to welcome your prime minister, Berlusconi."

I was a Canadian citizen, I was living in Canada, my kids were born in Canada, I had written a story about Canadian politics in an English Canadian newspaper. Still, for a prime minister of Canada, my prime minister was Silvio Berlusconi.

Of course, he was not trying to offend me; in fact, he thought he was being nice, and this is what is most concerning. While the majority of new Canadians try hard to become Canadian, they are pushed back into their cultural group and regain the hyphen that many have been trying to get rid of.

What kind of political involvement is the Canadian Italian community going to have in the future?

It is hard to predict because many independent variables are involved. There is the new technology that crushes barriers, changing international relations—the worldwide demographic osmosis that continuously recalibrates the cultural balances at home and abroad, the different economic dynamics shaping foreign partnership, and, most importantly, the chaos in the traditional media whose inability to deal with the new medium has left a vacuum in the information business.

It looks now like the new generations, more confused than ever, are pulling back from a constructive contribution and using their involvement to foster their own personal gain. I hope that, somehow, they will reignite their political interest in this country, helping everybody to get rid of their hyphens and shape a cultural identity that is presently foggy.

I hope so, even if the centripetal forces to keep the country together are weak, confused, with no competent leadership in sight, and the centrifugal temptations seem more appealing, more accessible, and more dangerous.

ITO SCHIPA
GIORGIO CONSOLINI
ICCOLA PUPA
APLE LEAF GARDENS
UNDAY MAY 16 730 PM
ITALIAN RECORDS
JOHNN
LOMBA
College St
PICCOLA PUPA
GIORGIO CONSOLINI
BOBBY CURTOLA
Guess Who?
BOBBY ENZINA VINCI BERTI
MAPLE LEAF GARDENS
RITA BERTI & TITO SCHIPA
SPECIAL 35¢
IN PERSON
PICCOLA PU
EXCITING WARNER BROS. RECOR
SUNDAY MAY 16 7:30 P.M.
MAPLE LEAF GARDENS

PHOTO: CITY OF TORONTO ARCHIVES

MEDIA

DANIELA SANZONE

The history of Italian media in Canada goes back as far as the second half of the nineteenth century. Italians have used the press, and later radio and television stations, mainly for economic objectives and political representation. Today, Italians are still quite prolific in the media. However, despite similar goals, the political, social, and economic realities have changed, as well as "la comunità," in terms of number, political orientation and interest, education and job market, and conditions for new Italians in Canada. Between the two wars and into the 1970s, even for Italians living in Canada, it felt important to be part of the Italian political arena overseas. Nowadays, the main objective of the Italian diaspora is to gain more political, social, and economic power in Canada.

In our connected world, with its information overflow, everyone has the opportunity to be constantly and instantly in contact with the news from their country of origin. Today, newcomers have a higher level of education, speak English, and are socially and economically integrated. Yet, while programming in Italian should keep the language alive for Canadians, news with an Italian angle delivered in English would encourage everyone to understand and appreciate Italian culture. So, the future of Italian media in this country could be to create content useful for the mainstream Canadian media, with an Italian flavour and perspective.

This article provides a historical overview of the Italian-language media in Canada, based primarily on research developed by Angelo Principe in his unpublished work about Italian Canadian newspapers since the nineteenth century.[1]

EARLY HISTORY

Archives and displays in the Canadian Museum of History in Ottawa show that multicultural and multilingual publishing grew from the 1870s throughout the first half of the twentieth century with the settlement in Canada. The earliest record of Italian media is *L'Italo Canadese*, whose first number was published in Montreal on March 15, 1894. At the time, Italian immigration was not very significant, although Italians are among the earliest Europeans to have visited and settled the country, as reported by *The Canadian Encyclopedia*: "In the early 19th century, a sizable number of Italians, many in the hotel trade, resided in Montreal. Throughout the century, Italian craftsmen, artists, musicians and teachers, primarily from northern Italy, immigrated to Canada. Italian street musicians (hurdy-gurdy men, street singers) were particularly noted by Canadians, and by 1881 almost 2,000 people of Italian origin lived in Canada, particularly in Montréal and Toronto."[2]

Angelo Principe[3] divides the Italian journalistic experience in Canada into three stages, based on people trying to survive in the new country while still involved in Italian politics, as well as on the increase of Italian immigration and its social integration in Canada. The first stage goes from 1894 until 1915, starting with the publication of *L'Italo Canadese* in Montreal. The second stage goes from 1916 until 1940, when another weekly magazine, *L'Italia*, came into existence, followed in 1923 by *Le Fiamme d'Italia*, an openly fascist journal. The final stage begins in 1940 and continues up to today, starting with the founding of *Il Giornale Italo-Canadese*, by Antonino Spada in Montreal, which became *Il Cittadino Canadese* the following year. *Il Cittadino Canadese* is still a weekly tabloid, with a circulation of 18,000 and distributed through more than 250 sales outlets across the island of Montreal. Nina Giordano has been its editor since January 2008.[4]

Principe connects these three phases to three periods of Italy's political and institutional life: first, Liberal Italy, 1861–1914; second, the year Italy entered the Great War and the Fascist dictatorship, 1915–39; and third, Italy entering World War II on June 10, 1940, to present.

In his research, Principe identifies fifty-one Italian Canadian publications over the years, in various formats: bulletins, daily newspapers, illustrated magazines, political and cultural periodicals, published in Montreal, Toronto, Winnipeg, Vancouver, and other Canadian cities.

In the pioneering period, between the end of the nineteenth and the beginning of the twentieth centuries, the number of Italian Canadians was small; they were not congregated in specific areas and most were illiterate. In 1901 Montreal saw the largest concentration of Italians, 1,398 people, mostly uneducated and destitute (Di Stefani, 1914).[5] W. G. Smith (1920), in his *Study in Canadian Immigration*, reports that during the period 1899–1909, almost 12 per cent of Northern Italian immigrants and 54 per cent of Southern Italian immigrants were illiterate; a large number of them were poor, almost indigent. In 1894, because of their poverty, few Italians were able to read or could afford to buy a newspaper. It was a difficult time for periodicals. In spite of this, Pietro Catelli started the adventure of *L'Italo Canadese*. In the first number, it was advertised that *L'Italo Canadese* was the only Italian newspaper printed in Canada, and it represented "the interests of more than ten thousand Italians." It claimed that "it is the best way for you to advertise your business."

It is not clear for how long the newspaper circulated, but there is evidence of at least two years of publication. As Principe writes, it was well made in terms of printing and content, considering that it offered only six pages, in tabloid format, and was composed mostly of business advertising and services for Italians. There were forty-four ads, thirteen of which were for Italian businesses; two mentioned an employment agency Pietro Catelli was opening for new immigrants; and one offered free letters written, which confirms the high level of illiteracy in that era. Twelve of these ads mentioned Italian economic activities, such as Italian "bed and breakfasts," restaurants, shoe factories, travel agencies, money exchange, legal services, and so on.

In Montreal, aside from Salviati's paper, *La Gazzetta del Canada*, founded by Angelo M. Puccini, there were also two competing weeklies, *Corriere del Canada*, founded by L. Nobile in 1896, and *La Patria Italiana*, founded by Bernardino di Francesco in 1903. By 1904, two of the most important Italian travel agents in Montreal, Antonio Cordasco and Alberto Dini, had acquired the two newspapers and used the publications mostly as advertising bulletins for their business. Besides the travel agencies, Cordasco and Dini also owned a profitable employment office. Their newspapers represented a means of advertising and a sign of prestige for their business enterprises.

Edizione Extra per il Circolo Colombo

il BOLLETTINO

ITALO-CANADESE

THE ITALIAN-CANADIAN BULLETIN

Great excitement prevales on eve of Election.

NOTE DELLA SEDUTA DI NOMINA DEI CANDIDATI

CIRCOLO COLOMBO

Commenti Post-Assemblea

IL BOLLETTINO, 1930

L'ARALDO DEL CANADA

Universalità del Fascismo

L'ARALDO DEL CANADA, 1933

l'EMIGRATO

PUO' UN CITTADINO ITALO-CANADESE ESSERE FASCISTA?

"PRESENTE!" dirà tutta la Colonia per il

GRAN BALLO PRO SCUOLA ITALIANA

SOCIETA' di M.S. FRATELLANZA ITALIANA

LUNEDI 18 APRILE 1932 COLUMBUS HALL

L'EMIGRATO, 1932

LA VOCE OPERAIA

COMIZIO ANTIFASCISTA DOMENICA 29 OTT.

TRAGICA COMEDIA

Una vittoria degli scioperanti a Stratford

DIFFIDA

LA VOCE OPERAIA, 1933

In Toronto, the first Italian newspaper was *Lo Stendardo*, published in 1898, with a Mr. Saporita as editor-in-chief. It was located on Yonge Street downtown, between College and Dundas, the heart of Toronto's first Little Italy.

In 1924, Henry Corti (real name Enrico Corticelli), owner and editor-in-chief of *La Tribuna Canadiana*, wrote that his weekly publication had been going for sixteen years, and over time various other new publications did not survive long.[6] As Principe notes, we know little about the "various publications" Corti mentioned. Even *La Tribuna Canadiana* was not published regularly, other than during the municipal, provincial, and federal elections, since it was financed by the Conservative Party. After the elections, it appeared "when possible." To offer a different and more liberal view, the deputy consul of Italy in Toronto, an honorary position at the time, started the publication *Il Pensiero Italiano*, but the newspaper, according to Corti, did not enjoy a long life.

Of several newspapers that appeared between 1894 and 1915, only two survived until 1930: *L'Araldo del Canada* in Montreal and *La Tribuna Canadiana* in Toronto. *L'Araldo* first published in 1905, and *La Tribuna* in 1909.[7] The latter, in the 1920s, replaced "canadiana" (a term that was assimilated to "americana") to "canadese."[8]

In the twenties, Italians produced a substantial number of publications. As Principe illustrates, some Italian fascists in Canada, dissatisfied with what they considered the "lukewarm" way the Italian local press treated fascism and Mussolini, created their own periodicals, two years before organizing their first fascist club in Montreal in 1925.[9] In 1923, the legionnaire Nanni Leone Castelli started the weekly magazine *Le Fiamme d'Italia* in Montreal. In a letter to the periodical *Il Grido della Stirpe*, Castelli wrote that he had been a volunteer in the Fiume military expedition led by the poet Gabriele D'Annunzio in 1919, stating that he was a fascist from "the very first hour."[10] *Le Fiamme d'Italia* had a short life, because Castelli was accused of murdering his girlfriend, for which he was found not guilty. At the end of the trial, and before returning to Italy, Castelli became co-editor-in-chief with Camillo Vetere of the weekly *L'Italia*. This magazine became a supporter of fascism, and the two owners, Luigi Capuano and Enrico Pasquale, pre-empted possible competitors and obtained funding allocated by the Italian government for the Italian press abroad.

Following the 1929 Lateran Pacts between the Kingdom of Italy and the Vatican, *Il Bollettino Italo-Canadese* was published in Toronto that same year, with the support of the clergy.

In these years, the anti-fascist Antonino Spada lost his job as editor of *L'Araldo* to the ex-lieutenant Camillo Vetere. A note from the Italian Foreign Minister to the Minister of the Interior stated: "With the new director … the relevant periodical *L'Araldo* has changed direction completely, assuming a patriotic character, totally in favour of the present Italian Government."[11] After *L'Araldo*, Spada created and directed, for the Order Sons of Italy, *Il Risveglio*, an openly antifascist weekly.[12] Not a single copy of this periodical has been found. Spada often mentions this newspaper in his book, but he gives no further details.

Gente Nostra, a bilingual weekly in Italian and English, appeared in 1926. It was edited and published by Francesco M. Gualtieri, a veteran of the Great War, but the magazine did not last long.[13] The Catholic clergy, Principe points out, did not like it because Gualtieri was a Protestant, so they made sure his newspaper was considered anathema to Catholics.[14] Three years later, in March 1929, the pro-fascist *Corriere Italiano* was founded, but despite some initial success, like *Gente Nostra*, it soon disappeared.

As Principe writes, Toronto was not dominated by the clergy as Montreal was, and antifascists produced a slew of five newspapers of different ideological orientations, but with socially oriented values: the Catholic *L'Emigrato*, the conservative *Il Messaggero Italo-Canadese*, the socialist *La Voce Operaia*, the communist *Il Lavoratore*, and *La Voce Italo-Canadese*. Also, the rather singular *Canadian Lakehead Herald* was published in three languages—English, Ukrainian and Italian—by the industrial and agricultural workers of Fort William and Port Arthur, Ontario.[15]

Financed by Giuseppe Bagnato, the first number of the antifascist weekly *L'Emigrato* appeared in Toronto on December 30, 1931, under the editorship of S. M. Rubano. *L'Emigrato* likely ended publication the following summer, at the same time as *Il Progresso Italo-Canadese*. The struggle against fascism in Canada was taken over by *Il Messaggero Italo-Canadese*, in 1933. Dante Colussi, who had worked for *Il Progresso*, was editor-in-chief.

FROM THE FIFTIES TO THE SEVENTIES

As Principe writes, there was little activity after World War II. Many Italians were interned in the prison camp of Petawawa for confirmed or suspected fascist activities. An exception to the dearth of publication is *La Verità*, a weekly that self-defined as anticommunist and debuted in 1948. Its publisher was the ex-internee, journalist, and writer Mario Duliani. The following year, the circulation of his paper was 5,000 copies, making it more popular than *Il Cittadino*, which had been publishing for over a decade.[17]

In 1953, the *Corriere Canadese* was established in Toronto by twenty-year-old Daniel (Dan) Andrew Iannuzzi Jr. After graduating from the Graphic Arts School in Montreal, Iannuzzi moved to Toronto and, following in his father's footsteps, started the publication, hiring John Grohovaz as editor-in-chief. Principe reports that Iannuzzi later created Daisons Publications, Ltd., with five weeklies published over time: *Il Corriere Canadese, Il Corriere Sportivo, Il Corriere del Quebec, Il Corriere del Niagara*, and

Teledomenica.[18] He was also a founder of the Ethnic Press Association of Ontario. In 1990, *Il Corriere Canadese* turned daily, publishing Monday to Friday.

In 2004 Iannuzzi passed away at the age of seventy, in Rome, where he was travelling on business. On that occasion, Canadian Prime Minister Paul Martin and Ontario Premier Dalton McGuinty issued a long statement, declaring him "a giant in the field of Canadian media." They also wrote that "as President and Chief Executive Officer of Multimedia Nova Corporation, he was a pioneer in multicultural communications and a significant contributor to Toronto's Italian community."[19]

ITALY CANADA TRADE, 2002

PARTNERS, 2009

In 2013, Multimedia Nova Corporation ceased publication of *Corriere Canadese, Tandem, Vaughan Today, Correo Canadiense,* and *The Town Crier,* newspapers distributed in downtown Toronto. *Corriere Canadese* was then purchased by Domenico Primucci, president of Pizza Nova; entrepreneur Dan Montesano; lawyer Anthony Pascale; and former Liberal MP Joe Volpe, who remain the current owners.

About a year after the publication of *Il Corriere Canadese*, Luigi Petrucci began the weekly *Panorama* (which would later become a monthly). Both weeklies defined themselves as independent, anticommunist, and supporters of Democrazia Cristiana (the Christian Democratic Party of Italy). In the Canadian context, however, while *Il Corriere Canadese* supported the Conservative Party, *Panorama* was for the Liberals.[20]

At some point in the fifties, Petrucci advertised an excursion tour to Italy, and many Italians bought the package. But a few days before the trip, Petrucci disappeared, and many people lost their money. Years later, however, Petrucci published a book explaining that he was kidnapped, robbed, and abandoned on a road in New York.[21]

Many Italian newspapers flourished during the 1960s and 1970s in Montreal, Toronto, and other Canadian cities.

In 1964 the magazine *Italy Canada Trade* was launched by the Italian Chamber of Commerce of Toronto, an independent non-profit organization founded in 1961. In 2002 the magazine was revamped under the name *Partners*.[22] In 1964, *Giovane Fiamma* started as a monthly publication, edited by a group of students from the Toronto Italian Canadian Youth Club. The left-wing publications were *Il Lavoratore* (1958–60), published in collaboration with left-oriented Italians, communists included.[23] Then, three newspapers affiliated with the New Democratic Party were published: *La Parola* (1960–63); *Forze Nuove* (1972–80), edited by Elio Costa, Odoardo Di Santo, and Angelo Principe, which lasted almost ten years; and *Avanti Canada* (1975–76).[24] Italian Canadian communists published two newspapers in the years 1975–79: *Nuovo Mondo* and *Lotta Continua*. Published by the Canadian section of Federazione Italiana Lavoratori e Famiglie, *Nuovo Mondo* was inspired by Enrico Berlinguer, new leader of the Italian Communist Party. In the 1970s, the trilingual (Italian, English, and French) arts magazine *Vice Versa* was launched.

Other newspapers subsequently appeared. In Toronto, the most important were *La Voce Veneta* (1960); *Il Settimanale di Toronto; Comunità Viva,* published and edited by Rino Citarella; *L'Eco d'Abruzzo* (1971); *Il Tevere* (1972); *Settegiorni* (1972); *Incontri* (1973); *Famiglia Italiana; La Città,* edited by Don Evasio Pollo; *La Settimana* (1975); *Il Laghetto* (1977); *Facts and Opinions*, a periodical published by the Canadian Italian Business and Professional Men's Association; *Il Settimanale* (1977); *La Lumera* (1980); *Oggi Canadà* (1980); *La Gazzetta di Toronto* (1981); and *Vita Sana* (1984), a health periodical for the family.

A special mention must go to *Lo Specchio* (1984), founded by Sergio Tagliavini and Giovanna Tozzi, who previously published *Il Giornale di Toronto*, and *Donna*.[25] With Dan Iannuzzi and Johnny Lombardi, Sergio Tagliavini Jellinek has been a pillar of the Italian media community. He has been also a key player in York Region. Unanimously defined as "a man of humility and integrity," always showing a strong sense of humanity and compassion, Tagliavini was born in Genoa, Italy, in 1935 and grew up in Milan. He began his career in journalism after he came to Canada in 1970. In 1973, he became editor of *Corriere Canadese* and produced public affairs programming for radio and TV shows. In 1984, he and Tozzi founded the Vaughan weekly newspaper *Lo Specchio* and turned it into an authoritative voice for Italian Canadians. *Lo Specchio* is still published today. Tagliavini was also a leader in the Italian community and actively cooperated in the Italian Fallen Workers project, built at the Woodbridge Pool & Memorial Arena. Two years after his death in 2016, the square in front of the arena was named Piazza Sergio Tagliavini in his honour. He had received a number of achievement awards from Italy and Canada during his long career.

In Montreal, in the sixties and seventies, the situation was similar to that in Toronto. There was prolific production of many newspapers and magazines, but none lasted long. Among other publications, *Il Ponte*, a daily edited and directed by Michele Pirone, which lasted only a few months; the Catholic weekly *Insieme*, directed by Father Domenico Rodighiero and then Father Morassuto; *Il Corriere Italiano*, a right-wing weekly, directed first by Umberto Sgherri, then Luciano Coraggio, and finally Pasquale Cifarelli. The monthly *La Tribuna* was also well received in Toronto after its editor-publisher, Camillo Carli, added an Ontario page, edited by Angelo Principe. In line with the paper's orientation, the page edited in Toronto reflected, with the contribution of open-minded young Italians, the stark and sometimes tragic situation of Ontario's Italian workers, suffering dangerous work conditions, mostly in the construction business. Their problems were presented to readers who suffered the conditions of that work environment themselves. Even Filippo Salvatore, who later wrote a book about the Italian community in Montreal, began his career as a contributor to Carli's paper.

In Winnipeg, Manitoba, where the Italian population was scarce, several attempts to establish press failed, in part due to illiteracy and poverty. In 1960, two short-lived newspapers were published, *Il Messaggero Italo-Canadese*, directed by Franco Gotti, and *Il Progresso*. These two publications covered the local community and gave ample space to sports, social activities, and local young Italians and their organizations, but these papers did not last long. In 1970, an intellectual monthly publication, *Umanitas*, appeared, aiming at elevating the sociopolitical discourse, but it never attracted an audience. *Umanitas* was followed by *Per Conoscerci Meglio*, a monthly published by the local Sicilian Club but directed at the community at large. Even the Winnipeg Casa d'Italia published a newsletter. All these met the same fate: a short life.

Other newspapers include *Il Marco Polo* (Vancouver), founded in 1974, *L'Ora di Ottawa*, and *Il Postino* (Ottawa), established in 2000 by a group of young Ottawa Italian Canadians to convey the history of the Italian community in the capital of Canada.[26] *Panorama Italian Canadian*, distributed in the Greater Toronto Area, is still being published and edited by Enzo Di Mauro and Roberto Bandiera.

RADIO AND TELEVISION

The peak of Italian immigration in Canada was reached in 1961. By then, Italians had replaced the Jewish Community as "Toronto's largest non-British ethnic group, and Toronto replaced Montreal as the top choice for Italian immigration."[27] Thus, the seventies and eighties represented a new opportunity for Italians to create Italian-language media. Several radio and TV stations were born. In Montreal in 1962, Casimir Stanczykowkski, a Pole, founded CFMB, the first multicultural radio station in Canada. The programming was mostly in Italian. Although CFMB gained an Italian cultural stronghold in Montreal, as Principe points out, the station's programming was often criticized for being old-fashioned, with no space for fresh and modern music or ideas.[28] To address this, the radio station introduced a short program on Friday afternoons, *Spazio ai giovani.*

Four years later, in 1966, Johnny Lombardi founded CHIN, a similar radio station in Toronto.[29] As advertised on its website, CHIN AM 1540 is the first multicultural/multilingual radio station to be established in Ontario, followed a year later by CHIN FM 100.7. Johnny Barbalinardo Lombardi, notes the website, was born in 1915, on a street still standing behind the Eaton Centre in the heart of downtown Toronto.[30] At twelve, Johnny's first after-school job was as a folder and addresser for the Italian weekly *La Tribuna Italo-Canadese*, but he soon graduated to the position of back-page editor, writing his own column, "The Snipper-Snooper." In the 1950s, Lombardi opened a grocery store, but he was always busy with other interests—concerts, radio programs, record importing, and food and specialty importing. In those years, Lombardi started a career as an impresario, bringing Italian singers from Italy for concerts at the Eaton's College and Bay store theatre hall, Massey Hall, and then Maple Leaf Gardens, O'Keefe Centre (now Meridian Hall), and Roy Thomson Hall. He produced Italian radio programs on CHUM and then CKFH to promote his supermarket, concerts, and community events, and started a record label—Bravo Records & Music—to promote Italo-Canadian singers. In the early 1960s, Lombardi applied for a licence for a multicultural radio station, and CHIN Radio was launched, opening its studios and offices above the supermarket in 1966. Later, he launched and ran CKVR Barrie for a few years, then approached Global Television in the early 1970s, starting a Sunday Italian show broadcast live from the Global studios on Barber Greene Road. In the late 1980s, when Global TV could no longer accommodate time in their programming schedule, Citytv welcomed CHIN Television shows to its broadcasting schedule. CHIN TV is still broadcast on Citytv every Sunday morning.

Lombardi was a member of the Order of Canada, and was invited by Prime Minister Jean Chretién to commemorate the fiftieth anniversary of the D-Day invasion of Normandy on June 6, 1994, in which he had originally participated. Often called Mr. Toronto, he died in 2002. Mayor Mel Lastman remembered Lombardi as "a pioneer of multiculturalism in the city." The City of Toronto officially named a segment of College Street, between Clinton Street and Grace Street, Johnny Lombardi Way in his honour.[31] A statue of Lombardi sitting on a bench was erected on Grace Street and College Street. In Pisticci, a small city in the Basilicata region in Southern Italy, a square was restored and renamed Piazza Johnny Lombardi (also known as Piazza Lombardi). His son Lenny and daughter Theresa, as well as daughter-in-law Grace Fusillo-Lombardi, along with the Toronto city councillor Joe Pantalone, established The Johnny Lombardi Multicultural Foundation on May 21, 2008.[32] Johnny Lombardi: The Great Communicator, an hour-long documentary about his life,[33] produced by Lenny and Grace, contains interview clips with many well-known Canadians, including Chretién and Ted Rogers.[34]

LENNY LOMBARDI

Today, CHIN Radio and TV, led by Johnny's son Lenny, reaches out in over fifty languages to more than one hundred cultural communities in the greater Toronto and southern Ontario areas on CHIN AM 1540/FM100.7, and in over twenty languages and cultures in the Ottawa/Gatineau region on CJLL FM 97.9.

In 1979, Dan Iannuzzi founded CFMT-TV in Toronto, the first multicultural/multilingual television station in Canada. Acquired by Rogers in 1986, CFMT became Omni TV in

DOLCE, 2019

2002. For eight years, Omni TV produced local and international news in five languages: Italian, Portuguese, Cantonese, Mandarin, and English/Punjabi. In 2015, Rogers announced a restructuring of Omni news programs for financial reasons. They claimed a loss of $5 million: advertising revenue in the newscasts brought in less than $4 million annually, in contrast to production expenses of $9 million. After shutting down the Italian news for a few years, today Omni, owned by Rogers Communications, produces newscasts in three languages: Italian, Cantonese, and Mandarin. Omni TV currently consists of all six of Canada's conventional multicultural television stations, located in Ontario (two stations), British Columbia, Alberta (two stations), and an affiliate in Quebec. Although the CRTC, which regulates ethnic media production in Canada, did not believe that Rogers' proposal adequately addressed the provisioning of programs for regions of Canada not currently served by an Omni broadcast station, or that it was financially sustainable. In 2017 the commission still granted Rogers a three-year interim license term.

CHCH-TV started broadcasting in 1954 and is still considered the news leader for Hamilton and the surrounding Halton and Niagara regions. In the seventies, it also used to broadcast two days a week in Italian.

Telelatino (TLN), a speciality channel focused on multicultural programming, began broadcasting in October 1984 in Toronto and Montreal and is widely available through cable distribution. Though it offers programs in both Spanish and Italian, 70 per cent of TLN's revenues are derived from the latter. There is also 25 per cent programming in English. TLN is owned by the privately held TLN Media Group, a consortium owned by three prominent Italian Canadian families and network president Aldo Di Felice. Corus Entertainment previously owned a 50.5 per cent majority share in the company; it later sold its interest to its existing partners and Di Felice for $19 million.

EIGHTIES AND NINETIES

In the eighties and nineties, Italians were very active in the Ontario media industry, with a large audience. Emilio Mascia owned TLN, Lombardi CHIN Radio, Iannuzzi Corriere Canadese and CFMT-TV, and Tagliavini published *Lo Specchio*. Therefore, there was an opportunity to create a big Italian media pole, which could have consolidated the political and social power of Italians in Ontario, really influencing Canadian politics. However, this opportunity was lost, partly because of the lack of professional figures in the media world, but most of all for the rivalry among the broadcasting players. As a result, TLN and CFMT-TV were sold to big Canadian companies.

In the nineties, Italians produced fewer newspapers. A few magazines, though, had a strong impact on the community. The groundbreaking quarterly *Eyetalian* was launched by Nick Bianchi, John Montesano, Teresa Tiano, and Pino Esposito in 1993 as a challenging, indepedent magazine of Italian Canadian culture.[35] It encountered commercial difficulty and leaned toward a general lifestyle magazine format before concluding its publication later in the decade. Along with *Eyetalian*, the already-cited *Vice Versa* has been one of the absolute top magazines in Canadian history.

Dolce, or *Dolce Vita*, after over twenty years, is still nationally recognized and internationally respected as a luxury lifestyle guide. On its website, it is advertised as the "product of the passion of brother-and-sister duo Fernando Zerillo and Michelle Zerillo-Sosa," and it "continues its tradition of uncovering the most stylish fashion, automotive and jewelry; the most desirable resorts and real estate locales, and profiling countrywide and international

PANORAM ITALIA, 2019

EYETALIAN, 1996

ACCENTI, 2001

VICE VERSA, 1983

businesses and entrepreneurs of high distinction." It is published by Dolce Publishing, Inc., and distributes over 290,000 pristine copies annually across Canada and select US cities, catering to a distinguished readership that includes VIPs and prominent social figures, including CEOs, presidents, doctors, lawyers, and national/local celebrities.[36]

Italo of Montreal was published sporadically in Italian, with some articles in French and English, focusing on current affairs and community news. *La Comunità* was taken over by the youth organization of the National Congress of Italian Canadians in Quebec in the late 1990s.

In 1992, a group of about fifty Italian Canadian journalists formed the Associazione dei Giornalisti Italo-Canadesi, with the objective of promoting initiatives aimed at improving the professional journalistic activity in Ontario. The president of the association was Angelo Persichilli.

THE NEW MILLENNIUM

In 2002, *Panoram Italia* magazine was founded in Montreal, by publisher Antonio Zara. It is currently published bimonthly in two different editions, one in Montreal and one in the Greater Toronto Area, with the objective of unifying Italian Canadians and rekindling their connection to their heritage.[37]

In 2003, Domenic Cusmano and Licia Canton founded *Accenti*. After thirty-one print issues, in January 2015 *Accenti* went to an online-only format. It also publishes a newsletter, which is emailed to subscribers nine times a year.

In 2005, Rai International, today Rai Italia, became available to Italians living in Canada, giving them the opportunity, on a daily basis, of following Italian programming, political debates, and news from Italy. Later, also Mediaset TV, packaged in Italy, has become purchasable.

Il Fatto Online was founded in Italy in September 2008 by Joe Infusini and developed into a monthly magazine in 2009. It was published in Italy, Rome, and Calabria, until it reached Toronto in 2016.

Today, the Italian Canadian media environment revolves around a few players, published and broadcast mainly in Italian, with some content presented in English: in Toronto, *Corriere Canadese*, *Lo Specchio*, Omni News, CHIN Radio and TV, TLN, with little programming produced in Canada, *Panoram*

Italia, available by subscription in Italian and English, *Dolce*, *Il Fatto Online*, also published in Italian and English, *Panorama Italian Canadian*; in Montreal, *Accenti*; *Il Corriere Italiano*, founded by Alfredo Gagliardi in the early 1950s; and *Il Cittadino Canadese*, founded in 1941, the oldest Italian-language newspaper still in circulation. It is not known how big their audience is and whether they are satisfied with the content. Because these media outlets are in Italian, most do not target the mainstream or the second and third generations of Italian Canadians.

TRANSITION TO THE FUTURE

In the twenty-first century, a multiplicity of ethnic communities are a normal part of Canadian life, where different cultures co-exist, interact, and blend. And yet, mainstream traditional media still lacks ethnic diversity, representation, and perspectives. Historically, Italian media helped Italians integrate in Canada. But in recent times, Italian media faces the same hardships as mainstream media in trying to compete with digital and social media, building the trust of their audiences, and finding new readers, listeners, and viewers among the new generations living in more integrated and diverse cultural and geographic communities. The markets for immigrant communities have changed: newcomers are better educated, more aware of global issues, and generally speak better English. Thus, to evolve or survive, ethnic and Italian Canadian media need to be restructured for the evolving Canadian market and provide a level of journalism and contents compatible with professional mainstream standards. Ethnic media should also try to reach all Canadians, which involves delivering and collaborating with multilingual digital media. An Italian newsroom should be able to produce information that is culturally relevant and sensitive to many Canadian communities, bringing a contemporary Italian perspective and style, while distributed in English. This would be one step toward a new form of media communication, intercultural journalism, aimed at integrating a melange of cultures, as opposed to simply acknowledging ethnic language differences within Canadian diversity.

Canadian society and mainstream media need to integrate journalists who can do more than speak several languages. Journalists should not qualify by simply belonging to an "ethnic group," but above all for having lived the experience of more than one culture, including mainstream Canadian life. This lived experience would support the creation of intercultural media and contents, a medium that can tell stories and mediate relevant conversations across cultural differences to all Canadians. Intercultural journalists should also be able to monitor the Canadian circulation of international and digital information, which is indispensable in a globalized world.

The journalists of the global Italian diaspora, along with those of other ethnic communities, are well placed to offer stories across different cultures. Italians in Canada are very well integrated socially, politically, and economically, and have an opportunity to create strong intercultural media. They can lead the way and leave behind the "ethnic" label, which no longer corresponds to a society where most people belong to several traditional cultures and many new ones.

ENZO DI MAURO

In 2021 the Italian Canadian community lost one of its most essential voices in the Toronto media landscape. Enzo Di Mauro worked with Ciao and CHIN Radio, Omni News and CFMT television. Besides his work in radio and television he launched the weekly print publication *Panorama Italian Canadian*, which eventually became a monthly. As a journalist and publisher, Di Mauro devoted himself to insuring that Italian culture would continue to inform and inspire all those of Italian descent that choose to call Canada their home.

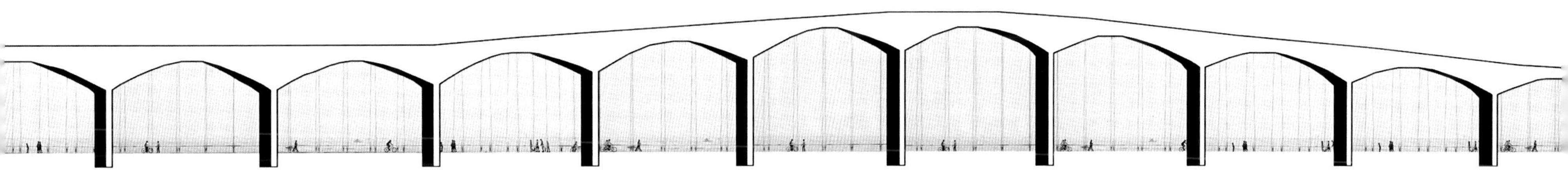

SOCIETA' ITALO-CANADESE
BAND
TORONTO

SOCIETÀ ITALO CANADESE BAND; PHOTO: ARCHIVES OF ONTARIO

COMMUNITY BUILDING AND PHILANTHROPY

PETER NORMAN

Although some of the earliest Europeans to explore and settle in Canada were Italian—notably Giovanni Caboto, the Venetian navigator who explored Canada's east coast—it was not until the late nineteenth century that Italian immigration to Canada began in earnest. In 1881, only around two thousand people of Italian origin lived in the country; by century's end, that number had grown by more than five times.

BAY STREET LOOKING NORTH FROM FRONT STREET
APRIL 1904, PHOTO: CITY OF TORONTO ARCHIVES

Toronto and its surrounding municipalities reflected this national trend. In 1891, only four hundred or so Torontonians were from the Italian peninsula; two decades later, the census reported 4,600 people of Italian origin in the city. Many Italians merely passed through Toronto en route to labour jobs in other parts of the province and country; because the census after 1911 was taken in June, when many such workers had proceeded to summer employment elsewhere, census numbers likely underreport the Italian population.

After the 1904 Great Fire ravaged Toronto, Little Italy needed rebuilding. Many of those formerly migrant labourers were employed in the reconstruction and then stayed on in the city, where they then pursued the opportunity to practice their trades—although they had come to Canada as "unskilled" labour, many were apprentices or higher in specialized trades and crafts, which they now contributed to the city's burgeoning Italian community.

Between the number of newcomers and the proliferation of business, the need grew for organizations to serve both immigrants and the business community. One of Toronto's earliest Italian mutual aid societies, established in 1888, was the Umberto Primo Italian Benevolent Society, which in 1897 convinced the City Council to commemorate Italian unification by raising the Italian flag over City Hall every June 14. By 1900, Toronto's Italian Canadian Association was on Ontario's Register of Benevolent Societies, and the Italian National Club was created in 1907. An Italian parish, Our Lady of Mt. Carmel, was founded in 1908. Whereas many of the smaller social clubs were devoted to particular regions of the Italian peninsula, these larger clubs, in the spirit of 'Risorgimento,' were apparently open to all Italians.

The Figli d'Italia, later called the Order of the Sons and Daughters of Italy, was established in New York City in 1905, and its first Canadian chapter opened in Ontario ten years later with a lodge in Sault Ste. Marie. In contrast to its Montreal counterpart, the Order in Ontario was province-wide in its jurisdiction; whereas Italians in Quebec were concentrated in Montreal and its suburbs, no fewer than ten Ontarian cities had one thousand or more Italian residents. Larger and more active in Toronto itself in the earlier twentieth century were the Società Italo-Canadese, formed in 1919 when three older societies amalgamated; the Trinacria Club, serving Toronto's large Sicilian cohort; and the Circolo Columbo, established in 1913.

Starting in the mid-1920s, the balance of the Italian Canadian population shifted: increasingly, its Canadian-born members outnumbered their immigrant parents. Organizations grew from this cohort, not only to assist immigrants, but to serve the thriving native-born population. The Comitato Intersociale was set up as an umbrella group for various organizations throughout the community. In 1931, the Italian Information Bureau of Toronto published a Direttorio Italiano, a listing of more than 700 Italian-owned businesses in Ontario.

Meanwhile, the interwar years represented a setback for the perception of Italian Canadians within the larger Canadian society. While Italy's eventual participation in the Allied campaign in World War I marked a high point of tolerance—Italian Canadian troops were honoured throughout the country, including an illustrated honour roll published by Toronto's immigrant-focused Central Neighbourhood House—many soldiers died on the front or stayed in Europe, and events there would soon create trouble for Italian Canadians at home.

After 1927, consular authorities representing Italy's fascist government became heavily involved in the creation and management of GTA clubs. Although most Italian Canadians were not active fascists—and some were nominally involved with the movement only for reasons of professional necessity rather than personal conviction—the mainstream press and many members of the Anglo majority looked favourably upon the fascist regime before Mussolini's international aggression turned the tide of public opinion. As war engulfed the globe and Canadian authorities interned prominent Italian Canadians, many members of the community suppressed expressions of national identity, some even anglicizing their names. Frank Iacobucci, whose highly distinguished legal career saw him appointed to the Supreme Court and named to the Order of Canada, recalls his Italian immigrant parents reporting monthly to the RCMP. It would take the end of the war—and the mass immigration of Italians that followed the lifting of the Enemy Alien Act in 1947—for healthy cultural expression to flourish anew.

The decades after World War II brought a great influx of immigrants. In the 1950s, Canada became the top destination for emigrating Italians, and Toronto surpassed Montreal as home to the most Italian Canadians. During any two-year period in the fifties, more Italians arrived in the city than already lived there. Various organizations emerged to ease the transition to Canada, offering information and tangible aid in areas like housing, employment, and training. These included the Italian Immigrant Aid Society and the Centro Organizzativo Scuole Tecniche Italiane, which helped newcomers obtain work and offered English lessons in preparation for professional certification and licensing exams.

By the late sixties, COSTI had opened offices throughout Toronto, Hamilton, and North York; it became a United Way member agency and expanded its focus to the wider immigrant community, notably reaching out to Vietnamese newcomers in the seventies. In 1981, it amalgamated with the Italian Immigrant Aid Society to form COSTI-IIAS Immigrant Services. Its work continues today; recently, COSTI has been active in addressing the refugee crisis provoked by the Syrian Civil War, and it now provides services to approximately 39,000 new Canadians in more than sixty languages.

Meanwhile, the postwar era saw the rise of the welfare system and the expansion of the insurance industry, diminishing the role of mutual-aid societies in maintaining a social safety net. Increasingly, Italian Canadians gathered into organizations based on regional, religious, and social affinity.

The Toronto chapter of the Canadian Italian Businessman's Association, later renamed the Canadian Italian Business and Professional Association, was founded in 1952 and incorporated in 1956 (the first Canadian chapter was Montreal's, founded in 1949). Its express goals were threefold: assisting new immigrants, supporting charities, and undertaking fundraising in the wake of natural disasters—one early and notable effort in this regard was the response to the 1951 Po Valley flood, which killed eighty-four people and left 180,000 homeless. CIBPA thrives today as a vital professional network in the GTA, and remains active in local charitable contributions—including the decades of work performed by Villa Charities.

Villa Charities originated in 1971 as the Italian Canadian Benevolent Corporation (ICBC), with the express purpose of providing seniors' housing. An ICBC feasibility study noted that Italians comprised the largest non-British ethnic group in Toronto, and that over 12 per cent of that cohort was over the age of sixty. Highlighting the theme of celebrating seniors, the ICBC used its inaugural ball to crown the winner of the Oldest Italian Contest, 101-year-old Cristina Cardona.

An intensive fundraising campaign ensued, with hundreds of events and a lottery to rally community support for the endeavour. Nearly fifty Italian Canadian clubs, unions, churches, and other organizations offered support. Construction began on a property on Playfair Avenue, near Dufferin and Lawrence; nearby community mainstays included St. Charles Borromeo Church, Dante Alighieri Academy, and Regina Mundi Catholic School. One of the most visible and effective ICBC fundraising activities was established in the early 1970s: an annual Mother's Day Telethon, aired on Citytv. All told, nearly ten thousand individuals and groups donated. In April 1975, the completion of the exterior structure was commemorated in a ceremony that saw Italian and Canadian flags raised over the roof. The home, Villa Colombo, was officially opened in April 1976. (Twenty-three years later, Joseph Culizia—president and CEO of its managing company, UniversalCare Canada Inc., would be honoured with the ICCO Community Building Award.)

The project was not simply a question of housing. For his book "Eh, Paesan: Being Italian in Toronto," social anthropologist Nicholas De Maria Harney, now at the University of Windsor, spoke to people heavily involved with the project at all levels—planning, funding, construction. They described a concerted effort to create, not merely a place to live, but a place that evoked Italian identity, going so far as to install a piazza and fountain to encourage the type of socialization familiar from the homeland. A word that surfaces repeatedly in these interviews is "pride." The goal was pride in two directions: pride in Italian origins and culture; pride in being a vital contributing force within Canadian society.

On the evening of May 6, 1976, Terremoto del Friuli struck. The massive earthquake devastated seventy-seven villages in Friuli, leaving more than 150,000 residents homeless, 2,400 injured, and nearly a thousand dead. The tragedy led to the creation of the Protezione Civile, and in Toronto it unleashed an outpouring of support from the Italian Canadian community. Repurposed as a quake relief fundraiser, the Mother's Day Telethon raised more than $700,000.

Through the 1980s and '90s, Villa Charities construction continued apace. The Columbus Centre, a community and culture hub, went up in 1980. Three years later, Caboto Terrace was completed, providing lodging for independent seniors. In 1987, federal and provincial ministers convened at the Columbus Centre to officially open the Joseph D. Carrier Art Gallery. And still more seniors' housing became available with the 1990 completion of Casa DelZotto. In 2004 ICBC—which had since changed its name to Villa Charities—opened an additional two facilities: a Vaughan version of Villa Colombo; and Casa Abruzzo, a 175-unit home for independent seniors.

Another vital aspect of ICBC/Villa Charities' outreach is Vita Community Living Services, established in 1986 to provide services for developmentally challenged adults. Vita CLS has since joined forces with Mens Sana, which focuses on mental health, and today offers a range of clinical, educational, treatment, and community participation services.

Over the decades that Villa Charities took a major role in philanthropy and heritage celebration, many other groups arose to bolster and celebrate the GTA's Italian Canadian community. The Italian Chamber of Commerce of Ontario was formally established in 1961, and has thrived since as an economic force, alongside its counterparts in Montreal, Vancouver, and throughout North America. The late sixties inaugurated the Federation of Italian Canadian Associations and Clubs, which morphed into the National Congress of Italian Canadians in 1974. Its efforts have included a push, starting in 1990, to prompt apology and compensation from the federal government for internment of Italian Canadians in wartime; this came closest to realization in 2009, when Montreal MP Massimo Pacetti introduced Bill C-302, the Italian Canadian Recognition and Restitution Act, which passed the House of Commons in 2010 but did not ultimately become law. Despite mixed reception among Italian Canadians, the effort did raise awareness of a relatively little-known aspect of Canadian history.

Italian Canadians in the labour movement had a significant role throughout the latter half of the century, particularly starting in 1960, when five Italian workers were killed digging a tunnel under the Don River, which collapsed, and another digger was buried alive in a dockyard accident. Major strikes and demonstrations followed—complete with derisive coverage in the English-language press—but ultimately bore fruit with government regulatory reviews and collective agreements. Unions today continue to contribute to working conditions and charitable causes alike; one example is the quarter-century-old Nick Barbieri Charity Bocce Ball Tournament, organized by Laborers' International Union of North America Local 506 and named after one of the local's beloved members. The Almagamated Clothing Workers of America is another union with a particularly strong Italian membership.

Recognizing that the Archdiocese of Toronto was an increasingly diverse jurisdiction that couldn't necessarily be run by blanket fiat, Archbishop Philip Pocock established the Italian Pastoral Commission in the early 1970s, which gave Italian-speaking priests and parishes a stronger voice within the city's Catholic Church. In addition to empowering Italian Canadian congregations and their leaders, the commission served as a forerunner to the Ethnic Pastoral Councils, which would serve the city's Portuguese, Hispanic, Polish, Filipino, and Vietnamese parishes.

In 1974, the Sisters of St. John the Baptist, the community of St. Charles Borromeo Church, and the Metropolitan Separate School Board (now the Toronto Catholic District School Board) co-founded Dante Alighieri Academy to serve the predominantly Italian Canadian population of Lawrence Heights. Two years later, with Prime Minister Pierre Trudeau exhorting Canadians to embrace multiculturalism, Alberto Di Giovanni established the Centro Scuola e Cultura Italiana. A native of Roccamorice, Abruzzo (where, in 2011, he helped create the Centro d'Arte e Cultura that bears his name), served as the school's director for thirty-five years, overseeing Italian lessons and, starting in the mid-eighties, trips to Italy for students of the language.

In 1996, Pope John Paul II bestowed the Cross Eccelsia Et Pontifice on Bruno Suppa. This was one of many awards, local and international, that Suppa would receive over his lifetime (he also received honours from the Ontario government, the Toronto District Catholic School Board, the National Congress of Italians, and the president of Italy—the latter naming him Cavaliere in 2013). It recognized the Vallelonga native's contributions to many crucial organizations in the life of the GTA Italian Canadian community, including COSTI, the National Congress of Italian Canadians, Villa Charities, and the Precious Blood Fathers and Brothers Mission Projects. This as on top of his contributions in leadership roles at the Metropolitan Separate School Board, the Immigration Appeal Board, and the Court of Canadian Citizenship, under whose auspices he bestowed citizenship on more than seven thousand new Canadians.

As the century entered its last half-decade, a group of businesspeople, convinced of the benefits of community-based banking on a small scale, began efforts to create an Italian Canadian financial institution. This came to fruition at the cusp of the millennium with the incorporation of IC Savings and Credit Union in April 2000. The list of founders includes many prominent contributors to Italian Canadian philanthropy in the GTA, such as Masters Insurance co-founder Sam Ciccolini—well known for his involvement in Sick Kids, Villa Charities, and the Sisters of the Sacred Heart—Fausto Gaudio, who has served as a director for VITA Community Living and was a founding member of the Calabrian Benevolent Association of Ontario, and World War II Royal Navy veteran James Mizzoni, founding member of the Columbus Lions Club and former CIBPA secretary.

By the beginning of the twenty-first century, the Italian Canadian community in the GTA had established a rich, fruitful history of philanthropy and community-building. The focus had largely been on charity and cultural heritage. Philanthropy in contemporary culture and arts, however, was not as prominent—Toronto's cultural institutions traditionally had been perceived as elitist outposts of the Anglo-Canadian establishment. Enter Tony Gagliano.

As CEO of St. Joseph Communications, a major publishing enterprise that included such magazines as Toronto Life and Canadian Family in its stable, Gagliano was eager to boost the profile of Italian Canadian philanthropy in the arts and culture sector. One evening in 2006 he met with restaurateur Felice Sabatino, developer and prolific philanthropist Mario Romano, and former Villa Charities president Toni Varone for dinner at Sabatino's Via Allegro restaurant in Etobicoke. They discussed the idea of pooling donations from prominent Italian Canadians into a single, impactful gift to a high-profile cultural institution. Thus was born the concept that would become the Galleria Italia, a stunning Frank Gehry–designed sculpture promenade that is now one of the defining architectural features of the landmark building.

SAM CICCOLINI

Gagliano was on the Art Gallery of Ontario board of trustees (he would go on to serve as gallery president from 2009 to 2013), and he was the driving force in rallying donations. Eventually, twenty-six Italian Canadian families gave $13 million towards the construction. Unusually in the realm of mega-donations and names on museum wings and galleries, the

GALLERIA ITALIA; PHOTO: ETHAN

space was named not for a donor or corporate sponsor but after Italy itself. "I saw the opportunity... to bring a community together," Gagliano told the Toronto Star, "and name a space, not after one family or one organization, but name a space after a culture and a country." He also said he conceived of the project partly as a tribute to his parents, who had immigrated to Canada in the mid-twentieth century, and their generation: "We've been given so much as a generation. This is an opportunity for us to do something for this country, to do something for the next generation as well."

Meanwhile, Gagliano had joined forces with David Pecault of Boston Consulting Group to establish Luminato, the annual arts/culture/ideas festival that launched in June 2007. Its inaugural instalment brought more than 1,500 artists to thirty venues across the city and attracted more than a million attendees; through 2019, the festival had cumulatively showcased more than 15,000 artists from over forty nations. Its impact on the civic artscape is incalculable, and it has become a source of pride throughout the GTA. According to the festival's 2018 annual report, 90 per cent of ticket buyers are "proud that Toronto can host an event like Luminato."

In 2009, another massive earthquake afflicted Italy. This time, the epicentre was in L'Aquila, Abruzzo, and devastation occurred throughout central Italy, with more than three hundred fatalities and aftershocks that numbered in the thousands. Prime Minister Stephen Harper reached out to Senator Consiglio Di Nino (who has been heavily involved as a leader in many of the charities mentioned throughout this article), who was travelling abroad at the time, to ask whether his relatives in Abruzzo were safe. They were, but the crisis remained dire. Further conversations between the senator and the PM eventually led to the construction of a $5 million student centre at the University of L'Aquila.

Within days of the disaster, volunteers under the leadership of Villa Charities had formed the Abruzzo Earthquake Relief Fund (AERF), which installed Frank Iacobucci, the former Supreme Court judge, as its honorary chair. The fundraising was immediate and prolific. Centro Scuola students raised $100,000. A luncheon featuring Sergio Marchionne of Fiat Chrysler contributed $600,000. That autumn, the Walk for Abruzzo, sponsored by the Carpenters Union Local 27, raised $60,000.

In April 2015, Villa Charities teamed up with the Toronto General & Western Hospital Foundation to host a fundraiser, paying tribute to two Italian Canadian "Pioneers in Excellence": Dr. Fred Gentili, inaugural director of the Skull Base Centre at the University of Toronto, who had made notable advancements and innovations in neurological surgery; and visionary developer Fred De Gasperis, who had passed away two years previous. The event raised $4.2 million. (De Gasperis, the legendary self-made billionaire, was a leading philanthropist and donor to the Toronto General Hospital and World Vision, among other charities; his family continues that tradition of philanthropy to this day.)

In 2017, in response to two more major earthquakes in Italy in two consecutive years (2016 and 2017), the AERF was reconfigured as TIERF (the Italy Earthquake Relief Fund). Aimed at providing long-term assistance for Amatrice, Accumoli, Arquata del Tronto, and Pescara del Tronto. Buoyed by organizational support from groups like the Canadian Italian Business & Professional Association, Centro Scuola e Cultura Italiana, Italian Chamber of Commerce of Ontario Canada, National Congress of Italian-Canadians, IC Savings, Order Sons and Daughters of Italy of Canada, Canadian Italian Heritage Foundation, the fund raised over $2.5 million dollars for the cause.

TIERF's work continues to this day. With an eye on permanent relief for affected regions, the organization has raised over $1.6 million—an amount that has doubled thanks to the federal government's pledge to match every dollar donated. In 2018, TIERF president Toni Varone, in recognition for his efforts on behalf of earthquake victims and for his philanthropy and entrepreneurship generally, was awarded the Premio Italia nel Mondo.

A primary concern—and sometimes a source of division—within post-war Italian Canadian organizations was supporting, promoting, and honouring the contribution of Italian Canadians to Canada, raising awareness of the incalculable contributions Italian Canadians have made to the fabric of this nation. In 2016, as plans solidified for Canada 150, a coast-to-coast celebration of the nation's century-and-a-half birthday, the Canadian Italian Heritage Foundation and the National Congress of Italian Canadians, Toronto District, urged the federal government to designate June as the national Italian Heritage Month. In a press release announcing the push, Italian Heritage Canada said: "The designation is significant to all Canadians of Italian origin in Ontario as it serves to acknowledge and validate all of the hard work and sacrifices of past generations who have left the security of their country of birth to arrive in a new land and make it their home." That campaign succeeded, and in May 2017, the federal government announced the new designation; Mélanie Joly, minister of Canadian Heritage, invited "all Canadians to learn more about the rich heritage of our fellow citizens of Italian origin and the inspirational role that they have played and continue to play in our country."

Individual, families, and organizations throughout the GTA's Italian Canadian community are carrying this legacy of philanthropy and community-building into the future. And they continue to rally to the aid of Italy when perils arise there. As this book was being assembled, the COVID-19 pandemic had the world on shutdown. At the time of writing, Ontario was a month into a state of emergency, and the premier had recently announced an extension of the province-wide lockdown. Worldwide, populations were reeling from the medical catastrophe and its economic and social side effects, and Italy was one of the nations hardest hit. The Italy COVID-19 Response Appeal, spearheaded by the Embassy of Italy in Canada and the Canadian Red Cross, was mustering donations to bolster medical supplies, ambulance services, and support to Italy's Ministry of Health. This cause, and other misfortunes to come, will continue to inspire Italian Canadians in the GTA to consolidate community support and reach out with aid whenever the homeland calls for it.

Over the last century and a half, the story of Italian Canadians in Toronto has been an epic chronicle of toil, hardship, hope, faith, and ultimately triumph. Like many immigrant communities, this one started small and endured overt, widespread discrimination. Out of necessity, it banded together for mutual aid, and out of altruism it came together to contribute to the wellbeing of its own, of its homeland, and of the larger society in which it found itself. Although the twentieth century brought many dark days, for the world overall and for Italian Canadians in particular, the resilience and optimism of this community—fuelled by the mainstays of family and faith—saw it prevail as a great force for good in the GTA.

DAVID PECAULT AND TONY GAGLIANO

2018

ICCO CANADA

THE ITALIAN CHAMBER OF COMMERCE OF ONTARIO CANADA SIXTY YEARS OF TRANSFORMATION

SARA RELLINI

GETTING STARTED: THE 1960S

Sixty years ago, the Italian Chamber of Commerce of Toronto started its adventure at 159 Bay Street, in the heart of Toronto's business district. At an anniversary celebration twenty-five years later, Ron Farano gave a speech commemorating the Chamber's origins. "It was composed by a group of businessmen from Toronto," Farano recalled, "put together by the Console Generale De Rege, who decided that it was probably a good thing to have an Italian Chamber of Commerce representing the unity between the two countries with the idea of developing trade links and cultural links. It was much smaller then, considerably less influential." Antonio Valeri, the first Managing Director, was vital to the early success of the Chamber, dedicating his life and passion to it.

Originally from Abruzzo, he arrived in Canada in 1961. He settled in Hamilton and started as a waiter at an Italian restaurant, but soon decided to move to Toronto and seek opportunities more suited to his skills. He found a new occupation as proofreader and City Editor for the Italian newspaper *Corriere Canadese*. In 1963, with the help of other Italian professionals, he founded COSTI, a school designed to help immigrants learn trades they could practise in Canada. Later that year, he was hired by the Royal Bank of Canada as an assistant accountant. After only eighteen months, he was promoted to Branch Assistant Manager. Valeri was the Chamber's original Managing Director, and in 1978 he became President, a position he held for the rest of his life. His passion for journalism inspired him to found the highly successful magazine *Italy Canada Trade* to promote the "Made in Italy" brand in Canadian markets. In 1983, the publication received the coveted Gold Mercury Award in Rome. As the voice of trade between Italy and Canada, it dedicated space to such Italian industries as handicrafts, fashion, food and wine.

Like Antonio Valeri, Ronald Farano is considered a major early figure in the Chamber's history. From 1966 to 1970, he held the position of President, after which he became Managing Director and, from 1990 until his passing away, he continued as Chairman. He was an esteemed lawyer, and in the pages of *Italy Canada Trade* magazine gave great lessons about business ethics and the challenges facing the Chamber and its members. It is impossible to discuss the

RON FARANO, 1989

Chamber without mentioning Farano—he was there for each and every event as the Chamber's representative. He dedicated his knowledge, leadership and charisma to the Chamber and its members. In September 2006, Farano was honoured by the Government of Italy as a Knight of the Order of Merit of the Republic of Italy. He proudly carried the title of "Cavaliere." As the Taylor family wrote in the blog *A Celebration of Farano's Life*, "when Ron was awarded the title of Cavaliere, I searched for a definition in English. A Cavaliere is a man of honour and loyalty, a gallant and chivalrous man, a gentleman in every way." He passed away on May 23, 2010, but his presence continues through the ICCO Ron Farano Mentorship Program created by ICCO's youth division, ICCO Forward, whose objective is to create a bridge between generations and provide an opportunity for personal, professional and cultural growth.

From the beginning, the Chamber was concerned not only with business and trade, but with Italian affairs in general. In 1963, when a landslide at the Vajont Dam ravaged the Piave Valley, Valeri and the Chamber organized a solidarity campaign. Earthquakes at Belice (1968), Friuli (1976) and Cilento (1980) prompted the Chamber to get involved. For these causes, Valeri raised $300,000 in relief donations through the Chamber's channels. In 2009, the Chamber was part of the Abruzzi earthquake relief fund created to help the people of L'Aquila, the capital of Abruzzo, when they were devastated by one of the most terrible earthquakes in Italian history.

REACHING OUT: THE 1970S AND 1980S

Starting in the 1970s, Valeri and the Chamber organized a variety of trade missions representing almost every Italian region. One of the first of these brought a delegation from Abruzzo to Toronto to display crafts and other traditional local products and arranged for then-Ontario Premier William Davis to visit Abruzzo. Representatives from Lombardia came to Toronto a year later, followed by a delegation from Friuli Venezia-Giulia. The eighties began with changes to the Board of Directors: Antonio Valeri became the President and Ron Farano the Managing Director. New trade missions promoting tourism and local crafts reached out to Abruzzo, Calabria and Umbria. Delegations from those regions were welcomed in Toronto by the Chamber staff and representatives from Canadian companies that recognized the business opportunities offered by the effort and enthusiasm of the organization.

A DECADE OF CHANGE: THE 1990S

On May 19, 1990, the Chamber, its members and the whole Italian Canadian community paid their last respects to Antonio Valeri. His wife, Concetta Valeri, would continue his work by becoming the Executive Director and working with Arturo Pelliccione, President of the Chamber from 1990 to 2002.

The 1990s brought new challenges to businesses; globalization and new technologies were rapidly reshaping communications, trades and business. In May 1991, the "Marco Polo Meeting," a trade event organized by the Fiera di Milano (trade show organizer in Milan) was held in Toronto for the first time. The Chamber, since its inception, had played an important role in advertising and supporting the Fiera. Every year, the Chamber celebrated its anniversary with a gala dinner and a special issue of its magazine dedicated to this very important trading event, which became a destination for most of Toronto's prominent Italian Canadian businesspeople. This increase in participation is one of the Chamber's great achievements.

CONCETTA VALERI

In the summer 1996 issue of *Italy Canada Trade*, Chamber President Arturo Pelliccione announced the launch of the Chamber's website. The Chamber continued its trade missions targeting specific Italian regions. In March 1998, for example, the ICCT received a delegation of Italian businesspeople from Parma, who wanted to meet with Canadian companies in the food packaging/processing industry to initiate a commercial collaboration. In April, they accompanied a Canadian delegation to Verona for the Vinitaly wine show. There, the delegates had the opportunity to visit several vineyards in Emilia Romagna and Tuscany, sampling world-class wines and learning about the techniques involved in their preparation. Many of the delegations the Chamber hosted under his mandate had been in non-traditional sectors such as biotech, high-technology and investments, but they could reach their objectives because the Chamber was able to expand the services it provided to its members.

In November of the same year, Nivo Angelone was elected President of the Chamber. The word the new President liked and believed the most was "multiculturalism." In his promotion of Canada as an excellent country where Italian business could have great opportunities, he stressed this concept because, in his opinion, the business community needed to be aware of how to take advantage of "the harmony of a multicultural community that creates a

NIVO ANGELONE

wonderful working environment for people to do business together" (from *Partners*, Spring 2005). In these years Nick Simone was hired as Executive Director. In 2005 Nivo Angelone was honoured with the title of Commendatore dell' Ordine della Stella della Solidarietà Italiana, a recognition of Italians abroad for their contribution in rebuilding Italy after the war.

Corrado Paina became the Chamber's Executive Director in 2006, after six years spent growing the Chamber as Deputy Director. His

CORRADO PAINA

creation of *Partners* magazine expanded on the original concept of *Italy Canada Trade* by engaging with a wider variety of business and cultural leaders and included everything from retrospective profiles of the great Italian design house Missoni, to interviews with lead-ing politicians like Prime Minister Stephen Harper. By working first with Nivo Angelone and later, George Visintin, he has pushed the Chamber and its members to play a central leadership role in municipal, provincial and federal arenas. He began in 2003, at the municipal level by organizing the twinning of the cities of Milan and Toronto. He has continued this outreach by creating the Greater Toronto Business Alliance (GTBA), an alliance of the ICCO Canada, the Toronto Chinese Business Association, the Indo-Canada Chamber of Commerce and the Federation of Portuguese Canadian Business and Professionals, with the goal of showing the federal government that the chambers of commerce in Canada are not simply representative organizations, but have become a new and particular business reality in this multicultural country. Paina believes that the mandate of the various chambers and their connection to home markets could serve as a prototype for cost-effective Canadian business centres all over the world.

The ever-widening networking capabilities of the ICCO Canada was perhaps most evident when the "Lombardia Agreement" was signed in April 2009 by Ontario's Premier Dalton McGuinty and Lombardy President Roberto Formigoni. It is a contract that ratifies the collaboration between the two provinces in fields of bio-technology, bio-medicine, R&D, environment, aeronautics and advanced technologies. The Chamber helped mediate the meeting of the Ontario Government with the delegation of 15 companies from Lombardy led by Formigoni. The relationship with the provincial government remains strong and the ICCO Canada has a contract with Ontario to facilitate trade with Italy. When asked why he has spent so much of his time building business networks and lobbying governments, Paina has an immediate response: "I feel strongly that we are in a phase where all the business organizations in the Italian community must unite to send a more effective message to governments in order to make sure that the voice of the Italian Canadian community is heard and recognized. We must promote our excellence at any level—at a business level offering markets for expansion, new networks where business can flourish—and at a social and cultural level where our people can be protagonists not only in the international and national business community but in the international and national scene."

In 2008 Nivo Angelone passed the presidency to George Visintin who well understood that globalization was permeating more and more areas of business, especially in Italy, where small and medium-sized companies needed to look beyond their national borders to discover new markets and diversify. The vibrant mood of these years affected the activity of the Chamber and its crucial role not only in Toronto but throughout the province of Ontario. So, after years of discussion, in 2010 the Chamber changed its name to the Italian Chamber of Commerce of Ontario (ICCO). In what has become the most important annual ICCO event, the Business Excellence Awards Gala was inaugurated on May 15, 2003, to recognize and honour individuals in the business community who demonstrate excellence in their field, such as Sergio Marchionne, who won the President's Award in 2006. Almost 450 members, friends and government officials attended the inaugural banquet, and that number has increased significantly year after year. The 2011 banquet celebrated the Chamber's fiftieth anniversary. Despite all the changes and challenges that the decades have brought, the Chamber continues its work with the energy and passion exemplified by its founders.

GEORGE VISINTIN

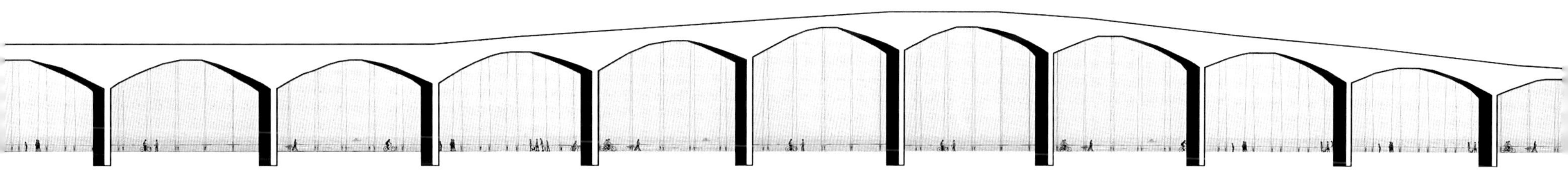

VAUGHAN
VOTES

PHOTO CREDIT: GIULIA STORTI

THE THREE Fs

MICHAEL GENOVA
DIRECTOR OF COMMUNICATIONS, CITY OF VAUGHAN

"When we think about that Italian Canadian connection, it is the three Fs. It's family, it's food, and it's faith. And the faith component is very key."

ICCO CANADA: You work for the city of Vaughan which has a strong Italian Canadian population yet you live in Missisauga. Why do you stay there?

GENOVA: I grew up in South Mississauga, the Lakeshore area, where everyone was principally Italian, Portuguese, Eastern European. And so, we had a connection through the elementary school, the church, then we all went to the same high school. Now we all stay in touch. We went from meeting in kindergarten to being barely men with children. And a lot of that had to do with the connections our families had, being Italian and being connected through our local parish. So, there's another reason I can't move.

ICCO CANADA: Yes, the parish thing. That's a whole family.

GENOVA: Absolutely. When we think about that Italian Canadian connection, it is the three Fs. It's family, it's food, and it's faith. And the faith component is very key.

ICCO CANADA: How does that affect your work here? Your job is to go out into the community, to communicate and intersect, and you also do pastoral care within the church. You see a connection there?

GENOVA: For sure. Whether it's a municipality or a non-profit group or a faith community, what they're ultimately trying to do is to safeguard and elevate the quality of life for people and for neighbours—it all overlaps entirely.

ICCO CANADA: I understand you did your BA in political science and history, and then a master's in political science, with a focus on elections.

GENOVA: That's right. I did an undergraduate degree at the University of Toronto, political science, history, and American studies. And then I went off and did a master's in political science with a concentration in elections and campaign management. And I went to Fordham University, which is located in the Bronx. I lived on Arthur Avenue, the original Little Italy of New York City. It was 2007, 2008, which was a fairly historic presidential election year. That was when Hillary Clinton was running against Barack Obama in the Democratic primary. But then on the Republican side, I had the opportunity to intern for Rudy Giuliani on his presidential campaign. I was in his headquarters as an intern in the finance office. It was very telling to see that Italian American connection, because New York, of course, is famous for larger than life Italian American elected officials, Rudy Giuliani being one of them, but also someone like Mario Cuomo, or Andrew Cuomo, his son, who's the current Governor of New York. So, I did that political science program, and after I graduated, I went off and I worked in politics. So, principally, I was at Queens Park working in a variety of different communications roles for the Ontario PC caucus when it was in opposition, and then I also worked for a member of Parliament, Gary Goodyear, who was a minister and an MP.

ICCO CANADA: And those were your first jobs after school?

GENOVA: Yeah. I would say those were my jobs out of school. And then, along the way, I got an opportunity to join the Brampton mayor's office as a press secretary. And so, I joined that in December of 2012, and the moment I arrived, I loved every minute of it. By the end of my first week, I had decided that I wanted to go back to school on a part-time basis to do a master's in public administration and local government. This is a program that's offered by Western, which really specializes in this role. Applied by January, accepted by February of 2013, and then completed that program in 2016. So, I worked for Mayor Fennell for two years, and then the election did not work out for her, so I was retired early, and then had the opportunity to then go join Mayor Bonnie Crombie's office, at the City of Mississauga. Eventually an opportunity came up to apply to the City of Vaughan to be director of communications, and that's how I ended up here. My department includes three business units, communications, stakeholder and community engagement, and intergovernmental relations.

ICCO CANADA: How many people would work under you for that?

GENOVA: So, in total, there's 15 of us on the team.

ICCO CANADA: It seems like you had a pretty clear idea of what you wanted to do all along. Were you a policy wonk in elementary school?

GENOVA: That's actually spot on. I've always loved politics. Speaking of being a wonk, I remember in 1993, I was seven, eight years old, and I watched the '93 election by myself. I was just a kid. I put it on TV, and something sparked. I've loved politics ever since. I volunteered in politics. I think the first election would have been 2000 actually, so I was 15 years old.

ICCO CANADA: So, when you went to do your BA, did you have a clear idea in mind that you wanted to go into the political world?

GENOVA: Yeah, entirely.

ICCO CANADA: So, you knew in high school?

GENOVA: I would say even elementary school.

ICCO CANADA: Really?

GENOVA: Yeah. I knew that I wanted to do political science. I knew that I wanted to go to the University of Toronto. I knew that I wanted to go to Victoria College at U of T because that's the school of Lester Pearson. And then what was pretty exciting was the Fordham Program that I did. When I entered it, it was only the second or third year that the program existed. And it's a new movement that's now happening: applied politics. And that is, people clearly see being in politics as a profession. I think Fordham was one of three schools in the United States that existed, the others being George Washington and the University of Akron. Nothing like this existed in Canada. Today, you can go to Carleton to do a similar program that I did at Fordham. But I remember finding that program. I was an intern for Case Ootes, who was a former deputy mayor of Toronto in 2006, and I found it online and I just knew when I found it.

ICCO CANADA: Right. So, you shifted into municipal politics early on. Why municipal, and not provincial or federal?

GENOVA: What I love about municipal is it's the opportunity to immediately be in government. You don't have to worry about the government/opposition divide. You work very closely with the elected officials, with Council, with the mayor. And cities really are transforming the way we live, the way we think, our approaches to policy. Speaking of being a wonk, a policy area that I'm really passionate about more than anything is education. And normally, we don't think of education as being part of the jurisdiction of municipalities. We think of it as provincial. I don't believe that's the case whatsoever. I really believe that municipalities need to plan cities with an education lens. What can be done to make it easier for people to access education: getting to school—how's the transit being built, where are campuses being located? When I was in Brampton, I got to work on the post-secondary university strategy. When I was in Mississauga, I got to work very closely with UTM and Sheridan College. But under Mayor Bevilacqua, I've had the greatest opportunity of my career, to help support the mayor in his efforts to bring the first university to the city, and that is Niagara University. And I've been able to provide support from a communications lens all along the way. Mayor Bevilacqua was able to do that in an incredibly fast amount of time.

ICCO CANADA: It must also be challenging for elementary schools, because in Brampton and Vaughan, you've both grown so fast, you had to build schools to keep up with growth.

GENOVA: Oh, absolutely, and you have to work with the school boards. But what I would like to see, and I'm doing this sort of on my own time, is I'd like to create a SHSM program. SHSM stands for something along the lines of "Specialist High School Major" program. When you drive past an elementary, or a high school, certainly in Peel, you'll see a big banner outside, and it says a concentration in athletics or arts or environment. I think we need one in public service, in public administration. Fifty percent of all local government bureaucrats are retiring within the next eight years. There's an incredible opportunity.

ICCO CANADA: Just here, or in the GTA?

GENOVA: Across Ontario. It's an incredible opportunity for people to find well-paying jobs, but most importantly rewarding jobs. But how many people in high school—or even in university—know to have that hook? I didn't know it myself until I was 26 years old and already had a master's under my belt. So, what

I've tried to do with the Dufferin-Peel Catholic District School Board is work with them as much as possible to put these various opportunities on the radar. I've been part of an organization called CAMA, which is the Canadian Association of Municipal Ad-ministrators. They've launched a really great promotional campaign called *Making Life Happen*, and that's about encouraging people to work in local government. So, this is how I overlay my profession with my personal interests. And again, I just want to highlight, what Mayor Bevilacqua has been able to do on the Niagara University file, to me, really helps explain why I'm in this work and why I'd like to continue in this work.

ICCO CANADA: I just want to go back to when you worked for Mayor Fennell.

GENOVA: I was with her for the full last two years.

ICCO CANADA: Right. At the end of her long reign, she was constantly under attack. For the spending, the salary, for financial record-keeping. At that point, you're still a fairly neophyte media relations person, so that must have been trial by fire.

GENOVA: Yep.

ICCO CANADA: What did you learn from that?

GENOVA: You know what I learned? I learned to recite over and over in my head the words of Saint Francis of Assisi, "If you do what you want, if what you want is right and just, the rest will work itself out in the end." What I learned was in my position as an advisor, all I can do is advise and give the best advice possible. Ultimately, it is up to my superiors to make the final decision. But in the end, if you're giving advice based on what you think is right and just, and is in the best interest, not just of the individual but of the office and the organization, you continue to push it, and you continue to push it over and over, and you don't back down.

ICCO CANADA: So, did you learn things about that time that you would advise the next mayor differently, with Bonnie Crombie?

GENOVA: Entirely. And I think a good takeaway coming out of that was the importance of a mayor and their council working very closely together. This is something that Mayor Bevilacqua is very mindful of—he works very closely with his Council colleagues and is committed to ensuring that they are full partners in city building.

ICCO CANADA: And that was less so in Brampton? There was a lot of fighting between them, right?

GENOVA: I would say that's the root cause of it. You need to remember too, in local government, it's not like party politics. If you're a Councillor and I'm the Mayor, you will have been elected in your own right and you'll be re-elected in your own right. I didn't have anything to do with that, more times than not, because we run as independents. Can't say the same provincially or federally where you have party politics in place. The Prime Minister will, in some cases, appoint private citizens to be candidates in specific ridings, and then those individuals, if they win, go to Parliament, and then the Prime Minister will then appoint them into cabinet at his discretion. The Prime Minister also has the discretion to expel people from the party as well. A very different dynamic. And that's not the case locally: everyone is one vote. You have to work collaboratively together. And if you don't do that, you could find yourself in a similar situation that the former Brampton mayor found herself in.

ICCO CANADA: Also, inertia kind of governs who gets to be councillors of municipalities, because often, once an incumbent's there, they stay there.

GENOVA: Oh, entirely. Federally and provincially, too, you have a number of marginal constituencies, and the local candidate, they say, is worth only three percent of the vote. So, however the chips may fall, Andrew Scheer and Justin Trudeau and Jagmeet Singh have a lot to do with the success of the candidates.

ICCO CANADA: Right. So, when you went to Crombie's office how did the kind of work you did there differ from Fennel?

GENOVA: It was similar work: communications, media policy support. It was a fascinating time, because Mayor Crombie had won a very competitive election and succeeded the larger-than-life Hazel McCallion. It was just a fascinating time to be in local government. There was a new mayor in Toronto. There was a new mayor in Brampton. And there was just a general feeling of goodwill across the board, with the large Urban Mayors' Caucus of Ontario, of which Mayor Crombie's an active member, the Big City Mayors' Caucus, which again, Mayor Crombie's an active member. I'm from Mississauga, so I love the city. It was surreal to be in the Mississauga mayor's office. The first campaign I ever volunteered on was my local ward one councillor in Mississauga. So, it was really great to see everything come full circle.

VAUGHAN CITY HALL, PHOTO: MHSHEIKHOLESLAMI

ICCO CANADA: Vaughan only legally became the City of Vaughan in '91, which really wasn't that long ago. And it's experienced exponential growth. So, what kind of challenges does that put upon you?

GENOVA: Well, for communications, ultimately we have to be very top of mind of the types of developments that are happening, making sure that the public is properly informed of what the planning process might be. Really, Vaughan is unprecedented when you look at council agendas of how many planning items are there. But the challenge is also an opportunity. The Vaughan Metropolitan Centre, the downtown, is like no other. There is no other municipality outside of the city of Toronto that is serviced by the TTC subway. So you get to see these exciting new developments and investments come in. You get off the subway and there's the KPMG tower: a global company. Inside there is Miller Thompson: a global law firm. Across the street is the building of the PWC: another global company, with our first YMCA that's going to be built there. But for me, what I find even more exciting is that there's going to be a Vaughan Public Library branch, the 11th branch, located right in the downtown core, that students who are two blocks away at Niagara University will be able to use. There are plans for other developments to go up, and they're going through the approval process now: a hotel, convention centre, additional residential dwellings, additional commercial dwellings. When Vaughan is fully built out, 40% of the community will be green space.

ICCO CANADA: I notice, that the Trump era especially, has really shown how much and how often the information we receive is manipulated by bad actors or algorithms or by the media silos that we associate ourselves with. It must be a communication challenge.

GENOVA: Social media makes it easier for two-way communication. I understand that the president uses social media as a 21st century bully pulpit—certainly his prerogative. Engagement's one of our business units. So, if somebody is providing us feedback over social media, we take that very seriously because it's an opportunity to help improve our service levels. And then a lot of times, too, there's positive feedback we hear from members of the community. We have made a conscious decision, certainly since I've arrived, to ramp up the level of social media: out to the community, and out to members of the council so they can then share on their own platforms. We provide them social media content that they can use every Monday morning. That content can be provided with images; it's topical, it goes out in real time, and people can be kept informed to the best of their ability.

ICCO CANADA: When you have plans here for the city or crisis management that you have to do, do you find you can effectively get your message out to professional news organisations?

GENOVA: We try to actively inform them and make ourselves as accommodating as possible. It's a very competitive media cycle. At the City of Vaughan, we're not within driving distance. And when I say that, it's not like we're at Queen and University going over to Toronto City Hall where there are bureaus, physical office spaces set up. So, it has its challenges. But overall, I'd say we have a very productive working relationship with members of the media, and we have a great team here who are actively on the phone working with our media. Also, we need to remember the era of Tom Brokaw and Peter Mansbridge is over. There's a number of online outlets that will accurately hold us accountable and work with us to ensure that we are providing accurate information to the public on a number of different stories. So, it's not just the 6:00 pm news.

ICCO CANADA: There's a huge Italian community here. Does it have an effect on the city?

GENOVA: Well, I think it does have an effect in terms of the types of community events that take place, the types of delegations that come to the council. We'll get requests to hold events at City Hall, official proclamations, official flag raisings. When you have a robust community, of course, they're going to be proactive and proud to share their culture and heritage and their identity with the entire city. So, we see that also in our economic development efforts as well, the Italian Canadian Chamber of Commerce Ontario Canada is an important stakeholder; the Italian Consulate General is another important stakeholder. And you have those synergies, because in this day and age, people, if they are moving to a new community because a business is moving, the top of mind is, "Well, what's the quality of life there? How can I make those synergies for ... because it's not just a new home for my business, it's a home for my family as well." So, to have those connections through language, through identity, through faith, it does make a difference. Our diversity and our connections to the Italian community enriches both culturally and economically as well.

ICCO CANADA: How does it affect you personally?

GENOVA: It's like being at home.

ICCO CANADA: So, you've carved a pretty sure-footed path on your career travels, and you're pretty young. How do you see career opportunities for young people today? Italian young people in particular.

GENOVA: Anything is possible; you just have to want it. That's what it ultimately comes down to. How badly do you want something? If it doesn't work out, how do you take a step back and say, "From this setback, what are the hidden blessings? What can I learn from this?" Because nothing is a missed opportunity in life. I truly believe something better down the road is going to happen but you have to want it, whether you're an Italian Canadian, or whether you're 25, 15, or 45.

ICCO CANADA: As we head into the second, third, and fourth generation of Italian Canadians, how do you see the culture changing? You still have that "food, faith and family" culture in your own life that we associate with the community. Is that going to hold, do you think?

GENOVA: I think it holds and I actually think it gets stronger as you end up marrying into perhaps other cultures that have similar values as well, and the appreciation will always be there. I think the ability for people to more conveniently access information, to learn about their family's history, whether it's ancestry.com, or whether it's a simple search engine, and the freedom—as we live in more of a globalized world—to hop on a plane to go to your community, wherever that may be, makes a huge difference.

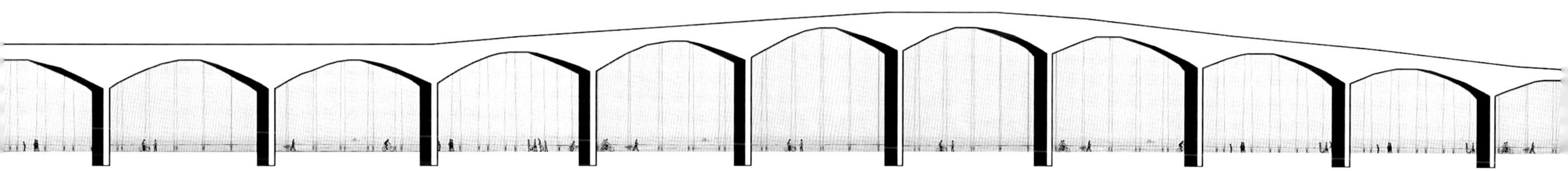

PHOTO CREDIT: GIULIA STORTI

WOMEN AND TECHNOLOGY
A PARTNERSHIP OF THE FUTURE

CLARA ANGOTTI
CO-FOUNDER & PRESIDENT, NEXT PATHWAY INC.

"I think technology has always had this idea of guys sitting in white shirts and in labs, not talking to each other in front of their computers and just coding all day. And if you look at what technology means today—it's about art, it's about math, it's about science, it's about creativity. There are so many more elements to it."

ICCO CANADA: Next Pathway is an automation cloud migration company. Can you give a little background, in simple terms, what that means and what challenges your service solutions address?

ANGOTTI: We help organizations migrate some of what we call 'legacy data warehouses'—storage facilities that maintained complex code and data on traditional servers that were typically in their offices. The movement to the cloud has a lot of operational benefits. When you use cloud storage, you only use the storage that you need, when you need it. You only pay for what you use. A lot of businesses are attracted to that proposition. The challenge is that what they have, legacy-wise, doesn't run on the cloud. You're talking about older traditional technology and code. It's not just a simple copy and paste to move that code and that data and think that it's going to work in the cloud. What companies have traditionally done, is say, "Okay, I'm not going to use that data and I'm going to start fresh in the cloud," which means they don't have any of that historical information to make insights on, or they'll say, "We will manually migrate and rewrite the code from one old system to the new system." And that takes months, sometimes years, and they have to test it. And then of course the businesses that are relying on that information with a lot of reporting have to retest all of their reporting in the cloud. It just doesn't work. And so, all of the beautiful operational benefits of the cloud sometimes can't be realized because of all of the technical complexity. What we've built is tools—think of it as a Google Translate—we take a code that's written in an older language and we run it through our processors and we basically translate it into a code that can be run in the cloud. It sounds really simple, but it's actually quite complex, because you can imagine the complexity of the code. Sometimes it looks like spaghetti and we have to figure out the pipelines. It's a lot of engineering talent. It's three years of research and development that's gone into doing this. So, when we say we automate the migration process, what I mean by that is we use technology to take what is written—ABC, translate it to XYZ, and it runs in the cloud.

ICCO CANADA: This is proprietary software you created? It didn't exist before?

ANGOTTI: Yes, it didn't exist before.

ICCO CANADA: When did you start Next Pathway?

ANGOTTI: We started I think in 2006.

ICCO CANADA: What was the focus of the company, because the cloud wasn't a big thing then?

ANGOTTI: That's exactly right. We started traditionally with professional services. Our base of customers were typically financial services in the downtown core in Toronto and then in New York, and we provided engineering and architectural services to companies that wanted to build new applications or manage their infrastructure. We did a number of different professional services. And then as we were looking at some of the development that we were doing, we couldn't help but notice certain opportunities that presented themselves and the cloud was one of them. And we said, "You know, this is something that we see missing that companies are going to need." So we started by building our cornerstone technology, which is a data lake that's built in the cloud. And then we realized that the next big challenge, once they've moved the data, is to move the code. And that's where we built Shift, which is the code migration technology. You know, success is one of those things where you can try for many, many years, and then you have the right product, the right time, the right audience.

ICCO CANADA: So when did Shift happen?

ANGOTTI: We built Shift over three years and it was launched in 2017. And then came Snowflake, which is a very new entry into the market, that builds data warehouses specifically to the cloud. They came to us early last year after doing a lot of research trying to find code migration tools, and seeing a lot of companies that claim to do what we do. We've created a license agreement with them. It's not exclusive, but it's a great validation that what we're building here in Canada is something that's very timely.

ICCO CANADA: So when you send it via cloud, are you using Azure or do you...

ANGOTTI: We run on Azure, we run on any cloud provider. The beautiful thing about our solution is that we're cloud agnostic. Whatever cloud a client wants, we can run on that.

ICCO CANADA: The technology sector moves so quickly, and you've seen so many changes already because we're all moving so much faster and further into the digital world. What changes affected you most since the company was founded and how did it affect the business mainly with Next Pathway?

ANGOTTI: I think the last 20 years or so have been interesting. The last 10 years have been a little bit quiet from a technology perspective. But in the last five years, with the advent of the cloud, there has emerged a lot of really interesting ideas in terms of the flexibility of migrating applications in code and data. People realizing how important data is to their business has spun a number of good and bad things about how people use data. It's created a whole interesting idea about how companies can compete with the right amount of information at their fingertips.

ICCO CANADA: Security must be a big issue—to take server farms that are in-house and to move them to the cloud.

ANGOTTI: Yes. The good thing is that it's not really our issue. Google and Amazon and Microsoft have spent billions of dollars ensuring the security of the cloud. So, for our purposes, I don't necessarily need to be overly concerned that the services that we provide and the products that we provide need to be relegated. We're just moving the code. I don't have to be burdened with that worry.

ICCO CANADA: Just to back up a little bit of history, you had two successful start-ups before this.

ANGOTTI: Right.

ICCO CANADA: Can you briefly give a description of what they are and how they relate to what you're doing now?

ANGOTTI: Our first company was Sage Information Consultants and we sold that in June of 2000 right at the peak of the dotcom boom. We provided professional services primarily in the Microsoft space and we built custom applications based on the Microsoft platform. And I think at that time it was good timing for us because it was really when online banking and e-commerce was starting to take shape. A lot of the banking customers that we had were still very much in brick and mortar. So, customers had to come in with their bank statements and do all their transactions inside the branch. And we assisted TD Bank with their first TD access PC, which was their first foray into online banking. I think that kind of set our company up for success and we ended up doing quite a bit of work in that area.

Then that business got commoditized. I think that's the one good thing about being an entrepreneur: you need to be able to understand when you have something that's really special and when to make the most of it, and then to move off of it when you realize that it's not really special anymore and it's been commoditized. What was happening in our business was that a lot of very large offshore companies were coming into the US, into Canada, and offering very cheap, very cost-effective development and we couldn't really compete with that. So we decided not to.

Then we went into an area where we knew there was still some interest and some specialty. At that time, email was becoming a lot more prevalent. People were moving off of Lotus Notes and onto Microsoft Exchange, but they didn't have a lot of experience in Microsoft Exchange, and so we built a very strong skill set and understanding of how to manage large email platforms. I'm talking hundreds of thousands of mailboxes: how to back them up, how to ensure that they were being replicated properly and all of the Edge services. That's exactly when Blackberries started becoming much more of a presence.

We had a managed service business that was called M Systems Group and we sold in 2006 to Bell. Then we took some time off and really thought about what we wanted to do. We built Next Pathway and we started with what we knew best, which was professional services, but we quickly started evolving that into building products.

ICCO CANADA: So Next Pathway is devoted to solving the problem that all businesses have with the legacy workloads they use. Technology moved so fast in the last 20 years and it has required constant updates to software, and the hardware horsepower to keep up with the expanding capabilities.

ANGOTTI: Right.

ICCO CANADA: But we are now at a point where computers bring more computing power to the average person than they are ever likely to need. Will this happen at the enterprise level you mentioned? With Next Pathway, it seems you've centered your business on this transformational moment, right?

ANGOTTI: Right.

ICCO CANADA: Or maybe it's not a transformational moment. Maybe there will always be legacy issues, because it seems like we have legacy products after three years—things become outdated so quickly.

ANGOTTI: No, that's true. But I think the legacy problem will eventually get resolved, but the thing is we will enjoy that ride for the next five years. We're constantly innovating in our office, so we're not going to necessarily ride on our laurels. You can see that the next things that are happening are with 'data exchanges.' So people are figuring out a way to monetize their data and they're putting them on data networks and opening that up so that people can decide. Maybe for example, for open banking, you may decide that you want to transfer one bank account to another bank account. Well today you have to complete a whole bunch of forms. You have to still do a lot of personal interaction with your bank. If it was open you could basically just do that electronically and have a much more open system. So I think the openness of where technology is going, is going to create more opportunities for innovation to take place and whoever comes up with the best idea first will have some staying power.

ICCO CANADA: I guess I'm trying to figure out whether there will eventually be some kind of common language that we all speak technologically. It seems everybody is agreeing on cloud as the way to go.

ANGOTTI: Yes. And the only way that open technology will work, is if we all agree on open standards. Right now the reason why you physically have to fill out paper when you want to open up a bank account or transfer money from one bank to another, or rent a car and whatnot, is that things are not open. Everybody has their own closed systems. When people start moving to the cloud, they will eventually adopt more open, what they call 'APIs,' and that will allow more free data flow and more data exchanges, and that will simplify things.

ICCO CANADA: Will that allow more entrepreneurs to participate?

ANGOTTI: I believe so, yes.

ICCO CANADA: Interesting. The tech sector is such a high wire act because it requires such expensive research and development before a product can be brought to market. As a result, risk and reward are both out-sized at either end of the spectrum. There are big failures and big wins.

ANGOTTI: Right.

ICCO CANADA: Do you find there is enough venture capital in Canada willing to take a risk on Canadian entrepreneurs?

ANGOTTI: It's a good question. What saddens me is that a lot of Canadian entrepreneurs tend to go to the US to make it big, and not only because there's more money there for investing, but there's a lot more revenue to be had there. Going forward, I think Canada needs to create an environment where entrepreneurs are valued. Whether it be tax breaks, or access to capital, Canadian companies need to recognize, "I want to support my Canadian entrepreneurs." It's a mind-shift to say, "What is best doesn't necessarily have to mean that it's foreign." The government needs to be a player in that. I think that there's more to be done there for sure.

ICCO CANADA: The question is, can Canadian companies scale internationally in the same way US companies are able to, because they throw so much money at them in the US?

ANGOTTI: Well what happens with most Canadian entrepreneurs is they hit a level of success and then they sell. We've seen that ourselves. We sold twice. And as you say, it's risk and reward, but it's also one of those things where you have to decide, "Is this the right time for me to sell and take the chips off the table and invest in something else, or do I parlay this into a much bigger operation?" You've got to have confidence that the market is willing to support you in that gamble. And so both times we've taken our chips off the table, whether it was at the right time or too soon. Certainly in the dotcom space, we timed that beautifully. Had we waited three more months, the company would not have been worth what we sold it for because of market speculation in the dotcom space.

But for our company today? I don't want to sell it too soon. I really want to see. I think there's a great deal of potential for our technology, and not only in Canada—we're selling a lot of our technology globally.

PHOTO CREDIT: GIULIA STORTI

ICCO CANADA: It seems like it should scale internationally quite well.

ANGOTTI: And it is scaling. A couple of things are happening—one is that internationally, people are seeing Canada as a good tech spot. It's not as fast as I would like, but I think people are realizing that while traditional San Francisco start-ups are doing good, that there are other places in the world that are also delivering some phenomenal innovation. And I think Canada is getting some of that attention.

ICCO CANADA: Do you feel government's doing enough to support innovation?

ANGOTTI: Honestly, I think government can always do more. If we said that government was doing great we'd be missing out on an opportunity. When I look at what the collective universe of entrepreneurs in Canada contribute to our GDP, it is quite significant. And then you see companies, for example, Amazon: when it was considering coming here to set up their head office, there were a number of concessions being brought forward to make Canada much more attractive to them. Those same attractions are not necessarily given to entrepreneurs because, as individuals, we don't necessarily contribute the same as an Amazon. But collectively when you look at the force of entrepreneurship in Canada, and I think that's how government needs to look at us, it is not just, "what can Next Pathway do for me today and tomorrow?" but, "what does the collective do for Canada?"

ICCO CANADA: So, to shift the conversation a little: Gender equality has been a big issue with a lot of bad stories in the tech field, but you've had such great success in your career. Are things getting easier for women since you started? And what are the major challenges for a woman starting out, particularly in the tech sector?

ANGOTTI: I think for women in the tech sector, or anywhere really, the more money we make and the more equal the playing field is from a monetary perspective with our male counterparts, the easier it's going to be for us to make choices. I think a lot of women are still required to fulfill very important roles at home as well as in the office. And that balance tends to be weighed in the context of how much money does a woman make versus her partner. If we want women to stay in the workforce, to be able to afford daycare for their children, to be able to take care of themselves mentally, physically, we need to pay them more. And that's going to keep them in the workforce longer. The number of female entrepreneurs is rising and the reason is that women are not given the same opportunity as men in traditional offices. They know they're not paid the same and they know they still have many more pressures than men do. And so they probably evaluate and they say, "Well I might as well work for myself. And that way at least I can have much more opportunity to make as much money as I want because I'm effectively paid for every hour that I work."

ICCO CANADA: Would you say it's a net positive for a young woman starting out these days?

ANGOTTI: I think it's a great opportunity. I think technology has always had this idea of guys sitting in white shirts and in labs, not talking to each other in front of their computers and just coding all day. And if you look at what technology means today—it's about art, it's about math, it's about science, it's about creativity. There are so many more elements to it. Every day that we're working requires a lot of creativity, and I find women as well as men have great skills in that area. And so those stigmas of what an engineer used to look like or what a software developer used to look like—I don't think those exist anymore. The jobs of the future probably also don't exist today because they're going to be a combination of so many things. Women tend to be very creative, good problem solvers and good communicators. Those are essential skills in technology.

ICCO CANADA: Are there singular opportunities within the sector—I'm talking about the future—where one should pay attention now, because that's going to be the next big thing or is it just that there's going to be opportunities everywhere?

ANGOTTI: Well I think to limit ourselves would be foolish. But if you look at anything relating to science and to mathematics, they will always be incredibly valuable. If you look at using artificial intelligence, understanding the logic of data and understanding its presentation and being able to make inferences around what the data means to what customers are feeling, what people *are*, what the pulse of individuals are like... that's just not only in basic finance. Look at it in health care—that's another area where artificial intelligence is becoming literally a game changer. I think that it's going to really impact our lives. I know that we deal a lot in enterprises, banking and stocks and groceries. But if you think about stuff that we all really care about, which is our health, we're going to see a great impact. Anybody that has a desire to do that is going to have a limitless opportunity.

ICCO CANADA: Family-run businesses are very common in the Italian Canadian community, but it's unusual for husbands and wives to work together at the top level of something of this scale. So not to be too personal, but how do you divide duties, resolve conflicts and separate out your personal life?

ANGOTTI: Right. Well, it's interesting. And you're not the first person who said this is unusual. People comment, "I could never work with my spouse." The thing with me and Chetan is that we started out working together, so it was more like work came first and then love came second. We weren't necessarily in any traditional roles per se and we were young when we started. So we sort of figured things out as we went in terms of the definition of our roles. As the business grew, we have very distinct responsibilities, although we do collaborate a lot and in fact, every office that we've had, we've shared. And that idea of us being able to bounce ideas off of each other and know that if we give any feedback, it comes from a place where it's intended to be a good place, as opposed to being critical for the sake of being critical. So we divide our roles—he's more on the sales and the strategy side. I'm more on the operations side, but we collaborate a lot. We also involve our personal life a lot. We're a family, so we operate as a family. We discuss what we're having for dinner and what we're going to do on the weekend and then we also talk about who's going to answer that email and how do we resolve that problem. It's all within the same breath.

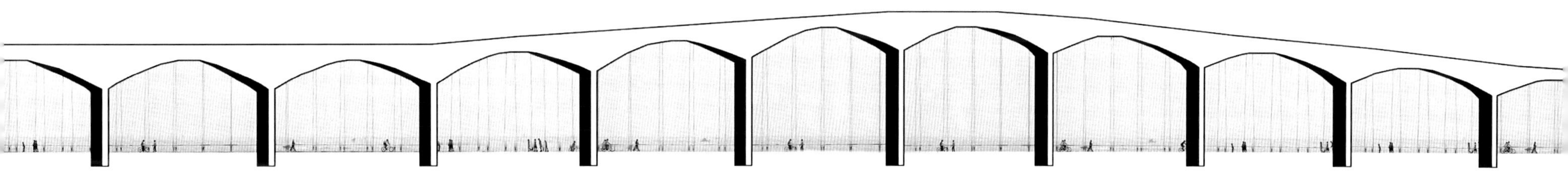

THE PATH TO SUCCESS

ENTREPRENEURSHIP AND VALUE CREATION

ANTHONY DI IORIO

CEO & FOUNDER OF DECENTRAL & JAXX, CO-FOUNDER OF ETHEREUM, TECHNOLOGIST, THOUGHT LEADER AND GLOBAL KEYNOTE SPEAKER.

"Every sector is going to be impacted by these technologies, just like the internet impacted information. The movement of value now, and agreements between people, are going to be automated and are going to have as much impact on people's lives as the internet did."

ICCO CANADA: You've been in the family business as a manufacturer of patio doors, you've been a DJ, run a web design company, experimented in geothermal drilling, and then were an investor in Bitcoin, and an innovator in the whole world of cryptocurrencies. What ties all these things together for you? Is there a common thread here? It doesn't seem like the most obvious progression if you don't mind me saying.

DI IORIO: I guess the common thread would probably be computers, and then entrepreneurship and learning, and then along the way tying all those things together to create a pretty good formula for trying to create value.

ICCO CANADA: So where did that entrepreneurship come from?

DI IORIO: I would say my father, he's always been a problem solver, a questioner of everything, someone that would go nuts until he solved the problem. He was an entrepreneur, and he liked to invent things. He's very good with his hands and fixing things. Problem solving really ties it all together.

A difference between me and my father is when you get into the technology side of things. He was involved in technology, but not necessarily with computers or tech per se. It was more about creating better products. I think my differentiation is maybe more aligned with the direction the world is going in terms of technology. And that was something that being born in the '70s, when personal computers were starting out, was big. Then the internet, and going through all that, and understanding where the world was heading. And then not just being a computer person but becoming an entrepreneur and being able to bring people together and work with employees and build teams.

ICCO CANADA: These are attributes that you associate with the Italian Canadian community because of the tight family, but also just the line of work that your family was in, as you were an early investor in real estate. Very common Italian Canadian thing to do, right? Making patio doors, investing in real estate, and then you really shifted to this new technology. Is the family supportive of that? Do they get what you do?

DI IORIO: Yes. I was building computers when I was eight years old. I've always been in technology and computers. And I didn't go to school for it because I knew it, and I thought it would be better to study business. So they've known I've always been a computer person. When I was punished, they'd take away my computer when I was a kid. So it's not really a change into anything new with technology. I've always been into seeing where the future is headed.

Economics has been something of interest to me since 2008 with what happened in the financial crisis and the housing crisis. That's where I really started delving into economics and limited government. I believe in individualism and volunteerism, so that everybody should be able to volunteer and enter into relationships—but not through coercion or force.

I've always been very big on doing things the way that I want to do them, and not be told what to do. And I don't like groups. I mean, the family thing on the Italian side, yeah, very much raised in that way, and having family dinners together, and I was involved in soccer and hockey. I guess I did learn a lot of little things from there, but the technology side was a little bit different.

ICCO CANADA: The use of cryptocurrencies has been gathering force for a number of years. You were there at the beginning really. But for the average person, it's very confusing to know which ones are secure and safe to use. We have six big banks in Canada. Will there ever be a similarly rational financial ecosystem with cryptocurrencies that will allow for people to contrast and compare services and security features as we do with regular banks?

DI IORIO: There will be. There's so much development and work that's being built on infrastructure and user experiences and trying to take this amazing technology and put it into something that the masses can understand and digest. So all of what you hear and what's been building up, it's very technical. A lot of new technologies are hard to understand, but everything's growing right now to the point that these technologies are going to be visible and available for their features in many different sectors, and a lot of financial activities.

Now you've got smart contracts on it—that is when you're talking about not just finance, you're talking about law, and the impact on insurance companies. Every sector is going to be impacted by these technologies, just like the internet impacted information. The movement of value now, and agreements between people, are going to be automated and are going to have as much impact on people's lives as the internet did.

So, yes, there will be a time when people will be using it. A lot of times they're not going to know they're using it, but the features of it will be used. Features such as trustworthiness and transparency, and all the things that the world needs these days to tackle the issues—mostly around trust.

Right now companies with technologies, like banks, are really not up to speed on where technology is. They're very much reliant on centralized systems that are prone to attack and they are going through disruption. And in the crypto space, you do have some people that take advantage of people not knowing what's going on, but that's not a technology thing, that's just a mankind thing.

The technologies are very sound, if used properly and understood properly. So it's not like they are to blame for people taking advantage of people. It's just very easy, when there is something technical, for people to get fooled and not understand things and be taken advantage of. But that's nothing to do with the space itself. It's to do, in general, with people.

ICCO CANADA: But you were the first chief digital officer for the TSE, right?

DI IORIO: Yes

ICCO CANADA: And you advised lots of clients like financial institutions. They're all going to undergo, presumably, a tremendous disruption. Banks especially make money by acting as a middleman for financial transactions. If money becomes virtual, cryptocurrency and the blockchain would make many of their services obsolete, wouldn't it? I mean, that has to be a major threat to their business. How do you advise them?

DI IORIO: Well, I mean, money is virtual right now, right? Everything is digital. There's very little paper money anymore, so it's already digital, and people are used to doing things digitally online. It's not much of a transition from what's occurring, except for things can be tracked better, people can have the ability to trust entities online, and know that code is going to make it so they can't be taken advantage of. And financial institutions are going to take advantage of these technologies, and they're going to utilize them. And the ones that actually do that first, I believe, and do it in a good enough way, will probably be the ones that excel in the future.

There are risks to these companies if they don't adapt and don't change and don't utilize the advantages of these technologies. And those that don't are going to be left behind, and those that do are going to do well. It's an opportunity, rather than a big risk; an opportunity to show that they could be more trustworthy and transparent to clients. These technologies provide so many solutions to world problems that are exacerbated by the internet.

There's going to be some issues that they're going to have. There's going to be a risk. But there's going to be much more opportunity that's going to emerge. You can see when the internet started, no one understood the amount of service work that was going to be created by it, and all the industries and businesses that started. And it's going to be the same thing for this space.

ICCO CANADA: So will some of the services at banks, or other sectors of the economy, become obsolete with the widespread usage of this technology?

DI IORIO: Yes, definitely.

ICCO CANADA: Can you give an example?

DI IORIO: The ways that lending is done is going to be different. People will be able to remove a lot of middlemen in terms of getting loans, and the payback of loans. It's just going to facilitate a lot more automation systems that can't be automated right now. And a lot of the non-value-added participants in the equation of middlemen right now are going to be cleared out. So it's going to radically change the way that loans are done, the way that real estate is tracked and maintained, and the way that digital assets move in terms of physical products. It's going to touch everything, just like the internet did.

ICCO CANADA: Would you say the government is supportive of this technology, aware of this technology, adapting to this technology?

DI IORIO: Very much aware of it—not very well understood—concerned with the impact on the people. There's going to be negative consequences, but there's going to be a lot more positive opportunities. And for the government to understand that enabling these technologies, and not looking at it as something that they are fearful of, would then remove the issues. But, if they don't get on board, other countries are going to be much better, and we're going to be left behind. And if there are too strict regulations put in place, it's not going to do much good. It's not going to create the jobs in these new sectors that I'm sure they would love to create. They are trying to understand it but it's very complex and moves very quickly. Canada so far has taken a pretty light-touch approach: wait and see what others are doing, which they generally do with everything, and then follow suit. So governments are aware. Some of them more than others. Some are setting up very good ecosystems that flourish in this new space. Others are trying to lock it down and are fearful of it.

ICCO CANADA: Right. So taking it down a notch from governments and global industries to entrepreneurs with smaller businesses, how would these changes affect them?

DI IORIO: It's going to give them new services and new products that are going to be passed along to their customers. It'll be a lower cost. With the payment gateway there's more competition. Cheaper products and services. They'll pick up a whole new realm of technology and new experiences and new offers that are going to be available for them, so they'll definitely be used. They'll be attracted to see which services benefit their businesses and benefit their customers. I don't see any way that it's not going to impact the small business side.

ICCO CANADA: Now, taking it down one more notch to the average person: your company Decentral created a wallet app called Jaxx so people can manage their portfolio of cryptocurrencies. Do you see this as something we'll all have on our phones one day?

DI IORIO: Yes. Everything is digital now, and there's a movement towards people being in control of their data, control of their identities, control of their money. And that's what wallets have done, given faces to these technologies. And wallets enable people to manage their new value, the digital information, the data. We want to be able to share information.

ICCO CANADA: So we won't need PayPal anymore?

DI IORIO: No, I think PayPal will still be around. There's still going to be government currencies. They're getting into the game now of potentially having digital currencies. But the dollar is not going anywhere anytime soon. And PayPal is a very useful service right now that millions and millions of people use. But there's going to be more choice, and there will be more choice in companies like that, especially as new features become available through blockchain technology.

ICCO CANADA: So the obvious elephant in the room is the coronavirus racing around the world. Businesses like the LCBO don't even want to take paper money now because it's unhygienic. So is this an argument for cryptocurrencies?

DI IORIO: I don't know if that's the best case for it, because of bills being dirty. Should they stop taking bills right now? If that makes sense, then do it. There's a lot of inefficiencies with cash, and there's a lot of issues with the tracking of cash and those will be benefits for cryptocurrency. Cash also enables people a level of freedom as well: to be able to have something physical, in case there are ever issues electronically. Resorting to something that's of value is easier, it doesn't require technology in the same way you can just hand someone a dollar bill. So it has its benefits. All technologies have benefits and I think it's best to have choice. I think cash is fine, I think digital dollars are fine. And I think cryptocurrencies that have value and that people want to use, and have the choice to use, will provide even more value.

ICCO CANADA: You've been an investor for a long time, but you've also been a real evangelist, so why is it so important to you? Beyond the fact that you made a lot of money from it?

DI IORIO: When I first got into it, I was really into this freedom movement, and personal responsibility, and not being controlled, and having the ability to choose what you want to do. And I think I recognized that we all had a lot of limitations in terms of people not really being free, and choices being diminished in terms of options of what they want.

I also started trying to figure out what had happened in the financial crisis, and really gained a passion for economics, and spent a lot of time around 2010, 2011, studying economics and different ways of thinking of the economic models. I tend to always focus on value creation and entrepreneurship, and I think they're the value creators.

Governments should be there to maybe place some order on things, but I also think people have been really accustomed to getting a lot of stuff for free, and entitlements. That leads to the degradation of countries and of society. There needs to be a push towards entrepreneurship and people understanding more, learning about the purpose of money, and the purpose of being able to have choice and make your own decisions. That was a thing I had passion for.

When I heard about Bitcoin in 2012, and saw that this was a way to be in control of my digital life, and not have others in control of my money and my communications and my identity, which gets co-opted and which people sell and put all over the place... when I heard about the ability to be my own bank, and the ability to have a lot more features and function than traditional finance has right now, and the way that it tied into freedom and tied into my passion for technology—I felt I had the ability to be a person that could make a difference and get in there early and start creating value.

The best way to learn about something is to bring people together. And then you become a center of gravity for that new space. And that's exactly what I did in 2012 when I started a Bitcoin meetup group. I ended up bringing people together that were passionate about the

space. And then from there, you start being in the middle of ideas being created. If you have the ability to look and see how you want to be a participant and create value in that space, there's a lot of opportunity. Building a community was important. And then building a business.

And now, I'm not as passionate in the space as I have been in the past. I've got a child on the way in a couple months, that's going to change things up. I'm a little more chill these days. When I go at things, I go at them very, very hard. And then I do lots of things. And then I need some time to reset and take a break. I'm trying to find that perfect balance myself right now. Being able to still do the change in the world that I want and to create impact, but also to make sure that I am mentally and physically and emotionally sound, and all those things that are required to stay in balance.

My mission over the last year has been really to find that balance and find the way that I can still excel and soar in what I want to do.

ICCO CANADA: You've done so much in the last eight years when you think about when the Bitcoin group started. We're only eight years later and I read that you're going to retire. What does that mean for you?

DI IORIO: My role right now is I am still CEO of Jaxx. I've gone back to that position, as my partner had stepped into that position, but now with her being pregnant and just two months away, I've taken the position back again and am running the company. So I'm not retired. And we didn't find out about the baby until after she had taken over the CEO role, so we've switched back right now and she's taking it easy a little bit more, and I'm running the operations again. What does it mean to be retired? I wasn't necessarily retired. I still have a lot of my investments. And my plan is to start working on health and wellness initiatives and use my problem-solving capabilities and formulas that I've developed to really help the world. So yeah, I wouldn't say that I was necessarily retired.

ICCO CANADA: Are these entrepreneurial initiatives or charitable initiatives?

DI IORIO: I believe it makes sense to do both of those things. I believe the more impact you can create, and the more good that you can do, will lead to a lot more things that you can collect as resources in order to then redeploy again to solve problems.

ICCO CANADA: For young Italian Canadians, you're basically a generation that made this grand shift and had great success with it. Can you speculate on the opportunities for younger Italian Canadians these days?

DI IORIO: There's opportunity for everybody. And I don't know if there's a certain cultural difference that would enable them to take more advantage of what's out there. I just think in general it's the idea of working hard, and being kind to people, and helping people, and being of service to people. And if you could figure out where technology and where the world is heading, there are ways to create value. And those that figure those out earlier are able to get ahead of the curve and do some great things.

ICCO CANADA: Would you say there's a sector for young people to focus on?

DI IORIO: I think it would be great if everybody was an entrepreneur. If everybody realized the powerful thoughts that you can have to create solutions to problems that exist out there, while at the same time creating things that people are using. The incentive model is to just make money. I think if it was aligned with the planet and with the future... I think things need to change towards a value in creating impact, which will in turn create more money for the person. So I'd like to see a shift with incentive models towards impact creation. And the better brands and the better companies that create better impacts on the world and help people, are going to be the ones people are going to want to associate themselves with. It's a cycle that needs to be created: Is what you're doing good for the planet? Good for people? Or is it about making money even though you're going to be a little bit deficient on certain things that people really like, like trustworthiness and transparency, and having social capital, and doing good for other people, and all those positive things? I think it would be great if people had those qualities.

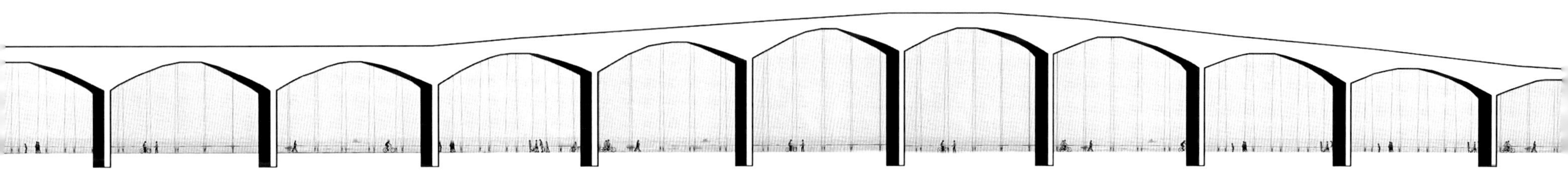

THE VERTICAL BUSINESS

ALEXANDRA DE GASPERIS
VICE PRESIDENT OF DECO COMMUNITIES

"I think it's really important for our children to know where we came from. I didn't have to endure the hardships that my grandparents or my parents had to endure. But I sure as hell want to tell my children about the hardships that they had to endure, because to me, that's what makes me, me."

PHOTO CREDIT: GIULIA STORTI

ICCO CANADA: You did your law degree, but you specialized in land use and planning?

DE GASPERIS: Yes. I went to law school in England. I came back and worked for a firm called Kagan Shastri which specializes in land use planning and municipal law but I did everything from litigation to small claims. Once I finished my articles, I really started focusing on planning and the municipal side of things.

ICCO CANADA: Did you know that you'd go into the development industry?

DE GASPERIS: It's funny—people say, "Oh, did you plan that out?" Yes and no. I fell into law a couple of ways. I'm the middle child. I think from the get-go, I was the one always mediating between my family. From a young age my parents would always say, "Oh, our little lawyer," because I was either defending someone, or I was mediating. I had a business degree and initially I thought I wanted to go into finance. And then I worked for the lawyer that I ended up starting my career with, and he made me fall in love with municipal planning law, which sounds like a wild thing because most people don't even know what that is. I could relate to it because it was closely tied to the family business but with such a different perspective. When I was working in law I always thought, "I'm really happy here. I love law." But there was always the idea of the family business.

ICCO CANADA: Was it expected of you?

DE GASPERIS: Not expected. If I stayed in law I think that my dad would have been happy. I think there was definitely hope. He was very much like, "If that's what you want to pursue, you go for it." But there seemed to be an opportunity to come to the family business and start something new and different. My father and I sat down and talked quite a bit and I ended up here. And you see all the empty office spaces around and so eventually...

ICCO CANADA: Why are they empty?

DE GASPERIS: This is a new division of our family business. We started our home building side of things about four years ago. Our family business is a vertically integrated company; there was at one point one home building company. As the family grows people started wanting to start their own companies. I've always been interested in land development, but more so in the mid-rise and high-rise side of things. So, more intensification. I thought it was a good opportunity for me to come in and start up that side of the business. My father and I entered discussions, and it seemed right, so that's when I left law and started Deco Communities.

ICCO CANADA: You're going to do mid-rise and high-rise? Is that the plan?

DE GASPERIS: Yes. It's about a year and a half old. We're currently working on two different projects. One of them is the redevelopment of the Angus Glen block—not the Angus Glen golf course—in Markham. That's a big project that has some mid-rise on it, but it's a single-family home development. So that's my big baby. And then I've been heavily involved in Lakeview Village, which is a community and it's the old OPG power plant on the lake in Mississauga.It's about 177 acres and that's all high-rise and mid-rise. It's going to be an incredible complete community.

ICCO CANADA: Are you doing all the buildings?

DE GASPERIS: It's a partnership. The partners are TACC Construction, Green Park, Road Development, CCI, and Grand Haven Homes. TACC Construction is the partner in the project. I've been kind of the development support that the group needs to keep things moving because it's such a huge project. It's not a Deco project, but Deco will be building out one of the blocks on the site. And hopefully more.

ICCO CANADA: What is your typical day?

DE GASPERIS: It honestly varies. I think the development industry over the past year, with the Conservative government being in power, has seen a lot of policy changes. We need to make sure that the policies are helpful to what we're trying to accomplish here. It's incredible for the government to go and pass policies that they believe to be helpful, but you have a very different perspective when you're on the ground and you're actually dealing with things day in and day out. A lot of my time is working with the government, going through consultations with them on different things that affect the building and development industry. That's been the past few days. Other than that, it seems to be back to back meetings and conference calls. We always have a strong group of consultants that support all of our projects. It's really keeping constant contact with them and moving projects forward. It goes from dealing with the environmental aspects of any given site to dealing with the marketing. There's a communications aspect to it, and there's a strategy aspect to it. But there's also the regular planning aspect and the building. I love development so much because you have all these multifaceted things that can come together to create the community.

ICCO CANADA: There's a lot of pressure now to build green communities, because of global warming and also to build up, rather than out. The designated greenbelt areas have changed things a lot. How has the development industry changed in this new environment?

DE GASPERIS: I think the whole industry, the province and the whole country moving towards sustainability is of utmost importance. I'm of the millennial generation, and it's important to me how our world is treated. We're not just developing a community and moving on to the next one. My father has always instilled that in us. He's proud of the communities he built, he invests in those communities and then he donates to hospitals in that community. I see it the same way but with my millennial goggles on, doing all those things, but also having the green take on things.

When we started Deco Communities, it was with an eye to do things differently. It was to build sustainable developments that people like me want to live in. Because a lot of my generation want to live in the city; they want to have everything at their fingertips. There's a lot of pressure on the industry. There's a lot of policy being put on the development industry for sustainability, and for green changes, and most of the time those policy initiatives are really costly. So, we're balancing that with trying to provide housing that people can actually purchase and buy. The affordability aspect of things and being green and sustainable makes trying to find that balance a real challenge. I think more and more developers are becoming accustomed to it and are trying to push that boundary. People I know aren't able to afford the types of houses that they want to live in, or raise a family in. When you add that green part to it, is it driving up the cost of housing so that it's even more out of reach? I think that's the balance. But I certainly know that for people in my generation that are in this business, it's no longer an option. We are looking to do things in a more sustainable way.

ICCO CANADA: We also need access to housing for working people.

DE GASPERIS: Absolutely. I have friends starting families right now. And they've been living in their condos very happily for a number of years, and for two people it's been great. They're now pregnant and on the verge of bringing another human to the world and at first it may be fine but when you're in a one bedroom condo it's very difficult. These friends are well educated, successful in their own right, working in good jobs, but they are priced out of the market. For the most part a lot of people need to move north in order to find the types of housing that they're looking for. How do we get that balance? Is it more affordable rentals? It's really tough. It's something we struggle with on every single one of our developments. And it's something that we are in constant communication with in every municipality that we work with.

ICCO CANADA: Are there any developments in technology or something in the development industry that is promising, that will help with sustainability or affordability?

DE GASPERIS: There's a couple of things. Modular housing has become really interesting, we're just at the forefront of that right now. You see housing being made out of shipping containers. We've been in discussions about how we can take that and build affordable housing. In a way, that's beautiful, that's sustainable. There are architecturally pleasing ways to do things. Modular housing is still a very new idea in the province of Ontario. I think government needs to open their minds up about that. But it could be a way to help with affordability.

ICCO CANADA: Does it have to be shipping containers? It could be...

DE GASPERIS: No, it could be anything.

ICCO CANADA: Prefabs?

DE GASPERIS: It could be prefab concrete. As we know, concrete's very expensive, but it could be prefab. There are a number of companies in the States that are already doing that. We're just not seeing it here. When it becomes a little bit more mainstream, that's when it becomes a little bit more affordable. It's something that I think a lot of different developers are exploring.

ICCO CANADA: Do you feel like the government is doing enough to support the build-out of the infrastructure in the GTA?

DE GASPERIS: I think so. It's a multi-faceted problem. I think the provincial government, is certainly trying to push transit. And I think that's a really key initiative for environmental concerns. It's a huge initiative around building up instead of building out. People want to live in condos, but they also want to be connected. As you look outside this window here you see the Vaughan Metropolitan Center. Now the subway is right here. I could walk there. This is one of the only examples that you'll see of transit coming first and then buildings being built second. What we've been doing historically is building and saying, "Okay, now we need the infrastructure to catch up." I think municipalities, regional governments and the province need to do more to do transit first, development second. Bring the transit and then let's build up around it, because you're bringing that value for people to actually be connected to the city. You can be downtown in 40 minutes. We're in a challenging environment where there's not enough money to do everything that needs to be done. The introduction of public/private partnerships is so important. If the government has a willingness to allow something to happen, and can help fund a portion of that, I think the private sector will come to the table and say, "Let's make this happen, because this is good for everyone." The challenge is always money.

ICCO CANADA: So just a little shift. You were the executive director of the Burgundy Brick Foundation. I know you've done lots of charity stuff and I guess you're not the executive director, is that because you're not a student anymore?

DE GASPERIS: The Burgundy Brick Foundation was founded by my sister and myself and actually, the Minister of Education, Stephen Lecce, in university when we were at Western. We came up with an idea that we wanted to do things a bit differently. We saw a lot of our friends were going out to the bars and spending money on drinks and other extras and we thought why not do all those things but contribute to a good cause at the same time. It seems like such a simple idea, but no one at the time was really doing anything like that. And we thought, "Okay, let's sit down and let's create this foundation that can support all the things that are near and dear to our heart." And at the time, my sister and I, both being children of a developer, thought affordable housing was an important thing.

I started getting involved with Habitat for Humanity when I was in high school. I was chosen to be part of this leadership—religion class, and as part of that, we did a ton of charitable work. We did sandwich patrol where we'd make sandwiches, go downtown and hand them out to homeless youth. We did a night where we slept out on the streets to raise money for homeless youth and those struggling with mental health and addiction. One of the most incredible experiences was traveling to Philadelphia and building houses for Habitat for Humanity and getting to meet the families who were going to be recipients of these houses. It was life changing.

Habitat for Humanity was at the forefront of what was important to me and my sister, and Stephen as well. We wanted to do something that we thought could make a tangible change. Youth homelessness was a huge issue in the city. Having children grow up with a roof over their heads and having a family have equity within a home that is their own is hugely beneficial to the community of the future. So these are the things we started the foundation on. We ended up throwing, I believe four events... I'll call them galas, raising over $150,000, which when you're a university student back in 2010 was great. Habitat for Humanity could not believe that this group of young individuals were so keen on helping such an important initiative. There was no youth involvement initially in their work. So we did that and supported a number of homeless youth shelters. It was a great time in our life and so much fun. Then once we started getting out into the work world, it just became impossible. Stephen took a step back, I think after the first year, because he was working in Ottawa at the time. My sister and I kept it up, and it ended up becoming a foundation led by all women, by fluke. We ended up being women build ambassadors for Habitat for Humanity. Every year we would bring out a huge group of women, or a huge group of men and women to come and build off-site and raise more money, etc. It fostered our relationship with Habitat, who I still have a very close relationship with to this day.

ICCO CANADA: Does the foundation still exist?

DE GASPERIS: We closed it down. There was a dream to pass it on to this next generation of university students to keep it going but we couldn't find any that were interested in taking hold of the reins.

ICCO CANADA: Great initiative though. So now you're on the board of the Ontario Arts Council, which is a shift or maybe it's not. What led you to that?

DE GASPERIS: I've always had a serious passion for the arts. When I was practicing law, I felt like I wasn't completely fulfilled—like I was missing some creativity that I wasn't receiving in law. When I moved over to the development side of things, I felt a whole lot more fulfilled. All of a sudden I'm doing what I love, creating these really incredible and fun communities, the way that I'd want to live in them. I think creative placemaking has become such an important part of doing this. It's no longer, "Let's build a cookie cutter house and move on." We really take pride in how these are designed, how a community is designed.

The appointment to the Ontario Arts Council came as there was a number of people moving out of board positions in the province. When I heard that, I thought, "I would love to sit on a board of something that I have a passion for." I was eventually appointed, which I was so thrilled about, because in a lot of ways, I connected what the OAC does with what I think our ethos is for this company, and the ethos I was brought up with. It's investment in the arts to help the community. And the OAC truly is the investor in the arts for the province of Ontario. Every community should have some sort of artistic component, some sort of creative placemaking. We can do more than just house people and move on.

ICCO CANADA: It's a good board to work with because it's cross-disciplinary.

DE GASPERIS: Exactly. I've been on the board for just shy of a year now and I've learned so much about Aboriginal art, and about dance, about theatre, and about writing. It's so great. The cultural things that I'm exposed to as a part of the OAC has been amazing and the individuals that I've been meeting, like Rita Davies, the chair of the board, has been great. She's an incredible human being. For Lakeview Community Partners, our project in Mississauga, we actually have a partnership with Artscape. We're trying to get affordable housing on site for artists. TACC Construction is a partner in that. I, as part of Deco, provide support for that. Deco will be building out on site, but I'm helping the development team with everything that needs to be worked through because there's a lot. So the entire partnership has a partnership with Artscape. We're trying to work out having a place on site where artists can work and create art for the community, and can also live in affordable housing. Because as you know, many artists are completely priced out of the areas that they gentrify because they're creating so much value with the art that they're producing. And then they're pushed out of the areas that they create and they make vibrant. I don't know how it happened, but I feel like I have such synergies being on the OAC board with how I'm trying to run this business and how we're building up communities. Having a sense of place above and beyond just a roof over your head is so important.

ICCO CANADA: That's encouraging to hear that you want to include that. I don't think that was always the case.

DE GASPERIS: No, I don't think it was always the case either. But the industry has changed a lot over the past number of years. And it's continuing to change. Developers get a terrible reputation, which I honestly can't understand. Obviously, I'm a little bit biased, but I know my dad would wake up every Saturday morning and go and drive around the sites. He loves every single one of the developments that he's building. And he truly starts investing in that community from the hospital to whatever else it may need. I guess I've taken that love of community and put my millennial twist on it.

ICCO CANADA: Just to shift a little bit again—is the Italian Canadian community important to you?

DE GASPERIS: Absolutely. I feel like my drive to work hard comes from what I've seen my grandparents and my parents go through. My dad is an immigrant. He came here when he was 12 or 13. I'm very proud of my heritage because I'm so proud of what my family has built. Not only on my father's side, and building up this incredible company, but on my mother's side too. My grandfather was a labourer, one of the individuals that helped build the subway in Toronto. And he was one of the individuals building the CN Tower. He was a labourer his whole life, but he was proud of the work that he did. They really sacrificed. I don't think we'll ever know sacrifice the way that our grandparents did.

ICCO CANADA: That generation were largely labourers when they arrived in Canada and they were a pretty tight community compared to some because there weren't the kind of services back then we have now. They needed each other's help just to get things done. Then you get the next generation, they're the ones that start having success. The labourer becomes a developer, becomes a contractor, becomes whatever. Huge success across the community, and now you've got doctors and lawyers etc. They don't really need each other for support in the same way as the earlier generation. I'm just curious if there's been a diminution of the community bond for you, and will the community be cohesive for your child in a way that it is cohesive for you?

DE GASPERIS: My grandmother has stories of her getting on public transit and them saying, "Hey Italian, get to the back of the bus." Right? They were not welcome. They were not considered citizens on par with Canadians. The Jewish community has really stuck together to become successful and build themselves up. I think the Italians have done very much the same thing. Your question is so interesting. How do I see that going in the future? My friend group, and my social circle is so broad. I did not grow up just around Italians. I'd say I probably grew up with more Canadians than I did Italians. But strangely some of my best friends today are Italian. My husband's Greek, so I guess very close.

It's an interesting question because we do have a lot of family friends and we still hang out together, we still do business together. I think from a business perspective, we always try to help out the people that we know and we care about. From a social perspective, things are changing a bit—my friends are black, white, Jewish, Asian, South American, you name it.

ICCO CANADA: Will you and your children be maintaining the traditions?

DE GASPERIS: Yes. For both my husband and I, tradition is really important. The Greeks have some beautiful traditions that I would like to carry forward in our family, and Italians have beautiful traditions that I'd like to carry forward. And a lot of that is the tradition of family and food. Who doesn't want to carry that forward? I think it's really important for our children to know where we came from. I didn't have to endure the hardships that my grandparents or my parents had to endure. But I sure as hell want to tell my children about the hardships that they had to endure, because to me, that's what makes me, *me*.

I've been lucky enough to have my grandparents in my life for 31 years. I just lost two grandparents over this past year. Before that, all four of my grandparents were at my wedding. I'm blessed because I really got to know them as humans, as people. I got to hear the stories of growing up in the Depression, and then the war, and then learning about all these things. It's things we can't fathom, when every day there's war. It's terrible. We're in a bit of a bubble here in Canada where we don't have to deal with any of that first-hand. Whereas they did. So I think carrying all those traditions forward is important. I don't want them to lose sight of the fact that they're Italian.

PHOTO CREDIT: GIULIA STORTI

EDUCATION, EXECUTION, CONSISTENCY
THREE RECIPES BEHIND SUCCESS IN THE FOOD INDUSTRY

JACKIE DALIMONTE
FORMER GENERAL MANAGER, HMR/PRONTO AT EATALY
CURRENTLY, CATEGORY SPECIALIST AT FRESHCO

"It's so funny: all we ever did was spend time with our family back in the day, or whenever back in the day was for the non-millennials, and all there was, was time. Weekends we're going to Zio and Zia's, or weekends we're going to a cousin's house. Now time is "me time." I just want to have time to do nothing. And that's why we're seeing, in the food business, everything becomes a snack, everything becomes grab and go or takeaway."

ICCO CANADA: How did you get interested in food?

DALIMONTE: I think the food thing started before schooling. My mom's favourite story to tell is "My kid could crack a lobster open by the time she was nine years old." I remember Food Network was very big. I grew up with my grandmother who was a chef. I had aunts who were chefs. I had grown up in the grocery business where food was constantly around me. My first oyster was in a Loblaws seafood department; I was 11 years old. I worked as a dishwasher when I was 12. I worked with Loblaws Cooking Schools to teach little kids how to cook, probably younger than I should have. It was going into the colleges that I knew that George Brown was going to be the only option because it was the best.

I went there at a funny time in 2007 when the curriculum was still the older curriculum. The school hadn't had their big massive renovation yet, so we were working out of this older kitchen learning banquet-style cooking in the very, very old format. Unfortunately, I got let go from chef school for one whole year because unbeknownst to Jackie-the-young-18-year-old, no one was going to tap me on the shoulder and say, "Hey, your grades aren't great." So they said, "Pull your shit together, go to night school." So I got that done and by the time I was back in chef school it was 2009, 2010. In those two years they had renovated the school, they had changed their curriculum, everything was fresh and fancy, and we were learning so many new things. And then I found out about an Italian program to go to Italy.

ICCO CANADA: Through George Brown?

DALIMONTE: It's an Italian post-graduate program. There were 150 applicants; 29 of us were selected. It was a gruelling process, too. That was, I guess, the first real interview as a semi-adult at 22 years old. I got into the program and I went in 2010 and I was there for about four or five months, and it was intensive Italian cooking at ALMA, the biggest Italian chef school in Parma, and then from there they send you off in stage. You stage with a Michelin star; you can go to an agriturismo; you can go to a mom and pop—there's so many options. The first restaurant I was at was called Giuda Ballerino in Rome, and the second was called Castello di Spaltenna. It was really exciting to go to Chianti to learn about the Chianti way of living and cooking.

ICCO CANADA: It must have been awful!

DALIMONTE: It was terrible. I got to wake up to vineyards every morning and then olive groves on the other side—it was great. I came back to Toronto and I worked, that's what you did. Everybody was trying to find great kitchens to work in and we were trying to find amazing chefs to work under and you come back with another boost. You've learned so much in another country that has a Michelin star standard and then you come back to Toronto and there's almost this—"Why aren't we there yet?" Or, "How do we get there?" It's just a different calibre of technique to an extent. When I came back to Toronto we had to finish off a couple more courses for this Italian program. I worked with Gabriele Paganelli for a little bit. He owns Speducci Mercatto now, but before he owned Romagna Mia. He was also one of my professors and I said, "Chef, will you teach me how to make salumi?" He said, "Of course," because he made his own salumi and it was some of the best in the city, and he said, "You have to work for me first." I said, "Okay." There were these shifts where we would work a whole day and we'd scrub down when shift was over and start production for salumi. That's what I waited for.

After that I worked for Local Kitchen and Wine Bar. In 2010 to 2012-13 Toronto had this massive shift in how we started to dine. We started believing in communal tables and feeding people at a great price, with smaller plates and we stopped taking things so seriously and just started using what we had. The thing that I loved the most was, not only were the owners exceptional and very, very nice, but their motto was, Italian-inspired but locally grown or locally sourced. Their father turned their backyard garden into the farm for the restaurant in the summer, so we were growing what we were eating and it was kind of back to your roots.

I think at this point I was about 23, 24, and I had hit the wall I think a lot of cooks hit, where they say, "Am I doing the right thing? Do I want to work this long?" It's that question of "Am I capable of more?"

Luckily for me, I got a phone call from somebody named Mario Moccia and he worked for Sobeys. He knows my mom, who works in the grocery business, and he had asked her, "Is your kid still a chef?" He called me, and we had a meeting and he said, "We want to create a catering business for our downtown locations. We don't know how to do it, but we need a chef to help us." I was like, "You had me at hello." So I got this job with Sobeys back in April 2013. It was a dream come true.

I was a 24-year-old working for Sobeys Urban Fresh as Catering Culinary Specialist. Did we know what that truly was? Nope! But at the end of the day, I'd like to think that I became the Jackie of all trades. I started to fall in love with something brand new, where I got to create a catering program with no budget and no employees—you just did it. Slowly you start to build confidence and you're like, "Okay, I'm building the program. I'm doing the catering, I'm taking the orders. We're building some infrastructure here." Next thing you know, I'm building an online program and then they're asking me to help with store openings. It's those times where I said yes to everything, to learn everything, that gave me so many moments now in my career where I'm like, "Yeah, I've done that. I know what we're talking about."

Ultimately, underlining all of it, I never thought I would end up in the business. My mother worked in the grocery industry. Growing up to see my mom, it was always, "We gotta visit her at a store, she's busy." It's just the way life was. There were no questions asked. Going to work with your mom on the weekend was like, "Go ahead kid, have fun, go walk the aisles." I guess I have this thing that's just in me. Customers first—we put things on a shelf for a certain reason and cross-merchandising is important. It's in my blood the same way that my family and my heritage is in my blood—it's what I was born to do, I guess, and I never want to turn back.

PHOTO CREDIT: GIULIA STORTI

ICCO CANADA: After Sobeys was there...

DALIMONTE: I was there for about six years. Sobeys was an onslaught of career paths, so, Catering Culinary Specialist, to being the project lead, to opening Canada's first Nutella Café. It's come and it's gone but getting to understand the Ferrero brand and work side by side with them was wonderful. They threw me on a plane and put me in Alba and I got to do a tour of Ferrero factories. At that point at Sobeys I was the lead specialist for all of Ontario in-store programs, food experiences, and taking care of all of our in-store chef programs. I did that for about six months, and then our GM said, "We want you to take care of all of in-store fresh merchandising." From operations that I had done for three years, I was now taking on merchandising, which was brand new for me. It wasn't a "we want you to take this job, —we need you to do both jobs at the same time."

I worked collaboratively with senior directors and category managers on 52-week flyer planning, so: strategy. We worked collaboratively with all the fresh departments to build merchandising programs—specifically where things were placed in the stores on a weekly basis, and in-store communications. It was a really interesting thing for me, and I ended up loving merchandising. From there I went off to become a produce developer with Sobeys, so I oversaw our produce departments and our HMR departments, which is prepared food.

"HMR" is home meal replacement. It was, again, something brand new for me. I guess this is where my life as a chef started to come into play. I know what I know and have the palate that I have, so I just applied it. Maybe I'm not the food scientist that a lot of product developers are, but it was really nice because the product developers on that team were super welcoming to say, "You're bringing a different perspective." Just earlier this year, in May 2019, I came over to Eataly, and I'm a GM for Pronto, which is our prepared foods, packaged prepared foods, ready to eat, ready to heat items. The title is HMR, so they've implemented the HMR mentality from Canadian grocery into our Toronto location.

ICCO CANADA: So there'll be one section for take home and home replacement?

DALIMONTE: We're going to have both. We're going to have 90 linear feet of prepared foods, packaged foods, some hot and ready to eat, all packaged and ready to go. This isn't new for the Canadian market. We do it in every grocery store, but I think we have Prontos in three other locations in the USA. We saw that there was a great opportunity to expand. We're doing things that we've never done in the Pronto realm, introducing a lot of hot foods for customers. We're going to have everything ready to go for a customer to just walk in and walk out if they're time-strapped. We're creating a solution to a problem. The problem's time—nobody has time.

ICCO CANADA: That's so true.

DALIMONTE: It's so funny: all we ever did was spend time with our family back in the day, or whenever back in the day was for the non-millennials, and all there was, was time. Weekends we're going to Zio and Zia's, or weekends we're going to a cousin's house. Now time is "me time." I just want to have time to do nothing. And that's why we're seeing, in the food business, everything becomes a snack, everything becomes grab and go or takeaway. I get to play in that playground and say, "Okay, how do I make this delicious, convenient, and time-saving for you?" Now, I'm not saying that every single thing that I make for you is going to be ready to eat. So maybe we're going to have the freshest ravioli and the freshest pasta sauces ready to go, you just have to go warm them up, and then you still have that feeling of, okay, I cooked it. I get to eat this on a Tuesday, but I didn't lose out on an hour of anything.

ICCO CANADA: Your role is merchandising?

DALIMONTE: Operations for sure, execution.

ICCO CANADA: Which means what to you?

DALIMONTE: Operations, number one, is leading and educating our teams and executing. Execution and consistency are... tattoo them on my arms! That's what I believe in the most. When we can stay consistent and a customer can come back every single time and get the same thing that they got last time, we're good. If we can execute it flawlessly, even better.

ICCO CANADA: Going from Sobeys to Eataly—were you compelled to do it because of the Italian thing?

DALIMONTE: The first time I walked into an Eataly was many years ago. You go to Eataly to get inspired. You can watch people do this now. People walk in for the first time and they just stop and they're like, "Where am I? What is this? Where do I start?" I did that, and I do it every single time. It took me back to Italy, to my roots and how I grew up, and it was so nice to be around all this Italian food. I grew up in Woodbridge, so I was exposed—overexposed—to all of the Italian foods, but they did something here: they made me feel like I was in Italy. I had always said from day one that if Eataly ever opened in Toronto I was going to try and get a job there. And I tried, and I got it. It was a one in a million chance I'd get it.

ICCO CANADA: Would you say your Italian heritage has influenced your approach to business?

DALIMONTE: Yeah, I mean hard work is probably the answer that you're going to get all the time, right? My grandparents on both sides came here, right after the war like so many people do. They worked hard from day one. My parents also worked hard but not in the way that they did. It's what sacrifice meant to my grandparents, versus what sacrifice means to my parents, versus what sacrifice means to me—which shouldn't be called sacrifice anymore. My parents took what they saw their parents do, working three jobs, taking care of families, coming home and making fresh pasta because flour and water is cheap. They got married in the '80s and my mom went to university. My father worked for Canada Post. Through university my mom worked for Loblaws. I think she started as a part-time cashier, moved her way up a little bit, went on to be a supervisor in the store, and then there was this turning point in their lives where my mom had this great opportunity. She had to have the conversation with my father to say, "Okay, this could be big... I want to go for it." My dad's like, "Go for it. I have a job that I work 6:00 am until 11:00 am, and I got the kids, I'll figure it out." My mom just went off and she hustled. My dad was the Mr. Mom or the perfect dad and he took us to soccer practice, took us to gymnastics, he picked us up, he went to parent-teacher interviews. My dad just was amazing throughout and he's been the cheerleader in all of our lives. So this is where the sacrifice, I think, starts to come into play for me. My grandparents did it all for us. I'm still reaping the benefits of those wonderful people and what they've given us—the love that they showed my parents and what our parents have given us. They left everything in Italy, but the best part is that they brought it all here for us to learn about too. Our traditions are the same, the food is the same, the way that I use my hands a little bit too much when I speak is the same. I don't know if I'd want it any other way.

ICCO CANADA: What do you see in the future for yourself?

DALIMONTE: I know for sure I will be in the food business no matter what. I never thought I would be here today. If you do the math, seven years ago I was a chef, that's it. Seven years ago I was cooking. I was working until 2:00 am some days, and now I get to wear heels to work. I get to put on blazers and feel a part of a team and a strategy, and to build big businesses. Did I get there through conventional vices of schooling and MBAs and all of that jazz? I didn't. Do I wish I did now? A little bit. I know that I can always go back and get more education. My career in the food industry will only grow because of the connections I've made, and the avenues that I foresee.

ICCO CANADA: Do you ever miss getting your hands dirty behind the stoves?

DALIMONTE: Yes and no. I'm pretty excited because I'm about to open an Eataly. We've got the works. We've got stoves, we've got operations, I have it all. If I ever wanted to, I'm sure we can have some fun here.

ICCO CANADA: That doesn't mean you have to work the line to still be a chef.

DALIMONTE: Right, but I didn't know that as a young cook, and a lot of young cooks don't know that, and they deserve to know that, because there's a lot more out there. The respect that we get as people who have more knowledge of food than others, is a respect that's waiting to be given. Chefs don't stop being chefs, and they should know that there's an opportunity out there to work for great companies as well. I'm interested to see where the food business goes. I mean, talk to me in 20 years.

ICCO CANADA: Given the generational change, first generation, second generation, third generation. What's going to happen with the fourth generation? Italian food culture has taken over Toronto. It's a huge part of our culinary experience. There's no corner you can go where there isn't some Italian influence somewhere.

DALIMONTE: It's good and it's good food. That's the other thing, we're not Americanizing it, we're still following what we know. I think that when it comes to what food will look like for the next generation, I'm not worried. I think we have to be a little bit more conscious about how we get our food, how much of it we are using, and what we do with it, because I believe that food waste is a problem, but as far as keeping it alive... it's not what it was. I think we can all see that Italians married Italians. Now it doesn't matter who you marry, but what's really great is you're seeing these children grow up with whatever heritage they come from, or it's the same heritage, and it's implemented in them. They're educated on it. I think travel's important. I think going back to see where you come from is very important. As long as we keep the family tradition, the food tradition, and the heritage tradition alive, what can go wrong?

PHOTO CREDIT: GIULIA STORTI

THE TWO FACES OF TECHNOLOGY

NELLO ALTOMARE
INTER-TRANSPORT LTD / FOODPIC

"I think there's a lot of distractions in the world. Technology is a great thing, but there can be a lot of negatives that come with that. Being distracted, and not getting to the stuff that you should be doing, and doing stuff that you shouldn't, is definitely something that's a little too easy for a lot of people."

ICCO CANADA: Let's start with a little about your background.

ALTOMARE: Sure. My parents are Tony and Vita Altomare. I have two older sisters, Rosie and Josie. I started a business with Rosie. It's called FoodPic. It's a food sharing app. My other sister is doing a residency in Kingston, at the hospital at Queen's University. As for me, I've been working with my dad at ITL for the past four or five years. For the first couple of years I was working summers while I was at University of Toronto.

ICCO CANADA: What did you study there?

ALTOMARE: I was at the Rotman Business School, and I got my degree in finance and economics. It was quite a challenge—University of Toronto is not the easiest school, but it was fun to be there. Rotman is a management school and as you go through each year, you get into the different fields of accounting, finance, and management. I was able to get a broad view of business. In the first year I was able to take a computer science course, which really broadened my horizon on technology and got me looking where the future is going. I also went to St Mike's, which was a phenomenal experience.

ICCO CANADA: Was it?

ALTOMARE: Really, really great. The brotherhood that I shared there—I have friends that I talk to almost every day, so it's really nice. I also played in the hockey program. In fact, I played hockey growing up from eight years old.

ICCO CANADA: You're a good Canadian!

ALTOMARE: Yes. I think it shaped me, because it instilled in me discipline and hard work. I was never really the best player on my team, and I never played at the highest level. But every summer I was on the ice, constantly developing, polishing up my skills. And as the years went on, I went to better and better teams. Eventually I was able to play for a junior hockey team my last year of high school.

ICCO CANADA: You must have been pretty good.

ALTOMARE: It was an awesome experience, and I really enjoyed it. From about eight years old until 14, my dad was my coach; every year he was mentoring me. He was a bit more tough on me, which, looking back now, was the best thing that could have happened, because the discipline and the hard work is really instilled in me, whereas if I had another coach that didn't care as much, that might have not been the case.

ICCO CANADA: So tell me about the FoodPic app. I know you did some computer science. Did you do that for fun, or because you thought you were going to need it in your career?

ALTOMARE: For me that was definitely a fun thing. I thought it was cool and something that I wanted to get into where I could see where technology was going, and not be in the dark. Plus, I had quite a bit of math background. That's why I went into finance. I thought computer science has those formulas, and it could be an easier jump to get into. It was a fun elective. I took Italian as well in my first year as one of my electives because I wanted to stay close to my heritage.

ICCO CANADA: So how did FoodPic come about?

ALTOMARE: When I graduated university, I was on vacation with my sister, and we were trying to figure out something that could be worldwide, something that could benefit a lot of people. We wanted to create a business that would help everybody. So, we thought, okay: What is something that everybody needs, or everybody uses? That's food. Everybody loves food.

We noticed that we were taking a lot of pictures of our food, but we weren't really showing them to anyone. We wanted a place that people could post pictures and have a local area, a local profile, where they can show friends and the rest of the world what they're eating. We created this app to have a community of foodies locally and beyond in the world.

ICCO CANADA: Did you hire a developer?

ALTOMARE: We did. He was able to create this app, and we're constantly updating. In the app world it's never finished, which is why we did a soft launch in May, to see what our users were using: what was beneficial, what changes we needed to make. From May until now, we've been solidifying our brand, figuring out exactly where we want to go and what marketing strategies to use. That's the biggest thing for something like this: you really want to be able to push the app and get people using it. Marketing and retention are the two main things, so we're going to start a marketing push in October. We feel we're ready with the app to get it out there.

ICCO CANADA: You work here at ITL full time as well as working on FoodPic. How about your sister?

ALTOMARE: My sister's working on it too. It's definitely not easy. There's a lot of work involved, because I'm here at ITL. There's not a lot of sleep involved. My 8:00 to 4:00 job is not finished at 4:00. I go home, I freshen up a little bit, I do a couple of hours of FoodPic, I'll go to the gym, then go home, work on it a little bit more, and go to sleep. It's never-ending. I'm very fortunate my sister is helping me. We've noticed too, that a big component of our business, or of any business really, is to have a team that works well together and can hit deadlines. I've never really worked as the head of that. In school you're kind of all together, whereas now, my sister and I are really forcing everything.

ICCO CANADA: You have to drive it.

ALTOMARE: Driving it is what I see in my dad. It's a great thing to see what my dad is doing. I can take what he has from his business and transfer it to what I'm doing.

ICCO CANADA: If FoodPic blows up big, how does that happen?

ALTOMARE: It's like a snowball effect. Word of mouth is really big on these types of apps. You have to get it out there.

ICCO CANADA: Did you always have an interest in food?

ALTOMARE: Since I was born. I love food. For the Italian culture as well, when you think of getting together with family, food is the central point of it all. For me it's always been important.

ICCO CANADA: For FoodPic, did the interest in food come first, or interest in technology?

ALTOMARE: I would say an interest in food is a thing that everybody has. Technology is something that can bring the food to everybody. It's kind of a mesh of both, where you see something that you want to eat: Wow, that looks delicious. It's on technology, but you still have to get out there and go get it yourself. It's kind of a combination of both, where this app came from. We wanted to get people involved in food in a way that is easier for most everyone.

ICCO CANADA: Would you say learning how to leverage technology is important in business?

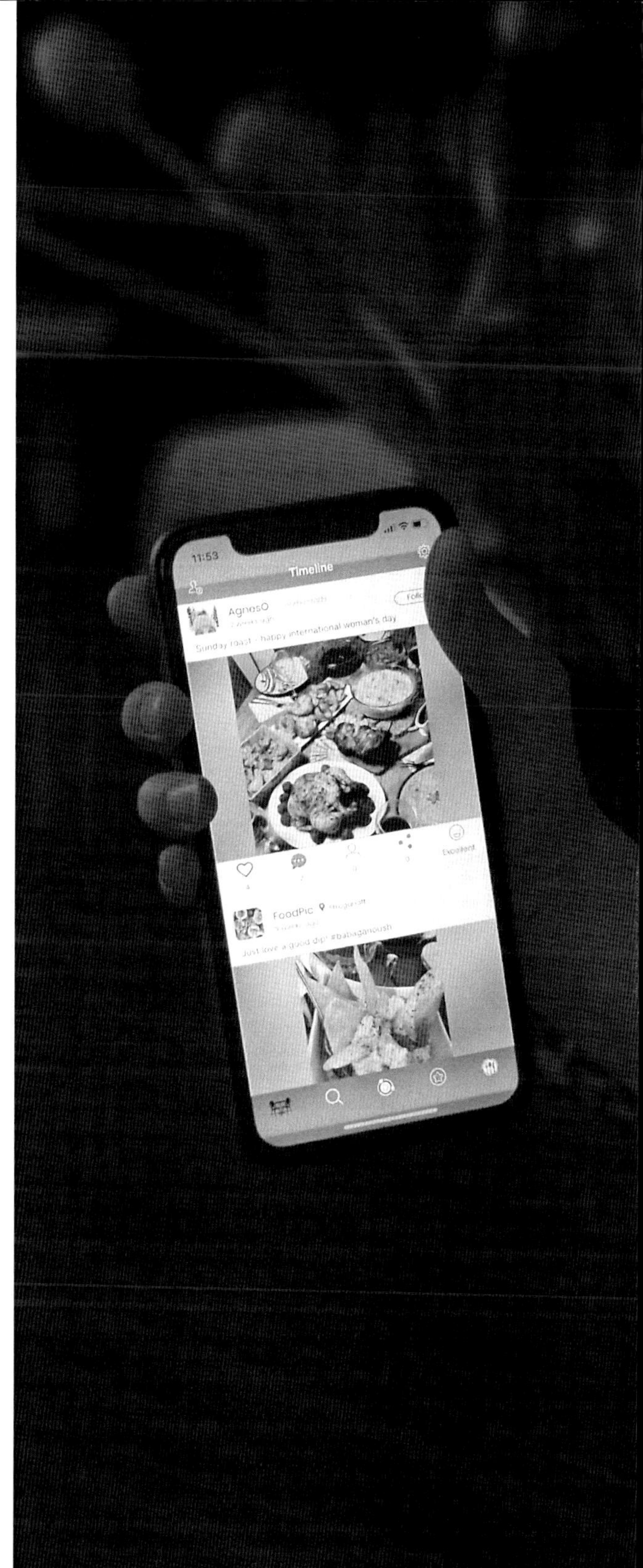

ALTOMARE: I think it's the most important thing as a young entrepreneur by far. We are so blessed in this day and age to have so many things right under our fingertips. You can find anything you want at the push of a button.

ICCO CANADA: Let's talk a little of your work at ITL.

ALTOMARE: We are a freight forwarding logistics company. We are in charge of connecting suppliers with their customers. We deal mostly with Canada, so we're shipping to Montreal, the GTA, even outside of the GTA; Vancouver as well. Those are our big main hubs. We deal a lot with European suppliers, mostly Italy, Germany, Spain, Switzerland. Those are our big markets.

ICCO CANADA: Helping them bring stuff here?

ALTOMARE: Yes. Basically, because Canada's not much of an export country, we have a lot of imports that we deal with. We're in charge of getting the freight, bringing it to our agent's warehouse, and then bringing it either through air or sea to our warehouse and sending it to wherever it needs to go.

ICCO CANADA: What's your role at ITL?

ALTOMARE: When I first started here in the summers, I did an accounting job, which didn't really have much to do with the freight as a whole. I went into approvals of invoices, just learning the business and what the charges are. Now my job is implementing processes and procedures, which means, because technology is growing, I'm finding ways to make the operations team and the sales teams' lives easier. Because our software is so vast, there's many different ways that you can do things. I'm trying to find the easiest way for our business to do everyday operations.

ICCO CANADA: I imagine the technological environment has changed quite a bit since the company began?

ALTOMARE: Yes, that's for sure. I came in at a good time, because we implemented this new software about four and a half years ago. We've been slowly integrating for the first couple of years, and now we can really see what the system has to offer. It was great that I had that computer science background because there's a few features in the system that have these macros and formulas that you need to input, and if I didn't have that background, I'd be pulling my hair out.

ICCO CANADA: Going forward, what do you see as challenges for ITL?

ALTOMARE: The biggest challenge that ITL has is we are at the mercy of our carriers. Basically, we have an obligation to our customers to get the freight here at a reasonable time; it's what they expect. But because we have to use third party services, we're at the mercy of what they do, as well as weather. We can't control everything. That's a big problem with our business, where we need to be always on top of our carriers and make sure that we can get the freight to our customers within a reasonable time. If that's not possible, we need to find solutions.

Another thing that we're trying to implement is the track and trace system, where we can really track from when it gets picked up to when it goes to the warehouse and overseas, to when it goes on the plane or on the ship, to when it gets here, to when it's de-palletized, when it goes to the warehouse, and when it gets to the customer. We have it for a few customers, but we're rolling it out slowly.

ICCO CANADA: What do you see in the future for ITL? What would your role be in the company?

ALTOMARE: Well, I see it expanding to Montreal, getting a bigger office there, expanding to Vancouver, becoming a bigger office there, eventually becoming multinational, getting to the US and getting an office there. It's baby steps, obviously, but hopefully I can spearhead something like that in the future. I'm working in different sections here to learn the whole business. I have a great opportunity because of my dad; I'm able to meet everyone that is involved with this business, so in the next few years it's important that I spearhead certain projects.

ICCO CANADA: I can remember when Amazon was a new thing and they were trying to encourage people to buy things online. Now everybody does and shipping's a big thing. Am

I right to say that this is a growth business for you guys?

ALTOMARE: Oh, I'd say for sure. I think we've got a business that can definitely grow and prosper.

ICCO CANADA: So, let's talk a little about your Italian heritage, and how you're connected with it. Did you hear Italian at home when you were a child?

ALTOMARE: My grandparents moved here around 1950. Both sides were living in Italy, and they moved here with just the clothes on their back and not much money in their pockets. They were able to create families, to sustain themselves, and create their own businesses and grow something. Then my dad creating his own business—he was very inspired by his father—and now me creating my own business, being inspired by my dad, I've kind of become close to that. I see how much hard work it took. They were looked down upon when they moved here. It wasn't an easy thing for them. I can see what they've done, and the values and relationships they've created. I can take that and create something based on the values they instilled in my parents, and then my parents instilled in me.

ICCO CANADA: So you would say that your Italian heritage formed you?

ALTOMARE: Definitely. And you know, seeing them be so down on their luck, and then come here and build something—the sky's the limit for someone like me.

ICCO CANADA: What did your grandparents do?

ALTOMARE: One of them was a shoemaker, and then he was able to distribute and sell shoes from Italy. The other one was a paver, so he was in the paving business.

ICCO CANADA: So these are common...

ALTOMARE: Yeah, they're all hardworking jobs, which is good. They were able to sustain.

ICCO CANADA: So when you were growing up, did your nonna make food for you and all that?

ALTOMARE: I was fortunate enough to live literally around the corner from my nonna, so after school I would always be going to her house, and she'd have food there. All my cousins were at the school too so it would be a whole family type of reunion right after school. I was fortunate to be there all the time. My nonno, on the other side, he passed away, but I remember going to his backyard. He had a fig tree in the back. They had a garden. All the Italians had one, so it was nice to be able to go there and pick something out of the garden and make a big pasta with it.

Food is the centre of the culture. I was brought up loving food and loving having a Sunday lunch with everybody. You look forward to eating and sharing an experience—so, I would say it's not just the food; it's the experience as well. That's important, because you experience people through food as well.

ICCO CANADA: Right. So, the different generations: we've got grandparents, parents, and now it's your generation. You've already expressed the differences, because you have resources that your dad didn't have, and way more than your grandparents had. Can you elaborate on the challenges that you face? Or maybe what the next generation will face? We touched on that a bit just with technology, which is a big difference from previous generations, and it can be quite disruptive.

ALTOMARE: I think there's a lot of distractions in the world. Technology is a great thing, don't get me wrong, but there can be a lot of negatives that come with that. Being distracted, and not getting to the stuff that you should be doing, and doing stuff that you shouldn't, is definitely something that's a little too easy for a lot of people. You can hide behind the computer as well. For me, looking towards my future kids, it's a little bit scary. I don't know what they're going to be seeing on the screen. I have no control over that. They can hide in their rooms on their phones and just be scrolling, and who knows what they're reading; they could be typing bad things. You don't know, right? But I have values that were instilled by my parents. I grew up in a religious family and I still practice my religion. That's something that I would teach my kids, and hopefully, with those values, they'll grow up away from all this negative stuff.

ICCO CANADA: In economic terms, things are different now. My father worked for the same company for forty years until his retirement. He was an immigrant too, but once he ended up at this company, he stayed. That's true of lots of people from that generation. It's not like that anymore.

ALTOMARE: Well, yeah. Nowadays, even all my friends, they're not really happy with what they're doing.

ICCO CANADA: Why is that, do you think?

ALTOMARE: They've been kind of switching.

ICCO CANADA: Because it's all contract work?

ALTOMARE: That's one of the things. Some of them have contract work where they feel like they're not getting the pay that they deserve.

ICCO CANADA: Or security?

ALTOMARE: Or security that they deserve. Another thing is that they feel like they're stagnant in their jobs, and they're not being challenged. That's kind of two things that they've noticed: they want to be moving up in the company, and the company is restricting them. That's why people are moving around a lot. In this day and age stability isn't really something that is on the mind, at the beginning, of anyone really.

ICCO CANADA: It is when you're 60.

ALTOMARE: Exactly. In this culture stability isn't something that people strive for. They don't look for it— I'm going to get a good job that can move me up. I want to hop around and see my options. And that goes for relationships, too, everything in this culture.

ICCO CANADA: It's definitely different. It's just the way people are interacting. So, would you say that young entrepreneurs have the same opportunities as previous generations?

ALTOMARE: I'd say we have even more opportunity. I think there's so much to be done. If you have a passion for something, you can definitely work hard and figure out what direction to go with that passion, whether it be eating or working out, sports or anything really. What you love to do, you can definitely find a way to make money off of it and thrive.

ICCO CANADA: In the old days, people would say you should go into the professions. You should be a doctor, lawyer, whatever. A clearly defined thing—now it seems it's not so clearly defined. Does that bother you or is that just the way it is?

ALTOMARE: I think that's great, because now people have the opportunity to do what they love. I love working here. It's an awesome job. The opportunity is astronomical to grow this, so that's something that I love to do. With the app as well, I love food. I love to help people post pictures of their food and share their meal experience. It's not a burden on me if I love doing it. There's a lot of opportunity for people nowadays to sell anything. The internet is there. You can literally sell anything online.

ICCO CANADA: What is your relationship with the Italian community now? Do you feel a part of it?

ALTOMARE: I am part of the ICCO Canada with my father. My father's the president of that, so I do go to all the events. I'm really enjoying that. When it comes to the culture, there are a bunch of Italian events that go on, I think, every long weekend. They call them club nights, so I attend all of those, and I'm supporting the community that way.

ICCO CANADA: Do you think that's of value, to have a business organization like the ICCO Canada?

ALTOMARE: I think so. It's definitely important to be part of the Italian community. Even in university I was part of the Utica Club, which is the St. Mike's Italian club and I went to those events. I try to stay close to my roots, and close to my heritage.

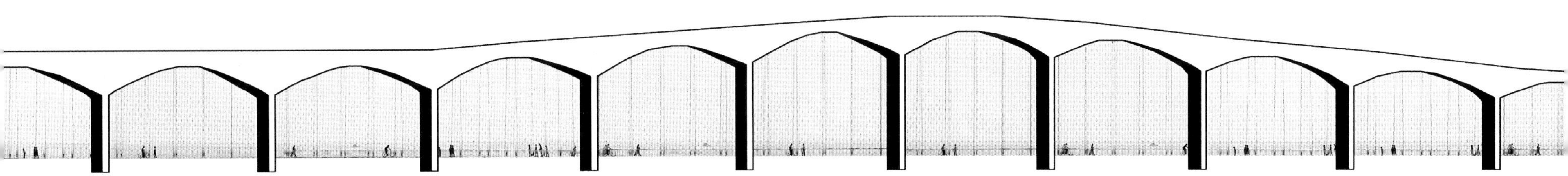

ANGELA, LEFT; MELISSA, RIGHT. PHOTO: DANIEL RICCI

FROM BUILDING TO WINEMAKING: AT YOUR SERVICE

ANGELA MAROTTA IS THE CEO OF TWO SISTERS AND THE DIRECTOR OF CIVIL MARKETING FOR SOLMAR DEVELOPMENT. MELISSA MAROTTA-PAOLICELLI IS THE CAO OF TWO SISTERS.

"We make it a point to go to Italy every summer, all of us with our kids. Sometimes we'll go throughout the year. But it's very, very important. I still speak Italian to my parents. I think, it's a core value of what it means to be Italian. It's that sense of a little bit of sacrifice. And, how can I put it? Certain principles. You need a good foundation of family for you to continue to make good decisions."

ICCO CANADA: Well the obvious first question: What's it like working with your sister?

MELISSA: It's wonderful. We push each other through our weaknesses and celebrate our strengths. And in terms of our roles, we've kind of evolved in those roles naturally. So I kind of have a little bit more of a creative spirit. She's a little bit more analytical as well.

ANGELA: I like business a bit more: the business planning and numbers and budgeting. But we're so lucky. We were raised in a very small family, just my sister and I and my parents. We don't have a lot of cousins. We were raised to be very close from a young age, and we just have a high respect for each other. So even with disagreements, we really do try to work them through. We're definitely a team. We share the same vision.

ICCO CANADA: Your family background as developers shows magnificently in the work you've done here at the winery. Now that it's built out, the job becomes more about the wine, the marketing, the events, the restaurant, and the whole hospitality side of owning a winery. It's a big departure from the family development business. Why?

MELISSA: I think it stems from things that our parents exposed us to from the time we were very young, through our travels, through beautiful dinners. It was something that we did every Friday night with the four of us. So, it was always a dream of our family to one day run a winery. And to share the love that we have of wine, and food, coming together. These experiences are so beautiful, and we wanted to allow for a place where the public can come and experience that as well.

ANGELA: But to answer your question directly, because I know you're trying to correlate it with Solmar, it's a departure, yes, because it's a completely different industry. But what aligns both is, we're very consumer driven. We already have an innate understanding of what the consumer wants—be it a house, a condominium, or commercial properties; and overall design, to wine, to food. It's about satisfying consumers and knowing what they want. I think with both companies, the standard of what we do is always pretty high because we do want repeat customers, whether it be in the wine industry or with Solmar.

ICCO CANADA: What was the trigger that made you finally say, "let's do a winery"?

ANGELA: Our family has a strong entrepreneurial spirit. Things for us are opportunities that we take on always driven by passion. And I know it sounds corny, but it's the truth. I mean, there's a passion for design. There's a passion for building. There's a passion for when we look at a piece of property: we can envision what it's going to be like years down the road. So that's always been something that we were pretty sensitive to. We always wanted to get into the wine industry. I think it was something in the back of my father's mind for a very long time. We love land. Our dad was a farmer. His whole family were farmers. So for them to cultivate or to have the opportunity to cultivate land, which was going to be vines, that was the focus: when we saw the property, we envisioned a winery or a vineyard on it.

ICCO CANADA: We're talking *here*? You saw this land...

ANGELA: This property. Yes.

MELISSA: There were no vines. It was a peach orchard, and the opportunity came up. Our father came to Canada many years ago holding on to the tradition of making wine. He was a stonemason as well. He came to Canada with that and he wanted to hold on to something from Italy. He knew how to make wine and it was always something in the back of his mind.

ANGELA: Back then, even in our initial discussions as a family, we all thought, "Oh my gosh, this is a crazy idea. How are we going to penetrate this market? There were so many challenges. But again, there's a level of risk that we always take, and that's something that we were ready for. We saw how the future generations of our family can carry it on. I mean, the most famous wineries in the world are carried on for generations. So I think the intent of my father from the beginning was: I want to do this because I want to know that my children, my grandchildren, my great grandchildren...

ICCO CANADA: A legacy business.

ANGELA: That's right. He wanted to create a legacy business, built from a labour of love—something we were all very passionate about, and that we shared from a very young age as a family.

ICCO CANADA: So you bought this land and you had to tear out the peach trees and plant the vines?

MELISSA: Yes. This was a peach orchard. So when we purchased the property, we did keep some of the peach trees in the back. We have peach trees, cherry, plum, we have table grapes. And we kept those for future use of the restaurant.

ANGELA: As a family, it is a tradition for us to pick cherries every summer. Our family still holds onto jamming and harvesting for our own use. So that was really important: I think my dad really thought that through in knowing that in the future, we'd continue to do that.

MELISSA: We knew we wanted to focus on just Bordeaux varietals here because our climate is very similar to Bordeaux, France. And if we're going to do something where we're going to be growing a particular grape, then it has to be a grape that we know will thrive in this climate. The terroir here is very similar to Bordeaux. Our soil was tested and the Niagara escarpment itself has a lot of the subsoils and all the rocks and minerals.

ANGELA: And the limestone.

MELISSA: Exactly. Beautiful for growing grapes. So we focused on Merlot, Cabernet Franc and Cabernet Sauvignon. We have that equally split on our property, and they're exclusively our own grapes. We don't purchase any grapes. Each vine is tended to up to 10 times in one year by the human hand. So we have that commitment to quality, and it shows in the grapes.

ICCO CANADA: When did you plant?

MELISSA: We planted in 2007. And our first vintage was in 2010.

ANGELA: The wines that we wanted to produce were going to be full-bodied wines that can age years and could be purchased and held in cellar. So that was the whole premise as well. And we have very low yields. So, while most wineries do between eight to ten tonnes per acre, we do two and a half to three and a half. So we drop a lot of fruit.

MELISSA: Our commitment to quality also shows when we release our wine. 2010 is our first vintage and we released it in 2014. From vine to bottle, we respect the time period that's needed to really produce a premium wine. When you open up that bottle, you let it breathe, and it's perfect. Our wines are aged two to three years in barrels and then two years in bottle before release. We're very patient.

ICCO CANADA: To go from "I want to build a winery" to "when will this winery be ready"—those first few years must have been exciting but frustrating, too: wanting to taste the wine; wondering "what can my winery do?"

MELISSA: And we understood that.

ICCO CANADA: So you planted. I'm imagining you've got some viticulturists—

MELISSA: We have a vineyard manager who handles the vines. And again, it's us as well, going through the vineyard and making sure that everything is the way it should be.

ANGELA: And we don't outsource the management of the vineyard: it is somebody that works directly with us. There are some wineries that outsource the management—that's very import-ant. Everything is done in-house.

ICCO CANADA: Who blends the wine?

ANGELA: Adam Pearce. When we met Adam, we knew right away that he was going to be the perfect fit for Two Sisters. He shared the same vision as us for the quality of wines. For him, it wasn't about production, it was about quality, because it's his reputation that's on the line as well. There's a mutual respect there. And we get along so well. He's very collaborative with us as a family. He understands what it's like to work for a family—a very different dynamic than most. We're not corporately run.

PHOTOS: COURTESY OF TWO SISTERS VINEYARDS

ICCO CANADA: So in designing the restaurant, despite the Bordeaux varietals, you went Italian.

MELISSA: For us to have an Italian restaurant was important because we are Italian, and it's part of our heritage, which we're incredibly proud of. And in regard to the main menu, it revolves around the wines, not the other way around. The thing about Italian cuisine is you don't have to have so many ingredients to make ingredients shine. Simplicity is key with Italian cuisine. That's what we're trying to project with the restaurant.

ICCO CANADA: So do mom and dad work here at the winery? Or are they just investors.

ANGELA: They're very much a part of the winery. The family owns the winery. And they have their opinions.

MELISSA: I think the biggest thing that we always speak about is the restaurant because we're so food-obsessed. Everyone has their say, absolutely.

ICCO CANADA: But you guys do the day-to-day?

ANGELA: Yes, but when it comes to the wine tasting, it is me, my sister, my dad and Adam, our winemaker. When it comes to the stages of barrel ageing and tank, we'll always go through that whole process of tasting before we finalize what that blend is; we all agree on the components of the blend before it goes into bottle. And then we taste it many times before it's finally released to market. That's definitely a group effort.

ICCO CANADA: Your first vintage was 2010. How many cases were you able to produce in the first vintage?

MELISSA: 3,700 cases of red. 900 cases of white.

ANGELA: So, 43,000 bottles of red and 10,000 bottles of white.

MELISSA: We're set this year to produce over 20,000 cases of red and white. So, 240,000 bottles. We've grown quite a bit.

ANGELA: And we have the capability to do more, which we will, based on further purchases of acreages of vines. Our intention is to grow.

ICCO CANADA: Just on property?

MELISSA: Well, this property grew from the original 76 acres, and now, we're just about 130 acres. But we have other pieces of property that we've just acquired. We plan on planting more vines throughout the area in very close proximity to the winery.

ICCO CANADA: Do you sell through the LCBO? It takes a while for that, doesn't it?

ANGELA: It does. And there have been discussions with the LCBO, and they do want to have our wines on their list. We will have our Stone Eagle on their 'classics selection,' which is online. We sell a lot of our volume, and we meet the demands of our inventory through our store online: we ship direct to your door. We have a huge wine club. So a lot of what we do sells right through our doors. We really don't need to have that much of a presence or that much inventory through LCBO. Who knows what happens in the future? But our Stone Eagle will be on their 'classic selections.'

ICCO CANADA: I can see over the short years that you have been open, you've been building up a program, different varietals, different blends of wine. Where do you see yourself in the market? What's your focus? What sets you apart from other people? What do you want to be known for?

MELISSA: To be a leading winery in Canada and to be recognized internationally as a result. There's so much potential for wineries within this region to do well on a national, international level. Because the production is getting that much better. I think we've helped in pushing the boundaries of that. And the wines are a testament. A lot of them, if not most of them, are award-winning wines.

ANGELA: In addition to that, we have the estate. What we do is give an elevated winery experience. Niagara has such a dynamic landscape of different types of wines, different experiences, different wineries. So we added to that landscape. Our wine consultants are also educators. We want to make sure that when someone comes into our doors, they're educated on our wines, to make it a very welcoming environment.

L TO R: ANGELA MAROTTA, MELISSA MAROTTA-PAOLICELLI, LOUISE MAROTTA, GIUSEPPE PAOLICELLI, DANIEL J. PATTERSON, FIFTH PRESIDENT OF NIAGARA COLLEGE

MELISSA: And we're connecting with them on an emotional level. I mean, who doesn't have a great experience tasting through wines and food? We recognize how much that can add to people's overall life experiences.

ICCO CANADA: Just to go back to the international question, do you produce enough wine now that it's worth trying to cultivate that market? Do you want to sell wine in Italy or is that bringing "coal to Newcastle"?

MELISSA: Well, anything is possible. Our wines are cool climate reds, they are different than what you could expect from the terroirs of the landscape in Italy. So there is a market for everything. There is an opportunity for us to export to the UK, which we're looking into, and other areas of Europe. There is definitely demand for it. But with regards to our production I think sometimes, too much of something isn't a good thing, either. So we're understanding what can be allocated for those markets, and we're doing that.

ICCO CANADA: On a more sociological level—you're two women in the wine industry. When I was working in the restaurant business, there wasn't that many women working in the industry. I don't know what it's like now.

ANGELA: It's changed.

ICCO CANADA: Have you come up with issues or unique challenges because you're women?

ANGELA: There's a lot of women in the wine industry. If you look even to Italy there's the Antinori sisters, I mean, there are so many women, second, third generation, that are running the wineries today and doing such a great job, as winemakers as well.

ICCO CANADA: But that culture in Italy has been around a lot longer, right? That's why I'm asking because here it's different.

MELISSA: There are definitely female winemakers in the region and also female-run wineries, as ours is. Not a lot though.

ICCO CANADA: So you don't find that an issue?

ANGELA: I think it sets us apart. We have an advantage, because there aren't so many. So that also brings attention to the fact that this is a great winery, and it's owned by women. So that is a good thing. And the market has been taken up by women as well with regards to who purchases our wines. And who comes.

ICCO CANADA: Your family has made a major contribution to Niagara College with the Marotta Family Innovation Complex. Can you speak a little bit about that and why you did that?

ANGELA: We have a lot of Niagara College graduates working in the winery. Our wine-makers are graduates. Many of our chefs and sous chefs in the restaurant are Niagara College graduates. Also the staff.

MELISSA: And it's a leading institution.

ANGELA: Yes. What they do, for that part of the industry is amazing, and they're very innovative. So again, coming here and seeing what they're doing, and seeing the quality of students that are coming out of the college, it was just a natural kind of thing that we wanted to do.

MELISSA: And we're investing in the future. So our place here in Niagara-on-the-Lake, whether it be the winery, whether it be at the restaurant, whether it be the hotel, which we're planning for, and we're going through the process of designing—we need those graduates. And we want to give an opportunity to expand on possibilities and give them hope for a great future regardless of what their backgrounds are.

ICCO CANADA: Will the hotel be on this property or somewhere else?

MELISSA: A very close walking distance.

ICCO CANADA: Is it an existing building or you're going to build something?

ANGELA: It does have four historical buildings on the property which we're going to be utilizing for certain programming within the hotel and for the hotel. The actual hotel itself—which we're aiming for about 130 rooms—that's going to be new construction, a new build. That's going to compliment the area, compliment the existing buildings and reflect the beauty of the heritage of Niagara-on-the-Lake.

MELISSA: And also it's an extension of the experience here. We're giving them another opportunity or option for hotel space. And I think the market here is only going to get bigger.

ICCO CANADA: So you've kind of addressed this already but in different ways. But is being part of the Italian Canadian community important to you?

MELISSA: Very. 100%.

ANGELA: Oh yes. We're very proud.

MELISSA: And I hope that the generations to come don't lose what it really means to be Italian. We make it a point to go to Italy every summer, all of us with our kids. Sometimes we'll go throughout the year. But it's very, very important. I still speak Italian to my parents. I think, it's a core value of what it means to be Italian. It's that sense of a little bit of sacrifice. And, how can I put it? Certain principles. You need a good foundation of family for you to continue to make good decisions. That foundation is really important.

ICCO CANADA: In the '50s and '60s, so many Italians came to Canada. Lots of working-class people. They came to build and dig the roadways and that kind of thing. And in a very short period of time, there were successful Italian Canadians in every sector of the economy. What do you attribute that change to?

ANGELA: The opportunity was here. I think a lot of the immigrants that came in, including my father, were intelligent. Although they didn't have the opportunity to go to school. I mean, they were so poverty stricken. But had a lot of them—and we know who they are, the leaders in industry—had they gone to school, they would have done so well. They would have achieved a lot of academic accolades. And a lot of them didn't have those opportunities. I know if our father had gone to university, he probably would have done extremely well. I think they're able to make really good decisions because of that.

ICCO CANADA: One of the things that this question is leading up to, basically leads to your kids. Because your dad's generation, they succeeded in a major way, that cohort of Italian Canadians, and they're in every sector. But now we're at an interesting time because everything's digital. Every industry is being disrupted. That's what your kids are going to be faced with.

MELISSA: Yes, it's a challenge.

ICCO CANADA: And how do you guide them? How do you see the future, especially as it relates to Italian Canadians?

ANGELA: Well, Italian Canadians have kids in family businesses. I think it's important for kids in general to build character, to really get to know themselves and who they want to be, rather than a mirror image of something or someone else. So I think it's important for us to be in this industry in that we're very much in tune with the general public. They have to work in the restaurant. And it's so important for them to be able to do things, where they are communicating with people, being forced to look people in the eye, and have that average and regular communication. And you can do that through this sector. So that's important for us.

MELISSA: It's very easy for kids, especially our kids, to grow up in a bubble and to protect them from so many factors and things in life. We don't do that. There's a lot of tough love in our family. And there's a lot of pushing them and just them being forced to jump and to figure out on their own, which is what our parents did with us.

ANGELA: Absolutely. Our father always pushed the boundaries for us and pushed us into situations, where we did feel uncomfortable. We weren't sure if we were ready. Figure it out and do it. That's exactly how we were raised, and how we raise our kids.

ICCO CANADA: Do you think, every generation that goes by, the Italian dissipates a bit? Is that what happened with your kids or...?

MELISSA: No. No. You know what it is? It's the responsibility of the parents to make sure that they hold onto traditions. Every year, we do tomatoes in the garage. There are family dinners that everybody has to be at the table sitting and eating. That's very, very important for us. So it's a responsibility of the parents to make sure that they hold onto that. And then that way their kids, one day, when they have their own families, understand the importance of taking that time for family.

ANGELA: But I think you have a point in that yes, some of it probably will dissipate a little bit. But I think what's important is the family values. And you hope that it doesn't.

ICCO CANADA: This is a bit more of an abstract question, but it's like wine is of the earth, is from the earth, but it's also something that travels, that everybody can share. And we live in that kind of transnational culture. You travel. Your kids are going to travel. Is there a relation between Italian Canadian roots and the actual physical roots out there in the vineyard?

MELISSA: Our terroir, I think, is our family. It really is. Even today, if my kids are doing something, they're like, "I want to make Nonno proud." Not us. They want to make their grandfather proud. It's a beautiful thing to have... You're blessed if you have a family, and you're even more blessed if you have a family that's united. And, speaking of roots, it's important, you know: as teenagers, they go through their things. And as new parents, we go through our things. But ultimately, knowing that as a family, we can always rely on one another.

ANGELA: But wine also: wine doesn't care about your culture. Wine doesn't care about where you come from. Everybody in the world enjoys wine. Unless, of course, it's restricted because of religion. But you can go anywhere in the world, and there's wine on the menus.

ICCO CANADA: But it expresses a culture, too, right?

ANGELA: It does.

MELISSA: Even when you're drinking wine, yes, you think of the wine: what varietal is it? what year is it? what are its tasting notes?— and so on? But it's also a very beautiful thing. We've shared many a bottle of wine having beautiful conversations. We remember where we were, who we were with. It's a very emotional thing. So that's the beauty of enjoying the wine as well.

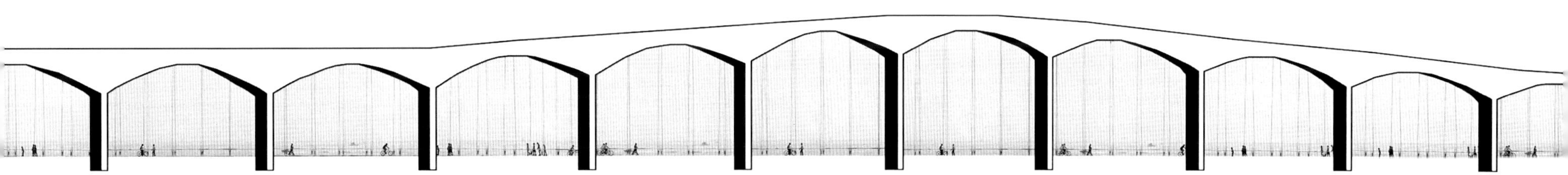

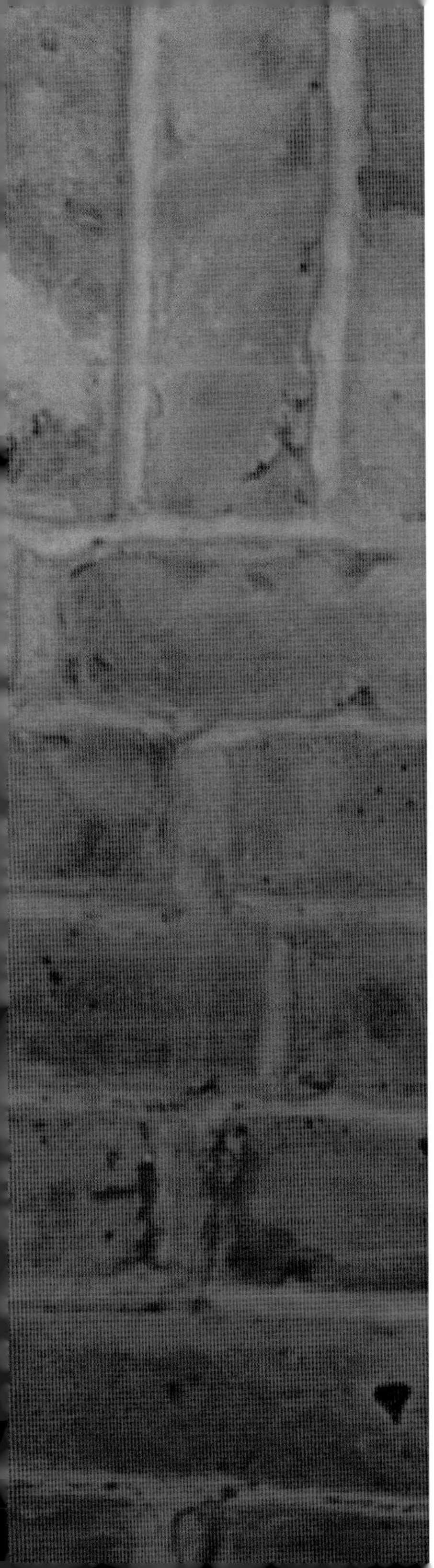

PHOTO CREDIT: GIULIA STORTI

CREATING COMMUNITY, CREATING HOME

CHRISTINA GIANNONE
VICE PRESIDENT, PLANNING AND DEVELOPMENT OF
PORT CREDIT WEST VILLAGE PARTNERS

"I think in the next generation of executives you'll see a lot more women at the table. Of course, we get support from men on that side, but predominantly it's still dominated by the baby boomers and that baby boomer generation is male."

ICCO CANADA: Your official title is Vice President, Planning and Development of Port Credit West Village Partners but one of those partners is FRAM, which is the family business.

GIANNONE: Yes. I worked for FRAM previously. Coming out of my undergrad, FRAM needed someone to sort of step in. I hadn't planned on coming to work for FRAM directly, but they needed help on a project right across the street and I jumped in. That was in 2007. I fell in love with real estate development on the planning side. And I have worked for FRAM ever since. I grew up in Port Credit, born and raised. My commute was from the west side of the river to here. Every day I would pass the site that I'm currently working on. It was vacant for 30 plus years, and when that came up for sale, I said, "I'm either working on that project or I'm moving, because I can't pass the site every day knowing someone else is shaping that." So our partnership was formed, the Port Credit West Village Partners. It includes FRAM, and also Diamond Corp, Dream, and Kilmer. So there are four partners in the group and...

ICCO CANADA: Dream is family related to you too, right?

GIANNONE: No. But my brother works there. I'm one of four kids, I'm the eldest, and then my brother who's a year and a half younger, he works at Dream. So the partnership was formed. We submitted an RFP to Imperial Oil. They were the former owner of the site, and the partnership was the successful bidder and then they formed the West Village Partners and hired a small team. I was the first one on that team to basically represent the partnership, oversee it, make sure that it's carried through from beginning to end. So it's myself and we've got three other people. Each partner brings their expertise and their staff, but our team sort of manages that process. So I no longer work for FRAM. I'm on the partnership side, representing the four groups.

ICCO CANADA: That means you deal with the permits with the city and the province?

GIANNONE: We're supported by the partners' teams, but I was involved in putting the proposal together, so from land acquisition. And then we've been going through the planning process, getting the zoning approvals, master plan approvals. Now we're into the design of our first three blocks—working and managing our design team, starting the sales and marketing process. We'll be launching our first phase in May of this year. So through that, and then once construction starts I'll start shifting to the next phase. When the condominium is completed, I carry it through to closings as well.

ICCO CANADA: It's 72 acres and from the pictures, there are a lot of buildings there. How many phases are there going to be?

GIANNONE: There are four big phases, but I'll say that it'll probably be broken down into 12 to 15 different phases as you move through. There's approximately 3000 residential units, 400,000 square feet of commercial—so retail and office: there's a proposed elementary school; proposed YMCA; we've got affordable housing on the site; we've got purpose-built rental on the site. So there's a broad range, and it's a really exciting opportunity to bring some interesting partners and tenants as part of the overall project, and to extend what makes Port Credit really special. I mean I was born and raised here so I'm a little partial to it. But it's a pretty incredible community and to be able to add to that is a once in a lifetime opportunity.

ICCO CANADA: Are the West Village Partners building everything?

GIANNONE: Yes.

ICCO CANADA: And Giannone Petricone Associates are working on it?

GIANNONE: They were the master plan architect. So they oversaw the whole thing. Everything that we've developed to date and that we've got approved, they managed that, and they designed that. Now in an individual phase by phase, they're going to be doing one of our first townhouse blocks, and another condo as well. They're not going to be doing all of the buildings, but we have them doing a couple.

ICCO CANADA: They actually laid out the streets?

GIANNONE: Yes. Master planning. They're very good at it, actually. Very, very good.

ICCO CANADA: So as construction begins, how does your role change?

GIANNONE: Because it is such a big site I've got a co-lead that oversees the single purpose vehicle, the partnership that we have. So he's on the construction end. There is sort of a handoff in the workflow, that I need to make sure that what's being constructed stays as per the intent and the vision, but he'll handle the construction end. So as that's happening, I'll be circling back and starting the next phase. Because what construction means is that we've hit our sales targets, and so we should be moving on to the next phase. That will happen for the next 8 to 10 years, that cycle.

ICCO CANADA: Eight to ten years?

GIANNONE: Yeah. I mean, if we can do it quicker, great, but we're anticipating an eight to ten year build out.

ICCO CANADA: You'll be in this office for a while.

GIANNONE: But this is home for me anyways, so I love it.

ICCO CANADA: You live across the street?

GIANNONE: I did. I've got two kids, and so after I was pregnant with my second, we said, okay, even though we love condo living, we have to move. So we live five minutes west of here.

ICCO CANADA: Family stays in Port Credit.

GIANNONE: Yep.

ICCO CANADA: So, obviously your family has been incredible. So many people are involved in the business. Did you always want to be in the business?

GIANNONE: At a young age, starting at the age of 13, I was doing summers here. So that was my intro to it. But, I'll say I didn't know that that's what I was going to do. I didn't know that I had a passion for that, because the stuff that I was doing was small jobs here and there. My undergrad was commerce and finance. If I knew that I wanted to be in the business, I probably would've done planning or engineering, or something like that. But I wanted to go into business, keep my options open. And then, as I mentioned before, FRAM needed some support on the 22-story condo across the street, and I jumped in and I said, "Sure, yeah, I'll try," and, "I'll help you guys out." And then I fell in love with the planning side. I loved sitting around a team of creative people, seeing a vacant piece of land, thinking what is it? What is it going to be? You're creating something that someone is going to live in. This is the biggest purchase that they're going to make for a long time. To be able to help shape that, and to offer that, was really exciting.

And then to also create the relationships with city staff and hear their comments and feedback, I just loved the process. I thought it was fascinating, and everyday there were different challenges. No day is the same. And I just kind of took off with that. I know that's a long-winded answer, but then I went back to school and took a certificate program through the Urban Land Institute to freshen up on the planning side, which I didn't have any background in, to help expedite the learning curve. And then I decided to go back and do my MBA at the Schulich School of Business. That was also focused on real estate, some of the finance side that, again, I hadn't really been exposed to previously.

So I went back to school for the passion that I discovered. But it was something that was already there. I'm the fifth generation in this business and so it has carried on. My grandfather was already the third generation, back in Italy. So there obviously was sort of a tie, but I was never pushed into it. It was always, do what you want to get into and push yourself, challenge yourself, and do that. And I'll say three of the four of us ended up in development. I'm still obviously working on a project with FRAM, but my brother, John, works for Dream. My youngest brother, Rob, moved to New York City, actually recently New Jersey now, and he works for a developer there. He did his master's in New Jersey. And we have another brother, David, who went and became a chiropractor.

ICCO CANADA: Where'd he come from?

GIANNONE: Yeah. He went a different path, a different passion. And he owns three clinics and gym facilities called SWAT.

ICCO CANADA: How does being a long-term resident influence the work that you do here?

GIANNONE: Every single decision I know is going to shape, not just my own future—because it will—but of my kids. I know they can move on when they get older. But for now, we go to the parks, we walk the area, we're walking distance to our site. So I know every decision that I make is going to impact that. It's exciting, because to be on the inside and to be able to really shape your own community... I've got relationships with neighbours. I know what people are looking for. So it's a different perspective than finding another parcel that you have no ties to, because I already know, sort of, what is missing in this area, and what we can add. Obviously there's a bit more of a heart string to it. So, I still always have to have my business hat on and make sure that I'm making decisions that are for the best for the partnership, but I'm also doing it for the community, too. I think I'm able to find win-win solutions, because I know what all the stakeholders' goals are.

ICCO CANADA: Has the community been supportive of the project, would you say?

GIANNONE: I'd say yes. Before we even were involved, the city of Mississauga—and I think it was initiated by the community—created something called Inspiration Port Credit, and it was a master planning framework. So the city and the rate payers actually created a document of what would happen if this parcel ever became available. This was before it was even put on the market—What could it be? What would people want to see? And I'd say that we stayed pretty true to what that original vision was. We worked a lot throughout the process with the multiple stakeholders, with the ratepayer groups, with the BIA. Obviously, you can't please everyone 100% of the time, in that people have different interpretations of what that vision could be, but it's been empty and gated for over 30 years. The community is going to get a beautiful park out of it, and we're going to get new amenities, new retail. I mean, it's an exciting opportunity to open that up again.

ICCO CANADA: In many ways this project is illustrative of the challenges and opportunities that your generation faces as a younger generation in business. An earlier generation was able to build up the GTA pretty freely on existing farmland. Mississauga, like many other communities, was allowed to sprawl. Development opportunities for your generation, especially by Lake Ontario, are quite different, because it seems the only available lands left are brownfields that often require extensive remediation. Do you feel that you have the same opportunities as the previous generation had?

GIANNONE: Well we don't have the same. I think the challenges today are to build differently and to build smarter, to make conscious decisions. The previous generation didn't know as much about global warming, the environment, the climate change side. I don't think that the infrastructure was set up to anticipate all the traffic congestion that there is, or affordability.

So these are challenges that we're facing that aren't necessarily the same. But it still provides exciting opportunities to shape based off of what we're facing today. And so with climate change and issues of car use, we need to focus on these areas to form underutilized old industrial sites, that are so central in our communities, and give them purpose again in a smart way that is environmentally conscious. We are creating something that will give back to the community, making conscious decisions of increasing density where transit is actually already there—where people don't need to get into their cars.

These are the decisions that we have to make that will benefit the community, will benefit society and the world. We have to start making those decisions now, because the previous decisions got us to the challenges that we have today.

ICCO CANADA: You've anticipated my follow-up question which was, what are the biggest challenges facing the industry as a whole in the coming years? Climate change, transportation, population density...?

GIANNONE: Affordability.

ICCO CANADA: Affordability will be another one. Are there any solutions to these issues on the horizon that excite you about future growth? We do LEED certification now. Is there anything in particular of interest that you think is going to be very helpful?

GIANNONE: It's a challenge, but investment in infrastructure, that's something that the city and the province have been talking about, especially in this area, which is going to be something that's really important to smart growth. On the affordability side, I'll say at this point right now there haven't been any great responses yet to that. So that's something that's exciting in the sense that there is a real problem that needs to be solved, and so we are working to try and incorporate affordability into our project and prioritize that. And there are a couple other of developers that are doing that, and it's important to focus on that. There is a big challenge to be environmentally sustainable. A lot of new technologies are coming out. There's a lot of options for alternative energy sources.

The government will need to respond to that, because right now there's a lot of subsidies on the current energy models that we have, which take away from prioritizing alternative energies. But we are exploring that even on our site—geothermal, solar. So there are a lot of exciting things. We just need to figure out how to implement them at a larger scale.

PHOTO: CREDIT: GIULIA STORTI

ICCO CANADA: Do you find the federal government and the province are...

GIANNONE: They need to step up.

ICCO CANADA: ... supportive of research, and that kind of thing, because you need that too, right?

GIANNONE: I mean, yes and no, but it changes. For instance, we had made an application for a grant on the energy side, and when we met, we made the submission. The program was cut a couple of weeks after that. So, it changes. We need the government to step up and really support that innovation. On our team we have an innovation committee that's focused on trying to find those new technologies to ensure that we are future-proofing and incorporating smart living abilities for our residents and for the neighboring community. But there needs additional support, for sure.

ICCO CANADA: To speak on a more of a personal level: the development industry has been dominated by men, traditionally. Has this been an issue for you in your career, or has the playing field been more level for your generation?

GIANNONE: A lot more women are in the real estate industry for sure. There's a lot of support.

ICCO CANADA: From women?

GIANNONE: For women, from women.

ICCO CANADA: From men?

GIANNONE: I'll say that as an executive I still sit in boardrooms with mostly men. For myself personally, I mentioned before, I grew up with three brothers, so I think that really helped set me up for some success.

ICCO CANADA: "You don't scare me."

GIANNONE: Exactly. I can hold my own in a boardroom. But I think it is changing. I think in the next generation of executives you'll see a lot more women at the table. Of course, we get support from men on that side, but predominantly it's still dominated by the baby boomers and that baby boomer generation is male.

ICCO CANADA: But aside from that have you felt held back at all? I mean, there's the sort of sexist com-mentary that just happens. But has it actually slowed you down?

GIANNONE: No, I'll say it hasn't slowed me down. I guess I grew up in that in-between of traditional women's roles versus 'women can do anything,' so I didn't get some opportunities. Not saying that I couldn't, but I feel like I sort of leapt over it. In my industry I didn't get the onsite construction experience, whereas my brothers did, and they got the office paperwork. So I missed that. It's, how do you make decisions to ensure that you're not left behind? In my role on the planning side and the development side, as the buildings were going up, I would go on site, and I'd ask questions, I'd want to understand what is happening. I could read plans, no problem, but how does that translate on the site? I also made sure that I worked very closely with the construction management team. So again, when they're going into detailed engineering drawings, even though I didn't have an engineering background, I wanted to understand what the implications were, what the challenges were, so that I could eventually take that on myself. So I think it's just having a personality of making sure that you aren't left behind. Obviously you need the extra support, but you can push your way through too.

ICCO CANADA: And that's not a gender thing particularly?

GIANNONE: No, it's personality.

ICCO CANADA: Italian Canadians have played a large role in building and developing the GTA. Is there something in the culture that makes them excel at this work?

GIANNONE: That's an interesting question. I mean they're very passionate. They're very proud, it's a proud culture. This could be just my own family experience, but I feel like what's shared in the culture is that when you're putting yourself into a project you work hard, and you put your best foot forward and you see it through. I think that getting in and working with your hands... Italians are very, I don't know, expressive. I think all of those combined give them... Gosh, this is a challenging question.

ICCO CANADA: That's the whole idea.

GIANNONE: Yeah. I think that being proud, being passionate about what you do and getting out there, working with your hands... I'm Northern Italian and Southern Italian, and there's differences between the cultures, but they're both industrious. I just see that translating here. And again, just putting forth the best of their abilities and in everything that they do. Regarding the housing industry specifically, again, I don't know if I'm digging too deep into the Italian culture, but I'll say family is everything, and family is home and home is family. And so again, being proud of where you live and setting that up for yourself is just something that's, to me, embedded in the culture. So being able to create that home for someone else and give someone else that basic human right of creating and settling and having that, I think that's also part of the culture too. Like, every memory I have is with my family at home. And so being able to do that and give other people opportunities to create their own memories in their own spaces is why I love my job and why I find home-building is so rewarding.

ICCO CANADA: It comes naturally to you?

GIANNONE: Yeah.

ICCO CANADA: I think that there is something in that. Part of it is when the big immigration came in the fifties, they were doing construction work initially. So that's a skill they learned, and they learned to excel at it. In the same way that Sri Lankans came and worked in kitchens, and now that community plays a huge positive role in restaurants throughout the GTA. I think what you said about the house-proudness of Italians is true. Somehow that, combined with the discerning sensibility that Italians also have, created a perfect storm of elements. So, is your Italian background important to you?

GIANNONE: To me it is who I am. So just the different aspects of the culture, again, family being so prominent, and it's how I make decisions in what I do. Again, it's how do people live? So if you're talking about it as tied to work, then yes, I carry that through. I'm also loud and vocal. I'm proud. I'm feisty. So I think those all come from the Italian culture. I mean, it's built who I am today, for sure.

PHOTO CREDIT: RICK O'BRIEN

GLOBAL AND LOCAL

ANTHONY DI DOMENICO
PARTNER | CO-LEADER, ANTITRUST / COMPETITION & MARKETING
FASKEN MARTINEAU DUMOULIN

"Thirty years ago, when you reviewed a case, you had a few boxes of documents, some interviews, that sort of thing, basic files. Now you have gigabytes of data that you have to go through. That's a big cost-time-intensive process."

ICCO CANADA: When I look at your CV, I get the impression you had a very clear idea of your path from an early age. You were very active in student affairs, serving as the chair of the University Student Senate Caucus, sitting on the Board of Governments, et cetera. Then you were vice-chair of the Alumni Board, and now you're on the university's Board of Governors. You've been an adjunct professor at Osgoode Hall Law School pretty much since you graduated from that same school. So, what led you to pursue a law degree, and what made you align yourself so closely to York? How's that for a question?

DI DOMENICO: Yeah, that's a great question. Let me start with an intermedial question first. I spent a lot of time at York, and I would say that York University is a fabulous environment for students to grow and develop. York has a significant number of students who are the first to go to university in particular families. And that is important because it facilitates inclusion and affords opportunities for students to take leadership roles. I think that York deserves a lot of credit for what it does, and that's why I continue to be quite loyal to York and to work with York even today.

It allowed me, for example, when I was at York, to pursue my academic endeavors, but to take on leadership roles. And again, it's the kind of environment where, if you have the energy and the wherewithal to do it, those opportunities will be available to you. In terms of how I became a lawyer, I was always fascinated with law, really for superficial reasons from the beginning, since I don't have any lawyers in my family. But I watched Law and Order programs and found the criminal justice system to be very cool and interesting. During my undergraduate degree, I was a political science and a Law Society major. I studied a lot about how the justice system and law interconnects with society, whether politically, socially, or economically. I found all of those issues to be fascinating, and that really percolated my interest and led me to go to law school.

ICCO CANADA: Your point is that York took a lot of first-generation—the children of recent immi-grants—and maybe that helped define how they proceeded as a university. Was that your case as well?

DI DOMENICO: Yes. But look, Canada is filled—and this is a good thing—with lots of first-generation immigrants. And I would say all the universities across Canada embrace that, so it's not just York. What I find special about York is that it has been very inclusive and actually is very proactive in giving opportunities for any of their students to take on leadership roles. In my case, I felt very empowered and encouraged to do that. And then once I started doing that, I became more and more involved, because I really did enjoy the experience very much.

ICCO CANADA: Did you start at Fasken right from graduation?

DI DOMENICO: Actually, I started there before. Many of the law firms recruit students out of law school. They ask you to join them in the summer programs that they have. I started at Fasken in the summer of 2004. And then when I graduated, I articled there, and that's a prerequisite of becoming a licensed lawyer. I stayed there ever since as an associate and I became a partner over time.

ICCO CANADA: You're a very loyal person.

DI DOMENICO: That's a very good point. I am a loyal person, but just because you stay with a firm doesn't really mean that things can't evolve. I've evolved a lot professionally. When I started at Fasken I was a commercial and class action litigator and did a lot of general litigation. But if you look at my career now, I specialized. I co-head the firm's antitrust competition and marketing group and basically focus my entire practice now on competition law.

ICCO CANADA: That's interesting because from 2014 to 2016, you worked with the federal department of justice as an advisor to the commissioner of the Competition Bureau. You had to leave Fasken to play that role, right?

DI DOMENICO: That's right. I took the leave of absence from the firm in order to do that job. That allowed me to work on competition law full-time for two years on behalf of the regulator. Like every country Canada has a competition regulator. What that competition enforcer does is enforce the laws about competition. What they're concerned about is too much concentration in certain areas of conduct that may be considered anti-competitive. Because if you engage in that conduct, it may lead to higher prices for consumers to pay, less innovation and just bad competition. In our market economy, we have a belief that vigorous and effective competition leads to lower prices and better products and services for consumers. That's what that agency does. So, I was their prosecutor. I would advise the Commissioner of Competition and the Competition Bureau and prosecute cases upon its behalf against companies and individuals who may be engaging in anti-competitive conduct.

ICCO CANADA: But what led you to that? Maybe I'm wrong, but I'm assuming when you go on hiatus from your company and then go work for the government, you probably make less money. There must have been some reason why you wanted to do this.

DI DOMENICO: I made a decision over some time during my career that I wanted to specialize in competition law. I did what many people do, especially in foreign jurisdictions like the United States, that if you really want to bolster your experience and credibility in that space, it's a good idea to spend some time with the competition enforcer in your jurisdiction, to really learn and understand how cases are thought through, the economic sort of thought process, et cetera. That's why I did it. It was always an intent to come back. I think it was an investment in me and my practice to go over there and to really roll up my sleeves and learn and experience all there is to know of competition enforcement from the government side so I can come back and use that experience to further develop my career and advise my clients on those points.

ICCO CANADA: So if you want to defend somebody in front of the Competition Bureau, you know how they work.

DI DOMENICO: You have a better understanding of the operations. And again, that's a very common thing. If you look at the United States, there's tons of people who do that. It's not as common in Canada though. And it's a big sacrifice in Canada because I had to move away from Toronto.

ICCO CANADA: But you went all in, because in 2018 you published the book "Competition Enforcement and Litigation in Canada." Has a nice ring to it, but 1200 pages! When do you find time to write that much?

DI DOMENICO: Well, it's very cold in Ottawa, and some of those late nights there's really not much you can do outside, so I spent a lot of time writing. But I should say that book, all kidding aside, took me about five years to write. I took my time with it because I really wanted to offer something. There's some excellent text on competition law but there wasn't a text in the marketplace that really outlined enforcing the litigation process from beginning to end. There was a gap there. It was a long endeavor, and 1200 pages is true, but it's actually more like 800 without the appendix.

ICCO CANADA: Wow. Before that, were there resources for this element of law available to lawyers in Canada? Or was it scattered in different places?

DI DOMENICO: I would say it was either scattered in different places or not available at all. That's what I tried to bring together. There are a lot of good books out there on competition policy as some high-level process, but not that detail. The book basically outlines: here are all the criminal offenses under competition law; here are all the civil matters under competition law; here's how they work; here's just laying it all out; here's the process for investigation; here's the process for litigation; here are the different kinds of courts you can go to. It's really meant for, I think, two audiences. It's a teaching tool for those who are new to the area, whether you are a student or a lawyer. And for the experienced practitioner, it's a very good reminder of things. If you need a quick reference guide to understand what the test is they need for that or this, you can go ahead and do that.

ICCO CANADA: Right. So now I've got an expert in front of me: this COVID-19 pandemic has really brought home our dependence on supply chains and who controls them and all that. As we all stay at home self-isolating, we're relying more and more on digital interactions, getting

PHOTO: RICK O'BRIEN

our goods through Amazon, engaging with the world mediated by Google and Facebook, Apple, and Microsoft. So how does this impact our ability to maintain fair competition in the marketplace? Because the marketplace is really changing. Do you deal with that?

DI DOMENICO: I do. I'd make two comments about that. I think that the supply chains, and how goods are supplied generally, is a focus of competition. What competition agencies worry about is how goods and services are brought down through the supply chain, and whether or not companies who have market power may be exploiting their position to enhance their own market power by preventing new competition or lessening competition from existing competitors. That's always been a matter of concern. I think that it was there even pre-COVID-19. With COVID-19 it's become even more important because there are these critical supply chains for companies that are vital for COVID-19-related goods. If you are a company that is in the supply chain for goods and services that are important in COVID-19, say for ventilators, for masks, food, certain food supplies, things of that nature, you can expect to be under closer scrutiny than you otherwise would be as a result. For sure, supply chain is definitely a focus.

ICCO CANADA: Right, and then the larger thing: Microsoft years ago was found to be anti-competitive. The actions that they did, basically forcing people to use their stuff, they fought that. But now we have the same thing with Google and Apple. And some are more benign than others.

DI DOMENICO: Yeah. Well, those are different. That is a fascinating debate. The role of big tech has become the prevailing issue now. When you think about a hundred years ago when competition law was huge, late 1800s, early 1900s, the issue of focus was control of the railroads. Because railroads were a critical piece of infrastructure to get goods and services across country. And with that, there was this characterization of the railroad being an essential service. If you own the railroad, you can't just restrict access to it, because it's so big and so important that you need to have other entities to have access to it. And you think about the Googles of the world, the Facebooks—those entities have become so large and so important in our lives that antitrust arguments are now arising, such as, that those are important and critical services for consumers; that there should be more access allowed on them, whether by way of selling products or services or otherwise. The focus has really become these entities having so much, so large in their scale and their ability to do things, which is really fabulous for consumers, right? When you think about what kind of benefits Google has on our lives—we use that every day. When do you not Google something to find something?

ICCO CANADA: True.

DI DOMENICO: And you think about social media platforms. I use mine every day, and I would say a significant amount of people around the world do too. But the question that antitrust regulators are thinking about is: how big is too big? And these entities engage in conduct. I think they're just under more scrutiny than you would be, just given their size and their ability to change dynamics.

ICCO CANADA: I guess one of the interesting things is they have so much money. A company creates some new software, they could just buy them up. Isn't that anti-competitive? Partly it's just the market economy working as it should, in one sense. But the other sense, they're the only ones that can afford to keep buying up everybody and consolidating their central role. Right?

DI DOMENICO: But again, buying entities, they can't. That's why we have merger control provisions in our Competition Act. So, if you want to merge with someone, any merger in Canada can be reviewed by the Competition Bureau. And in the United States and Europe and other countries, mergers are reviewed. So, to the extent that any of these entities want to buy someone else, that can be reviewed by those agencies. And that's what those agencies are doing. They're reviewing these potential purchases to make sure that they won't have an anti-competitive effect. So that's the check on that.

ICCO CANADA: I see.

DI DOMENICO: It's a big part of what competition law is all about, right? Merger control is a big factor. That's why companies face competition issues all the time, because of that reason.

ICCO CANADA: Would you say the Competition Bureau has more work now than they did before or less?

DI DOMENICO: I think it's just changed. They've always had a lot of work, but the work they're doing now is much more complicated, because big tech has increased their costs and ability to look at things. Thirty years ago, when you reviewed a case, you had a few boxes of documents, some interviews, that sort of thing, basic files. Now you have gigabytes of data that you have to go through. That's a big cost-time-intensive process.

ICCO CANADA: Well, the digital economy is also transnational too. I guess that makes a difference because you have to work in jurisdictions, maybe, that you're not completely familiar with.

DI DOMENICO: That's a great point. That's why the Bureau has to work with a lot of different agencies. What ends up happening is that sometimes you have mergers that are mobile, more profitable, and as a result of that you end up having to work with different agencies on the same competition issue.

ICCO CANADA: So just from your personal experience, I note that the Canadian Italian Advocates Organization, [CIAO], began life in 1984 to give a voice to Italian Canadians. They must've thought that their voice was required. It begs the questions: are separate Italian Canadian organizations like that still necessary now that Italian Canadians are so in the mainstream? And when you started, did you think it was necessary? And has it changed?

DI DOMENICO: I think those organizations are very helpful. Any organization in law, whether based on certain ethnicities, cultures, or otherwise, are good opportunities for awareness to get together, to network, exchange information, and just do things to help each other. This is a very tough business. And it's one of those businesses where people really do rely on each other for all sorts of things. If you have some sort of commonality, whether it's because you happen to be Italian Canadian or otherwise, I think anything that can form connections to people is a helpful thing.

Italians have established themselves well, and there are hundreds of Italian Canadian lawyers, if not thousands, across Canada that are doing terrific things. They would do that with or without organizations like the ICCO Canada and others. But I do think those organizations play an effective role in terms of connecting people and allowing for information sharing.

ICCO CANADA: Do you feel it's different from when you started out in 2004?

DI DOMENICO: I think it has evolved. I think Italians, certainly then, were still further advanced than some. I think what's happened is that Italian Canadians have generationally evolved. Right? And so, you're seeing Italian Canadians getting into all kinds of different areas of law that are different from the traditional areas of law and the practice. I think that Italian Canadians historically have been very strong at the real estate business, the construction business, and things of that nature. As a result, you've seen a lot of Italian Canadian lawyers choose to specialize in those areas, and that's been very effective. I would say, in addition to that, now, you're seeing Italian Canadian lawyers who are choosing all sorts of different areas of law, like mine, and others that are different. I think that that has changed.

When I look at professional organizations that I am active in, they tend to be focused on my area of competition law. And that would be on an international basis. It's not so much focused on Italian Canadians. But I do welcome opportunities to be involved in Italian Canadian organizations.

ICCO CANADA: I guess what you're saying is that being Italian Canadian doesn't necessarily play a role anymore in the pursuit of your profession? Would you agree with that?

DI DOMENICO: Yeah, that's correct. It's not a driving factor now of what kind of areas of law you practice. I think there are so many good things that come from being Italian Canadian—you think about the things we all talk about: having a strong work ethic, having regard for the immigrant family coming to Canada, working really hard and pursuing those cultural virtues we all cherish. That never changes. And I think that helps people have the drive to chug along in this business. Italian Canadian culture gives people a good foundation that I think is necessary to make it in this business. But at the same time, I think that Italian Canadians are very confident in their abilities to pursue whatever they want to pursue. They've made that transition to really focus on anything that they're interested in. And there's really nothing Italian Canadians are not into right now, insofar as law is concerned.

ICCO CANADA: Just to finish up with a broader question: you've mentored a lot—your experience at York seems to have impressed you, and you've really given back in a big way. When you advise young lawyers, not necessarily Italian Canadian, but any young lawyers, about the future of your profession, are there any issues that they should watch for, or opportunities that you might point them towards in the profession?

DI DOMENICO: In terms of professional organizations, I think it's very important to get involved in them. Because I think it takes a long time for you to find what area of law you want to specialize in. I think lawyers tend to start broad in terms of their practice. I was a general litigator when I started, and I began to narrow my practice to competition law. And that's a natural progression. You want to start with general skill-building abilities and then specialize with an area. I wouldn't say—go run off and become a solvency lawyer, or a tax lawyer, or whatever the case may be. I would say take it slow, find your way. But realize that there are all kinds of specialized areas that are very exciting. If you're doing your general practice and you want to specialize, you should feel free to do that. Because there are all sorts of areas that are very exciting, very complex, but are very much a challenge for people once they get into it. But it takes a little bit of time.

ICCO CANADA: So you're basically for a broad humanist education at the beginning?

DI DOMENICO: Yes, very much so. I think that's the way to build your skillset.

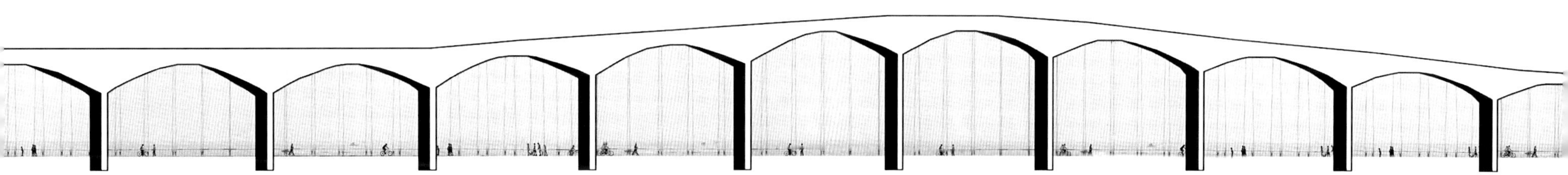

MAKING HOSPITALITY A GLOBAL ENTERPRISE

JANET ZUCCARINI
CEO, OWNER, GUSTO 54 RESTAURANT GROUP

"My leadership team is female-heavy in a male-dominated industry, but I'm not looking to hire women. I'm looking to hire the best person for the job. I don't see gender and I don't have a problem being a female boss out there."

ICCO CANADA: Your dad brought the first espresso machine to Toronto and I think the first pizza oven. Were you conscious of Italian cuisine when you were a kid? Was that a big thing?

ZUCCARINI: My father came to Toronto in 1954 and opened up a cafe and a restaurant called The Sidewalk Caffè. That's where Toronto had the first espresso machine, it had the first wood-burning pizza oven, it had the first heated patio. It was at the corner of Yonge and College. My father started in the restaurant business on his own and then immediately switched to selling and distributing espresso coffee machines in Canada. But he had a deep love of food and cooking and was always working in restaurants starting at the age of 14 in Rome, at the Hotel de Ville, and then the Hotel Savoy in London.

By the time I was born, he was already in the coffee machine business, but he brought to the family his love of food and cooking. And my father was at the level of a chef. So, we ate very well and kids going to school begged to come over to my house because everything was made from scratch. Pasta made by hand, and tomato sauce made from scratch and all the really wonderful Italian food that my father loved to cook. He taught my mother. She is German and so my father had to teach her. His recipes were also my nonna's recipes. The love of food, my whole life, was very much ingrained, very much Italian.

ICCO CANADA: When did you first start thinking about the hospitality business as a career path?

ZUCCARINI: When I was 18, I moved to Italy and lived in Rome. I went to the American University there. I did my undergrad in business. Then I did my MBA at Boston University, but in Rome. I lived there for eight years and being a student with not a lot of money, I would cook at home. I'd call home and get my mother to give me recipes over the phone. I started basically recreating my father's recipes, which were my nonna's recipes. I did a lot of entertaining and my friends would always say that I needed to open up a restaurant. It never crossed my mind that that's what I would do. My father was an entrepreneur and a pioneer, so I knew that I would be an entrepreneur. I wanted to work for myself.

When I came home, I dropped into Toronto for a friend's wedding and the corner of Yorkville and Bellair was under construction. It's a long story, but basically, I met these two guys that were opening up a restaurant in Yorkville. It was called Cafe Nervosa. And they inherited some equipment from my father—an espresso coffee machine from another restaurant that went bankrupt. So, I walked in and I said, "oh if you have any problems with your machine, it came from my father's company." We ended up talking and they said, "why don't you be our partner?" I was fresh out of university. Two weeks later I was in the restaurant business. It really happened that fast.

ICCO CANADA: You never worked in restaurants?

ZUCCARINI: Never. I had never even served a table. I didn't know at the time I was marrying two passions: business, and hospitality and food. I think that to be successful in the restaurants, you have to be astute in business. With my father being an entrepreneur, I worked as a young child starting at the age of 12. I saw this entrepreneurial side of my father—the restaurant business is the toughest business out there. You have to know numbers so well. Having an MBA, and being really comfortable with numbers, I was able to go into the business and look at it from that numbers point of view. I don't think a lot of restaurateurs have that background. I think it's the only reason why Nervosa is still there. It's going to be 24 years in June. It's there and thriving because I look at numbers very carefully.

ICCO CANADA: It must be more than numbers though, to last 24 years. You have managed to keep Trattoria Nervosa relevant for so long. Why has it stood the test of time?

ZUCCARINI: Nervosa found a niche. There were no good value restaurants at that time in Yorkville. We were one of the first to bring a good value neighborhood vibe to a higher end neighborhood. I felt as a businessperson, that model of bringing a neighborhood restaurant to a higher end neighborhood was a formula that was really going to work. Plus, we had a triple A location. We're on the corner of Yorkville and Bellair. So, we had all the pieces to really create a stalwart restaurant. But there are so many restaurants that were great that don't last 24 years. And the only reason why I'm there is because I really manage the numbers well. It's this combination of all these pieces coming together. But I have this passion for hospitality and food, and an understanding of what's the right location for the right concept. I feel very comfortable that I'm good at that. All of my restaurants are one-off. I don't have anything that I duplicated. When I came to Los Angeles, I decided to create a chef-driven restaurant, not so much a good value neighborhood restaurant. And then I wanted it to be on a certain street in Los Angeles and I got a location on that street. I'm a visionary and I think of what I'm going to do and where I'm going to do it. What's the investment going to be? Do I buy the building? Do I lease the building? So, I'm on the business side of things. It's a very strong reason why I'm here 24 years later. It's a combination of many things, but a strong reason is business.

ICCO CANADA: It seems to me that something changed along the way. You had Trattoria Nervosa for many years and then Gusto 101 was 2012, right?

ZUCCARINI: Yes.

ICCO CANADA: Then you went crazy with growth. You've got Chubby's Jamaican Kitchen, so you're not just doing Italian anymore. You've got two Thai restaurants. Now you've got the Felix restaurant in California, which is considered one of the best restaurants in North America at the moment, which is pretty amazing. What happened? Did you take a special pill or something?

ZUCCARINI: Yeah, you would think. There were a few reasons. Again, thinking from the business point of view, I wanted to build a very strong foundation. Now what makes me an anomaly in this business is I've grown the business with my own money. I only take on debt to purchase real estate. I knew that the real estate was very important. So I set my sights on purchasing the corner of Yorkville and Bellair and for those 10 years that I leased the building I didn't buy a house. I saved my money so I would be able to buy the corner of Yorkville and Bellair. And once I purchased that piece of real estate, I felt that I had built enough of a foundation to go out and buy another building. That's when I purchased 101 Portland and I started to invest quite a lot of money to build this restaurant that has this retractable roof, almost like the SkyDome. I put money in, but all cash. I didn't take on any debt; I don't have backers. I saved my money from selling margherita pizza and then I buy real estate and invest a lot of money building nice restaurants. So, I slowly started accumulating buildings. I bought the building where Chubby's is, then created that restaurant, doing something I would say is a little bit riskier. I'm taking the formula—not Italian, not neighborhood—but okay, let's try Jamaica now, which is a passion project for me.

My Thai restaurants are in partnership and that was a different model for me. I thought, "let me back this amazingly talented Thai chef and I will bring in all my systems and procedures and training." We're quite sophisticated as a company on the operational side. I also financed the project. So I come in with a certain talent, but I give the food over to Chef Nuit to completely run it and I just support that. Right now we're slated to open another one at Young and Eglinton. So we're growing with Nuit and her husband Jeff. We're going to have more under our belt in the coming years with them. I'm really hoping to bring them to Los Angeles. So I'm growing in these different ways where I'm purchasing buildings and developing them.

I had to wait to grow when I felt security. I took the long road, but I have built a very strong foundation. I feel secure enough to take some slightly bigger risks right now. Opening in Los Angeles was a bigger risk, and we can roll the dice a little bit more—the foundation is strong. I've also taken my time to build an incredible team. So right now I have a proper company. We have a head office. I hired incredible people. My chief operational officer has been with me since day one for 24 years. I have a chief culture officer, I have a head of expansion, so I have a proper corporation. I only expanded when I felt very, very ready to do so.

ICCO CANADA: Well your way of doing things was prescient, because well-known restaurants like Prego closed because the landlord wouldn't re-sign the lease. Le Bistingo closed because the rent doubled. The restaurateurs weren't in control so owning the building was very smart. It gave you a lot more control.

ZUCCARINI: Well, yes. I mean, I knew that the most important thing that I could do is buy the corner of Yorkville and Bellair, forget about any of the restaurants. To lock up that corner. That was going to set me up for life, and I knew that. But again, there's not a lot of restaurateurs thinking that way. It's the only reason why I'm here and we're thriving 24 years later.

ICCO CANADA: It sounds like your Thai partnership has gone very well. In the future, are you looking to partner with people, or do you still want to be mostly the sole owner of everything?

ZUCCARINI: You know, I'm opening a Middle-Eastern restaurant on Islington, and I'm partnered with a chef for that project. His name is Stewart Cameron. I am absolutely open to going into partnerships with really, really talented chefs. I feel like I now have a good instinct when I meet people and if I like what they do and I like them as people, then I definitely am completely open to partnerships and will continue to do that. And I love my partnership with Jeff and Nuit.

ICCO CANADA: What led you to L.A.? Taking on the American market is quite different from what you were doing. Did you know people there?

ZUCCARINI: Did I mention it's 80 degrees today?

ICCO CANADA: Oh right! You don't need to know anybody.

ZUCCARINI: I was making a lifestyle move to get out of winters and also a life and a business move to expand and be more of a global company. So, the first step was checking out a couple of cities. I landed in Los Angeles and fell in love within 24 hours. I started shopping for a home and putting together a restaurant business. I bought a house. I found it before I found the location of the restaurant. The house and the restaurant are about a 10-minute walk from each other. So, it's a lifestyle move, a business move, and now we're under construction for two more restaurants in Los Angeles.

ICCO CANADA: One of those is Gusto Green, is that right?

ZUCCARINI: One is, yes, Gusto Green.

ICCO CANADA: And that's going to have cannabis infused foods? Eventually?

ZUCCARINI: Well not yet. It's not legal. What we're doing is we're opening in downtown L.A. and it's a complete lifestyle brand. So, we have a cafe, restaurant, and private dining room. It's more of a health focused restaurant where the food is infused with adaptogens, so you know—natural herbs and botanicals to help boost your health. And then we have a rooftop and we can do private events and private dinners. We can do infused THC dinners, but that's under construction and basically, we want to be ready for when it's legal. And you know, do it in a very responsible way. It's a complete lifestyle brand. We're also launching a food product line, which will be infused and be distributed through dispensaries.

ICCO CANADA: Is that legal here in Ontario, or will it be anytime soon, compared to California?

ZUCCARINI: In California it's legal to have consumption lounges. So, we're going after licenses for lounges where you can consume cannabis and be in a setting where it's social and have food. In West Hollywood there is one open consumption lounge and there will be more. Ontario is also pushing to have consumption lounges and we're going after licenses. We want to be ready for when it's completely legal.

ICCO CANADA: I was in the restaurant business for years working mostly front of house. It was always male-dominated because I tended to work in high-end restaurants. Has this been an issue for you as a female entrepreneur in a business that is so male-dominated?

ZUCCARINI: Specific to North America, female chefs and female owners make up 7% of the entire industry. It's a male-dominant industry. My father was an old-world Italian father who, you know—really celebrate the boys being born. But my father had three daughters and it was very upsetting to him that he did not have a son. I was maybe a little bit of the tougher girl in the family. I don't see a difference between male and female because of the way that my father raised me. He raised me to think "you can do anything." We had these three group espresso coffee machines that were so heavy, and he would just tell me, "get on the other side, you're lifting this up and you can do it." In a way he treated me like the son he never had. So yes, I'm in a male-dominated industry, but in my business, I call the shots, I'm the boss. I didn't have to fight any other males really, so I don't have any issues. My leadership team is female-heavy in a male-dominated industry, but I'm not looking to hire women. I'm looking to hire the best person for the job. I don't see gender and I don't have a problem being a female boss out there. I just don't.

ICCO CANADA: I guess the difference is you are the boss. I've worked in restaurants where women in the kitchen were treated quite badly.

ZUCCARINI: I've set up a company where we don't do any of that, because I'm a woman. I am absolutely equal opportunity, treat people with respect, and I've built a very respectful, loving company. I'm really proud of that.

ICCO CANADA: Italian Canadians had a huge impact on the way all Canadians eat. You can't walk down the street without one of your dad's espresso machines showing up, not to mention the food, the pasta, the pizza. For the future generations of Italian Canadians, do you think there'll be the same kind of influence and dominance, at least in the GTA?

ZUCCARINI: Yeah, I would say that Toronto, first of all, as we all know, is the most multicultural city in Canada with one of the largest Italian populations outside of Italy. It also has more recent immigration than the United States. When I go to the States, the Italian restaurants have more of an Italian American vibe as opposed to authentic Italian food, which I experience a little bit more in Toronto. I think in the restaurant scene, everybody's only getting better. Italian food is getting better. With every restaurant that I open, I want the food to be more authentic. I think peoples' palates are becoming far more astute as the world becomes smaller and people are traveling a lot more. They demand better.

ICCO CANADA: Do you think the Italian Canadian community will maintain a cohesive identity? Is maintaining that heritage even important to you?

ZUCCARINI: I love that Toronto is distinct in being multicultural, but again, I've been living in the States for four years and I see it compartmentalized here. We meld together in Toronto, yet we keep our cultural identity. And I feel like in the States they'll say I'm American, but I'll say I'm half Italian and half German. People don't say that in America as much. Don't ask me what's happening in a hundred years, but I think right now that's how we still identify ourselves. It's a more recent immigration that happened in Canada, obviously, so we hang onto our roots a little bit more, and I like that. But we're very inclusive. Look at me, I have a Jamaican restaurant, a Thai restaurant, I have an Italian restaurant, but they're distinct and they hold onto their culture. I'm not melding them; I'm not doing fusion.

ICCO CANADA: Well, that's what they say, right? The USA is a melting pot, and here, we're more of a mosaic. We don't melt together completely.

ZUCCARINI: Yes, I like that.

ICCO CANADA: So, what's next for you and Gusto 54? What do you have on the horizon that's exciting to you?

ZUCCARINI: This year, 2020, I'm opening five concepts. One restaurant, Gusto 501, just opened up in Corktown. It's 8,000 square feet and it's a very, very ambitious project.

ICCO CANADA: It is gorgeous.

ZUCCARINI: I think we're going to win design awards. It wasn't done for that purpose, but it's a special building and an ambitious project in that part of town. I'm doing a lot of ambitious projects this year. I'm opening a Middle Eastern restaurant. I'm partnering with Larry Gagosian, the largest art dealer in the world, and we're opening a 6,000 square foot restaurant. I want that to be an incredible Italian restaurant in Beverly Hills. I'm launching in the cannabis business. I am going in a thousand different directions, but I'm ready for it and I'm excited. Today I have a meeting to possibly partner in New York City. I had a meeting yesterday to open three concepts in Las Vegas. I don't know what I'm going to do, but we're going to keep going. The future is bright. We're very excited and we're set to grow this to be a real global restaurant group.

Linda Hasenfratz
Linamar Corporation
Flavio Volpe
APMA
John Zianis
Woodbridge Group

LEADERSHIP BEYOND BARRIERS

FLAVIO VOLPE
PRESIDENT, AUTOMOTIVE PARTS MANUFACTURERS' ASSOCIATION (APMA)

"I have a theory that advocacy can't be done the old ways. You can't do it with white papers and quiet discussions. I negotiate through the front page of The Globe and Mail. We were in The Economist, the New York Times, the Washington Post, CNBC. And I never once wrote a white paper."

ICCO CANADA: In 2009 you were chief of staff with the Ministry of Economic Development under Sandra Pupatello when the automotive industry needed a massive bailout. So you've been at the centre of crisis management in this industry for a long time...

VOLPE: Well, in 2009, when the world fell apart, the first call from any of the automakers was from Chrysler. This is pre-Fiat/Chrysler days. It was a call to our office from Bob Nardelli, who was the CEO at the time. And the first meeting was the Ontario Minister of Economic Development and the Ontario Minister of Finance, going to Ann Arbor to hear Chrysler say, "We need a billion dollars." We had been tracking it. And by the time the third quarter results came out, we knew that Chrysler's burn rate meant they had five months cash left. General Motors had nine months of cash. And I think Ford had something like 20 to 26, because they mortgaged everything, including the logo. We set up a task force, our office, within the Ontario government, to say, "The world's falling apart. We're at the centre of it." Chrysler asked for a billion, which would last them about a month. We were the only sub-national jurisdiction that ended up in the bailout. It was the U.S. Treasury, it was Canada. And then we paid one third of the Canadian bill. And because we were able to be proactive on it, we guaranteed a footprint in Ontario for another 10 years. I mean, it cost us money. But nobody else had those guarantees.

I always was a car guy, but I became an auto guy in the middle of that. Car guys, we like the products. Auto guys, it's "how does the industry work"? That was my doctoral studies on the ins and outs of the auto sector.

ICCO CANADA: It gave you an overview of the whole ecosystem?

VOLPE: Yeah, I left that job. I went to go build solar power plants. It was a great run for about three years or so, and then somebody called me about this job because they remembered me from that job. And I said, "Yeah, let's go." And here we're in a crisis that's even more acute than that one.

ICCO CANADA: Well, you jumped from the frying pan into the fire. In 2016 Trump was elected and demanded the renegotiation of NAFTA. That was a big thing for the automotive industry because we're so reliant on cross border trade. How do you feel your members fared in those negotiations?

VOLPE: Well, you may or may not know that I was at every single round.

ICCO CANADA: I knew you were at some. I didn't realize every one.

VOLPE: Oh man, are you kidding me? At one point we did an inventory here. I think I did 567 media interviews over the course of that year and a half. And we did it as a matter of course. What we said was, "This is a new system." I was there during the TPP negotiations as well. We were the only voice that raised the curtain that the Canadian government just got sold out on a deal by the Americans and the Japanese on local content. And we made it an election issue in 2015. Because of us, there were two additional rounds of TPP. And I think because of what we did, the new American administration walked away from TPP. So we roll into NAFTA and we say, "You know what worked was negotiating in public. Pushing the government in all three countries to respond to us, to the clips in the morning." And I'll say this, that the new NAFTA, is the first agreement in history between major trading nations, where the local value content in automotive has gone up. So it means Canadian automotive suppliers are looking at an incremental $6 to $8 billion a year, at full implementation of the agreement.

I have a theory that advocacy can't be done the old ways. You can't do it with white papers and quiet discussions. I negotiate through the front page of *The Globe and Mail*. We were in *The Economist*, the *New York Times*, the *Washington Post*, *CNBC*. And I never once wrote a white paper. If I couldn't say it in public, there was no point in saying it. We had meetings at the White House; had dinner with the President of Mexico. It was crazy. But we got out there, and the only thing I said was, "We need more content, not less. And if we get more content, that means the American suppliers get more content. And you win." And we did. I think if you look at the media coverage on it, there's a lot of people who say that we lost on NAFTA. A lot of different sectors will say that, but I think everybody agrees that the automotive sector, especially the supply sector, won. It didn't happen by accident. We would have been the biggest losers in TPP.

ICCO CANADA: You wanted them to walk away from TPP?

VOLPE: We implored them to walk away from TPP. I tried to scuttle the whole thing. If you look at November 2017, the Trudeau government walked away. The only voice that said, "Thank you for doing that," was me. Because we said, "You have to hear the consequences. The Americans aren't in, you've got to walk away." Then they did it overnight. They came back in, in January 2018, while we were at a NAFTA round in Montreal. I woke up to news that we signed the TPP overnight. And I said, and my quotes were everywhere: "We could not have done a dumber thing at a worse time." You know, everybody thinks I'm friends with the government in Ottawa. I'm friendly but I called them dumb, in a media scrum, at a NAFTA round in Montreal. I got carried around the world, and I walked them through it. So what are we going to tell the Americans right now? We just gave the Japanese access to a market share Americans think they should have a bigger share of. And then go with a straight face into the rooms, and tell the Americans we're a fortress across America?

ICCO CANADA: So now we've got another crisis on our doorstep, with COVID-19. And closing borders is the pragmatic solution for health reasons, but economically it must be hard for the supply chain. Right? How have you guys responded to that challenge?

VOLPE: So we saw in the middle of March—I think it's the weekend of the 14th and the 15th. We were all still making cars. The borders were not closed. People were still buying cars. But the EU was saying, "We'll do export restrictions on medical goods." Because of course Italy was in trouble, the Brits were in trouble, Spain was just getting into trouble. And we kind of looked around and said, "All of this stuff comes from somewhere else. If they shut down, not only are we going to end up with the disease, but we're not going to have the stuff we need to defend ourselves." So we put out a call to action on the 15th and 16th. We said to the government. "You give me the volumes, the product that you want, and give us the specs. I'll tell you if we can make them." And we scrambled to get what I think is the biggest peace-time mobilization of Canadian industry, to make PPEs. And what's important on that, is that kept us on the essential list, in Ontario. So we were never shut down by the government. Every other jurisdiction in North America, every state in North America that had a shutdown, automotive was not on the essential list.

ICCO CANADA: Was that by design? Making PPE in order to be on the essential list?

VOLPE: Well look, these are congregate workplaces, right? Hundreds, and sometimes thousands of people. I mean, for health and safety reasons they had to shut down. Which is what they did. They did it in Michigan. The capital of the auto sector in the world shut down. We negotiated with the premise to say, "Look, if I've got 25 companies making PPE, we've got 77 to make proposals. We had 165 that expressed an interest. If you keep us off the essential list, how are we going to make gowns, and ventilators, and shields and masks? And now some of them are making test swabs." Critically, we were kept on the essential list, which allowed auto parts makers, even the ones that weren't making PPEs, to build up inventories. I mean, they had to change their workplaces to COVID-conscious workplaces. The distancing, and the PPE, and everything else. Screening on the way in and screening on the way out. When the assemblers decided to go back and make cars we were the only ones ready. And it's been trouble for everybody. But we've had the least trouble.

ICCO CANADA: So was the goal to help the country with the PPE as a national thing? Or was the goal just to keep the industry running? Or was it both?

VOLPE: The automotive sector ships a hundred million dollars a day of parts in Ontario. And the total amount of sourcing that we've been able to negotiate, is about $350 million in total for medical supplies. $350 million versus $35 billion a year. So we did it just for the right reasons. And to be honest, most of them started without purchase orders of any kind. But the consequence of it, and what we've always preached is, as long as we take a leadership role, we've got something to negotiate. We took the initiative without being asked.

ICCO CANADA: The interdependence of supply chains has come into such sharp focus now because of COVID. It made people realize that a lot of the resources we need to run our businesses and maintain our health are not available locally, right? Will this crisis change the manufacturing landscape in your industry? Will we produce more locally going forward, do you think?

VOLPE: Well, I think it's a combination of that and the new NAFTA, because the new NAFTA will raise the content by law. A vehicle that's sold tariff-free in the current NAFTA, 62.5 percent has to come locally. In the new CUSMA, it's 75%. So you're legally obligated to raise your local content. Also to get the 62.5% on NAFTA, there were 29 parts categories that you had to hit a check mark on. Now there's about twice as many. So, it was going to happen anyway. I think what COVID has done to people, is shown everybody why maybe you want to get a better price when you're pricing the plastic takeout containers for restaurants, but probably saving 10 cents on a test swab, and leaving you without a test swab, is a problem.

And if there's no other legacy of what we've done during this COVID process, it's that people better understand the value of manufacturing than they did beforehand.

ICCO CANADA: For sure.

VOLPE: There's a dignity in making things that has escaped us over the last few decades. Before the original NAFTA, Toronto was the geographic centre of textile manufacture in North America. And I'm not saying we should be making textiles, but the point is, in the city I grew up in, we were a manufacturing city. Yes, the banks showed up down the highway from Montreal after the PQ came into power. But we transformed to a city that is service sector. It's a financial capital. It's an IT capital.

We're such an international cosmopolitan destination. There's tourism. Who makes anything in Toronto anymore? And yet, even when I was at Queen's Park, that affects the mind-space of legislators. Doesn't matter what political stripe they are. Taking the subway to work. You're not driving a car. Your neighbours aren't making cars. Your neighbours aren't making cigarettes. They're not making shirts like they used to. I live at Dufferin/Lawrence. Rothman's used to have their massive facility on Orfus Road. And that was until 1990. But nobody does it anymore. It's out of the consciousness. Now, it's back.

ICCO CANADA: Now, it's back?

VOLPE: Now, it's back. I think people understand now that maybe you need to make stuff. If you're going to be a global power in a post-COVID-19 space, some of that power comes from your ability to take care of yourself. And I'm not being protectionist. Canada needs access to global markets, but the new currency will be: can you take care of yourself?

ICCO CANADA: That is a skill set, that in a lot of cases, we've lost, because we live so much in the virtual world these days. Everything's mediated by the computer, by television. It's just like, how do you make things, actually?

VOLPE: Yeah. And none of us go anywhere without our phones. And they're made by somebody, but who are they made by? If you have an Apple phone, you might think that you have a California phone, but you have a Chinese phone in your hand. And you don't go anywhere without it. I mean, the emotional

and social investment we have in a phone, it's made somewhere else. And no one denigrates a phone. If you're young and you're renting, and you don't have a car, your most prized possession is the one that you will not spend a minute without, and it's in your hands. You think it's cool with all the things it can do. But somebody makes it. And by the way, it's not you.

ICCO CANADA: Can we shift just a little bit? Because the Italians, especially the Italians that settled in Canada in large numbers, in the fifties, they were known as makers and builders. Do you think there's a respect for this today among young Italian Canadians? Or have they also been swallowed by the digital world like everybody else?

VOLPE: They've been swallowed completely, and that includes my children. But it's not a long bridge to go back to understanding. They've been swallowed by the digital world. The second and third generation have become consumers, probably disproportionate-sized consumers. And whether you're into the digital world or you're in the service world, you reward yourself by buying things. And so they do covet things, and they don't see... It's a pretty short bridge to come back and say, "You know that house that you really like, that you live in? That you feel great in? And that car that you're in? Somebody made it." We reward ourselves with things that people make. But what we do is we glorify pursuits that are not manufacturing. So it's not that far.

You almost have to just hold up a mirror to people. I'll say the Italians that settled in the city, in the fifties and sixties especially—although my family came here first in 1902, and then went back to Italy, and returned in 1958—but this last postwar wave—a lot of people found their pursuits in making the houses, and the bridges, and the schools, and the offices that we're in. And all those houses that we've all had to sit in for the last three months. And I think people are starting to get back in touch with what you actually have and you can hold, because you were stuck. You're there. What do you have? That's the only thing you have, is the things you have.

Look, in the PPE effort—one of the first companies to stand up and do face shields, and then stand up and do test swabs: Joe D'Angelo. An Italian Canadian guy who grew up in North York, moved out to Kitchener, Waterloo, and set up a company called Mitchell Plastics. He moved out there and he's manufacturing. He's making consoles for Dodge Rams and Toyota RAV4s. But if you get a face shield in this province, as a frontline worker, chances are you got it from Mitchell Plastics. If you get a mask, a non-N95 mask, chances are you got it from Woodbridge, a company called Woodbridge Foam. It's privately held, but a lot of the management is Italian. My chair is a guy from Niagara. He's senior exec at Woodbridge. An Italian guy, Sicilian guy.

ICCO CANADA: Now wasn't that where Premier Ford was loading his truck?

VOLPE: That's right. And so the plant manager there is Italian, the production manager's Italian, the senior VP responsible for Ram's an Italian guy. And he happens to be my chair. I mean, what I found in this job that I didn't know was the case, was there are Italians all over the province making auto parts. A company called Windsor Mold. The head of production at Windsor Mold is a guy named Dave Mastronardi. They're making 10 million face shields. I mean, I leaned on a lot of our companies to come up with solutions on PPE. In a surprisingly disproportionate number, there was an Italian guy on the other side of the phone.

ICCO CANADA: Okay. So here's a bit more of a personal question. So, so many Italian Canadians came here in the fifties and sixties, and the comm-unity's obviously really grown and changed since that time, right? They started as labourers and moved on. They didn't used to play prominent public roles, but you have. And your father has, too. Is that because of how you were raised? Or was there a larger cultural transition within the community, do you think?

VOLPE: I don't know what the answer is on that one.

ICCO CANADA: Sorry, a bit personal, but...

VOLPE: Well, my best shot is... My father was the public figure. My mom had a lot of fight in her. And in the eighties, she was a stay-at-home mom with a university education, who became chair of the PTA. Ends up fighting the school over getting a computer lab. The school principal slanders her, she takes on the school board, wins the fight with school boards, standing up for the parents and the kids and that lab. Ends up on a front page of the Toronto Star as local Toronto mom takes on the school board and wins. I think if I'm an advocate, it's because my mother, who told me never to back down from a fight. And of course I learned a lot at the feet of my father.

Now what's the second, the third generation of Italians? I think the first generation of Italians, and there was a whole bunch of them, were a part of Paul Martin and Jean Chretien's governments. There were a few of them in the David Peterson government and the Bob Rae government. They were community organizers. They were able to get Italians to think of themselves as—"look, if we work together, we could...." First of all, we'd get leaders from our community elected, but then also our people could be part of the decision making process. Success for us has almost dispersed that sense, right? We've been so successful in all aspects of life, that I'm not sure anybody my age is teaching their kids the Italian language. I think we all are kind of proud of our heritage, but it isn't the same because we're all interspersed in a very multicultural city. I think you might find as you do this, a lot of Italian Canadian leaders. But they're not leaders because they're Italian Canadians, and the fuel didn't come from the community.

ICCO CANADA: I've observed the community and it used to be that everybody was all about how my parents or my grandfather came here. And there was this whole narrative of Sunday family meals, and the whole cultural kind of thing. But you're right. Now it's kind of dispersed. People are successful in basically every sector now. They're not outsiders. They're leaders, and they're insiders. It was such a cohesive community before, is it still going to be? For your kids, for instance, will there be an Italian Canadian community for them?

VOLPE: I don't think there will be. I think the ties for them is a neighbourhood, interests, who their friends are. As you move up economically over the generations, you move from neighborhoods that are predominantly your culture to places you want to live. And the second and third generation go to colleges and universities away from their cities, and they come back and they've got a different idea of where they want to go, and they kind of disperse. And so what's missing is that... Since my mom passed away, we don't do the Sunday lunch. Okay. And I think that's probably like everybody else. That first generation was the anchor for that. And it's one of those things where you lament it a little bit.

It's like that period has gone. But I think if you asked my grandfather in 1957, when he came, and said, "What would be the best thing? How do you see this for your grandkids?" I think he would have said, "It doesn't matter to me—the link to Monteleone. I want them to be leaders in whatever it is that they're doing, and they're Canadian." And so our lament, perhaps, because our memories are the warmest, are probably the opposite of what our grandparents intended. Yeah, they may have left to leave Italia, but they were coming to a place where they wanted more for their children and their grandchildren. And if their grandchildren said, "I just want to go back to Monteleone," he would have said, "Well, what did I eat dirt for?"

ICCO CANADA: Do you think young Italian Canadians have opportunities now that weren't available to you or your father? Or is there something in their future that they should watch out for, or look forward to, or...

VOLPE: I think when I was growing up in it, I mean, certainly there's a bias that was in my father's house. But when I thought about Italian Canadian leaders, the ones that I saw were in politics or they were in construction development. Okay? And so it is said of ethnic communities, you become what you see is possible. I think if I'm growing up Italian now, and whatever that means now, compared to what it meant in the eighties, my children see people with Italian names in every single discipline. They don't even think that way. They see themselves everywhere. And so if nothing else, our success has made it possible for our children's imagination to be fertile. And we're everywhere.

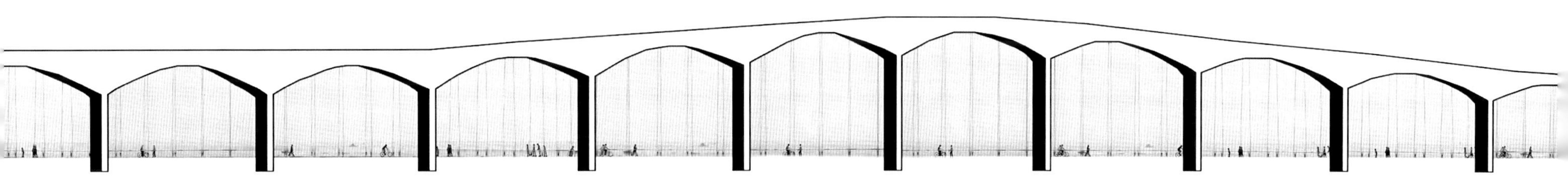

PHOTO CREDIT: GIULIA STORTI

WAKING UP TO TORONTO

DINA PUGLIESE
JOURNALIST, CO-HOST OF BREAKFAST TELEVISION

"I look at every day as, "Wow I get to do this. What a blessing." I need the show and the viewers and the laughs as medicine as much as the people at home do to take them away from something going on in their family or their job. Maybe they're tired or sick or whatever—we all need those breaks and we all need to connect."

ICCO CANADA: What led you to pursue journalism as a career in the first place? Were you a news junkie?

PUGLIESE: Not at all. I didn't know what I wanted to do with my life throughout all of high school. I wasn't sure where I belonged, who I fit in with, so I was part of every committee and high school group that you can think of. They called me the Oprah of the school back then. I hosted Mothers Against Drunk Driving. The milk marketing board: I sold the most milk in the school—they gave me a cow chair! I really loved just being around people and doing things that brought them together and got them out of their funk—whatever they were going through hormonally. I never thought I could parlay that into a career.

I changed my major three or four times in the first year at York University, and then I finally settled on mass communications and sociology. By the fourth year, I still didn't know what I wanted to do until there was a media class, and we had to do a mock-style news program. It was a little assignment and I named myself Dina Black. I got a rush out of that so I went to the Humber College post-graduate journalism program. We got to do the whole radio class and TV in the second term. I loved the immediacy of it. It was all of us working as a team in these mock little newsrooms, and one minute you're directing, and then you're working the camera, and then you're out in the field as a videographer, and then you're on air as a presenter.

I always wanted to work at Citytv. I wanted to be a VJ. They weren't hiring interns and I was devastated. That's when I landed at Global News shadowing Mary Ito, who is my mentor and good friend to this day. Because of her I stayed the course. She had an incredible work ethic and cared about the people she interviewed. She had a health beat at Global News for the five and six. She's the reason I stuck it out. They offered me a job as an editorial assistant. From there I worked six years behind the scenes and I did every job you can think of. The assignment desk; on Christmas Eve and New Year's Eve I was there listening to all kinds of things on the scanners; I was rolling prompter for the 11:00 news; I was writing kicker stories if there was a cat stuck in a tree, and then I worked on The Bynon Show as a segment producer.

I was getting a lot of experience, but I didn't have the guts to put together a demo tape. Mary encouraged me: "When we go out on shoots, do a top and tail. Do an intro and an extro. Put together a faux piece." She literally pushed me to put together a demo tape. I sent it out. I thought it was terrible, and within two days I got call-backs for two different jobs. One was for a national entertainment talk show program, and the other one was for Toronto 1, which was a news station that was starting, and they needed an entertainment host. I went with the little known Toronto 1 station because they said you can be yourself. Be crazy, be loud. You're going to do all your own writing. Catch is, it's all going to be done by 4:30 in the morning, and then you go live. So I was getting up at midnight, and getting to the station at around 2:30, and I'd wash out all the stories, but I had total control of it, and I got to be myself. I feel that really led me to Breakfast Television.

It's been an incredible privilege and ride. It's so funny how I've had these mentors push me every step of the way. It wasn't something I was aggressive about. I wasn't one of those people who's tenacious and felt like I could do it. Every step of the way was like, "I'm not worthy, I'm not worthy, I'm not worthy." My story's very different than most. I don't know how I'm still here.

ICCO CANADA: Well, you're in a damn good mood every morning.

PUGLIESE: That's true.

ICCO CANADA: Your journalism career coincides with a massive shift in media consumption. Journalists have been particularly hard hit with the rise of the internet. There are YouTube personalities who work out of their home studios now, and they have millions of followers, which is crazy. But I watch them myself. How has that changed how journalism is practiced now and how you work as a journalist?

PUGLIESE: Loaded question. I mean, I feel so privileged, again, to have been able to be a part of the golden era of cable television, because when I first started on BT, it was. Everything was a behemoth at the time, and then you saw it slowly die down as other options became available through digital streaming. It's very much changed, so the fact that we're still here with our audience base is amazing, otherwise we'd be replaced by all the apps. You get your news, your weather, your traffic on your phone now. But there's that thing you can't really put your finger on—the organic nature and the authentic chemistry of the people on the show that keeps people coming back despite all of these new ways to consume information.

ICCO CANADA: Because you're responding to events as they happen, in the moment.

PUGLIESE: Yeah. I was the last one on Twitter, I was the last one on Instagram, because I knew it would be so much more work on top of everything else, but it also is awesome because you get to connect right away with your viewers when they chime in.

ICCO CANADA: You're on Twitter a lot.

PUGLIESE: I try. Because that back and forth is so important, otherwise it's just us giving out information, disseminating it one way. I love the back and forth, that's what it should be and I think that's how we learn the most.

ICCO CANADA: Do you think young journalists have the same opportunities now that you had? More, less?

PUGLIESE: I think they do, it's just different. Back when I was in school there was a certain way to go about things. You go to college, university, you get your internship, and then you hopefully land a gig, whether it's behind the scenes or on air. Now it's anything goes. You have everybody with a YouTube page, or they're just using their phone app, and boom—they're a video journalist. And sometimes they'll break news before traditional broadcast news agencies do because they're there first, and now it's worldwide and everybody can consume it. I worry about the integrity of journalism as a whole because of that, because maybe they aren't formally trained.

ICCO CANADA: In ethics?

PUGLIESE: Yeah, ethics, and what they're liable for. At the same time, it seems to be the way it's going. You have all these stars now, these kids in their 20s rolling in dough. They've got millions of followers, and it's them in their bedroom unboxing some outfit or some nonsense that we can't get into but the kids love, and we don't know what it is, but it sticks. I think there's just a different way of consuming information, but there's never been more of it out there. People can really tailor to their needs.

The point is there are more ways to communicate with, not just your local community, but also with the world through social media platforms. It's even more opportunity. The same goes with stars. Back in the day, there would be one hot star in comedy or in a movie, and they'd be seen in 10 or 12 movies over five years. Now, you see all these actors who've been away for 20 years. Now they're back. It's the golden era of TV in the sense that streaming has allowed this platform to produce incredible shows that look like they could be feature films. Now they have so much more opportunity to work. It's working in a different way, but there are more opportunities than ever.

ICCO CANADA: But specifically for journalists, and maybe we kind of know, but what are the special skills required by this generation that weren't required in your generation?

PUGLIESE: I guess it would be the ability to just connect, go live, and just talk off the cuff, rather than be bound to a prompter, because you need to be able to look at something and relay it and react right away in order to connect so that people find it interesting. The stilted way of doing this is dying because people are so used to things that look raw and real, as opposed to perfect and polished.

ICCO CANADA: Which is positive for your career because that's actually your skill set.

PUGLIESE: That's my thing.

ICCO CANADA: That you're very good at, right?

PUGLIESE: I don't know, let's hope. From your lips to TV god's ears.

ICCO CANADA: So just to shift a bit just to the local community, you've been on BT since 2006. It's basically a 14 year live documentary of daily life in the city of Toronto, right? The skyline, just to give a concrete example—no pun intended—

has changed dramatically in those years. Your audience, their concerns, and the stories you cover must also have shifted since you began. What's changed? What's remained the same? It is a very broad question, so...

PUGLIESE: Yeah, my gosh. That's so hard. It's like I need way more time to think about that one because what we've done is in essence always the same, which is a mixed bag of current events and then lifestyle and some news you can use. In terms of the pulse of the city, on BT we always just try to represent it well, that it is this beautiful cultural mosaic and celebrate whatever events are happening. I have noticed of course an increase in violence, unfortunately, on the streets, which is incredibly disturbing, and the fact that we have to worry about other things like terrorist threats.

ICCO CANADA: There's a lot more tension.

PUGLIESE: A lot more looking over the shoulder. A lot more, "am I safe right now?" But that's also what happens with a growing city. We're just bigger. Everywhere you look, there's a new condo coming up. We're more dense. And still relatively safe compared to other cities in the world that are as large as ours. Most people are good. Most people are kind. It's just "if it bleeds it leads." It's the bad stuff that makes the news. So we do have to provide that balance too.

ICCO CANADA: So just to switch gears: You're probably the only journalist I know to create your own skincare line. It seems like a left-field kind of thing. What is "The Care Principle," and why did you create it?

PUGLIESE: Oh, thanks for asking. I still can't believe I have my own business. It's still so new.

ICCO CANADA: Were you an entrepreneur before?

PUGLIESE: Never. But I'm married to one. And I was like, "How do you do this? You're on your own? All the decisions rest on your shoulders?" I like being a cog in the wheel. I know my part, and I do it, and that's it. But then a lot of family health issues came up in 2014 where one family member after another got sick. Right after BT I'd go to one hospital and then another hospital. Literally going through everything you could imagine with them, all in the prime of their lives, so it started making me evaluate what I put into my body and on my body.

My husband and I did a complete 180 change in our diet, our lifestyle—what we consume, what we put on our skin. We started reading a ton of books. That's when I discovered the importance not only of skincare, but of safe and effective clean beauty products, because our skin is our largest organ. It is a sponge. If you think of the birth control patch, you slap it on, it goes inside, or the smoking patch. I wanted to create something that I knew would make people feel a little bit better about themselves every day. I wanted it to be as affordable as possible with the best ingredients and with no toxic ingredients.

If you read the studies, it says on average, women in particular, leave home with up to 126 different chemicals on their skin between makeup, lotions, potions, perfumes. And if you look at cosmetics that are banned, the States have 11. That's it—banned substances and cosmetics that are known links for their toxicity to various things like cancer or affecting your hormones. And then there's Canada which sat at 600. And then you look at Europe, and our friends across the pond are at 1300. So I'm like, "oh, we have 700 ingredients that they've banned from their shelves that we're slapping on our skin." Not okay. We have a lot of work to do, and I think awareness is key.

ICCO CANADA: So how are you going to market going forward? Are you in stores now?

PUGLIESE: We're not, to keep costs down. We've been invited to be in certain boutique shops, salons, and spas. They love it. But the thing is, I don't want to have to increase the price. What happens is you have to mark it up in order to be in these stores because of the overhead. It would typically be two to three times the price in stores, so this way of doing things makes me happy. It's like when people say, "Sure I want to buy organic products for my family. I can't afford it. You think I don't want to buy organic products?"

This is something they can actually afford and enjoy and it's safe and it's effective and it works. We're still finding that balance of "if we grow, can we still keep the costs down?" If we can't, then to me, I'd rather keep the business digital and online. I feel better knowing more people can access this and have worry-free, amazing clean skincare.

ICCO CANADA: Where did the name come from?

PUGLIESE: It's called The Care Principle because I named it after the ethos of the golden rule—do unto others as you want done unto you. I wanted to put something out there that I know I feel good about, that I would want my family to use, that I know is clean and safe for them. And listen, I'm 45. One of the biggest questions I always get is, "But come on. You had work done. Everybody has work done." Millennials have these Botox needle parties and everything else. I don't knock it if that's what you want to do and you feel good about yourself. But Botox has the word toxin in it for a reason. You want to take that risk? They say a small amount is safe. I don't know. For me it's like I've been embracing my aging process because, yes, I'm in front of the camera, but I do like to set that example of another alternative. You can have some lines. You have some crow's feet. You have a little bit of gray. You don't have to look twenty forever—that's an idea Hollywood is constantly perpetuating.

ICCO CANADA: On your show you haven't been shy about showing your Italian background...

PUGLIESE: Love it!

ICCO CANADA: Has it ever been an issue for you?

PUGLIESE: I think in the early days. When I was working behind the scenes, I was kind of the... "Ask her how to pronounce this last name." "Ask her about the Sopranos." And over and over I was like, "I don't watch the Sopranos!" I guess my look was deemed too exotic to give a shot to me doing any sort of on-air work. And then Toronto One, and City was the opposite. Embrace it, embrace it, embrace it. That was a blessing because they were always the trailblazers when I was growing up. Seeing Laura Di Battista. You know what I mean? Jojo Chintoh. Everybody you see on the street was presenting. It was amazing. Harold Hosein, Monika Deol—Citytv has always been about referencing the city.

ICCO CANADA: Would it be different if you were on CBC back in the day?

PUGLIESE: Maybe I would have had to change my last name, and I wouldn't do it. Or maybe I would have to tone down my Italian roots. My mom and dad were both born in Italy. I grew up living with my grandmother. We grew up with all the authentic traditions. So for me, it's so ingrained in who I am, in family, in faith, in food. Sitting at the table for hours. And being full of life. Expressing yourself in a passionate way. Not worrying about being too big or bold for TV. When I first started BT actually, I did get some people going, "Whoa! She's too much! Who's this crazy lady?" But again, they took

PHOTO CREDIT: GIULIA STORTI

that risk and said this was the time to pivot. City has always been amazing. They allow us to just be ourselves. They go for authenticity over anything else.

ICCO CANADA: Does it influence the way you work, your Italian upbringing?

PUGLIESE:: Yeah... to stay as humble as possible while having a strong work ethic was very much ingrained in me from when I was a kid, and not take anything for granted. I look at every day as, "Wow I get to do this. What a blessing." I need the show and the viewers and the laughs as medicine as much as the people at home do to take them away from something going on in their family or their job. Maybe they're tired or sick or whatever—we all need those breaks and we all need to connect. The beauty of what I get to do is connect in a real-time way with everybody. And that's awesome.

PHOTO CREDIT: GIULIA STORTI

THE STRENGTH AND THE GROWTH—THE EVERGREEN PRODUCT

JOHN PORCO
CHIEF OPERATING OFFICER FOR UNICO, INC. AND PRIMO FOODS

"Now everybody sells food. You've got the Walmarts of the world, Shoppers Drug Mart sells food, Costco, the big warehouse clubs. Food is being sold online. It's just completely changed. The traditional grocery store where we used to do our weekly shopping, is no longer."

ICCO CANADA: Unico and Primo are two companies with the same owner but they don't operate under the same roof...

PORCO: Unico's based in Vaughan and Primo is based in the city of Toronto. Unico is a brand that is recognized from coast to coast. We have distribution from Newfoundland all the way to Vancouver Island, and our products have been in distribution for a long time. As we evolve, there is an opportunity for Unico to continue to grow because Mediterranean-type products are something that consumers are really interested in. They're healthy and economical. People continue to experiment, and that really bodes well for our brand moving forward. We currently sell well over 600 products under the Unico brand. We also have some brands we represent, like De Cecco pasta.

ICCO CANADA: How do you divide your time between Primo and Unico?

PORCO: Well what's happened here is we have good people. We have a great team and when Primo was acquired, we had different strategies to manage that business. We restructured the company so that we had people move from Unico over to Primo to help get that business up. We had people retained from Primo, and now we have a good team at both ends. We have some senior people that are involved with both sides of the business on logistics, distribution, and to a certain extent sales and marketing.

Behind the scenes, people that work in the actual facilities, whether it's a Unico facility or a Primo facility, do a great job on a day to day basis. We've been very successful, both with Unico since the 1997 acquisition by the Iacobellis, and then the Primo acquisition in 2006. I'm responsible for the day to day operations and the performance of these two companies. There's a lot of work but we get it done.

ICCO CANADA: How many work directly for Unico and Primo?

PORCO: We have approximately 100 people in both facilities, on and off. It depends on certain things. There has been more automation than we used to have. For example, in the Primo building, we had a lot of manual labor that's now been automated. The same thing goes with Unico, so automation has taken place in a big way in both facilities.

At Primo, since the acquisition, we've made a tremendous amount of investment in technology. We've basically upgraded the whole facility from a structural standpoint, but also from an automation standpoint with new machines. We brought in three big new pasta machines that are the biggest pasta machines in Canada right now.

We produce a tremendous product and we know consumers are very astute. They really understand quality. To try and provide a product that's not, let's say, up to standards...consumers will realize that really quickly and they'll just shy away from buying it. I think people have understood that since we acquired the brand, we've really focused in on better quality, and this comes right from the top. From our owner Henry Iacobelli. So, to improve the quality—new machinery. We only use number one durum wheat from western Canada, which is important.

ICCO CANADA: Who builds the machines?

PORCO: The machines are built in Italy by a company called Fava. They are recognized as almost the 'Cadillac' of pasta machine manufacturers in the world. There are other ones, but they build the best machines in the world. All three provide strong output and excellent quality. It is very important that we have the right tools to produce the quality that we're after.

ICCO CANADA: Now you use a lot of local suppliers in Leamington too, for Sun-Brite?

PORCO: Yes.

ICCO CANADA: Could you quantify the employment effect on local economies?

PORCO: Yes, it's critical. We are very much focused on 100% Canadian. We have six facilities currently and we are building a new warehouse in Leamington. That's seven warehouse and distribution facilities across the province. In all the various plants we employ hundreds of people. We also have seasonal workers that come in the summertime. The

PHOTO CREDIT: GIULIA STORTI

offshoot of all that is we buy local corrugate. We work with the local transport companies. We have packaging requirements, local label requirements. So, there's a big infrastructure. We support the local economies in Ontario in a big way—in the GTA with our facilities here, but also in southwestern Ontario with our Sun-Brite facility that's based in the Leamington area. We're very proud of that and we think consumers should really understand that by supporting Canadian companies, you basically support the local economies and it's healthy. It's a good thing for us.

ICCO CANADA: So, we talked a little bit about this, but modern technology in the digital age has disrupted so many businesses in the last 30 years. They don't know how to digitize a tomato yet, but it must have an effect on your business. Mechanizing jobs is one thing. Anything else?

PORCO: Yes, I'll give you an example. For years we always looked at the weekly flyers to see what's going on at the local retailers. Whether it's food or hardware or high-tech. A lot of the big retailers are slowly moving more to digital. It's like the newspaper industry. People are going online to look at all this stuff. So that's important. We talk to our customers about being on the digital side of the business. How do we improve, how do we get the message across to consumers? One of the major retailers will flash something on their website directly to a consumer that they have in data banks that indicate they buy a lot of our products. If you, as a consumer, bought a lot of Unico products, the retailer flashes a digital message saying, "Hey, you have an opportunity this week to buy Unico tomatoes because we know you're a frequent purchaser and we have a deal going right now." It's a direct approach, which is really amazing, instead of having this broad mailing where you don't know if people are really getting the message. So, it's very, very effective.

ICCO CANADA: At my place paper flyers go straight into the recycling bin but as a kid the flyers would come in the mail and my mother would save them. On grocery day she would circle the things for sale that she wanted.

PORCO: I'm old school. My wife and I still do that—my kids, forget it. But that's the evolution of everything. It's slowly going to fade out of that and more into the digital world. It's very effective because we all have loyalty cards. If you have one from one of the big retailers, they've got all your purchase patterns. They can determine if you're a very loyal customer on certain types of products. So, it's very interesting and we're certainly looking at ways to improve how we go to market digitally.

ICCO CANADA: Also interesting because you want to be front-facing to your customers on one hand. On the other hand, your product is represented by somebody else.

PORCO: Yes, that's right.

ICCO CANADA: So, I guess that's what makes it challenging.

PORCO: It is, but how do you get consumers to buy more? Having a big ad in the paper is one way and is still out there. But digital is becoming a bigger part of everything we do from a retail and marketing perspective. Traditional TV commercials are still effective, but there's other ways to get through with social media. We have started to move into that whole area from a marketing investment standpoint, and it's the future. But traditional marketing is important. Primo pasta was the pasta supplier to the Toronto Raptors. It was part of the marketing campaign. You'll see it if you go into the stadium, you'll see it on TV. As we all know the Toronto Raptors won the NBA title.

ICCO CANADA: Everybody was watching.

PORCO: It was great, and we've done some other spin-off opportunities with the MLSE, specifically on the Raptors with Primo pasta.

PHOTO CREDIT: GIULIA STORTI

We are very proud of what we've been able to do. What's interesting is the way we approached the Raptors with our Primo pasta. The Raptors fan base is different than the Leafs. When MLSE came here and made a presentation when we got involved, they said they broke down the demographics for the Leafs and the Raptors. The Leafs are a traditional sort of approach or business type, less females. Whereas the Raptors are more multicultural—a lot of visible minorities are big fans of the Raptors. They love their basketball. It is more female-oriented and younger. So, we said, okay, what are we going to do with the Raptors? We support the Leafs through our Unico brand. It seems to work well there, and you'll see it at the games on TV and things like that. With the Raptors, we use Primo because of the pasta and the younger crowd. It has been a smart strategic move on our part. We align the brands with the different teams. Primo with the Raptors, Unico with the Leafs and then both brands with Toronto FC. It's been a very effective marketing program for us. We've been involved for over 10 years now with MLSE.

ICCO CANADA: My pantry is full of Unico products and Primo products and the average consumer will say okay, that's two different companies. But you must view them as complimentary and also competitive with each other. How do you decide what's going to be an exclusively Primo product, and what's going to be exclusively Unico?

PORCO: That was one of the questions we had when we acquired the brand. There were specific parts of the business we were very interested in, especially the pasta manufacturing with Primo. But Primo also has a great brand of pasta sauces that dovetailed well with what we do within Sun-Brite, then also Unico. So, we strategically decided Primo will be more of a pasta brand and ready-made sauces. That's their focus. Unico's more Mediterranean foods, a full line.

ICCO CANADA: Unico does more importing?

PORCO: More importing, a wider range of products, more categories to compete in, more products that are used in preparation for meals. Primo's more quick, ready-to-serve sauces, whereas Unico's got all the ingredients to prepare a Mediterranean dish. Capers, roasted peppers or balsamic vinegar—that goes within Unico's brand. Pasta and sauces and those types of products are more with Primo. That's how we structure the thinking. Sun-Brite Incorporated owns both brands but we operate them, from a go-to-market strategy, as separate companies. It's one ownership group in the same way Loblaw owns Fortinos and Loblaws.

ICCO CANADA: We have a changing demographic in this country, and you are really associated with the Mediterranean diet. Do you want to open to other ethnic markets?

PORCO: It's interesting because we know that we were originally identified with Italian-type products. Then we went to Mediterranean products. But within Mediterranean, we know that some of the new immigrants to the country, whether they're south or east Asian or east Indian, they do use a lot of our products. Let's say tomato-based products: there is huge consumption within the east and south Asian community. So, although we are Mediterranean, those new immigrants use our products. Our beans are heavily consumed by a lot of new immigrants, especially the Arab, or the Persian community that buys chickpeas and things like that. We are the number one brand within their community. All this new immigration is driving part of our growth because they love our products.

ICCO CANADA: Well, you are the Mediterranean guys. That has great value I'm sure. You rose at the same time as Italian food took over Canada and much of the world.

PORCO: Italian food is consumed by everybody; we all know that. A lot of the new immigrants are looking for good, economical, nutritious foods. Pasta and sauces are things they can feed their family in a very inexpensive way and still provide tremendous quality and nutrition.

ICCO CANADA: Do you export your products outside of the country?

PORCO: A little bit into the U.S.

ICCO CANADA: Is that a goal?

PORCO: It is a goal to do more, of course. We'd like to do more, it's not easy. It's a very comp-etitive market, especially in the U.S. What we're finding in the industry is it's no longer like 30 or 40 years ago, where you would go shopping at your local grocery store on either a Thursday or Friday or Saturday. That's where you went and did all your food shopping. Now everybody sells food. You've got the Walmarts of the world, Shoppers Drug Mart sells food, Costco, the big warehouse clubs. Food is being sold online. It's just completely changed. The traditional grocery store where we used to do our weekly shopping, is no longer. Now you can buy anytime you want, seven days a week, 24 hours a day. New avenues are selling food that never sold it before. So, you've got to be thinking in a way that says, okay, where do we need to go to position our products? We look at every retail opportunity, whether it is online or direct sales as somewhere that can sell our food.

ICCO CANADA: So, you guys do a fair bit of importing.

PORCO: Yes.

ICCO CANADA: We have the new CETA trade agreement. Has that affected you in any major way?

PORCO: We're in favor of it. It's a good thing both for Canada and Europe to have that open market approach. Our olive oils are all packed in Italy. Gallo is the number one brand of olive oil and growing like crazy over the last several years. We are bringing a lot of other products and in some cases, it has helped reduce the cost slightly. It's just an opportunity to open the doors between Canada and Europe. I think it's a good thing for Canada to open its doors wherever possible to have open markets, and I think we have tremendous opportunities both ways.

ICCO CANADA: So now just to touch a little bit on the future: You're part of a company that began with the Iacobellis packing tomatoes by hand. Now you have Unico, Primo, and Sun-Brite, which is incredible. It seems the first generation creates it, the second generation builds it further, maybe the third generation maintains it? So, for young people today in the Italian Canadian community, what are their options? Is it a rosy future? Will they be part of a cohesive community?

PORCO: You know what, it is amazing because we're a family-run business, owned and operated, we have the next generation coming through the organization. Whether it's Sun-Brite or Unico, we have a lot of second and third generations coming through. But we feel that they have to be passionate about the business. So, we try to give them direction, give them the tools. We quickly realize whether they're excited about the opportunity, whether they're passionate. To be honest, we've been very successful. The new generation that's coming through the business, whether it's at Sun-Brite, Unico or Primo, they're very passionate, they're very in tune with what we're trying to do as a company. They understand the history and they try to respect that, but also provide us with a lot of new ideas.

We've been around for a long time, we've had so many ownership changes, and we've changed. We think the future is very bright for Unico and Primo. Consumers continue to look at our products as being good nutritious products that have great value. We need to continue doing all those things, while also looking at innovation.

It's like the car industry. It has been around for a hundred years, but they continue to introduce new products, new cars. They still have four tires, they still have four wheels, but they try to reinvent them, they reposition them. We think similarly. There are products that we've had for years and all of a sudden, we produce them in a different way. We slice them up, we add this, we add that. They're new and people get excited about them. They think "I didn't realize you could do that with this product, I'm going to try it." So we're looking at that through our marketing people, through our salespeople, our R&D people.

ICCO CANADA: So, going forward, the Italian part of the Italian Canadian identity in the community, is it going to play as big a role as it has in the past?

PORCO: It is hard for me to predict what's going to happen in 50 years from now, hopefully I'm around to see that. But I think the whole Italian image of everything we do is going to continue to be very strong in consumers' minds whether they're Italian or not. I can't see it slowing down. It's just something that has a lot of legs. When it comes to food or fashion for sure, Italian is top of mind. Italy leads the world in fashion, it also leads the world in food—everyone loves Italian. So that will continue to be a growth opportunity and a trend opportunity that we need to capitalize on as a company.

ICCO CANADA: Do you think there's an Italian Canadian way of doing business? For instance, Italian businesses are often family run. To me that's one of the identifying factors.

PORCO: They are family owned and operated, yes. But as much as we're Italian Canadian, we really believe in the 100% Canadian angle—we're proudly Canadian. We're of Italian background, but the Canadian angle is really important to the economy. Yes, we buy Italian too, don't get me wrong. Italian products are fantastic. But as you support Canadian products, I think that's really critical to local economies.

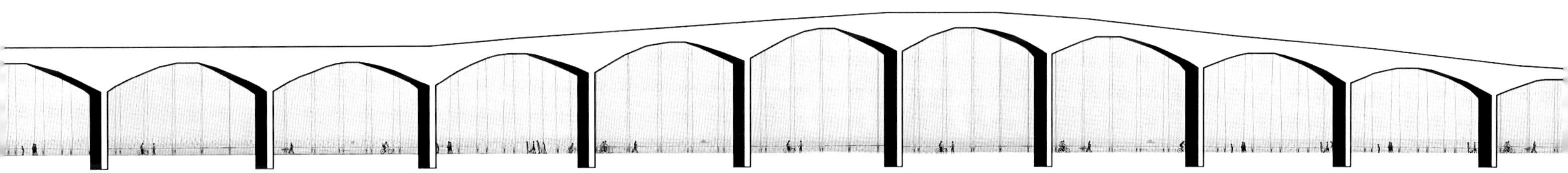

PHOTO CREDIT: GIULIA STORTI

THE DIGITAL AGENDA AND THE FUTURE

DANIELA CARCASOLE
ASSURANCE PARTNER, EY CANADA

"The best experience in anything is to actually try it and create and fail, and not be afraid to fail. My biggest lessons were the hundreds of failures I had. You'll learn from it. You won't do it again. You may do it again. You'll learn from it again."

ICCO CANADA: When you started out in this kind of work you went to the power utility sector. Why?

CARCASOLE: It's so interesting. You go to business school and then if you want to become a CPA, you get hired by a public accounting firm. It's almost like university all over again because you get hired in this big cohort of people. When you start, you have no idea what you're getting into. You don't even know what it means to be a professional. But one of my first engagements was a power and utilities client. I didn't even know what a megawatt was at that point in time! There was a circumstance where my manager was unable to come for the first few days, and a partner calls me and says, "Daniela can you handle it?" I had no idea. Luckily, I had this fantastic client. They knew that they had their auditor here and I didn't know what I was doing and they taught me about the power and utility business. So, it was an incredible experience. I started to really learn and the clients I had were also in the renewable space. I found it fascinating that this new technology of wind, solar, and clean energy was becoming a thing. I was lucky that those were my clients. I did more and more of them. And so, I got to work on a lot of IPOs and go to market...

ICCO CANADA: In renewable energy?

CARCASOLE: Yes. I got to learn how to do that. Every day was different and that probably was what really suited my character. It wasn't so much, "I'm graduating from university, I must go into power and utilities." What I found was that I came into a firm where there was a tremendous amount of support. I could test all of these industries and I just happened to find one that was interesting enough for me and it felt transformational.

ICCO CANADA: Do you work with more traditional utilities?

CARCASOLE: I've done that as well. I've spent a lot of time with utilities.

ICCO CANADA: So, how do you advise them? Because there's a great transformation going on now with solar power, wind power, and battery power, which is huge because of the car.

CARCASOLE: Electric vehicles are a huge deal because it's going to come and it's just a matter of how it's going to impact all the energy industries, mainly oil and gas and power and utilities. Their infrastructure will need to figure out how to support EVs. The grid will be important. I think for almost everyone in the energy industry, there's an element of renewable, or being carbon neutral, or sustainability, that everyone is considering. All of them are doing that in the best way that they can.

ICCO CANADA: But that's the big struggle right now. Governments try and put pipelines through and then everybody's talking about global warming and it's...

CARCASOLE: It's polar opposites.

ICCO CANADA: It's a no-win situation for any politician because we want to deal with climate change but we're a resource-based economy.

CARCASOLE: Absolutely.

ICCO CANADA: So what do you advise people to do?

CARCASOLE: That's a loaded question. Actually, it's not about what do I advise people to do—there's so many players in this game. There are a lot of companies and a lot of industries that are impacted and we wouldn't comment on the politics of the whole thing. We've got a lot of oil and gas companies and we've got a lot of renewable companies and a lot of utilities. So, it's really hard to say, "No, you must go in one direction and climate change is here and everyone go carbon neutral and let's all have clean energy." Because that's just not the way the world works. And I don't think that's the intent as well for governments globally.

What I think you'll see with a lot of these long-term power purchase agreements globally is that governments are saying, "Look, 20% of our energy needs to be clean. Let's do what we need to do." We're not at 100%. They're saying 20%. So, let's support developers in giving them long-term contracts. Because it's expensive to develop for clean energy. So, let's give them rates that will help underwrite this so that they can help the cause of cleaner energy across the globe. I don't think anyone is saying that any of these industries need to go away. What I would say to most of my clients is, "Are you thinking about an alternative revenue stream?" And most of them are. Every time I speak to a CEO and I say, "What makes you lose sleep at night?" or, "What are you thinking about?"—it's their next revenue stream.

ICCO CANADA: They see a change coming?

CARCASOLE: Oh, absolutely. CEOs are the visionaries, or are working with the visionaries of their companies. If they didn't see technology coming, or if they didn't think technology was going to impact them, then the company would be dead. I don't think anyone out there right now is saying, "No, technology is not going to impact me." But it is interesting times when you see, just from an investment perspective, that you've got Airbnb, the biggest hotel chain in the world that doesn't own a hotel, and you've got Uber, the biggest taxi company in the world that doesn't own a taxi. It's definitely different than how we've thought about companies since the beginning of time from an investment perspective. And also millennials—their spending habits change the way we're doing business. I think that's important.

ICCO CANADA: You see it everywhere: work is being decentralized and not just for the younger generation. That will just be normal for them.

CARCASOLE: Right. You don't see them owning as much. I don't know how you felt growing up, but I certainly felt that—and maybe this is just a generational thing—but my parents instilled in me that you save your money and make sure you own something and invest.

ICCO CANADA: Same thing.

CARCASOLE: Right? Buy a home. But I don't know if that's the direction you always have to go in. I don't think millennials feel that way at all. They don't see value in owning a car.

ICCO CANADA: My parents were in retail. And for them it was, "Get a job and stay there for the rest of your life. You'll have a pension."

CARCASOLE: And isn't that huge? Here's the thing. Millennials aren't going anywhere. And we need to understand them. We're 65% millennials here. Talk about it changing the way your workplace, and the workplace of the future, and the future of learning is different! We need to consider that because they do have a different mindset than we do and that's not going to change. They have grown up with iPads and with this technology and quite frankly, they're using it in such an amazing way. They just have different skillsets. It's not better or worse, it's just different. And so, the workplaces need to figure out how to best utilize that skillset.

ICCO CANADA: So, what advantages do they bring?

CARCASOLE: They are tech savvy and they are multitaskers. They do their work with earphones in their ears and they can listen to it. And actually that's the only way they know to work. I think their use of technology is important... again, it's not better or worse. It's just a different way they want to work. They're going to learn through YouTube. So, videos. The classroom setting is no longer as useful. I think that's important.

We've had to change the way we work in terms of flexibility. We used to just put our heads down and we worked, and you work your 12 or 14 hours but that's not cool anymore. They don't want to do that. They want to be able to work from home. They legitimately go, "I can do this at home. Why do I need to commute here? Why don't we use that time? This computer works here perfectly for me." They like the ability to be doing multiple things. I don't think they like to do the same thing every single day. Their attention span is maybe a little bit different than ours. I think they want to be part of something bigger. They want to be part of a movement.

ICCO CANADA: Technology must be having an impact on your profession—data verification and collection has changed dramatically with the digital revolution. There's so much more information available now. Are there methods and technologies in place to make sense of all this data now that we have an overwhelming amount of it?

CARCASOLE: Yes. That's a really interesting question because, power and utilities for example—there's a lot of data. Utilities used to gather four data sets a day. I don't know, maybe even ten or five years ago. And now they collect like 340,000 data points every 15 minutes or something. So, they're data rich. And in general, all of our clients have data. The challenge is how do you get the data in the format that we need it in.

So, we do have tools like the data analytics tool called EY Helix that allows you to take this data and slice and dice it to determine correlations and relationships and look at it in different ways and through a different lens. And that can provide a lot more insight, and maybe a different insight, than the way organizations would look at it.

If you're used to a pattern of recording entries and that pattern deviates, then using our tools will show you where that deviation occurred. In the past when we used to do audits, we would go test 25 invoices out of a pool of a hundred, let's say. And if those 25 invoices all checked out to be correct, then that told us statistically speaking the rest of the pool must be correct. So, the number in revenue must be correct. I'm simplifying this a lot.

ICCO CANADA: I understand.

CARCASOLE: Now, with data analytics and our data analytics tools, we look at 100% of the population. Our tools can show us where there are deviations and then we test those deviations. Because maybe that's where there was a transaction that was not in the normal course. It's really impactful because now we're looking at a hundred percent populations and honing in on where we think the difference would occur. This ensures that you're going after targeted deviance. The other thing it does is show insight into a company. It shows you how quickly a company's books are closed and it shows you if there's someone who's not in the accounting department that may have entered an entry and why would that be? Because we've got so much insight, we can benchmark against other companies and we can say, "Well, you guys close your books in three days, but on average companies of your size close in one day." This is all examples, but it just provides us a lot of insight into what we're looking at differently.

ICCO CANADA: How has that affected the requirements of regulators and compliance? Because they would have more access to information too, right?

CARCASOLE: Which regulators? Our regulators?

ICCO CANADA: Well, depending on the sector, right?

CARCASOLE: Sure. It's all clients' data. In terms of the regulators... we'll take power and utilities: I imagine they'd be collecting their own data as well and gaining their own insights. I do think, we're not there yet. There's so much data in the world right now. I think the statistic was 90% of world's data has been accumulated in the last two years. I think we're still trying to figure out what to do with that.

I do think that the company or the industry that figures out what to do with that data will win in the competitive landscape—because you get insight. What data can do is it can determine buying patterns... I was reading an article the other day about Huggies. You know the diapers?

ICCO CANADA: All too well.

CARCASOLE: Right. And they had transformed their advertising and it literally put them at the top as the number one brand for people who buy diapers. And it was because they looked at their data and they said, "We are targeting our campaigns to moms because that seems logical. Of course, they're the ones that change the diapers." But what they realized is when they start to look at the data on when individual moms buy diapers, it's not when they had the baby. Moms buy diapers when they're pregnant, which is a very big difference. So, they changed their marketing campaign to target pregnant moms. Generally speaking, you're going to buy the diaper when you're pregnant. And then you're going to probably stick with that diaper as you go along the way. And so, they realized quickly that they had targeted the wrong group of moms. I find it fascinating that you can change your decision making, your branding, the people you target in your business, if you really hone in on the data and look to see other patterns that maybe you had not paid attention to before.

ICCO CANADA: Do you find that the businesses that you work with are switching from analog to digital?

CARCASOLE: Yes. But I don't think it's easy. I think we say "data" and "digital" and "innovation"—the most overused words these days—a lot. It's not very easy to do overnight. These are big implementations because not only are you changing the way you do things, but you're also have to change the mindset of everyone around you.

ICCO CANADA: So many companies are working on legacy systems for what's called "Enterprise Resource Planning." And then we have the blockchain, right? Which I'm not sure I completely understand, so forgive me.

CARCASOLE: No, no worries.

ICCO CANADA: But when I hear the words blockchain and Bitcoin, I think, "Oh, hackers holding Baltimore for ransom or whatever and they want to be paid in Bitcoin." And I know it's not just about that, but...

CARCASOLE: With anything, it can be used for bad and good.

ICCO CANADA: But your industry is all about due diligence and it's about trust.

CARCASOLE: Well, blockchain is disruptive for us. I'll tell you in simple terms. What blockchain does is it creates an immutable system. What that means is it automatically certifies that a transaction is true. So if my profession is doing an audit, we check, and we confirm to investors, stakeholders and shareholders that these financial statements are materially correct.

It means that I did my due diligence to give them assurance that these numbers are right. But if blockchain comes along, and all of a sudden, a computer can do that for me or an IBM comes around and says, "Let me show you how to do an audit," then that would disrupt our whole industry. So, we need to get in front of that to say how we're going to use blockchain. That's not tomorrow. That's the future. That is five years out maybe. And we're still learning how we're going to use blockchain in our industry and developing the tools that we need to use to help us. But the reason that it's effective is because it gives you 100% certainty that a transaction is true.

So, the best way I can explain it is if I tell you my favourite colour is blue, then, in fact, it's blue. Now, you can tell someone else, "Daniela's favourite colour is blue and my favourite colour is red." We've created a blockchain and that transaction is verified and true. That's what blockchain does. It confirms the transaction to be true and it can't be reversed. There are some really good YouTube videos that explain blockchain. And they explain it in real terms. That's how you have to learn it in the beginning.

ICCO CANADA: Right. So, that's the simple explanation. But when you're auditing a major corporation, using blockchain, so everything's guaranteed and provable, I still find it hard to believe that you would be out of the job, because you need human oversight, don't you?

CARCASOLE: Absolutely. And that is a really good point. There is a level of professional skepticism that's required in our job to be able to speak to people and look at transactions and understand how they're meant to be disclosed in financial statements and how investors are meant to understand it. So, for sure, what digital does in general is it takes routine procedures and makes them efficient so that we can spend our time on areas of risk and estimation. A computer is only as smart as you make it.

So, do I think that artificial intelligence is a big player in this game? Yes. And over the next few years it can take over a lot of roles and responsibilities. I'm not the type of person that thinks, "Oh, the computers are coming. So, we're out of a job." I think that we have to up-skill. I call it up-skilling. The skillset that I have today is definitely different than the skillset I had five years ago. You need to be personally curious. You need to learn about what's happening in the digital world and you need to use it to your advantage to help you get creative in how you're going to conduct your business.

That's what we've had to do in the digital world when it comes to an audit. So no, I don't think blockchain will take over, but it's certainly going to force us to adapt. The audit profession, to give you an example, has been the same for the last 50 years. We haven't changed. Up until five years ago, when all this started to come, and now, we've been forced to get creative and figure out how we're going to do this differently. Very transformational, very different.

ICCO CANADA: But somebody still has to say, "This is where you spend too much money."

CARCASOLE: Yeah, there's a human element. But you can get AI to figure that out too.

ICCO CANADA: Really?

CARCASOLE: Absolutely. But I think nothing replaces professional skepticism and nothing replaces the human element of any relationship within business. The digital world will enable us differently and allow us to spend more time in those areas of risk. I think we used to be pretty manual. You look at the invoice and you tick it. It's how you reconcile a bank statement, or your chequebook. But now we've got so many tools that can do that within 30 seconds. That's great because now you can use those hours to actually look at something holistically and go, "Wait a second, there's an issue here." Something that I couldn't look at before because I was in the weeds. And that's different.

However, I can say that when I was a junior, when I was 23, it was doing that ticking that taught me what a bank reconciliation should look like and how the inner workings of a company worked. I think what the challenge is for us is that you're going to have millennials come in and now they've got a bot that's going to do that reconciliation in 30 seconds. So, they miss that opportunity to really have that hands-on learning. What we are challenged to do now is make sure that we are teaching them differently so they still get that experience. Probably through technology but in a different way so that they're able to have the insight that I have now. But the insight I have now is because I was doing things manually.

ICCO CANADA: So, going forward, if you're telling a young person what they need to know...

CARCASOLE: I'll probably ask them what *I* need to know. I have a lot of time for younger people in this industry because they inspire me every day. They know so much. We just have to combine the skillsets.

ICCO CANADA: Just focusing on your skillset, how would you advise them? "You should focus on this because this is going to become important in the days to come." What would you say those things are?

CARCASOLE: I would advise them to say yes, to try almost everything. I think that's important. You don't want to regret not trying something because it was out of your comfort zone. The best experience in anything is to actually try it and create and fail, and not be afraid to fail. My biggest lessons were the hundreds of failures I had. You'll learn from it. You won't do it again. You may do it again. You'll learn from it again.

That's the best advice I'd give them. And to try multiple industries because you're so young when you're coming out of university. They're younger than I was because they had four years of high school. They need to try all the industries and see what they like to do.

ICCO CANADA: But the technological innovations that are happening all around, is that an essential thing now that they have to do?

CARCASOLE: I think that if I were competing for a job today, it'd be a lot harder because before we used to just look for business students that had accounting background. Now we're looking for business students who have an accounting background and can code in four languages and have a digital mindset. If you put them against someone who just has their business degree, they will get hired because they've got that additional skillset that we're looking for that's going to help us into the future.

PHOTO CREDIT: GIULIA STORTI

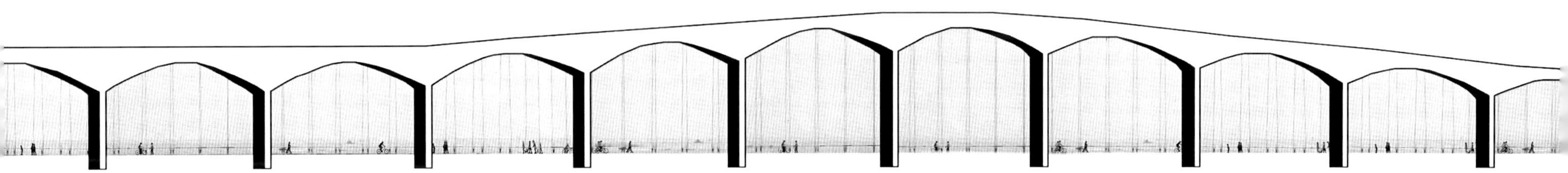

MIRABELLA
LiUNA!
FENGATE
PCL
ULMA
mirabella
condos.ca

DIAMANTE URBAN CORPORATION'S MIRABELLA LUXURY CONDOMINIUMS UNDER CONSTRUCTION IN APRIL 2021 AT 1926 LAKESHORE BLVD. WEST, TORONTO.
PHOTO CREDIT: SIWEI LI

LEGACY, HISTORY, AND OPPORTUNITY

INTERVIEW BY BRUNO MAGLIOCCHETTI

JULIE DI LORENZO
PRESIDENT DIAMANTE URBAN CORPORATION

"Developers must continue to seek out best-in-class innovation. We happen to ride out cycles and when the cycle wanes, we scratch our heads and say "what is next?" But we should not wait for the "softening" of market cycles to invest in solutions. How can anyone do anything anymore without being aware of environmental concerns?"

MAGLIOCCHETTI: Julie Di Lorenzo has achieved much. You have created an impressive corporate brand and have become a dominant, innovative and influential force in your sector. What is the recipe for that?

DI LORENZO: Everyone knows I work 24/7. People get emails at 3 am in the morning from me. I also am an information sponge. I love reading and read at least five newspapers and third-party news sources a day. I start reading sometimes at 4 am and continue for hours so that I have news from overseas and continue with our news cycle. Reading as many primary sources as possible and comparing them is more important than ever because of bias and politicization of the news.

MAGLIOCCHETTI: Is there a particular skill set that an individual must possess to be a successful entrepreneur?

DI LORENZO: Resilience, stamina, and leadership skills are probably the most important skills/attributes one needs. There are many smarter people than me but bringing the smartest people together, as a good leader does, and persevering, while also being able to fine-tune the strategy on an ongoing basis, is essential.

MAGLIOCCHETTI: Looking back to the time when you, as a very young woman, decided to embark on this career path, can you tell us what motivated you? In other words, why this as opposed to something else?

JULIE DI LORENZO, PHOTO BY BRUNO MAGLIOCCHETTI

DI LORENZO: I did not want to do what I do now when I was young. I wanted to be a lawyer because I love the written word and its power. I got into business because my family needed me to, and I always dreamed of going back to school. It took me 37 years to finally go back to school and get my Master of Law. Talk about perseverance! But don't misunderstand me. I adore business and adding value and creating things and helping people be their best self in their career. I had an epiphany that it doesn't matter as much whether you sell windows or you are a bricklayer—the key is in the "how." How do I apply myself? How do I get better at what I do? How can I contribute more?

MAGLIOCCHETTI: Was there a link between your formal education and the ultimate career choice? If I am not mistaken your background in university was in the humanities and here you are a leading developer in the GTA. Was the educational experience in a different discipline formative? Relevant?

DI LORENZO: My grandmother who raised me was a brilliant entrepreneur and she raised a daughter who was one of central Italy's first lawyers. She believed women could do anything and I was raised watching her. My education was in medieval history and religious iconology because as a questioning young person, I wanted to test my religious faith. I already had an apprentice-style business education, but my mind and heart needed to test my Catholicism, so I studied the humanities as they related to Christian religion. The funny thing is that the methodology of good research skills that you learn in the humanities is perfect for business. The appreciation of different perspectives, assessment of source material, primary or not, and thesis building, is all fundamental to business.

MAGLIOCCHETTI: Was being a member of an Italian Canadian family influential in your career path? Why do you think there is a disproportionate number of Italian Canadians in the industry and why do you think they have been so successful?

DI LORENZO: Being Italian Canadian was fundamentally important to my success in business because Italians who immigrated mostly started in construction or the restaurant business and as we became experts over time, knowledge transfer happened throughout the community and great leaders evolved. Truck drivers became the largest home builders and plasterers now run billion-dollar development companies. We matured as a community and excelled in construction and then development. While I wanted to be a lawyer, I learned to love a business that is tangible and involves more disciplines than any other vocation.

MIRABELLA CONDOS, PHOTO BY SIWEI LI

MAGLIOCCHETTI: Whenever your corporate history is recounted one cannot ignore the issue of gender. In underlining your great success in an industry which traditionally has been male-dominated, what were the major hurdles that you, as a young female, had to overcome?

DI LORENZO: This is a funny question for which I will give you a surprising answer. It was easier when I started than in the present. When I started the senior Italian leaders treated me like a daughter. They appreciated my ambition and capability and made a "seat at the table." I was shocked to go into a room recently where my peers by age did not even move to make space for me and I sat at the back with someone taking notes.

Someone asked me why I didn't assert myself and sit at the table. Firstly, I was shocked. Secondly, I already have been a leader for 37 years, so I did not need to prove the value of my contribution. But the shock now makes me more sensitive than ever to helping other young people advance.

MAGLIOCCHETTI: Have conditions changed between "then" and "now" with regard to challenges female entrepreneurs have to overcome? Has the gender gap narrowed or are many of these obstacles still present?

DI LORENZO: In some ways nothing has changed. It's better in some ways and worse in other ways. No matter what, I will not be going to Vegas with the boys to gamble or play golf, and I don't stay out late, so the networking is diminished. I need to bridge that by getting deeply involved in philanthropy and industry issues during the day and creating contacts in that way. Recently I was on a board where I was compelled to dissent on a major issue. If I was a man, I am certain the dissent would have been considered differently. But after 37 years, you have attracted enough momentum and support from good persons that slights are less meaningful. We still have to work harder. Thank God I consider hard work as a joy.

MAGLIOCCHETTI: As for the future? Where do you see the trajectory of female entrepreneurs going?

DI LORENZO: I am concerned for all entrepreneurs. Businesses are larger and more powerful, and smaller creative businesses have a harder time competing. Female entrepreneurs have more flexibility than female executives to live the dream of work and family, so women should continue to be attracted to the independence that comes from entrepreneurship. But all entrepreneurs will have a harder time in the future because big tech and big retail and big power will snuff out entrepreneurial business unless anti-trust legislation is dusted off and re-invigorated. The playing field is not equal if power is aggregated and that power can choke creative enterprise.

MAGLIOCCHETTI: You have always been very active in the Toronto community through your generous philanthropy and social activism on urban issues surrounding the different aspects of 'city building.' Why is this role important?

DI LORENZO: Business is not enough to keep me satisfied. I am inspired by good and bright people, and through philanthropy and community advocacy I can meet a beautiful range of personalities and characters. City building must include a philosophy that no one can be left behind. What is the point of success in one area of the economy and then some other people need to go to a foodbank? How is capitalism successful if wages stay stagnant for decades in some sectors? What is the point of laying off people to improve the bottom line when those same people that were laid off were clients and consumers who no longer have opportunities? Once, in Italy, it was not unusual for a major business leader to be having a coffee with an employee, and each knew the other, and their families, because major businesses were located in "towns." Town-based major businesses have been gutted because of globalization. We are in a new era of 'city building,' 'community building,' and 'economy building,' and leadership is more important than ever. Hopefully power has not aggregated so much that it is an uphill run.

MAGLIOCCHETTI: Urban landscapes are changing so quickly and the process of city building is burdened by many concerns and many pressures: from demographics to accessibility, to the availability of capital, to the role of public vs private capital, to sustainability, and the role of new technologies to mention a few. How do you see the process unfold in terms of priorities and what role can developers play in this?

DI LORENZO: Developers must continue to seek out best-in-class innovation. We happen to ride out cycles and when the cycle wanes, we scratch our heads and say "what is next?" But we should not wait for the "softening" of market cycles to invest in solutions. How can anyone do anything anymore without being aware of environmental concerns?

Priority number one is the well-being of the community. That challenge is bigger than it has been before because of Covid-19. Now we need to fix and heal the damage, while leading us to a better place. Nothing is the same. Ironically development works in a 7-year biblical-like cycle and a lot can happen to the economy while the natural evolution of the development cycle evolves. Because of that, resilience and flexibility are key. Anyone in my business who is not thinking about the environment and affordability and best-in-class building solutions will have a difficult time.

MAGLIOCCHETTI: What does being an Italian Canadian mean to you and is it important for you to be part of an Italian Canadian community?

DI LORENZO: I am 100 percent Canadian and Italian. The DNA of walking to the piazza, praying at the church with my grandmother, and eating at large tables of family and friends celebrating life and community is who I am as an Italian woman. Waking up in a still-young country, knowing that "everything is possible," is me as a Canadian woman. The combination of legacy and history, and opportunity, is full of wonderful possibility.

MAGLIOCCHETTI: Looking back at your fruitful professional history as you move forward toward future accomplishments, is there anything that you would do differently?

DI LORENZO: I would not tolerate negative people that waste time and I would have gotten my law degree earlier to serve the community at large more effectively. Education and credentials are as important as experience in an active, engaged life.

MAGLIOCCHETTI: One last question: imagine fifty years from now a visitor to Toronto is walking by one of your 'artifacts.' Is there an emotional, purely subjective reaction that he/she could have that would please you immensely?

DI LORENZO: When a friend of the family says to me, "are you proud of your accomplishments?" I often ask: "have I improved the life of one person? Then I am proud. Material accomplishments aren't as meaningful to me as knowing I added quality to persons and community. If someone says, "I enjoy living here" or "this place makes me happy," then I did my duty.

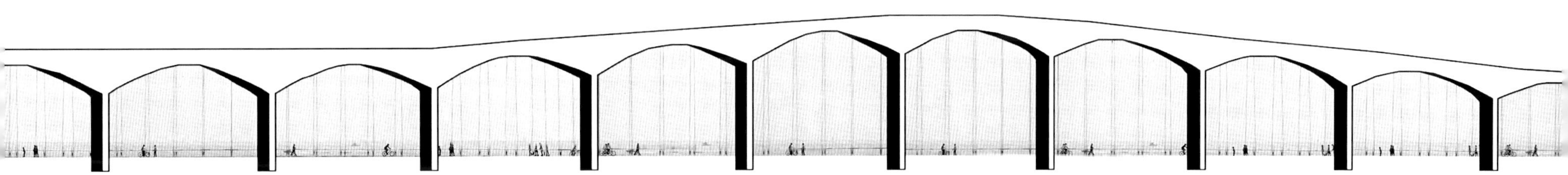

PHOTO CREDIT: GIUL A STORTI

INVESTING FOR THE FUTURE

JOHN RUFFOLO
FOUNDER & MANAGING PARTNER AT MAVERIX PRIVATE EQUITY.
FOUNDER, OMERS VENTURES AND CO-FOUNDER, COUNCIL OF CANADIAN INNOVATORS

"I said I was trained and shaped as a professional, and yet I had this entrepreneurship fighting in me to get out, and that was the Italian heritage that was fighting to get out. I was holding it down and now it's embraced and released. I feel like I have come full circle now."

ICCO CANADA: So, just a little bit of background: you started out as an accountant, right?

RUFFOLO: You say that with such disdain!

ICCO CANADA: Ha! No, I don't mean it disdainfully, it's just that you don't associate accounting—no offence—with a daring kind of venture capital. I wouldn't want my accountant to be overly adventurous, you know?

RUFFOLO: The reason is the influence of my parents' immigration. My dad went to grade five, my mother to grade seven. I was the first kid of my dad's brothers, sisters, et cetera, to go to university. All of my cousins, my aunts and uncles, are in some sort of manual labour or construction-related activities. And my mother got a job as a bank teller. Success for me needed to be professional, and professional was really defined, through my family, as an accountant, lawyer or banker. But it was shaped because of my mother. It was, you know—break out of manual labour and be legitimate. This was the frustrating thing when I reflect back. It wasn't just me, it was Canada. Canada is not predicated on being a nation of entrepreneurship. The US has been, but Canada—the ruling class, at the apex of society—is the professional. You go into the UK, it's still the landowner, so you get the aristocrats—but the highest paid folks in the UK are the accountants, lawyers, bankers, not the entrepreneurs. Canada followed the same model. The US didn't. In the US entrepreneurs are at the apex and professionals are somewhere down there when you look at compensation. In Canada I was groomed to be a professional. At 16 years old, I started with the Bank of Montreal. At 17, I was the youngest bank manager in Canadian history for BMO. My mother was the oldest at 71. I was in high school managing that. I thought I was going to be a banker. Yet starting when I was six or seven years old, I actually read the criminal code thinking every year I was going to be a lawyer.

ICCO CANADA: I'm not sure what I was doing at six, but it wasn't reading the criminal code!

RUFFOLO: I was. It was called Martin's Criminal Code. I thought I was going to be a lawyer. I got a job in a bank because my mother was working in the bank. I took accounting in high school and I was the top student in Ontario. I liked accounting, I wanted to be a lawyer and I was working at a bank. So, the three things that I was subconsciously streamed for was out of my control—it was purposely embedded in me. The irony was, in third-year university, I was going to switch into investment banking and all of my buddies were taking accounting summer intern jobs. One of my buddies said, "Are you going to apply to an accounting firm?" I said, "No, I'm going to be a banker." And he said, "but you get to party in Chicago if you go to this one firm called Arthur Anderson." And I thought, that's pretty cool. So, I applied on the last day and I got the job offer.

In your fourth and final year, you have to make your full-time decision. I was going to go into investment banking for BMO and they were offering, I think, $45,000. Arthur Anderson offered me $22,000. I went to BMO and I'm being interviewed by this vice president. I remember asking him how long it would take for me to be in his position. And he said, "Oh, my position, it's going to take you 20 years." Which was, you know, "20 years! I'm 21 years old. Are you kidding me?"

ICCO CANADA: It's an eternity at that age.

RUFFOLO: At Arthur Anderson I asked the same question, and the partner said, "as fast as you can move, maybe 9 or 10 years." So, I took a pay cut, and I became a partner in that time frame.

ICCO CANADA: Within 10 years?

RUFFOLO: 9 years. The irony was, I ended up in accounting because of the attitude of the folks there. And after auditing for a couple of years, I went into tax law. So, there was my legal.

It's amazing how you get streamed for what your perception of success is. The reason I tell that story is that's no longer the case. I stream my kids to be entrepreneurs and to create things. And as opposed to creating physical things, create digital things, i.e., be a coder or develop technology, but develop it on your own. So, my kids, that's all they hear, and they will never, ever hear banker, lawyer, accountant.

ICCO CANADA: You got involved with tech pretty early on.

RUFFOLO: Yes, 1992. For Arthur Anderson.

ICCO CANADA: Why did you pick technology?

RUFFOLO: I became a manager, and if you recall, this is the depths of the '91, '92 recession. Horrible. And I'm now a tax guy. But when the recession was on, it was boring because there were no transactions, and I wanted to be involved in transactional activities. I was getting bored and frustrated that I didn't understand the decision-making of entrepreneurs. So, I really wanted to shift from being a tax advisor into a business advisor. I went through the various industries, and here is the problem: I'm 25 years old. Which CEO is going to listen to me? It's not going to be a bank CEO; it's not going to be these big companies. But there was this small, burgeoning sector that had shockingly young founders and CEOs, and I had two clients at the time that I inherited in the tech sector, which I liked. And these two small companies were Microsoft and Oracle. So, I went to a few of the partners, and I said, "Hey, you know, I kind of like that tech sector. What do you think if I just try to build this one here?" And their response was, "Go knock yourself out." Not one of them wanted to touch it because, a) they didn't understand it, and b) it was shitty. And I have to go after the shitty stuff because I'm only 25 and I'm not the partners, you know, in their mid-forties, et cetera.

ICCO CANADA: They're going to pick the low fruit.

RUFFOLO: Correct. So, I started in 1992, by virtue of opportunity, to build a business inside of a business. I didn't realize it at the time but that was the start of my entrepreneurial career. From '92 to '95, I basically ended up with three years of zeros, trying to teach myself technology and understanding it—it was really rough. And then in '95, the magic started to happen. Netscape launched their browser. Internet surfing was born. All of a sudden, I became hot, and millions of dollars started coming in. I'm a young kid and I'm delivering revenues more than most of the partners. The supportive partners knew, but most of them were not supportive. I remember them turning to me in 1995 saying "Wow, you got really lucky." And I'm like, "That was three years of zero. Zero! You would have been fired; you would have been gone." I suffered horribly but I picked a sector that was just on the cusp of the rise. So, I went through '95 to 2001, through all the ups and subsequent downs. That's when I really became a tech guy. I probably spent three months a year in Silicon Valley back then, and really was at the epicentre of the rise and fall of the companies.

ICCO CANADA: That was a transformational moment for our economy, but I don't think very many people understood what was happening, that it would grow into what we have today. Did you understand that then?

RUFFOLO: I didn't understand the technical aspects to it, but I was one of the biggest Kool-Aid drinkers, saying "This is going to disrupt and destroy everything..."

ICCO CANADA: That's not Kool-Aid, that actually happened.

RUFFOLO: But it didn't happen when we said it was going to happen. '95 to 2001 was the building of the infrastructure of the Internet, really. "How do you get onto the highway?" That's all it was really about. But if you recall back then, we were promising that you're going to get what you want, when you want it, and how you want to do it. That eventually happened. But not until 2008, which gave rise to the next wave. So, it was actually a complete failure. What was a success was, people saw the dream and saw the possibilities. On the making money front, in those six years I became the biggest business guy in Arthur Anderson, amongst all of the partners, because I dominated that sector so greatly. The real reason was that I was a tax guy, but no one knew that. Why? Because I didn't care about taxes per se. I really cared about the entrepreneur and I spent the vast majority of my time trying to understand their business. By the end of it, I was starting to get very comfortable, and I no longer felt that I was a tax advisor. I was helping them build their companies and helping them develop their strategies. That was very, very critical to me. The irony was, I ended up attracting so much of their business, and a small proportion of that was actually on the tax front. Most of it was on capital raising, refining their business models—how to make money, et cetera. So that financial accounting acumen was very powerful for these highly technical folks that were largely young males who had zero of this. They thought I was, you know, so smart, and I'd be saying, "Dude, I don't know what *you're* doing!" I thought they were so smart, but it was the coming together that was really the powerful thing.

ICCO CANADA: And when the market tanked...?

RUFFOLO: 2001, the dot com.

ICCO CANADA: Did you have second thoughts?

RUFFOLO: No. It was the best thing that ever happened, because '95 to '98, a lot of these companies—it was really about the technology, it was so exciting. By '99, you start with these valuations going through the roof. And I go back to my accounting, thinking, "I don't understand this anymore. Why is this company valuable?" My core beliefs would suggest that it's worth zero. The market got so overheated. So, by 2001 everything that I thought was a piece of shit, was a piece of shit. And that was really the first time I started to trust my own instincts, that I actually do know what I'm doing, so that felt pretty good.

ICCO CANADA: You said earlier that the basic infra-structure was starting to be put in place in '95 or something like that. Now we have Google, we have Facebook for the social side of it, and they're worldwide. We also have cloud computing, which has transformed everything, basically, right? Because that wasn't there in '95.

RUFFOLO: Correct. So, '95 to 2001: when I say the infrastructure layer, I'm talking physical infrastructure. Telecoms, fibre optics, servers. This is the rise of the telcos, the Ciscos, the Nortels, the Lucents. Those were all the main companies. But that was making stuff in order to get onto the highway. Think of it as the highway builders. When everything imploded, starting in 2001, the companies that rose from the ashes were Google, Facebook, Apple—the ones today. What do they do? They started building the cars that were driving along the highway—or the application layer. So, they started taking off. In Canada from 2001 to 2008 we were just reeling from all of the drops of the physical layer, which was Blackberry and Nortel, et cetera. They were all on their descents. 2008 was my next real major inflection year. In 2008, three magical things happened at the same time: mobility first. Basically, people no longer cared for the PC-centric world—it was the mobile-centric world. Number two: cloud computing became real. AWS was born in 2006. And then the third thing: social was born. Really, those three forces in 2008—remember that promise of, "you can get what you want when you want?" It actually happened in 2008, just 7 years or 10 years after the internet had promised that. That created this cataclysmic next wave. You layer on three years for the entrepreneurial lag effect where people try to figure things out and 2011 is the first year of the rise of the next investing wave of venture capital. That's when I left to build it at OMERS. I didn't know for sure, but I thought we were back to my 1992 to 1995: come in and ride the wave. And I did it again. I came in at the perfect wave, and that wave was powerful from 2011 to 2014.

ICCO CANADA: But it was a different time too, because before you were advising and then this time you have skin in the game, you've got to make bets.

RUFFOLO: Yes. I finally had the opportunity, through going to OMERS, to focus on helping these companies really build.

ICCO CANADA: Just prior to OMERS and then OMERS, was your focus international?

RUFFOLO: Yes.

ICCO CANADA: But you also had a focus on promoting Canadian innovation and start-ups.

RUFFOLO: Correct. The environment in Canada, from an innovation perspective, was horrible. No venture capital, start-ups just basically failing, and we were dying. And here I am looking at it, thinking, "this is the future of our country." By 2008, in the financial crisis, the banks and the pension funds all abandoned the sector. So, no capital.

ICCO CANADA: Was that here in Canada or the States, too?

RUFFOLO: It was both. But in Canada it was very acute. In the States you had some level of activity, but in Canada it was abandoned completely. Around 2008, I took matters into my own hands and started really focusing on public policy, and helping the Canadian tech sector in particular, resurrect itself, because I was worried it was going to be permanently damaged, because people were leaving the tech sector and going on to other sectors because there were no jobs. And so...

ICCO CANADA: Was that for patriotic reasons or financial reasons, or both?

RUFFOLO: Patriotic. My first kid was born in 2005. So here I am thinking, "What do I want my kids to do?" I don't want them to be an accountant, lawyer, or banker. I want them to be innovators and there's not going to be any job for them. That was my impetus. And in 2010, Michael Nobrega, the CEO of OMERS, came to me and said, "We've got a problem. We want to put money in innovation." I said, "You do? You pulled everything out." He said, Yeah, we didn't want to put into venture. We want to go into the tech sector. We want you to help as an advisor." I said, "Of course, I'll help you." This was June of 2010, and by the third meeting—they were looking for help—they said, "No, no, we want you to come over." And at this time, I'm gunning to be the CEO of Deloitte. I was on the board of Deloitte, and I thought, I'm going to be here for the rest of my career. I loved it.

ICCO CANADA: That's a big shift.

RUFFOLO: It was a huge shift. I said to Michael, "Hey, I'm an advisor. I only *advise*—I don't *do*. But I felt like I was a fraud if I didn't come in. So, I started OMERS Ventures in the beginning of 2011. And I came at a time where every single senior person thought it was the dumbest thing to do, to go into the sector: no one's ever made money. And Michael Nobrega was the one guy who backed me and covered me for three years. I credit him for covering my butt. I had every target on my back saying it was impossible to make money. And it turned out that that was the perfect time to build it. It was the greatest run in venture capital history.

ICCO CANADA: Well, those things that you took bets on were all huge successes.

RUFFOLO: You know what's funny? People ask, what was it? Why was I so successful? It was the greatest financial results in Canadian history in venture investing. And the timing was a fluke, in that if Michael Nobrega never asked me, I never would have had the opportunity. I was not in control of the timing. I only did one thing right: when I started seeing the opportunities that were starting to pop up, I recognized that we were in an unbelievable cycle with low valuation entry points to make your investment. So, when other people, other competitors, particularly in Canada, were pussyfooting around and you know, maybe saying, "Okay, here's $1 million," or whatever, I'd be like, Bam! "here's 50. Here's 40." I bet big on the ones that I really liked: the Shopifys, the Hootsuites, the Wattpads. Wave Accounting was my very first one. The value of my first investment was four and a half million dollars. We just sold it for 537 million.

ICCO CANADA: Nice profit.

RUFFOLO: A hundred times the return. That's how incredible it was. So, I was acting like they were in Silicon Valley. You'd say, "So, how did you know that?" Because I spent so much time with the top VCs, top companies, et cetera, I had this great pedestal to see that this is really what behaviour should be like. All I did was emulate the best in the world because I was interacting with them. I brought the best that the world had to offer, and I imported it into Canada.

ICCO CANADA: Were the governments behind that, or only after they saw some success?

RUFFOLO: The government doesn't create companies or jobs, really, right?

ICCO CANADA: But they're supposed to create an environment in which...

RUFFOLO: They're supposed to create the environment. Chrétien and Paul Martin started off, cutting the red tape, cutting the taxes, et cetera. Harper continued in on that. This government increased taxes, they're actually making it harder. But then at the same time they're making it harder, they're taking money away—and then they love to hand out money, but they're handing out the money that they're taking away. They're being very interventionist, but they are supportive. I would say the last three governments have largely been very supportive. And the best way to be supportive is get out of the way, make it easier for folks. Where this government has been fantastic is on the immigration file, from a talent perspective. They've been the best that I've seen, in a long time.

ICCO CANADA: Because we need that intellectual...?

RUFFOLO: This goes back to the Italians. It's always that history repeats itself, just with different people. And you know, the people now are largely from India, or China—probably the two biggest—but we need them. And as we go into the digital world, they have great skill sets. Just like the Italians beforehand—the difference is, we *physically* built the country, they're going to *digitally* build the country for us.

ICCO CANADA: India, as you just mentioned, China obviously, and the United States—they're global leaders, they have so much infrastructure already in place. Can we do that here? Can we compete?

RUFFOLO: When I went to OMERS I really zeroed in and said, "Okay, it is about the Canadian companies." It's kind of funny, I went from global to: "we need this or else we're not going to survive." In 2016, myself and Jim Balsillie founded this thing called the Council of Canadian Innovators. That was designed specifically to focus on Canadian-based innovation companies that were scaling up, and using public policy to help shape that environment, with politicians, largely. The battle is on. China and the US in particular, they know it, they recognize it way better; our government is so naive about it. And where our government really screws up is they think the great thing to do is to provide labour pools for them. And I'm like, no, no, no.

ICCO CANADA: India already does that.

RUFFOLO: I want their labour pools over here. Immigration: you live here, and we will build the value here. We'll create it and we will own it. This is going back to colonialism. Remember the whole argument of having foreigners coming and sucking out our resources? Well, talent is our capital, and it's the same thing. It's your people resources. If you can't do that, you won't lead, and you won't achieve sustainability. Everything I'm doing today is all about the future of this country. And again, it really stems from my kids and making sure that by the time they enter the workforce, they will have an opportunity to have a great future because we built it and kept it here. And what I can do best is provide the capital.

The world is changing dramatically. If we want to have jobs for tomorrow, we need to build the Canadian-based companies that are the category killers of tomorrow, just like Shopify is today. Because that's where the jobs are going to be. And if there's not somebody there who's going to provide that significant risk capital to take these companies from 30, 40, or 50 million in revenue to 500 million, a billion plus—if you don't have somebody doing that—then we're going to end up becoming a nation of subsidiaries.

ICCO CANADA: You know, we've been a resource-based economy and you've been at the forefront of saying, "There's something else we've got to be paying attention to." So, for the next generation, for your kids, what should we be focusing on? Where should we be putting our energy?

RUFFOLO: There's three things. Number one, in order to achieve prosperity, i.e., creating wealth: it is created by the ownership of the property. Simple job creation doesn't create wealth. It just creates economic activity, but not the wealth of a nation. We need to build stuff. Prosperity without sustainability is hollow prosperity because you're just mortgaging the future. So, taking stuff that's physically in the ground, whether it's timber, water, minerals, oil, and just selling it to another bidder is the path to destruction. The great thing about the 'intangibles' economy is we can be environmentally sound and at the same time create wealth for Canadian-based businesses. But what that also means is, the future for the next generation won't be in the job creation of industries that don't meet that definition. For example, large-scale manufacturing industries like the GMs and the Fords, all those jobs are gone, basically. And that's what we relied upon. We will need to transform the next generation into a nation of subcontractors, not employees. And we are only one generation away from seeing that dramatic transition, and what we're going to have to train our kids in is: you will be an independent contractor. Some of them, will be able to engage other independent contractors to help build the business that they're creating, or they're going to be selling their wares to each individual businesses on an ongoing basis. And this whole idea that a company will take care of you, give you a pension...

ICCO CANADA: It's already gone.

RUFFOLO: It's going. And it was one of the other reasons why the future of the defined benefit pension plan is over. All of them are maturing. So, what's replacing all this? I think that teaching our kids that you're going to have to figure it out yourself, that you will have to be entrepreneurial, is going to be the single biggest transition. Certainly, when I was going to school—I told you this—success was predicated on being a professional. That's no longer the case. We will have to be a nation of entrepreneurs. I think most are going to be single person shops as an independent contractor, but that's a very different mentality. "Oh, you don't feel like going into work today?" Well, you don't get paid. You don't get any benefits. It changes all of the services supporting us, it changes the way we think about things, and this is why I am deeply troubled by a number of the government policies that are going on that are basically anti-innovation, anti-entrepreneurship and penalizing you if you're taking risk. That's ass-backwards. A lot of the programs are designed for you to work for a US subsidiary: get your compensation, don't make too much money or we're going to tax you really, really high. Oh, and by the way, you don't need a pension plan or what have you. Let's just average everyone out and all be good workers. And that's just a fallacy.

ICCO CANADA: I'm in that boat. I'm basically the contractor.

RUFFOLO: You are. You're constantly eating what you're killing all the time, right? Now, it's great that you don't have to worry about the other stuff associated with working for someone else. But it's stressful.

ICCO CANADA: It is. I don't have a retirement fund. I have no pension.

RUFFOLO: But you know what though? This is what happens in Italy, for example. Unless you work for the government, which is part of the cancer there, they work for the rest of the land, and they're all small businesses. They are a nation of entrepreneurs. The problem is they're not scaling up, and you can't just have small businesses. You need to have some businesses become big that will then... I use the word in quotes, "employ," hundreds if not thousands of other people in order to create an economic engine and to create wealth for a variety of folks

ICCO CANADA: Do you identify with Italy, with being Italian?

RUFFOLO: Yes. I didn't for the early part of my life. When I was growing up, very, very young, I thought I was in an Italian-speaking world, and then I quickly realized I was in a... I don't want to use the word... but I'm in a WASP-based world, and I didn't want to be different. I tried to be the same as them.

ICCO CANADA: Very common story.

RUFFOLO: Yes. It wasn't until I was in my late twenties, realizing what actually made me different. And I really have embraced those differences in the last 20 years—including making sure that I go to Italy every year. It feels like my second home. I now know who I am, and I am so proud of my roots. I said I was trained and shaped as a professional, and yet I had this entrepreneurship fighting in me to get out, and that was the Italian heritage that was fighting to get out. I was holding it down and now it's embraced and released. I feel like I have come full circle now.

ICCO CANADA: You owe that to your heritage?

RUFFOLO: Absolutely. Because at the end of the day, irrespective of formal education, when Italians came over here, there's a simple reason why they were entrepreneurial: no one wanted to hire them. They had no choice. And that's why they went into the trades. So now here we are, having a choice. I think building that entrepreneurship was really the greatest thing that they could have done. In the fifties the Italians really did build the city, physically. Now there's an opportunity for the Italians to build it, but in a far more cultural, spiritual way, like we've never done before.

SIXTY YEARS: THE LEGACY OF THE ICCO CANADA

CONVERSATIONS WITH ARTURO PELLICCIONE, PATRICK PELLICCIONE AND TONY ALTOMARE

ARTURO PELLICCIONE

ICCO CANADA: You were there at the beginning of the ICCO Canada?

ARTURO: Almost at the start.

ICCO CANADA: Why did you join the Chamber?

ARTURO: I always believed in the Chamber because the relation between Italy and Canada was not developed. So, I thought that the best way to overcome that was to have the Italian Chamber of Commerce. It was here, but it wasn't strong enough. At the time it was Tony Valeri that had started it. I was a member; I was on the board and we tried to support him and help him. He really did a lot for the Chamber and he truly believed in it. For him, it was his future. Then his wife got involved too because Tony wasn't well, and she was taking over a lot of responsibility. She kept it growing and we always had new members, and had a stronger board, and it worked out well.

ICCO CANADA: What was the business community like back in those early days in the Italian community? Were they cohesive?

ARTURO: Well, it wasn't as it is today because it was sort of the old mentality. You know, we've got to do this, but you got to watch that guy, or you got to watch that guy, or don't get that guy involved. I said, "Look, we can't keep fighting people."

ICCO CANADA: Regional fighting?

ARTURO: Yes. I would say, "We've got to go easy. We've got to be a unit. We've got to do things as us, not as me." As me, I could only go so far. As us, we go a lot further and it's better for everyone. I got involved for a while with the Italian club that was on Brandon Avenue, one of the original Italian clubs. And that was unfortunate. It was more Friuli club than Italian club and it tended to keep others out. I don't know why they got me in there because I was Abruzzese. The friends that I had were

Friulan. They wanted me in so I went in. In a way that helped.

ICCO CANADA: Break the barrier down a bit?

ARTURO: Break those barriers that existed from day one. And we did a pretty good job, I think. They started coming around and then they joined the Chamber of Commerce. And you could see that they were working as Italians, not as Abruzzesi, or Friulian, or Calabresi, or this and that. That helped a great deal.

ICCO CANADA: So, in creating the Chamber, what do you think it addressed? What was the thing that you needed help with?

ARTURO: A Chamber is to convince the Italian companies that there were opportunities in this country, and there were a lot of Italians that wanted their products. It wasn't just food, but everything else. And we spent a lot of time doing that. And I think it worked.

ICCO CANADA: So, you wanted to build up the export business?

ARTURO: The export was helping them more... It was helping us get the products that we wanted.

ICCO CANADA: Because you were creating a market basically, on this end.

ARTURO: That's what we were doing. The Chamber was different. We were the community. We worked in the community. We wanted the community to grow. So those are the things that mattered to me as a businessperson and as an Italian because I wanted to see the Italian community flourish in this country. It's no good to just have one, two, three getting rich and flourishing—we want the whole community—and not just financial, but cultural as well. Because that was important. I always strongly recommended that we teach our children the same values and the same things that we were brought up with. I said, "Keep the culture." That doesn't mean to neglect your Canadian culture, the country that you were born in, because that's first and foremost, but at the same time if you're of Italian descent and Italian culture, you should keep that strong at all times.

ICCO CANADA: Today we have a community that is extremely accomplished and extremely integrated. What does it mean to be a young entrepreneur of Italian origin? Does it still make sense to have a Chamber today?

ARTURO: There is always the need, regardless of the era, as long as we can guide it, to adjust it according to today's environment and today's way of doing things. You're no longer in the immigration era, you're into the second generation. So, what does the second generation like? Some of them couldn't care less. Some of them are exposed to the Italian culture, and Italian way of doing things, and they like to keep it. The trade between Italy and Canada will always be there, and it will always be better if there's an entity here that is capable of helping them do a better job. Because markets expand, markets change, new and different products are needed. Who could tell you better than someone who's in the market, rather than looking from there to here? So, the need is there. And to say that need is looked after by the government side? It will never be... politicians work differently. They're not business-oriented, but the Chamber is business-oriented and can create a better environment for whoever wants to export into our country. As needs change, we have to change, and adapt. Pro-act rather than react. It's no different than in business. If you pro-act in business then you're successful; if you react, 9 times out of 10, you're going to fail.

ICCO CANADA: You developed as a businessman in the '70s. Looking at the second and third generation, what has changed? Are you happy with what you see today in the business community?

ARTURO: That's the wrong question to ask me: I'm never happy. What I see today is a new generation that wants to do things. Given the opportunity, they're ready. But they also need help accomplishing what they want to do. We don't just have to tell them what's available, we have to tell them how to sell it; how to present it, what to do with it, what market to go to, who to target. It's no different than running a business. You have to look at what the market needs today. Yesterday's too late. What my grandchildren do is different than what their parents did, and what I did. We have to look at this generation. What do

BOARD OF DIRECTORS, 1965: LEFT TO RIGHT: ANTONIO VALERI, MANAGING DIRECTOR; ANTHONY PAUL, TREASURER; JOHN DE TORO, DIRECTOR; RONALD J. FARANO, 1ST VICE PRESIDENT; LANFRANCO AMATO, PRESIDENT; GINO SALVETTI, DIRECTOR; MURRAY HENDERSON, 2ND VICE PRESIDENT; V. F. GRUADIS, DIRECTOR; D. IANNUZZI, DIRECTOR

they want? Will they accept it? If it's presented to them right, they'll accept it. If it's presented to them that they should be members of that entity in a proper way, and the reason why, they'll join. But we have to do it at their level. Our level, it's yesterday. They don't react favorably to that. Not because they think that we're crazy or anything like that. We're not pushing the right buttons. They want to know what's good for them. What you did: that's fine, that was great; that was yesterday. But tell me what I have to do.

ICCO CANADA: They want to make it their own.

ARTURO: Yes.

ICCO CANADA: Your obligation is to mentor them?

ARTURO: Yes. Is it any different than our generation? They might look different. They might present a little different. But there's no difference. We used to think that our grandparents were dumb. Or, our parents knew a little more, but not enough. It's the same thing today.

ICCO CANADA: In the Pelliccione family your sons also got involved in the Chamber and the community in a similar way to you. How did you get the younger generation interested?

ARTURO: It's a combination of things. Think in the same line that I was saying before: what is good for them today? And then you try to present it that way and the reasons why you do it—the reason why you should be involved, if you want to be in business... Now, if you don't want to be in business, you want a nine-to-five job or whatever it is, that's fine, that's different. But then you're not involved in the business. You're not involved in the community. If you're happy with that, God bless you. But if you want to be involved and you want to be successful, then these are the things you should be doing, these are the entities that you should be involved with. You have to give them a reason. It's no different today than it was in my days.

ICCO CANADA: Today, international trade has changed dramatically with all the new trade rules, with CETA and the revision of NAFTA. How does that present challenges to the new generation that wants to do international business, as you do international business?

ARTURO: Changes will be constant. Now and in the future: some are for the better, some are for the worse. In business you have to look at what's

PATRICK AND ARTURO PELLICCIONE

available and the reasons why it's available, and then you try to adjust that to what you want to do, fit within the business plan that you have. Because, yes, it's more regulated today, but even within the regulation you can still start a business, and you can still survive—you might have to do it different... In my day, if you had a room that you could put some products in, you bring them in, put them there, and you go and sell it. But that was when I first started.

So, it's according to the times and the environment. At the end, two and two has got to make four. So, is there a need for the Chamber? Yes, and more so today because it's much more complicated to do business here than it was 20 or 30 years ago. So, if you have someone who can help you with connections on the other side, it's a help: at least get somebody on your side. Because everybody else is there to take, and your competitor's not going to help you.

ICCO CANADA: Today we have different businesspeople, right? Maybe we are the same in a way, but we have scientists, professionals, every sector represented, so what does it mean to be...

ARTURO: To be a successful businessperson is no different today than it was years ago, as long as you had an open mind and observed, learned as you went along, and adapted with the environment and the changes that society and the business community brings. It doesn't make any difference. It's a new generation that comes along and brings the changes, but you have to have an open mind to continuous learning and prepare for the changes that will come. You have to prepare for that change ahead of time. And this way you try to build for the future. Not just your generation; the next one and the next one. That's what is needed. And that's where we come in, the Chamber: give them some advice for the future generation. See, even entities like Chambers change. If you hadn't changed it, you wouldn't be here today. You're making the changes according to the time.

PATRICK PELLICCIONE

ICCO CANADA: Your dad was involved in the Chamber from the beginning. You're the next generation and you're currently the co-President, so you must've considered this work important. When did you first become engaged with the Chamber and why?

PATRICK: Oh, probably more than 15 years ago; I think it was a legacy because my father did it. I decided, out of respect for what he had done with the Chamber, that it would be nice if one of our family members stayed involved so there was some continuity. Right after my dad left, Corrado called and he said, "Look, it would be really helpful if we have a Pelliccione as a director. You guys are pretty successful with food. Foods are a mainstay for the Chamber, so if you'd like to come in, I can offer you a director role on the board." This is how it came to be. It was out of legacy for what my dad did, but I thought a second generation was going to be tough. It's a totally different society—different cultural generation.

At that time, social media wasn't as prevalent as it is today. It was different back then. The Chamber had meaning. There was a reason to connect people from Italy to Canada. There weren't tools that are available now. Email was still in its infancy. Communication was different and the Chamber played a role.

When we first got involved, it was scary. My dad's generation was very fortunate because they had a lot of funding from the Italian government. When we came in, we were at the high point of the economy. We were flying, and it was like spend, spend, spend. Money coming in with a big supplement from the Italian government to support the Chamber's activities because the government saw it as a viable method to promote trade between countries and especially with Ontario, which was a big sector within Canada. Then the 2008 recession comes and the Italian government says, "Okay, we used to fund at 25-30 percent of your annual budget. We're going to get down to three percent." So, we had to cut. The magazine went.

Sitting around the table, we had bankers, we had lawyers, we had accountants, we had some businesspeople and we're just looking around the room and I'm thinking, "They just destroyed this place," and I'm part of it, right? I don't know if you know, but there's, I think, 10 or 11 of us around the table at that time. Each of us takes part, and we write cheques at the end of the year to make up the deficiency. It's not for profit, but it's also not for loss. We have an obligation to run it. Tony Altomare and I were new to it and we just looked at each other and said, "You know what? We've got to run this place like a business. No business is going to be allowed to run a deficit balance sheet or budget or income statement. We've got to produce profit and we've got to become self-sufficient."

So, we said, "Look Corrado, we've got to do something different. We've got to figure out how to fund ourselves. Any money that comes from the Italian government would be a bonus. You're going to turn this place into a revenue generation sheet." We turned the Chamber into its own profit center, and we said, "Look, everything you do has to generate income. We would prefer it if you provide services instead of going with event-based revenue because every time you do events, it costs us money. If the event doesn't work, we're in trouble." So we turned our office into almost a virtual office. We sold space down there. You're probably saying this is where this model came from. It came out of necessity to survive, and we did that. Then we said, "Okay, let's have some key hallmark events that produce revenue as well so that we can count on them consistently from year to year." So, this is where we ended up in those early, formative years before Tony and I took on the presidency.

ICCO CANADA: Just to back up a little bit, before you joined, did you go to the events?

PATRICK: We did attend. I remember even as a young boy attending events. Later, I showed up to a lot of events because Corrado had just started the Business Excellence Awards. I remember they brought over Missoni Fashion, et cetera. And you know what, I liked what they were doing. It was innovative. It was driving trade between Italy and Canada, and with our business [JK Overweel], I was just in the infancy of going back and forth to Italy and Europe about four to five times a year. And it was a fun time because I was starting to work with the Italians. Normally I was on the Canadian and American side, developing customers for the business, then as I started hiring sales reps, I could take more time to focus on the Italian side. And that's where, as I started doing that, I had the Chamber. I said, "Okay, I can relate to these guys. I know what these companies need when they want to come to Canada. They're all mixed up so we can help focus them."

ICCO CANADA: Your dad spoke about the early days of the Chamber and how the Italian community was often divided by regional factions, and he fought against that. Do you consider the community today to be cohesive, because we're a couple of generations past that now?

PATRICK: Is it a north, south or regional division based on where somebody came from in Italy? We don't see that so much. There are still regional clubs, but our members overlap into these. The biggest thing our generation is facing are the different organizations within the community claiming to support and develop Italian heritage and culture, and in trade that is competing with the same group of people that all of us have to go to. This is the challenge that we have today and we're trying to break it by putting everybody together.

ICCO CANADA: Right. Now the Chamber has evolved a lot since the beginning due to changing economic conditions, and also because the Italian Canadian business community has matured and become established in all sectors of the economy. There are people who did really well. Your father's generation started something. How has the Chamber changed for your generation compared to your father's generation, do you think?

PATRICK: That's a great question. I guess I would have to answer by saying we have not done the best job to change and meet the needs of our generation and this is what we're trying to do now with the new board. It is made up of people from different sectors of the economy. IT people, accounting, business organization people, lawyers, merchandising people, people with travel, hospitality, people from trade itself. We're trying to put forth a platform and develop a service, and this is something that we haven't moved forward fast enough for our generation to take advantage of. The question that we always have at our board meetings is what value is somebody getting by joining the Chamber? What are we going to provide to them? How do we differentiate ourselves from the other organizations that exist in the community? This is our biggest problem right now. Have we differentiated? Not enough? Are we going to? Yes, we're trying to. And that value-added proposition has to be something like today's society. The new people, the millennials especially, have got to have value for the money. If we're not providing a networking service for them, if we're not providing something that allows them to grow themselves as people, they're not coming on board.

My dad's generation, you could say, was almost the same thing. But not really. I think it was a base for a cultural connection back to Italy and it was also just a place to get together. Because they had problems back then. They couldn't assimilate. I remember the times when they were telling stories back in the '60s, police didn't allow them to congregate together, even on Sundays. So, what did the businesspeople do? They established this as a basis to get together in a hall or in a room, talk about their issues,

PIAZZA ITALIA EVENT ORGANIZED BY THE ICCO CANADA, 2011

talk about life in general and have a collective group. If they had to deal with the government, they had somebody that they could put forth. Our generation is beyond that because, like you said, we had success, or our parents had success that made it a lot easier for us.

ICCO CANADA: What would you say in today's environment is the most important role for the Chamber to play?

PATRICK: Our mission statement is to foster trade and relationships between Canada and Italy and to provide Italian companies with a doormat into Canada. That's part of it. But I think the most important thing for it is just to exist. I look at my children and do they have a connection with Italy? Well maybe in my case, yes, but I look at their friends—they don't. They are further away from it. They don't have the language. We're trying to keep the culture with them but it's really tough.

As far as business is concerned, wherever there's a mechanism that takes off the top, where there's a cost to doing something—most of it is being eliminated. It's just the business model that exists in today's market. Nobody wants middlemen. Nobody has the ability or margin to pay somebody to help. So, it's changing a lot. That's why I say existence. That's why we're trying to change to be more self-sufficient to service the community. We understand the trade aspect of it. We're trying to establish an office in Italy. We had one in Milan. Now we're trying to put another one back there. The federal government usurped us and they're putting some funds there for a Canadian office in Milan. We probably need our own if we want to provide a service and pick up regions to come over. But businesses themselves... it's been difficult to pick up individual businesses from Italy to come over to use the Chamber.

ICCO CANADA: Are there any particular initiatives you guys have been doing the last two years that you're proud of—that worked well?

PATRICK: Self-sufficiency—just being able to be self-sufficient. In fact, in 2019 we actually ended up positive. We ended up being able to start up our reserve fund just in time for this coronavirus thing because we feel it's going to affect us. And we did that. We put a governance program in place for the board members. We actually have a document. We set up committees on the board. We're proud of doing that as well. The other thing we did was try to change over Corrado's mandate from an event-based revenue stream to a service-based revenue stream. And the fact is, we still exist and we're meaningful and we have the ear of the federal government, which is a very big thing. Because Corrado can call the PMO office. They look to us to lead the Italian community. They called us to organize the last trade mission to Italy that Prime Minister Trudeau and the International Trade Minister, Champagne, attended. We're working diligently with the Canadian ambassador in Rome and helping her to promote CETA between the two countries, helping her to establish a base for businesses looking to come over. So, I think that's our legacy. That's what we're doing and that's what we're proud of.

TONY ALTOMARE

ICCO CANADA: When did you first become involved with the Chamber?

ALTOMARE: It would have been in the early '90s.

ICCO CANADA: And what drew you to the Chamber?

ALTOMARE: I had just started an international freight forwarding and logistics company in Toronto, and one of my principal markets was Italy. I thought what better way to get to know the Italian business community in Toronto than to join the Italian Chamber of Commerce.

ICCO CANADA: It was a smaller organization back then, right?

ALTOMARE: I recall that the Chamber was not as active in those days. There were far fewer events and the focus was limited to assisting businesses here in Canada. Today the Chamber has strong relationships both with businesses and governments in Canada as well as with businesses, investors and all levels of government in Italy.

ICCO CANADA: Did you imagine you would one day be president?

ALTOMARE: Never in a million years. It wasn't even on my radar. It was like: I'm going to be a member of this organization. I'm going to support it. I'm going to attend the functions and so on, all with the purpose of getting to know the Italian Canadian business community.

ICCO CANADA: How did it help you over the years?

ALTOMARE: One of the things that it did was expose our company to the Italian Canadian importers here in Toronto. And also, by being a member, it lent some credibility in the early days when we were just trying to get a footing in the Italian Canadian import export markets —being part of the community and active as members of the ICCO Canada helped to raise our company's visibility to a certain degree, for sure.

ICCO CANADA: And did that change over those years— the help you got in the early '90s compared to the help you got later on? Because the Chamber changed a lot over time.

ALTOMARE: The Chamber had its ups and its downs over those years, depending, I suppose, on economic conditions of both countries. It had some fluctuating periods. I would say that some periods were almost nonexistent as far as any business development was concerned, but others were quite active. I remember there was one year where we were involved in the twinning of Toronto and Milan and that was very beneficial for me in my business. The credibility of the Chamber and their relationships with the various levels of government, plus the delegation of people that attended the twinning in Milan enabled me to expose our company in Italy with some of our customers and strategic partners.

ICCO CANADA: I remember when that happened. It was a big deal.

ALTOMARE: It was a big deal. The Chamber organized that entire event. At that time, I was a director. I believe I'm one of the oldest directors in the Chamber right now. The only one that is close is Pat Pelliccione, the co-president. We are, I believe, the longest standing board members, having seen several different administrations come and go.

ICCO CANADA: Are you happy staying on the board? Or are you anxious to get off?

ALTOMARE: Well, the answer is twofold. The first is that I'm very proud to be on the board and to represent the Chamber as co-president. It's important to serve the community and I am happy to be actively involved in an organization whose primary focus is the development of business and investment between Italy and Canada. But it's a lot of work, a lot of time, a lot of volunteer hours. Our positions as co-presidents are strictly volunteer and our objectives are first and foremost to leave the Chamber a lot better than how we found it. And that's not to say we didn't find it in good order. It just means we want to make it better financially, operationally, administratively, and in all the other aspects of the Chamber's services. We try to develop processes and build structure for how things get done. Really, most of the credit must go to Corrado Paina, who's the heart and face of the Chamber. He's done incredible work in bringing credibility and purpose to the Chamber.

Of course, there is our executive committee and board members. Our treasurer, John Fabbro, has really stepped up and gone above and beyond what a normal treasurer does. He's a professional accountant with KPMG and he spends hours and hours making sure that everything is reported correctly. The board is aware of the financial situation at any point in time. He's been phenomenal. Then we have Greg Farano, who's our secretary. He's a lawyer by trade, the son of Ron Farano, one of the ICCO Canada founding members. Ron was a director with the Chamber for many years. Greg has been incredible in maintaining all the legal aspects of the Chamber—the contracts, the agreements, and so on. Again, all volunteer work. We have a vice president who is based in Italy. His name is Vittorio Turinetti and one of his primary responsibilities is to maintain relations with the Italian governments including Assocamerestero, the umbrella organization of the Italian Chambers. Vittorio, a lawyer by trade, does a phenomenal job in maintaining the relationship and attending all the meetings that take place in Italy. He's instrumental in these relations and being a lawyer he represents the ICCO Canada in all legal matters in Italy. We have a pretty good executive committee that includes Daniela Carcasole. She is an accountant at Ernst & Young. She's been phenomenal in leading the business development committee, in modifying and bringing new ideas to how we do events. For example, we do an 'Aperitivo' series throughout the year. That all came out of the business development committee. A lot of innovation comes out of there, a lot of ideas. And of course, we have a phenomenal board made up of leading business people and legal professionals. They participate actively and really contribute to the direction of the Chamber.

TONY ALTOMARE

ICCO CANADA: What would you say is the most important role that Chamber can play in today's environment, and how has it changed since you started?

ALTOMARE: What I see more today than I did years ago is the effort to be a liaison between Canadian and Italian business and investment. There's been a lot of work done in terms of developing relationships with government officials and other trade associations and so on in Italy. There's been an effort to develop relationships with government at all three levels here in Canada—all for the purpose of creating an environment that will be helpful to companies and investors wanting to do business in Canada, or vice versa. I think the Chamber has morphed into a true business organization, basically becoming a bridge between Canada and Italy.

ICCO CANADA: Have the new trade agreements changed the Chamber at all, do you think?

ALTOMARE: What the Chamber has done is taken a leadership role, particularly with regards to CETA, the Canadian European Trade Agreement. The Chamber was one of the first organizations to begin doing seminars. We were doing seminars both here in Canada and in Italy, on CETA and its regulations and requirements, outlining the benefits to businesses. I recall a couple of years ago, maybe shortly after CETA had passed, our co-president, Pat Pelliccione, went over to Milan to the office of our vice president and did a seminar with 20 or 30 people on CETA, which was quite informative and quite beneficial. Those are the kinds of leadership activities the Chamber has undertaken over the last few years that perhaps we weren't as much involved with historically. I think the past was more events-driven. We do have the Business Excellence Awards, and the Pentola d'Oro and those are the type of events the Chamber has focused on. Also, in the early days we published *Partners* magazine.

ICCO CANADA: I used to edit it, so I remember it well.

ALTOMARE: That was a great magazine for the time, but with the evolution of the internet people became more focused on online articles and online magazines rather than printed ones. At the time, when the events and activities were not as polished as they are now, I think the magazine did a lot to give credibility. However, I've got to give credit to Corrado and his team for the polished events and the very professional activities they have put on throughout the years. That's really what brought credibility and made the ICCO Canada the leading Italian organization in the province.

ICCO CANADA: Moving forward, is there any particular initiatives that you're proud of, interested in, nervous about?

ALTOMARE: Well, going forward, I think this whole COVID-19 pandemic has made it necessary to re-evaluate how we do things. The big five, six, 700 people events that we normally put on probably won't happen for a little while, at least not in the short term. We've had to look at ways to reinvent, to stay relevant. Corrado has done a great job developing a plan with his team and with the support of the board, has managed to keep the Chamber in the forefront. We've been holding webinars where, I think, the first webinar had eight or 10 people. The last webinar we had over 350 people.

ICCO CANADA: I didn't know that. Wow.

ALTOMARE: With virtual events we lose the networking part of it, but we can still provide that same information to our members. Those are the kinds of things that we've had to do. We've had to transform our ideas into different things. Covid-19 has really changed the Chamber because we had delegations coming from Italy every month—wine promotion, cheese promotion, you name it, they were here every month, and now they're not coming. They can't come. The borders are closed. There's a lot of changes, a lot of things that have happened. But we've been able to roll with the punches.

ICCO CANADA: Just to shift things a little—has the Chamber played a role in making the community more cohesive?

ALTOMARE: I think the Chamber has definitely created an environment for the community to be more cohesive. A lot of the events we have are geared towards bringing the community together. For example, we have 'Aperitivo in Maschera' at Casa Loma. That brings in a lot of people from a lot of different parts of the Italian Canadian community—not necessarily members. In fact, non-members are in greater proportion than members, which is fantastic. These are the things that I think puts the Chamber at the center of the Italian business community here in Ontario.

ICCO CANADA: You know, I interviewed your son for this book. His generation is establishing itself in a very different economic environment from the one that you developed your business in. Can the Chamber play a role for him and his generation?

ALTOMARE: Yes, of course. I think it's important for the up-and-comers, the new generation, to be a part of organizations like the ICCO Canada. I think that they can evolve the Chamber so that it meets the needs of young entrepreneurs and young professionals. We see that already with some of the people on our board, and I'll mention Daniela Carcasole again. She's done tremendous work in bringing us up to speed as far as social media is concerned, trying to get our events, and all our activities on an app available to members. She's really forward thinking in that area, which I think is important for the younger generation who live and die by their cell phone.

And obviously, trade between Italy and Canada, and the investment between the two countries, is going to continue. It's a very strong relationship. For it to continue, the young people are going to have to get involved. I think the Chamber can evolve, just as it has for as long as it's been around. It will evolve with the new leadership that comes in and make changes to meet the needs of young entrepreneurs. Together with existing members, they will have the opportunity to make those important connections that will no doubt be beneficial to their businesses.

A UNIQUE CANADIAN CULTURE
AN EXCERPT FROM A SPEECH BY THE HONOURABLE CONSIGLIO DI NINO ON HIS LEAVING THE SENATE. JUNE 27TH, 2012

Immigration has been a critical factor in the development of Canada and many other nations. I do not believe there is any disagreement in this chamber on that. Immigration brings many benefits to the host country. These benefits span all facets of the nation. Economically, socially and culturally, immigration has enriched the nations in which people have settled.

As a trading nation, Canada constantly assesses its trading relationships. However, we must also focus on the incomparable value of immigration. Countries that welcome immigrants benefit in many ways. Their prosperity is directly related to those who choose to build their futures in the host country.

There is another side of the coin, however. Europe is facing very serious economic challenges and, in my opinion, these economic difficulties, to a large degree, relate to immigrants. The countries where the problems seem to be most serious—Greece, Portugal, Spain, Italy, Ireland and others—are those whose human capital drain over long periods and in large numbers has certainly impacted their prosperity. They lost generations of their best. They lost their most precious asset at an enormous cost to their economy and social fabric.

CONSIGLIO DI NINO

Whether in the past or today, immigrants bring with them courage, determination and focus, and they are strong willed. They are risk takers and entrepreneurs: the people a country least needs to lose. When they leave in large numbers, they weaken the fabric of a nation. The benefits to the host countries are enormous and last forever.

Examples of this are, of course, countries of the New World like Canada. Everywhere immigrants have gone, they have contributed to creating prosperity. The results are undeniable.

When the Europeans first landed in the New World, they did not come to an empty, uninhabited place. They found people who, for centuries, had built cultures based on strong values that contributed to building the nation of Canada and that continue to shape and edify our country today.

As well, I must remind honourable senators that the beautiful face of Canada today and that of the future now strongly reflect the faces of the millions of Canadians, the women, men and children who came from every corner of the world, from every shade of color, from every creed, from every race, who have contributed to making Canada the envy of the world. They came with their values, their customs, their vision, their hopes and their fears to build a place for their families and build their future —Canada's future.

Yes, thanks to the legacy of the first peoples, joined by the French and the English and later by the more recent arrivals, including my family and those of many other senators, together we are building a unique culture, a Canadian culture which will include the best of us all. The world is envious, and if we continue to do this right, the world can watch and learn, because it only takes understanding, respect, commitment and patience.

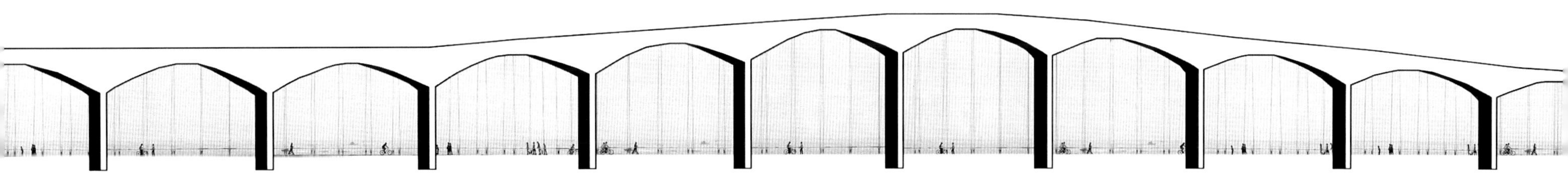

PIER 2
HALIFAX
CANADA

PHOTO CREDIT: WLADYSLAW

JOHN RUFFOLO

THE "CANADA" WE CHOOSE TO BE

(*Remarks originally offered at the Italian Chamber of Commerce of Ontario Canada Business Excellence Awards May 27, 2021*)

"While other countries shut immigrants out, Canada remains inviting, despite the ravages of the pandemic. Diversity is our most important natural resource. And we should continue to express this by being a haven for those seeking a better life, including refugees and family reunification."

ITALIAN MEN, ELLIS ISLAND, 1910. PHOTO: SHUTTERSTOCK

As a member of the Canadian-Italian business community, it is a profound honour to provide the keynote speech while we celebrate the achievements of these inspirational leaders. Frankly, I am blessed to be providing any speech, given my personal challenges recently.

I am a proud Canadian. I am a proud Italian living in the greatest country in the world. Sure, there is a catastrophic pandemic going on around us, but like all terrible things, it shall soon pass. And when it does, it will be a time of restoration and renaissance. We as a nation can choose to move forward and reshape this country in the vision of the "Canada" we choose to be.

Our country faces a tall order. Since the start of the pandemic, Canada's financial house has deteriorated badly compared to most countries. But there is a unique opportunity for our future —a future based on growth.

The Federal government believes we have a problem with our stagnant gross domestic product growth, averaging about 1.5 per cent annually since 2008. Notwithstanding the need to restore Canada's balance sheet from the financial effects of the pandemic, we also need to identify ways to overcome the challenges posed by an aging population in seeking to achieve sustainable, long-term growth.

Without higher growth, where will we find the revenue to pay for health care, education and infrastructure? Some economists suggest that if we don't generate sustainable GDP growth of 3 per cent a year, our treasured social programs will suffer. We are currently a long way from that target.

There are essentially two primary methods of stimulating GDP growth—by increasing productivity, largely through innovation, or by increasing the available labour pool. I have built my career focused on stimulating productivity through innovation. The CEOs of our fastest-growing innovation-based companies will tell you this approach is the most sustainable path to long-term growth.

While the path to sustainable long-term growth and prosperity is largely linked to the adoption of innovation, the proven link between demographics and growth cannot be ignored. As Peter Zeihan, author of *The Accidental Superpower*, has observed, the mass retirement of Canadian baby boomers also means a big increase in the consumption of health care and other entitlements. Zeihan also notes that Canada has one of the world's fastest-aging demographics, with one of the smallest replacement generations in Generation X and Generation Y. By 2025, Canada's demography will almost be identical to Japan—30 per cent of the population will be 60 and older, and less than 25 per cent will be in the critical 20 to 39 age band.

Responding to this shift means also pushing hard on the available labour pool pedal as the other path to long-term sustainable growth. The more talented working-age people we can attract and keep, the better positioned we will be to increase our productivity. The CEOs of Canada's fastest-growing companies will also tell you that access to talent is their primary barrier to scaling up to be globally competitive.

This is precisely where a population boost can help. For 25 years, Canada has welcomed an average of about 250,000 immigrants a year. This number has been increasing in recent years as Canada has opened up the valve for economic immigrants. We should continue to increase immigration levels.

Since by 2025, 30 per cent of our population will be 60 and older, we should focus in particular on skilled newcomers between the ages of 20 and 39.

Without such a strategy, Canada may face stark choices: tax increases, greater national debt or scaled-back social programs.

Some people might call this plan bold. But I hesitate to say that, because scaling up Canada's economy through immigration is an old idea. But that's where we come in. That's who we are. We helped build Canada, from the ground up—literally in most cases!

During Canada's third wave of immigration, from 1901 to 1911, our country's population increased from 5.4 million to about 7.2 million people, with immigration accounting for the entire net increase. That's a 33 per-cent increase. The following year in 1912, immigration peaked to 400,000 or almost 6 per cent of the entire population of Canada. It was during this third wave of immigration in which some of your stories in Canada start.

But, it was the fourth wave of immigration to Canada which the vast majority of our stories commence. The fourth wave came from Europe following the Second World War and peaked at 282,000 in 1957. With many of these migrants coming from Italy, Pier 21 in Halifax proved to be an influential port for Italian immigration. From 1928 until ceasing operations in 1971, the Pier would receive 471,940 Italians, becoming the third-largest ethnic group to immigrate to Canada during that time period.

Like many of you, my story in Canada starts at Pier 21 with my parents Anna & Santo. They both fearlessly and unselfishly emigrated to Canada from Italy in the 1950s to seek a better life. I was born not too far away from where I am speaking now in a largely ethnic neighbourhood where my parents still live to this day. They instilled in me (and sometimes the hard way), a passion for family, a sense of honour, support, generosity, and integrity—not to mention the incredible Italian food around the dinner table. My newer parents, Soon Bok and Yul Chee—also immigrants, from South Korea—share those same core values.

While other countries shut immigrants out, Canada remains inviting, despite the ravages of the pandemic. Diversity is our most important natural resource. And we should continue to express this by being a haven for those seeking a better life, including refugees and family reunification.

It worked for us. This is our story. Let's turn the pages to a new chapter and allow other people to live our story.

POSTFACE

CORRADO PAINA

We opened "Yesterday, Today, and Tomorrow" with a moving speech by Frank Iacobucci, who delivered it at the ICCO Canada Business Excellence Awards in 2017. Iacobucci, who is arguably one of the most significant Canadians of Italian origin in the country, remembers the burning words of his professor who once suggested he not choose a career in law because of his Italian last name. He also remembers the monthly visits his parents had to make to the RCMP because they were considered enemy aliens. It was only recently, on May the 27th, 2021, that the Prime Minister officially apologized to the Italian community for the treatment inflicted on them during the Second World War.

Things are changing. I want to believe they have changed forever for the better. The Canadians of Italian origin now occupy influential positions in politics, in science, in education, and in business. In his farewell speech to the Senate, Con Di Nino, another pillar of the community, talks about the difficult road to integration and how he became a businessman, a community leader, and finally, a senator. It has not been easy for the Italians; it has not been easy for anybody. Most communities in Canada have had to face marginalization, intolerance and racism.

We close this book with a speech given by John Ruffolo at the 19th edition of the Business Excellence Awards, on the occasion of the 60th anniversary of the ICCO Canada. Ruffolo, who is a top financier and a visionary, proposes a solution for a Canada that has been ravaged by Covid-19 and scarred by a growing economic deficit. The solution starts with immigration. That word, "immigration," that scared so many people years ago, still scares a lot of people in the world. Every day we see reminders in images of overcrowded boats, and in the waves of human beings that leave their countries, where poverty, unemployment, war, and natural disasters have taken their toll. The word stirs up the irrational fear of losing jobs and other nationalistic nightmares.

At the end immigration is always the same. People come and go for economic reasons. This is the perennial kinesis of human beings. According to Ruffolo, communities like the Italians have paved the way for other communities that followed. We must welcome and help to settle the newcomers. For a better tomorrow—a tomorrow where work, education, peace, and a clean environment offer a nest of serenity and creativity. A tomorrow that stands in the yesterday and in the today. We cannot move without all of them.

Yesterday, Today, and Tomorrow. Indeed.

ACKNOWLEDGEMENTS

Thanks to the ICCO Canada Board of Directors: Patrick Pelliccione, Tony Altomare, Vittorio Turinetti Di Priero, Joseph Balsamo, Riccardo Bressan, Daniela Carcasole, Andrea Chiaramello, Mary Dalimonte, Ernie De Carlo, Enrico De Pasquale, Antonio Di Domenico, John Fabbro, Greg Farano, Giuseppe Fiorella, Jenny Longo, Bambina Marcello, Mario Nigro, Corrado Paina, Ron Sedran, Deanna Stea, Richard Trevisan, Italian Ambassador in Canada Andrea Ferrari, Consul General of Italy in Toronto Eugenio Sgro'.

Thanks to the staff of the Italian Chamber of Commerce of Ontario Canada: Corrado Paina, Tiziana Tedesco, Mary Chirico, Marisa Guida, Astrid D'Urzo, Ilaria Venoso, Richard Bressan, Monica Gammarota.

Thanks to the generous business, organizations and individuals that helped sponsor and contributed to the creation of Yesterday, Today and Tomorrow: City of Vaughan, CHIN Radio, Empire Communities Corp., Fortinos, Italpasta Ltd., Jan K. Overweel Ltd., Pizza Nova, Policaro Group, Solmar Development Corp., The Arlington Estate, Two Sisters Vineyards, Unico Inc. & Primo Foods, UniversalCare, Villa Charities, Zanchin Automotive Group, Diginess, ITL Inter-Transport Ltd., Liberty Entertainment Group, Masters Insurance Ltd., R.Ferri Automotive, Stikeman Elliott LLP, Util Canada Ltd.

A special thanks to Julie Di Lorenzo, President, Diamante Urban Corp., for her generosity.

Special thanks to all the people that have been interviewed and the contributors.

Thanks to Hon. Frank Iacobucci, Hon. Consiglio di Nino and John Ruffolo.

A special thanks to Alexandra Bugailiskis, Canada's Ambassador to Italy.

Special thanks to Veronica Manson, director of the Italian cultural institute of Toronto.

Special thanks to Claudio Taffuri, Giuseppe Pastorelli, Alessandro Ruggera, Mario Giacobbe, George Visintin, Nivo Angelone, Clemente Benelli, Oscar Farinetti, Cosimo and Elena Mammoliti, Pietro Abate, Matteo Abate, Giovanni Da Pozzo, Simona Battiloro, Benedetto Reitano, Flavia D'Auria.

Special thanks to Pat Pelliccione, Arthur Pelliccione, Tony Altomare, and Concetta Valeri.

Special thanks to Bruno Magliocchetti.

NOTES

SOME REFLECTIONS ON ITALIAN CANADIANS

FRANK IACOBUCCI

1 Frank Iacobucci, "A Tribute To Giovanni Caboto"
2 *Canadian Encyclopedia*, "Italian Canadians," https://bit.ly/303gt6b
3 Kenneth Bagnell, *Canadese: A Portrait of the Italian-Canadians*, p.9
4 *Canadian Encyclopedia*, "Italian Canadians", https://bit.ly/371X12v
5 *Canadian Encyclopedia*, "Italian Canadians", https://bit.ly/33ahstd
6 Franc Sturino, *Forging the Chain: A Case Study of Italian Migration to North America, 1880- 1930*, p. 100
7 *Canadian Encyclopedia*, "Italian Canadians", https://bit.ly/2UURndo
8 Sturino, *Forging the Chain*, p. 109
9 Bagnell, Canadese, pp 23-30.
10 Sturino, *Forging the Chain*, p. 94
11 From Bagnell, *Canadese*, p.51
12 From Bagnell, *Canadese*, p. 26
13 Bagnell,*Canadese*, p. 42
14 Bagnell, *Canadese*, p. 78
15 Bagnell, *Canadese*, p. 78
16 Bagnell, *Canadese*, p.82
17 Bagnell, *Canadese*, pp 65 & 87
18 Bagnell, *Canadese*, p. 101 19 Bagnell, Canadese, p.114
20 Bagnell, *Canadese*, p. 129
21 Bagnell, Canadese, p. 142
22 Alberto Di Giovanni, *Italo-Canadians: Nationality and Citizenship*, p. 35
23 Di Giovanni, *Italo-Canadians*, p. 36
24 Bagnell, *Canadese*, p. 131
25 Bagnell, *Canadese*, p. 129
26 Bagnell, *Canadese*, p. 177
27 Bagnell, *Canadese*, p. 178
28 Statistics Canada, 2011 National Household Survey, https://bit.ly/396wQKV

THE INEVITABLE GROUP IMPACT: THE ITALIAN IMMIGRANTS' CONTRIBUTIONS TO THE CONSTRUCTION SECTOR

MONICA CONTRERAS

1 Stat.Can 2016
2 *The Canadian Business Journal*, Sept 13, 2020
3 Build Force Canada's Key Indicator Data, www.buildforce.ca. sourced from Statistics Canada.
4 Canadian Museum of Immigration at Pier 21, Italian Culture Trunk, History
5 Zanini,B. *City Builders*. 2007 Robarts Centre for Canadian Studies, York University
6 Zanini,B. *City Builders*. 2007 Robarts Centre for Canadian Studies, York University
7 Harney, Robert F. "Italophobia: an English-speaking mal-ady?," 1985
8 Canadian Museum of Immigration at Pier 21, Italian Culture Trunk, History
9 Familiari, plural of familiar (family)
10 *Forging the Chain: A Case Study of Italian migration to North America, 1880-1930* Franc Sturino, Multicultural History Society of Ontario 1990
11 http://www.costi.org/whoweare/history.php
12 Acculturative knowledge defined as knowledge necess-ary to adapt and work within another culture
13 Interview with James McCreath, "Italian Canadian As Enemy Aliens: Memory of WWII." www.italiancanadian-ww2.ca/collection/details/icea201100560001
14 https://canada.constructconnect.com/Leaders2017/top-50.html
15 https://canada.constructconnect.com/Leaders2017/top-50.html
16 Kapusta B. & McMinn, *J. Yolles: A Canadian Engineering Legacy*
17 Poplak, Lewis, "The Flying Form and Development in Toronto"
18 "Flying Form Construction," Greenrock Real Estate Advisors, Oct.4.2019
19 "Celebrating the Life of Angelo DelZotto," George Brown College, Aug. 4 , 2020
20 Zanini,B. *City Builders*. 2007 Robarts Centre for Canadian Studies, York University
21 *Globe & Mail*, Nov 26, 2004 Obituary Harold Green
22 Principe, A. (2015). Review of *The Italians Who Built Toronto: Italian Workers and Contractors in the City's Housebuilding Industry, 1950-1980* by Stefano Agnoletto Ontario History, 107 (1), 149–151. https://doi.org/10.7202/1050690ar
23 CAN Patent 1015993, Field of Invention
24 https://www.youtube.com/watch?v=JuqMTnZtrbE&t=2s
25 *Toronto Star* Obituary, 2018
26 https://patents.google.com/patent/US4004767A/en
27 http://www.zentil.com/about.htm
28 https://patents.google.com/patent/US3561223A/en
29 https://www.ic.gc.ca/opic-cipo/cpd/eng/search/results.html
30 https://www.tunneltalk.com/Honours-and-Awards-Dec12-Recognition-of-a-life-time-in-tunneling-for-Richard-Lovat.php
31 https://www.youtube.com/watch?v=2YRsv7ak-jQ
32 https://www.youtube.com/watch?v=I7tQB4hoIOs
33 Bianchi, A. "The Plastic Kingdom," 1993
34 https://www.canplastics.com/canplastics/vision-extrusion-getting-1-5-million-ontario-government/1003448078/

35 Thorandpartners.com, Video, ICCO Award Winning Interview

36 Del Zotto, A. "Real Condo Life: What it Really Means to be First," *Condo Life*

37 https://www.referenceforbusiness.com/history2/29/Tridel-Enterprises-Inc.html

38 https://www.referenceforbusiness.com/history2/29/Tridel-Enterprises-Inc.html

39 https://www.tridel.com/blog/tridel-85-years-of-history-and-still-rising/

40 Interview with Dino DiStefano, November 2020.

41 Interview with Dino DiStefano, November 2020.

42 Interview with Dino DiStefano, November 2020.

43 Interview with Dino DiStefano, November 2020.

44 Interview with Dino DiStefano, November 2020.

45 Colantonio, F. *From the Ground Up*. Between the Lines, UofT Press, Toronto. 1997

FROM GARMENT WORKERS TO FASHION DESIGNERS IN A GENERATION — ROSA FRACASSA

1 *How the Italians Created Canada*. Josie Di-Sciascio-Andrews. p. 199

2 *How the Italians Created Canada*. Josie Di-Sciascio-Andrews. p. 218

3 *Eh, Paesan! Being Italian in Toronto*. Nicholas De Maria Harney. p.21

4 *Such Hardworking People*. Franca Iacovetta p.78

5 *How the Italians Created Canada*. Josie Di-Sciascio-Andrews. P. 199

6 *Such Hardworking People*. Franca Iacovetta p.93 and 220

7 Earl McRae, "Let Us Now Clothe Famous Men," *Toronto Star Weekend Magazine*

8 Earl McRae, "Let Us Now Clothe Famous Men", *Toronto Star Weekend Magazine*

9 George Russell, *The Ottawa Journal*, "This burgeoning clothier sells more than a touch of class"

10 Earl McRae, "Let Us Now Clothe Famous Men", *Toronto Star Weekend Magazine*

11 George Russell, *The Ottawa Journal*, "This burgeoning clothier sells more than a touch of class".)13 (Kenneth Bagnell, "The Cutting Edge" Leisure Ways

12 Joyce Carter, "A Tailor and a Tough, Tight Softy" The *Globe and Mail*

13 Judy Barr and Nancy Sandrin, "Hot Stuff! Ontario's fashion designers are big on style, fair, and fashion smarts" *Canadian Living*

14 April 6. 2012, Nathalie Atkinson, "Dennis Merotto, the invisible man" *The National Post*

15 (http://www.clothingcanadafashion.com/canadian-fashion-10-years-on/ Clothing Canada Fashion, website)

16 Deirdre Kelly. June 17, 2006. *Globe and Mail* "Wingold Rush! The fashion World heads uptown."

17 Jeanne Beker, *Globe and Mail*, October 16, 2012, "Why we need more than Fashion Week for Canadian Talent to thrive."

18 p 13, INES bridal Magazine https://www.inesdis-anto.com/ines-the-magazine

19 *Toronto Sun*. May 8, 2020. By Rita DeMontis. "Canadian fashion designer creates clothing for front-line workers."

20 [http://gayinfluence.blogspot.com/2012/10/dsquared2-twin-gay-brothers.html]

21 [https://the-talks.com/interview/dean-and-dan-caten/]

22 [https://ww.fashionnetwork.com/news/Dsquared2-the-caten-twins-on-a-quarter-century-of-dressing-sporting-stars-and-superheroes,1173369.html]

23 [https://www.ctvnews.ca/canada-s-dsquared2-launching-into-limelight-1.465463]

24 [http://www.catwalkyourself.com/fashion-biographies/dsquared/]

25 [https://ca.hellomagazine.com/profiles/dsquared/]

26 [https://www.ctvnews.ca/canada-s-dsquared2-launching-into-limelight-1.465463]

27 [https://ww.fashionnetwork.com/news/Dsquared2-the-caten-twins-on-a-quarter-century-of-dressing-sporting-stars-and-superheroes,1173369.html]

28 [https://ww.fashionnetwork.com/news/Dsquared2-the-caten-twins-on-a-quarter-century-of-dressing-sporting-stars-and-superheroes,1173369.html]

29 [https://www.ansa.it/sito/notizie/cultura/moda/2017/07/17/gemelli-dsquared2-cittadini-di-frosinone-_7d3e6d4f-e3d1-45b0-acf8-1e0b700a7a9c.html]

30 *How the Italians Created Canada*. Josie Di-Sciascio-Andrews. p. 221

MEDIA — DANIELA SANZONE

1 Angelo Principe made his invaluable research available for this article in 2019. For over 40 years, he collected information about the Italian press in Canada, producing an incredible amount of work, and only a small part of his effort is presented in this article.

2 *The Canadian Encyclopedia*, 2018

3 Angelo Principe, "Un secolo e più di stampa italo-canadese: 1894–2000," in *Studi di Emigrazione/Migration Studies* XLVI, no.175, 2009

4 See https://iicmontreal.esteri.it/iic_montreal/en/la_biblioteca/quotidiani_e_riviste/

5 See W. G. Smith, *A Study in Canadian Immigration* (Toronto: Ryerson Press, 1920); for a comprehensive statistical study of Italian immigration to Canada till 1940, see Angelo Principe, *The Concept of Italy in Canada and in Italian Canadian Writings from the Eve of Confederation to the Second World War* (first chapter, PhD dissertation, University of Toronto, 1990); for a general view of Italian immigration to Canada in the first year of

the twentieth century, see Bruno Ramirez and Michele Del Balzo, *The Italians of Montreal: From Sojourners to Settlement, 1900–1921* (Montreal: Les Éditions du Courat, 1980); Robert F. Harney, *Dalla frontiera alle Little Italies: Gli Italiani in Canada, 1800–1945* (Rome: Bonacci Editore, 1984); Gabriele Scardellato, "Beyond the Frozen Wastes: Italian Sojourners and Settlers in British Columbia," in *Arrangiarsi*, ed. Robert Perin and Frank Sturino (Toronto: Guernica Editions, 1989); by the same author, "Italian Immigrant Workers in Powell River, B.C.: A Case Study of Settlement Before World War II," *Labour /Le travail* 16, Fall 1985, pp. 145-63; John E. Zucchi, *Italians in Toronto: Development of a National Identity, 1875–1935* (Kingston and Montreal: McGill-Queen's University Press, 1988); *Polyphony: The Bulletin of the Multicultural History Society of Ontario*, volume dedicated to Italians in Ontario with a preface by Robert Harney, Fall/Winter 1985, vol. 7, no. 2; Antonio Pucci, "Canadian Industrialization Versus the Italian Contadini in a Decade of Brutality, 1902–1912," in *Little Italies in North America*, ed. Robert F. Harney and J. Vincenza Scarpaci (Toronto: The Multicultural History Society of Ontario, 1981), pp. 183–207.

6 *La Tribuna Canadiana* (special number), November 11, 1924, p. 17

7 Antonino Spada, cit., p. 110.

8 Corti, "Il Dominio del Canada", in *La Nuova Antologia*, Vol. XIII, 1897.

9 Angelo Principe, "I Fasci in Canada," *Il Fascismo e gli emigranti*, a cura di E. Franzina e M. Sanfilippo (Roma-Bari: Laterza & Figli, 2003), pp. 101–14.

10 Castelli wrote that he had published a short monograph of his experience in D'Annunzio's expedition: *L'opera di Fiume* (Albany, La Capitale, n.d., n.p.). All attempts by Principe to locate a copy have failed.

11 See *Il Cittadino canadese* (special fiftieth anniversary issue), no. LII, October 27, 1993, p. 25.

12 Not a single copy of this periodical has been found, Principe writes in 2019. Spada often mentions this newspaper in his book, but he gives no further details.

13 Antonino Spada, op. 114.

14 Angelo Principe. "The Multicultural Press," *Polyphony: Bulletin of the Multicultural History Society of Ontario*, Spring/Summer 1982, vol. 4, no. 1, p. 94.

15 Principe, 1982.

16 Principe, 2019

17 See Stanislao Carbone, *The Streets Were Not Paved with Gold: A Social History of Italians in Winnipeg* (Winnipeg: Manitoba Italian Heritage Committee, 1993), p. 78.

18 About Dan Iannuzzi's journalistic and business activities see *Corriere Canadese*, November 22 and 29, 2004, and *Tandem*, November 28, 2004.

19 David Helwig, "Italian community loses a pillar", *Sootoday.com*, Nov 22, 2004 – Retrieved from https://www.sootoday.com/local-news/italian-community-loses-a-pillar-95031

20 Principe 2019

21 Luigi Petrucci, *Accadde in Canada*; Principe says that a copy of the book could not be found.

22 Daniela Sanzone, "Italian Canadian Mass Media in the Digital Era," in *The Virtual Piazza*, ed. Monica Stellin. Toronto: Frank Iacobucci Centre from Italian Canadian Studies, University of Toronto, 2006

23 Principe, 2019

24 *La Parola* was first associated with the Canadian Democratic Socialist Party, which in 1960 became the NDP.

25 Sanzone, 2006.

26 Il Postino was available online up to March 2020 at https://ilpostinocanada.com/

27 Daniela Sanzone, "From Mass Immigration to Professional Workers: A Portrait of the Present Italian "Comunità" in Ontario," *Italian Canadiana*, vol. 26–29 (2012–15).

28 Principe 2019.

29 Jerry Fairbridge, *Lombardi, Johnny (1915-2002)*, Biographies. Canadian Communications Foundation. Retrieved 2010/04/10.

30 https://www.chinradio.com/johnny-lombardi

31 Broadcasting-history.ca, "Lombardi, Johnny (1915–2002)," July 13, 2016, 2:36 a.m.

32 ic.gc.ca, "Federal Corporation Information." July 13, 2016, 2:36 a.m.

33 omnitv.ca, "Johnny Lombardi: The Great Communicator," July 13, 2016, 2:36 a.m.

34 Edward Samuel (Ted) Rogers Jr., OC, founder and CEO of Rogers Communications, was a businessman, philanthropist, and a pioneer in the Canadian communications industry who established Rogers Communications. At the time of his death in 2008, Rogers was the fourth-richest Canadian. Rogers Communications owned Canada's largest wireless telecommunications company and cable TV company; 52 radio stations; more than 70 consumer and trade magazines; and numerous TV stations, including City TV, OMNI, Sportsnet and The Shopping Channel. (https://www.thecanadianencyclopedia.ca/en/article/ted-rogers)

35 Domenico Servello, Manage, negotiate, and challenge identities: Young Italian-Canadian identities from the Eyetalian perspective, *Quaderni d'italianistica*, Volume XXXIII, No. 1, 83-108, 2012

36 https://dolcemag.com/

37 https://www.panoramitalia.com/, homepage

CONTRIBUTORS

Mark Cirillo is a Toronto-based writer and food industry consultant. He is the author of the book "Pizza Cultura," and the founder of Cucinato, a boutique agency that produces culinary events, like olive oil and wine tastings, cooking classes, chef dinners and in-home catering.

Monica Contreras is a registered architect and project manager of award-winning, strategic, sustainable, mixed-use residential/commercial complexes, institutional infrastructure, and transit-oriented developments. She leads the Architectural Program Delivery for Bell Real Estate. In conjunction, Monica has taught at the Institute without Boundaries at George Brown College design and systems thinking since 2005.

Denis De Klerck is a writer and editor, and the publisher of Mansfield Press.

Consiglio Di Nino is a businessman and philanthropist with a deep involvement in the Italian Canadian community. He was appointed to the Canadian Senate in 1990 by Prime Minister Brian Mulroney and served there until 2012.

Luigi Ferrara is an architect, designer, educator and storyteller. He is the Dean of the Centre for Arts, Design & Information Technology at George Brown College in Toronto, Canada and Director of the internationally acclaimed Institute without Boundaries (IwB). He has served as President and Senator of ICSID and lectures around the world on topics as diverse as design and sustainability, design management, urban planning, information technology, digital media, telecommunications and the network society.

Rosa Fracassa is the Chair of the School of Fashion and Jewellery at George Brown College. Rosa has been a Professor and Program Coordinator at the School of Fashion at George Brown where she has been teaching for many years in the Fashion, General Arts and Science and Theatre departments. Rosa's academic background includes a Master Degree in Italian Studies and a two year Master degree in Drama; she is at the dissertation stage of her PhD.

Roberto Fracchioni hails from two of the finest food-producing regions in the world: the Emilia-Romagna district of Italy and the Niagara region of Canada. He has been the Executive Chef or a consultant at some of Canada's most renowned food destinations such as Niagara's Inn on the Twenty, the Millcroft Inn and Spa, the Monk Kitchen at the Templar Hotel and the Hockley Valley Resort. With a passion for coaching as well as kitchen and menu design, Chef Fracchioni currently lends his skills as a mentor and business advisor to cooks and restaurateurs throughout Ontario, while teaching and providing faculty coordination support at the culinary program of Centennial College in Toronto. In addition, Chef Fracchioni works with the ICCO Canada, providing cross-border negotiation, and event organization designed to educate Canadian chefs on authentic D.O.P. and I.G.P. food products.

Frank Giorno lives in Toronto. He was a reporter for the *Brandon Sun, Mining Life*, and *Timmins Today*. A provincial & municipal civil servant, he was a Research Director, Canadian Environmental Law and a manager of Mushkegowuk Environmental Energy Conservation. Frank wrote 4 poetry books: "Elvis in America," "Arrivederci! Plastic Covered Couch," "MoPoPoMo," "My Nation is a Train." He co-authored "Internee 328: Camp Petawawa." Frank also writes *A Northern Blog*.

Eva H.D. is a poet and journalist. She is a winner of the Montreal International Poetry Prize and her books "Rotten Perfect Mouth" and "Shiner" became international bestsellers when her work was featured prominently in the Charlie Kaufman film "I'm thinking of ending things."

Frank Iacobucci began his storied career practicing corporate law before pursuing a career in academia as a Professor and Dean of the University of Toronto Faculty of Law. He has served as the Deputy Minister of Justice and Deputy Attorney General of Canada before being appointed as the Chief Justice of the Federal Court. In 1991 he became the first Italian Canadian to be appointed as Justice of the Supreme Court of Canada. The Frank Iacobucci Centre for Italian Canadian Studies at the University of Toronto was named in his honour.

Bruno Magliocchetti is an Associate Professor in the Department of Italian Studies at the University of Toronto.

Peter Norman is the author of four poetry collections, a novel, and numerous short stories, articles, essays, and reviews. His most recent book is "Some of Us and Most of You Are Dead" (Wolsak & Wynn, 2018); his first was the Trillium Award finalist "At the Gates of the Theme Park."

Corrado Paina lives and writes in Toronto. He serves as the Executive Director of the Italian Chamber of Commerce of Ontario Canada. He was the editor of "College Street—Little Italy Toronto's Renaissance Strip," a finalist for the Toronto Heritage Award and his poetry and fiction has been widely published in Canada and Italy.

Angelo Persichilli is an Italian Canadian journalist. He has been an editor of Corriere Canadese, the communication director for former Prime Minister Stephen Harper, a columnist for the Toronto Star, the Toronto Sun and others as well as working for OMNI Television and RAI-TV.

Sara Rellini is a former project assistant at the ICCO Canada. She currently lives and works in Bologna.

John Ruffolo is the Founder & Managing Partner of Maverix Private Equity. John is also the Founder of OMERS Ventures. He is the Co-Founder and Vice Chair of the Council of Canadian Innovators and the Co-Founder and Chair of the Board of AI Partnerships. John sits on the board of a number of leading innovation based organizations including engineering.com, OneEleven, and Ether Capital.

Daniela Sanzone is an Italian Canadian writer and journalist. Sanzone was born and raised in Rome, Italy. She began her Canadian career at *Corriere Canadese*, a Toronto-based Italian newspaper, before joining the team at Omni Television as a news anchor and reporter. Sanzone was also the Canada News coordinator for the Italian Press Agency ANSA and worked as a freelancer for publications in both Italy and Canada. Her novel, "La Guerra secondo Michele" (The War According to Michele), was published in 2016 and she is currently a PhD candidate at York University, in Communication and Culture, with research interests in Canadian broadcasting policies, journalism, and ethnic media.

Giulia Emanuela Storti was born in Milan and is a photographer and videographer. She has a Bachelor in Media Design and Multimedia Arts from NABA in Milan and was admitted to the Stage Photography course at the Scala Theatre. She lives in Toronto, where she has worked for different film festivals and as an assistant on a movie sets. She works at RTG Group as a YouTube content creator and collaborates with the ICCO Canada for different projects.